SHORES OF KORANTIA

A Complete Setting for
MYTHRAS
In the World of Thennla

By
Jonathan Drake

Shores of Korantia, Korantia and Thennla copyright © 2014 by Jonathan Drake and Used by Design Mechanism with Permission

Mythras is a trademark of The Design Mechanism. All rights reserved. This edition of Shores of Korantia is copyright © 2014.

Published under license in the UK by Aeon Games Publishing
www.aeongamespublishing.co.uk
ISBN 978-1-91147-100-4

This book may not be reproduced in whole or in part by any means without permission from The Design Mechanism, except as quoted for purposes of illustration, discussion and game play. Reproduction of the material in this book for the purposes of personal or corporate profit, by photographic, electronic, or other methods of retrieval is strictly prohibited.

Printed in Great Britain

CREDITS

Created, Developed and Written By
Jonathan Drake

Additional Material By
Lawrence Whitaker and Pete Nash

Editing
Lisa Tyler

Proof Reading
Carol Johnson

Design and Layout
Alexandra James

Artists
Lee Smith, Dan MacKinnon, Mark Stacey
Cover by Antonio José Manzanedo Luis

Cartography
Colin Driver

Special Thanks
John Hutchinson, Pete Nash and Lawrence Whitaker.

Playtesters
Tony Burns, Ian Carr, Marcus Pailing, Miles Peterson,
Neyah Peterson, Jonathan Ratty, Peter Whitelaw and 'Rhaskos'

CONTENTS

Introduction	4
Korantia	9
The Wider World	28
Characters	38
Magic	61
Korantine Wealth	71
Cults	83
Travelling Korantia	106
Encounters	117
Thyrta	135
Varoteg's Rascals	163
The House of Valsus	177
Prishad's Daughter	186
Index	233

Shores of Korantia

INTRODUCTION

Welcome to Shores of Korantia, a book which examines a key region within Thennla: a fully detailed fantasy world that has been specifically designed and created as a setting for Mythras.

This setting's genesis goes back to the days of Chaosium's 2nd Edition RuneQuest; however, it was first published by Mongoose Publishing, using the Legend system; Age of Treason: The Iron Simulacrum and Age of Treason: The Iron Companion. If you have those books then you already have a wealth of material that you can use alongside what is provided here, with only minor adjustments. Some elements have been repeated, but only as much as was necessary to make it possible to use this book as a stand-alone publication. The vast majority of what is presented here is new, and exclusive to Mythras.

About This Book

This book is designed to give the Games Master everything needed to get started with devising a Mythras campaign in the setting. The world is described, the region of Korantia with its peoples, customs and cults, is detailed, and a specific area for adventuring is fleshed out, with maps, city plans, personalities, plot hooks, scenarios and statistics for key NPCs. Three scenarios are also provided, of varying length and complexity, and these can be woven together into a mini campaign to last for several sessions of play, with enough background detail provided to readily spin off into many more.

The Land of Korantia

Korantia is a place you can find on a map, set between the Ozyrian mountains and the sea, on the continent of Taygus – home to the largest share of humanity and where civilisation has reached heights unknown anywhere else. However, to those who call themselves Korantines, any land can be Korantia; wherever they settle, and wherever there are people who share their languages and customs, deserves to share in the name. For all that, Korantia is made up of many city states, some of them very large with a population numbering in the hundreds of thousands, but many rather small and yet still fiercely independent, each with its own cults, laws and constitution, its own military, its own coinage. Over them all sits an Emperor, the mortal representative of the sun god the Korantines call Lanis. This Emperor has no real power to command his subject states, and the notion of a Korantine Empire is little more than an echo of a long-lost past when such was the reality... before the Empire's capital sank beneath the ocean waves.

Korantia is situated by the Inner Ocean, a great expanse of water on the other side of which lie continents whose lands and peoples are barely known, but that are a siren's call for those seeking adventure and new resources to exploit. While the northern routes across this ocean are dominated by Korantines from Sarestra and Kipsipsindra, the southern routes are almost monopolised by foreigners from the lands of Assabia; – Sharranket, in particular. Two Korantine cities, Borissa and Himela, compete with each other for first place in taking on these foreigners and carving a new Korantine presence in this part of the ocean, but, at the same time, the hostile Jekkarene

Introduction

Theocracy and its protector, the Taskan Empire, are dipping their toes in the Inner Ocean for the very first time.

Neighbours and Threats

Even in the Korantine heartland, there are other people – most of them disenfranchised and poor, descendants of the indigenous Thennalt people, whose lands were seized and populations absorbed or dispersed when the city-states were founded. These folk are regularly referred to as Pagans, a word that denotes simple country folk or 'bumpkins', slaves to old ways and to obsolete beliefs. Sometimes these people turn to revolt or resort to banditry, but they are scattered and, disunited people and never pose a serious threat.

Korantia is under sustained pressure from rivals and enemies on its land borders. To the North is Marangia, a Thennalt kingdom where barbarian folk still live in accordance with traditions that include taking every opportunity to break into civilised lands in search of plunder. Not so long ago, the border state of Tysil and its allies mounted an expedition into Marangia and inflicted a major defeat on the kingdom, but it is, surely, only a matter of time before they recover sufficiently to pose a serious threat once more.

To the East is the Taskan Empire, a growing and energetic power ruled by the immortal god-emperor Zygas Taga through his viceroy, an animated statue known as The Iron Simulacrum. The Taskan Empire looms large in the minds of those Korantines who appreciate that unless its power starts to wane Korantia may soon be on a collision course with its further expansion. Fifty years ago, Korantines from several city-states took part in a war between rival factions in the Thennalt land of Camtri, in which the Taskans took the other side. That war ended in a victory for the Taskan-supported faction and ultimately the absorption of Camtri into the Taskan Empire. Many feel these events are likely to be repeated in other lands that lie between the Korantine and Taskan spheres of influence.

South of the Korantine heartland, beyond the borderlands of Brotomagia, is Methelea, home to the Jekkarene Theocracy. The matriarchal Jekkarenes are the ancient enemy, credited with the destruction of the Korantine Empire when the oceans were summoned to swamp its shining capital on the isle of Korantis. The Jekkarenes have until now shown little appetite to expand beyond their natural borders, but they have become a protectorate of the Taskan Empire and are surely weaving nefarious plots with their Taskan friends to lay Korantia low.

The World of Thennla

Korantia is just one region of a world named after its primary earth-goddess, Theyna. This world is one in which humanity is not only the dominant sentient race, but according to many, is the *only* sentient race.

Geography

The world is a disc upon which the major land masses encircle an Inner Ocean and which are, in turn, surrounded by the Outer Ocean. Beyond the Outer Ocean is the Edge of the World and it is variously reported that crossing over is impossible, is certain death, or offers transport to other worlds or dimensions. Above the world is the realm of sky, which stretches all around at least as far as the Edge of the World, and above that is the Vault of Heaven, which so far as is known is solid and impenetrable. The distance from one side of the world to the other is about 7,000 miles. The Vault of Heaven's height is unknown, but it is assumed to be dome-shaped and at least 1,000 miles high at its centre. Some scholars suspect that it is, in fact, the upper part of a sphere within which sits the earth, with the vast majority of the sphere's volume being beneath the earth's surface, which is where the Many Hells are to be found.

One can walk overland from one end of the world to the other, for there is only a single break in the encircling land-masses that separate the Inner from the Outer Ocean. Nobody, we can be sure, has ever done so; but Aristentorus of Hypata made a circumnavigation of the Ocean 300 years ago and confirmed this to be true.

The Outer Ocean

Lashed by epic storms, whipped up by divine powers and stirred by magical tides and currents, the Outer Ocean is unfathomably deep and makes for unbelievably dangerous sailing. Having said that, it is not such a broad ocean – the Edge of the World is disconcertingly close if you can survive the crossing.

The Inner Ocean

The principal route of communication between human cultures, the Inner Ocean is generally kind to shipping, and its shores support the greatest concentrations of human population. The Ocean has its own geography of underwater volcanoes, treacherous shallows, deep-sea trenches and stormy capes. It is at its most violent and hazardous in the South where it meets the Outer Ocean. Powerful currents can help or hinder the seaborne adventurer or merchant, and frequently dictate the

most commonly used navigation routes and the siting of key settlements.

The northern and southern reaches of this ocean are different in character, and this includes the weather gods who rule the skies above. In the North, Palaskil drives the winds in a more or less anti-clockwise direction, while in the South Somadsil drives them the other way. Both these deities appear to be banned from a stretch of ocean east of Fierla, known as the Doldrums of Hiolanta., and Hiolanta is said to be the name of their divine mother, yet she is not an entity that anyone worships.

The Continents

(See map, opposite)

Reading clockwise from the southernmost, the continents are:

Uxmal
A southern land comprising of a huge, cool, central plateau pierced by rivers and surrounded by forested mountains descending to hot tropical lowlands.

Jandekot
A warm, humid land, much of its interior covered by a vast tract of rainforest and home to the greatest concentration and diversity of life, but thinly populated by humankind.

Kasperan
A land of sparse vegetation with a near barren interior, which is dominated by a chain of fierce volcanoes.

Thurina
Framed by tall mountain ranges to East and West, at its centre is a forest of massive pines surrounded by broad plains. Thick glaciers spread across its north-eastern reaches.

Taygus
Temperate lands of rolling plains, hills and forests, give way to hot subtropical lands in the South. Considered the most amenable to settled life and home to perhaps two-thirds of humanity. At its heart is Lake Taygus, the largest body of fresh water in the world.

Rasputana
The hot desert interior is thought to be the driest place in the world, but the southern tip is home to lush forests.

The Sky

Every day the sun follows a path from East to West across the sky, passing just South of the centre of the world and meandering slightly on its way. Depending on where in the world it is viewed, the sun's orb has a subtly different hue; only from Korantia does it appear to shine with a pure, golden-yellow light. Once the sun has set, you can see that the night sky contains both stars – which do not move – and planets, which look like stars but *do* move (which is how you can tell the difference). Some planets travel around the sky in set patterns, others stay static but change their aspect or appearance as they turn on their axes. Planets are agreed to be living entities and for many people they are gods. The stars are mostly thought to be there for decoration, each star or constellation set in its place to serve as a memento of some legendary event, or as the heraldic badge of a god rather than the god itself. The moon is stationary and, as the world is flat and nothing is ever over the horizon, it is always visible on a clear day unless blotted out by the sun's glare. It does, however, look rather small if you are on the other side of the world from the point above which it is anchored. The moon has phases, but this is the result of changes in the glowing light emanating from within as it rotates, marking out the months of the year.

The Year

A Thennlan Year is 366 days long, measured by the time it takes for the sun to complete a full cycle of the various stations he may visit on his daily travel across the Vault of Heaven. His gradual shift from one path to another and back again is the primary cause of seasonal changes. For most people, this year is divided into 13 months of 28 days each, and two additional days are inserted ('intercalated') at the end of the year to make 366. However, for the Jekkarenes, the year consists of 13 Lunar months that conform directly to the phases of their moon goddess, and two of these months are 29 days long: an extended full moon in mid-winter and an extended dark moon in mid-summer. Legend has it that the Lunar and Solar years were once completely in harmony at 364 days, but upon the divorce of the moon goddess and sun god some 1,200 years ago they became fractured, and the moon was forced to alter her step to prevent a disaster of cosmological misalignments. There are some cultures, such as the Jekkarenes, who do not use the Solar Calendar at all.

A day is 24 hours long, and a seven-day week is a measure of time traditional in Korantia and based upon the observance of certain astrological cycles, but little used elsewhere. In Tarsenia

the month is divided into nine-day 'weeks', the 9th day, and the additional (28th) day of each month being reserved for market and holidays. Seasons are experienced in all parts of the world, but they are not necessarily the same seasons at the same time.

Games Master Note: For ease of reference the term 'week' in this book always refers to the Korantine seven-day week

THENNLA

KORANTIA AND ENVIRONS

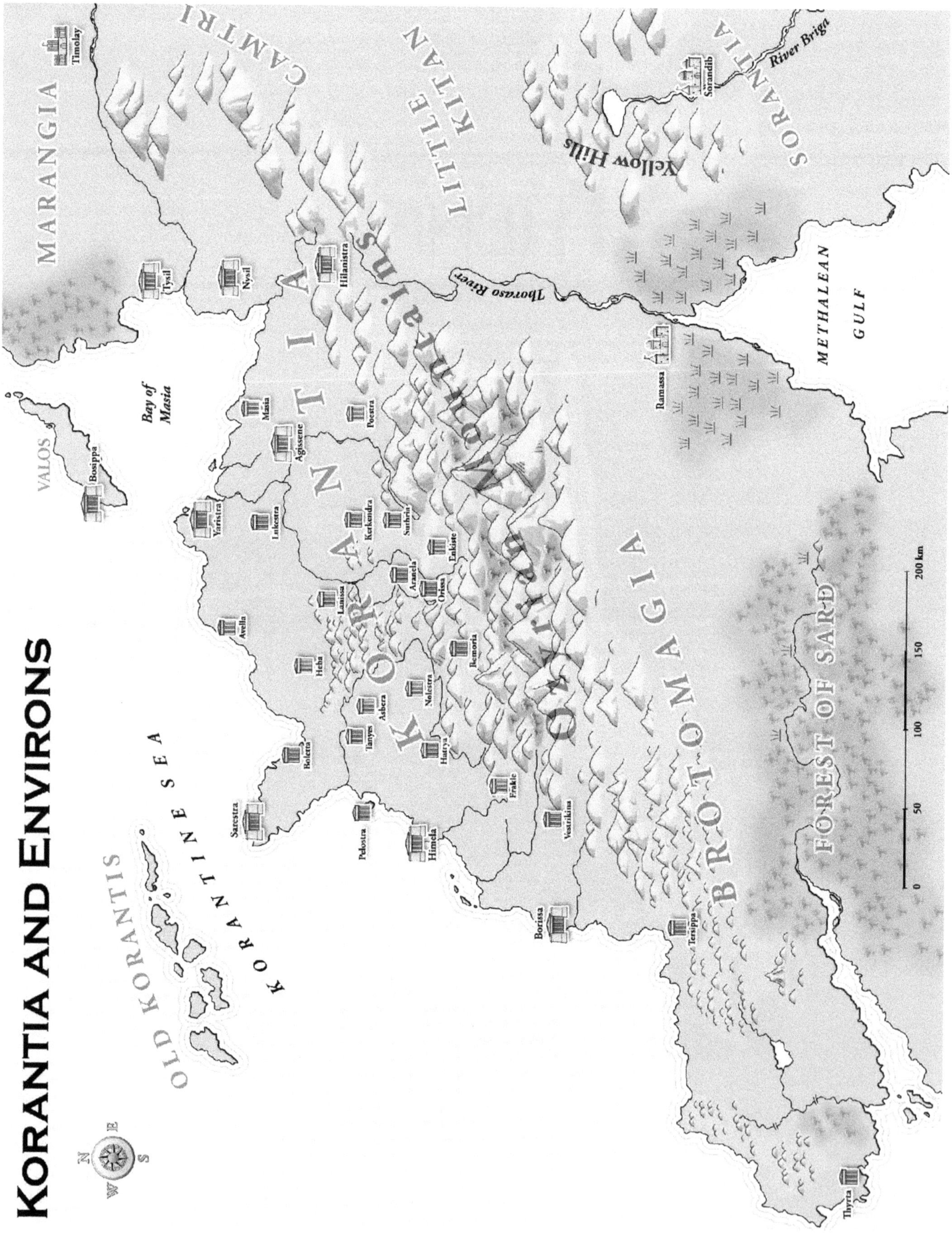

KORANTIA

> *'Wherever the Korantine tongue is spoken, and wherever the customs of our people are followed, that is Korantia. Korantia is not a country but a way of life.'*
>
> *Korantine Saying*

A Brief History of the Korantine People

More than a millennium ago the forefathers of the Korantines lived in Methelea, where the first civilisation, as it is said, was created as a divinely sanctioned and ideal society headed by a royal couple in whom were vested the powers of the sun and moon. Their king stood for prowess, authority, truth and justice; their queen for wisdom, empathy, harmony and magic.

Something happened that broke this union apart; as the Korantines now tell it, a female revolution that attempted to overturn the proper order of family society and state and enable the women to wield power over their husbands through their control of magic. As the Jekkarenes tell us, it was the opposite; the patriarchs began to assert power and control over every aspect of their wives' and children's existence, to force the womenfolk into seclusion at home and so to prevent them forming independent bonds of community either in public or between themselves.

Physical violence was matched against magic; sides were taken, lines drawn that cut even through families. When King Arribates was murdered in his bath by his own wife and daughters, his chief priests, foremost among them Phereleukus, declared the outrage to the gods was permanent and irredeemable; as society could not be healed, a new one must be made, and a plan was formulated to subordinate every aspect of the nation's life to the King and his Solarist followers. Yet the Queen's people controlled the land, and in withholding its fertility, and their own, from her enemies, the King's people were forced by famine and want to abandon their cursed homeland. They set out in desperation, either by land across the Quickwater River or by sea along the coast, to where they might settle new territory where the earth would yield its produce to them. Upon their departure, the Queen lifted her curse; however, not only had a full third of the population departed with Phereleukus and his followers, but also countless thousands more had succumbed to starvation.

It took generations for the new cities planted by Phereleukus and his exile nation to establish themselves in new territory. The common approach to colonisation was at first to beg the permission of some local people to settle, perhaps even to buy a place to build their homes and farms with gold, or to offer to fight for them in return for land; but later, to turn on their hosts and seize them as slaves or tenants. At this time, the Korantines went by many different names, according the name of the leader of each party. There were the Hilantri, the Velontes, the Dorasdi, the Byotyes, the Agissei and the Sisanayontes, among many more whose names are lost to posterity. The Hilantri had the greatest start, arriving at a large island that was almost completely devoid of human settlement, called Korantis. Their new city would grow to become the capital of an empire to which Korantis would give its name.

The Age of Heroes

By the time many of the early settlements were a hundred years old, their ruling dynasties had thrown up a class of warrior-aristocrat, who would seek out conflict and violence to prove their worth and win new glory, and, of course, serve their own communities by defending them from other such heroes doing the same. This situation became so endemic that the consequences for ordinary folk were becoming unbearable. Even those not directly affected by violence were subject to constant uncertainty, as crowns and lands were transferred from one hero to another as their fortunes rose and fell; loyalties were constantly tested, agriculture interrupted. These wars were ended by the growing power of the common people, who demanded an increasing say on whether they should be dragged into dangerous battles or not and what sort of benefits should come to them as a result. A political reformer by the name of Tygorus ultimately took control of the city of Borissa by declaring that, 'All men are equal under heaven'. While at the time this was merely an equal right to the spoils of war (after Tygorus himself), this ultimately set the precedent for the notion of citizenship that Korantines enjoy today. Tygorus' example had to be followed by those in other states who found themselves with footling little private armies compared to the Borissan horde of rapacious citizen-plunderers that Tygorus had assembled. The aristocracy responded by turning the many local cults dedicated to the sun-god Lanis into clubs for a narrow elite; people entitled by their wealth, their exploits and their learning to exercise power among their fellow men as the sun exercises power in the heavens. This was all very good until the rulers of Korantis, King Kribsion and his son King Koibos, conquered them all, forced the acceptance of a single solar cult of which Koibos was the head, and, in doing so, created the Korantine Empire.

Expansion 228-1034

The growth of the Korantine Empire was, initially, an exercise in depriving neighbouring peoples of their lands so that excess impoverished Korantines could be settled there and raised to respectability as peasant farmers. In the process, many smaller peoples were absorbed, assimilated or enslaved and their names all but forgotten. Yet once the borders of Korantia fell upon mountain ranges, or seemingly unconquerable barbarian lands, the Empire eventually looked across the sea for its next opportunity. Korantine traders had early found their way to the archipelago that led them on to the shores of Kasperan, and traffic already flowed in both directions. However, in the late 7th century, efforts were made to exploit these far-flung islands directly by establishing a colony on Kipsiperan. The new colony was a great success, attracting both farmers in search of a bigger or better lot than they had at home, and also the boldest spirits in the Empire lured by the whole new world they might access and exploit from Kipsipsindra's harbour. The most adventurous of them even established a trading post near the delta of the Saa, the immense river that appeared from the impenetrable jungles that choke that continent's unexplored interior.

By the turn of the first millennium – at which time the Taskan Empire was about to spring into being off to the East – the Korantine Empire was at its zenith. With trade networks that almost spanned the world, the ability to summon fleets and armies that outnumbered the entire population of any potential foe, the universal confidence in the magnificent gold coins bearing the Emperor's image on one side and a griffin on the other, the Korantine Empire looked destined to last another thousand years. And yet… Emperor Enkilos II harboured two ambitions, one of which he enacted in his lifetime; the other he passed as an obligation to his successor, Koibos XVIth. These two things would, in roundabout ways, lead to Korantia's darkest hour.

The Follies of Emperor Enkilos 1002-1055

The first folly was the outlawing of sorcery, something that had long been regarded as an arcane and philosophical way of looking at the world and that was a pursuit for some bookish members of the leisured classes. The bad name attached to sorcery had come about more recently, largely through the influx of foreign, particularly Assabian, sorcerers willing to sell their services to all and sundry and thereby threatening to put the high arts to ugly demotic purposes. A particular fashion for the female variety to dress their arts up as 'Jekkarene Rites' in order to make them sound more exotic, mysterious and dangerous, got the particular goat of the Emperor and a purge was declared. Many regarded this as an unnecessary measure, over-zealously pursued, and among the spell-slaves, street magicians and confidence tricksters there were certainly some genuinely powerful individuals who found themselves the Emperor's enemy.

Even respectable people who had indulged in sorcery were ordered to destroy their books, avoid further public discussion of the matter and certainly not to actually practise it. Those who failed to comply were, after a few warnings, duly exiled to

Korantia

somewhere unpleasant unless they decamped to a place of their own choosing first.

The second folly was the charge Enkilos set upon his son Koibos: that he should attempt to restore the Korantines to their ancestral homeland. What this meant was that Koibos should venture upon the conquest of the Jekkarid, an undertaking of immense cost and danger that would require the subjection of a population whose hostility to the Korantines was a matter of cultural tradition. As it happened, Koibos put off this undertaking as long as he possibly could while promising it was the first priority of his reign. In the meantime, he sent out a couple of expeditions to kill wizards lurking on the borders of his realm in order to satisfy his father's ghost. He also despatched the famous hero Zartos of Horaia on missions to bring Korantine power to distant lands, particularly the wild islands that dotted the inner ocean, to satisfy the hotheads in his court. This era even saw the trading posts in Jandekot converted to a full colony at Zarendra.

Koibos had his reasons to procrastinate over starting a major land war close to home. Around the start of his reign, the Unification of Tarsenia under Zygas Taga – a Jekkarene no less – had placed a significant new military power on the Eastern flank of his Empire, which may have a direct interest in the future of the Jekkarene Theocracy. He also began to hear rumours of an immense pact being woven between the Jekkarene moon-priestesses and the Ocean, something that Koibos was ill-equipped to understand or investigate, due to the deficit of arcane knowledge that was the result of the purge of sorcerers during his father's reign.

The Cataclysm

Koibos was already approaching his old age, and going increasingly mad thanks to the constant jabbering of his father's ghost berating him for not having conquered the Jekkarenes as he had been instructed, indeed brought up, to do. It was only now that Koibos realised that he and his father had courted disaster – his father for turning ancient enmities into a thirst for war and conquest, and he himself for having failed to either go through with his father's plans or else publicly set them aside. For the Jekkarenes had not been idle in the face of sabre-rattling by the Korantine emperor. Through their own offices, and with the help of powerful wizards who had an axe to grind, the Ocean had been persuaded to crush Korantis in a pre-emptive strike. This it duly did, a great wave sweeping the island and much of the nearby mainland shore clean of any vestige of habitation, while terrifying sea monsters gulped down any who attempted to ride out the wave in a boat. Untold thousands lost their lives. Eleven cities were lost forever, many more were abandoned and refounded away from the coast. Korantis itself was so shattered that only its uplands remained above the water, even when the wave subsided.

While Koibos drowned with most of his court, some of his family survived, being on the mainland at the time. They took refuge in Himela, a place shocked and wounded by the Ocean's power just like every other coastal city. All across the former Empire the survivors of the Cataclysm set about dealing with the catastrophic change to their circumstances. The Korantine system of local city-states federated under the Emperor proved a strength, as each community set itself up now as a truly independent body, self reliant and self-sufficient. Many were really quite happy that there was no longer an Emperor to whom taxes were due to support the great armies, navies and civil administration that had been such a burden in recent years. When Koibos' nephew Antekos was declared Emperor from his temporary digs in Himela, nobody took any notice, not even the Himelans.

In foreign lands, the Cataclysm brought chaos, as the Korantine Empire had been integral to international trade and the power relationships between states. Everyone had to reconfigure their world – and into this vacuum stepped the Taskan Empire.

Korantia after the Cataclysm 1055-1111

Once things began to return to normal, Korantine city-states continued to set their own agenda, and, inevitably, internecine wars sprang up as they vied for power with one another. Despite a population less than half that of the Empire at its peak, within 100 years new colonies were being established, some in the lands swept clean by the Cataclysm, others in entirely new areas. Thirty years after Korantis was lost, the Imperial household founded a new capital. Its location was a peculiar choice, set in a mountain pass to the east of Korantia proper, in striking distance of many of the Empire's potential enemies. Of course, Antekos II had been refused land grants sufficient for his needs by the city-states over which he was supposedly Emperor, who had no intention of seeing external authority over their affairs restored, so his choices of location were limited. His son Koibos XVII, who completed the project, turned this humiliation into a virtue. Koibos was an energetic fellow who named the city Hilanistra for the founding fathers of Korantis itself, and set about showing that he and his followers had the strength

and spirit to carve themselves a kingdom of their own in barbarous lands like the heroes of old. By the end of his reign, Koibos had raised the status of the Imperial throne to such a level that many Korantines now cursed the distance they had to travel to see the Emperor and ask his support and favour in disputes with rival city-states. He even made a success of the only war ever actually fought against the Jekkarenes, and successfully prevented their expansion out of Ramassa into the lands immediately to the south of his city. In the last years of his life, he had the joy to sit upon the Sapphire Throne of his ancestors, which had been retrieved from the waters covering the ancient capital by an enterprising band of his Paladins and transported overland with great ceremony to the new capital.

Recent History 1112-Present

The last 100 years of Korantine history have seen further threats from abroad. In the North, the warlike Marangians, a Thennalt nation, swept into the territory of Tysil four times in a decade. With help from allied cities, the Tysilots successfully resisted these invasions at great cost each time, but only when other barbarians, who had suffered cruelly at the hands of the Marangians, offered to change sides in return for resettlement in their territory did the tide turn. Nysil was created as a new city-state to house these same barbarians, who accepted Korantine gods and Korantine customs as part of the deal. In 1136 a stunning victory saw Tysil, with their new allies and even the support of the King of Zathrum, slaughter a Marangian army of over 70,000 near the cult centre of Oster. Hostages were taken, treaties forced on the losers, and enough treasure was brought home to make up for at least some of the depredations suffered over 11 years of war.

A generation later Korantia had a much less successful time, in a war in which, for the first and only time Korantines found themselves drawn up in battle against Taskan soldiery. The battleground was Camtri, a fine and well-populated Thennalt country that had long been in the Korantine sphere of influence, but now was increasingly falling under Taskan power. The Korantine war effort was led by the city of Borissa, the most militaristic of them all, whose population were all for a new conflict in which to enhance their fame and fortune. This war involved a series of inconclusive battles, disappointing amounts of plunder, and the eventual retirement from the field of the Borissans and contingents supplied by Himela, Tersippa and Agissene. Their Camtric allies had tired of the struggle early on and requested the Korantines should leave so peace could break out. The Borissans conducted a few desultory raids out of spite on the home towns of their former allies, and went home sulking.

The fallout in Himela was significant. The aristocratic leaders who had urged their fellow citizens to participate in this war were now in very bad odour, and a democratic revolution was the result. The Borissans were horrified at this destabilising turn of events on their border, and quickly placated their own disgruntled veterans with a redistribution of land annexed from neighbouring Vestrikina. Nonetheless, the Borissans were increasingly unhappy that their larger rival's new democratic government did not swiftly produce the chaos and internal strife expected of it, and eventually attempted to assist the plotters of an aristocratic coup to tear it down anyway. Their army marched in support of the self-declared Himelan Council of the Talents, led by a man who was clearly mad, bad and deeply unpopular, with spectacularly humiliating results. The Borissan army got lost in a confusing maze of orchards and dry stone walls, and were eventually surrounded and forced to surrender or face annihilation from swarms of dirt-poor Himelan militiamen armed with slings and arrows.

A more successful, if one-sided, struggle was the expedition to conquer Valos, an island that lies across the entrance to the Bay of Masia. Since the Cataclysm, it had been variously a struggling Korantine city-state, a trading centre for adventurous Kapolans and Guyuntars from across the ocean, and latterly the home of some rather daring barbarian warlords who threatened the vital sea lanes in and out of the bay. This was allowed to go on for far too long, as nobody wanted any rival state to gain the glory of rooting out these 'pirates', and thereby to win control of the sea lanes. Eventually, Kalacho of Agissene matched diplomacy and military skills to assemble a federated army of 40,000 men, supported by a fleet manned by 20,000 more, and cracked this small but awkward nut with an enormous hammer blow. So successful was this enterprise, and so delighted were the Korantines to have pulled off a cooperative expedition without any more blessing from the Emperor than the loan of a few Paladins, that federalism fever took hold. The military alliance that took Valos was continued as The Korantine League, and a capital built on Valos, named Bosippa – some say after Kalacho's favourite horse. Here Korantine cities would settle their disputes and think upon important matters as a collective – at least that was the idea. Kalacho was soon being pressed to accept a dictatorial role as the only man who could actually weld the quarrelling delegations from across Korantia into something that could work as a body; however, he had the wisdom to decline the invitation, spoke of how Korantia did

not need two Emperors, and disappeared into retirement on one of his favourite estates.

The Rediscovery of Zarendra

A bare two years ago something remarkable happened that gave Korantines even more cause to think their stars were once again in the ascendant. A strangely dressed foreigner who spoke fluent if rather heavily accented Korantine, and carried a banner emblazoned with a burning sun, appeared by ship at Sarestra and demanded directions to Hilanistra. This man called himself Redanger, the Regent of Zarendra-in-Jandekot, and he had come to declare his loyalty to the Emperor of the Korantines. Redanger duly processed to the Emperor's capital, announced that the long-lost colony founded by Zartos in the reign of Koibos XVI still thrived on the other side of the Ocean, and declared himself the Emperor's loyal servant. When he went home the following year, Redanger had taken the name of Koibion and acquired some proper Korantine manners to boot. It is unknown whether he will ever be seen in the East again, but there are already many Korantines asserting that their people now have a demonstrable first claim to the riches of the Occident, and that something must be done to protect their Western cousins from the Sharranketan merchants who appear to be enjoying a monopoly over the shipping lanes anywhere south of Kipsipsindra.

The Emperor of the Korantines

Emperor Koibos XXIV of the Korantines is the 27-year old chief priest of the sun god, Lanis.

Koibos is steeped in traditions of heroism kept alive by the stories of famous Korantines of the past. While it is normally the Emperor's duty to sponsor and reward acts of bravery and heroism amongst his Paladins, Koibos is at an age where he dearly wishes he could be a participant in adventure. The responsibilities of his role limit his ambitions to extended hunting trips into the forest of Sard, often accompanied by local Thennalt chieftains with whom he is very popular; but he cannot go anywhere without an extensive retinue.

The emperor of the Korantines has no actual power over any of the city-states that recognise his leadership, a source of great frustration that he is powerless to do anything about. The city-states now refuse the ancient right of his forebears to raise taxes from their citizens, and send him gifts rather than paying tribute. The extent of his power is to make pronouncements that lend weight to the position of one side or another when internal strife breaks out between factions within a city, or that relay his opinion over the right argument when two cities are in dispute. Sometimes Koibos may actually send an arbitrator to attempt to settle such disputes. Increasingly, the Korantine League is assuming this role in his stead. His final sanction is armed intervention, yet the forces he can raise are a fraction of what can be fielded by some of the powerful city-states in his Empire. He may endorse local interventions by his Paladins resident in a troubled city to lend their services to one side or another, but had better be certain that such intervention is either decisive or deniable when he does.

Hilanistra

The Korantine Emperor's capital at Hilanistra was newly founded by his ancestors after Korantis was lost to the Ocean. Hilanistra is situated in the highlands on the Eastern flank of the Korantine heartlands, astride a route through the Ozyrian mountain range. Here it is perhaps exposed to potential enemies but also is an ideal place to act as a hub for trade and diplomacy between Korantia and neighbouring lands, so while the city-states of Korantia make great efforts to keep their Emperor out of their internal affairs, he is still seen as a very useful figurehead for relations with the rest of the world.

Hilanistra is organised not as a city-state but as the extended court of the Emperor, and administered by the cult of the sun god Lanis of which Emperor Koibos XXIV is the chief acolyte. Its constitution is therefore unlike any other Korantine city, being ordered entirely as a reflection of the Lanist cult hierarchy with the Emperor at its apex, advised by a council of priests, supported by a cadre of senior acolytes, and its citizenry being formed of a body of warrior-initiates supported by an extensive peasant class. Hilanistra's citizens are also unique in that many are resident on lands situated in other city states but still owned by the Emperor.

Bosippa

A new foundation on the Isle of Valos, Bosippa is the centre of the Korantine League, which is now the preferred forum for the various city-states to deal with one another. Only 15 years old, Bosippa has been colonised by settlers drawn from nearly every state in order to ensure that it feels truly cosmopolitan.

Historical Timeline for Korantia

Year	Event
1	The forefathers of the Korantines migrate out of Methelea, and begin to conquer and colonise the coastal lands of Taygus.
112-217	Wars of the Heroes: A period of constant conflict between rival aristocrats and their followers provides the source material for the classic cycles of Korantine epic poetry.
228	Following a decade of conquests, Koibos I, King of Korantis, declares himself Emperor of the Korantines and chief priest of Lanis.
703	Korantines found their first overseas colony on Kipsiperan.
936-938	Aristentorus of Hypata circumnavigates the Inner Ocean.
987	Emperor Entekos I founds a library at Yaristra, which proves to be a key act in ensuring the preservation of Korantine culture when Korantis is later lost to the sea.
1002	Outlawing of Sorcery by Emperor Enkilos II.
1003	First settlement of the Aspalian peninsula, at Keba.
1019	Foundation of the Taskan Empire.
1020	Korantine hero Zartos founds a city across the ocean in Jandekot on the site of a trading post, and names it Zarendra.
1034	Zartos killed while attempting to conquer the wild land of Fierla for the Emperor (now generaly called Zarland in his memory).
1055	The Inundation of Korantis. The Korantine capital is completely destroyed. Jekkarene magic is blamed for the disaster.
1057	Marriage of Zygas Taga to the Moon-Goddess Jekkara aligns the Taskan Empire with the Jekkarenes, traditional enemy of the Korantines.
1061	Kipsipsindra emerges as a dual monarchy and rejects the authority of the Korantine Emperor Koibos XVIII.
1072	The Aspalian Synoikism: Four small states in the Aspalian Peninsula unite as the Aspalian Tetrapolis to better resist the growth in power of neighbouring Keba.
1086	Hilanistra founded by the Korantine Emperor as his new capital.
1091	New city founded at Mersin following a land purchase from the King of Zathis.
1098	The Wilderness War: The Emperor sends help to the chieftains of Brotomagia to resist the incursions of Jekkarene forces supporting the foundation of Ramassa.
1111	The Sapphire Throne restored.
1125-36	The Marangian War: Korantines fend off several waves of invasion from aggressive Thennalt warlords striking out of Marangia, culminating in the Battle of Oster.
1135	Thennalt migrants and mercenaries allowed to settle in Korantine territory in return for accepting Korantine customs and laws, and found the city of Nysil.
1160-63	Korantine-Taskan War over control of the Thennalt land of Camtri. The Korantines and their allies are defeated by the Iron Simulacrum and leave the country, which becomes a Taskan province soon thereafter.
1164	Democratic revolution in Himela, as the so-called Oraynist movement achieves universal suffrage for all citizens irrespective of property and wealth.
1196	The Orchard War — Borissan forces attempt to restore aristocratic rule to Himela, but are defeated.
1205	Borissa converts trading post at Thyrta to a colony.
1207	Submission of the Marangian king at Timolay to Taskan rule.
1209	Korantine hero Kalacho of Agissene conquers Valos; foundation of the Korantine League at Bosippa.
1210	Kalacho refuses the offer of 'lifelong dictator' of the Korantine League and goes into retirement.
1214	A semi-barbarian warlord named Redanger appears from across the sea and travels to Hilanistra to announce that the long-lost colony of Zarendra in Jandekot still exists; and declares it to be a loyal dominion
1216	Current date.

Korantia

The Korantine League meets annually at the time of the Great Festival of Orayna and attempts to resolve any issues and disputes between states that have caused or threatened inter-state conflict. It also attempts to set some common policies concerning matters such as trade, sanctuary and the pursuit of fugitives across borders. New as it is, Bosippa's founders have every intention of making it a model of archaic living; scholars compete with one another to seek historical authority for each and every choice that has to be made about its governance and customs. Ancient buildings and monuments have been transported block-by-block from the mainland to ensure that Bosippa can claim ownership of some venerable structures. Its modernity, however, is ever visible in Bosippa's port of Nesterin, a substantial settlement in its own right and superbly equipped with all the best facilities for both civilian and naval crafts.

Bosippa's other claim to fame is as the leading clearing house for the slave trade, something that began with the wholesale enslavement of the native population but has continued to be a lucrative source of revenues for the new city-state.

The City-States of Korantia

Korantines live in small independent nations formed around a single city. At present, there are some 40 city-states that are considered Korantine by language and custom, and because they send gift-tribute to the Emperor at Hilanistra or send a delegation to the Korantine League when it convenes at Bosippa. The vast majority do both.

Leading City-States

Agissene

The most powerful of the Korantine states, Agissene has very much taken the lead in the key events of the last generation – the capture and resettlement of the Isle of Valos and the foundation of the Korantine League by their general Kalacho. Agissene's leaders have tried to turn the League into an instrument of their will, but face significant challenges in doing so while there is no serious external threat to galvanise the city-states to greater cooperation. Agissene's chief representative at the League, a man named Thenodemos, is famous for his rousing speeches warning of the danger posed to all Korantines by Taskan expansion.

Borissa

A Southern city keen to assert its credentials as a military and maritime power. Rootless adventurers often make their way here to sign up for mercenary service. From time to time Borissa attempts to grab land from nearby peoples, or plant an overseas colony or enclave, of which Thyrta, a coastal town right by the Forest of Sard, is a current example.

Himela

This city has the most vigorously democratic constitution. The old aristocracy of Himela keep any notions of superiority to themselves or risks swift and eager retribution from the public assembly, which is only too happy to confiscate their estates and/or send them into exile. Himela has a rich source of silver within its home territory, and produces the most highly regarded wine of Korantia (known as Solarnian), and its dominion includes the island of Tempigone off the coast of Methelea.

Mersin

A Northern colony close to the territory of the powerful Thennalt king of Zathis, to whom it pays tribute. It is the chief source for grain, slaves, timber and metalwork imported from 'barbarian' lands.

Keba

The chief among five colonies that were been planted on the Aspalian peninsula to the North, which nevertheless strive to maintain close contact with the heartland.

Kipsipsindra

Far away across the Ocean, this city remains a bastion of Korantine culture among the Oceanic peoples; the shipping link between Sarestra and Kipsipsindra is vital to the interests of both cities. Kipsipsindra does not recognise the Emperor as head of state. Nevertheless, it sends a delegation to the Korantine League.

Sarestra

This bustling port city takes the largest share of the shipping trade between Korantia and the West; its sailors and shipping guilds are legendary. Sarestra relies on close ties with the city of Kipsipsindra, and acts as that city's ally and centre of operations in Korantia itself.

Tysil and Nysil

Twin cities with a symbiotic history. Tysil is an ancient Korantine city, Nysil a more recent foundation created to house a

mass influx of settlers from barbarian lands as a separate community rather than merging populations. Tysil has a militaristic leadership, its situation near barbarian lands a constant opportunity for elected officials to prove their worth by inflicting some small defeat on her barbarian neighbours.

The Tetrapolis

This city-state is actually four small cities who have united into a single polity in order to present a unified front against their powerful neighbour at Keba. One of the constituent cities, Ostyra, was chosen to be the cult centre for them all. Keba's ambitions to take control over the Aspalian colonies thus thwarted, serious competition remains over hunting down trade and resources in the largely uncharted continent of Thurina to the North.

Yaristra

The most populous of the Korantine cities and a centre for culture and learning. Well-to-do Korantines strive to send their sons and daughters there to be properly educated. Yaristra is regarded as highly conservative, its chief magistrates and its major priesthoods being one and the same.

The Small Cities

About one third of Korantines live in what is referred to as a small city; that is, one where the male citizenry is less than 10,000 strong. Technically, Bosippa should fall into this category; however, its importance as a league centre means it is counted among the leading states. There are currently 31 small cities, and the leading states compete for influence and control over their affairs. This struggle usually revolves around attempts to support or sponsor a faction within a small city in its efforts to gain or retain control of the government, and guarantees of military support against their aggressive neighbours or access to reserves of magical power. The major city-states have even co-operated in a movement to exclude their smaller cousins from independent representation at the Korantine League. To date, the Emperor has taken pains to veto such bullying behaviour, a rare example of his interference in the League's affairs.

The City-State

A city is founded when its prospective citizens first come together and enter into a compact with one another that produces a constitution (the rules they agree to live by) and a new goddess, an aspect of Orayna, Queen of Heaven, who represents the soul of the nation. The site chosen for the new city is consecrated in her name, and all the important temples and public buildings are laid out within this consecrated space together with as much of the residential street plan as can be accommodated. Agissene famously permits no private houses, businesses or tombs within the consecrated limits of its city, which is an immense 246 hectares in size, with the result that the inhabited area sprawls around the core in a number of disconnected suburbs.

The lands controlled and exploited by a city come in two parts. The *chora* is a city's divinely sanctioned and internationally recognised home territory, which cannot exceed an area greater than three square kilometres per 100 citizens. All land within it may be blessed by magic cast at state level to ensure the fertility of the fields or protect the land from some external threat. The chora must consist of a single parcel of land; however, it can be an irregular shape, as the founders seek to define its boundaries in such a way as to take in the best of what the terrain offers. Its limitations are not only imposed by the size of the citizen body, but also the land available to secure for the city's use. Borders with other cities have to be carefully negotiated and sanctified by the priestesses of both the city-cults involved.

Most cities also have additional territory, land that they can control by might rather than by right. It could be economically useful, or, perhaps, a buffer zone for defence, or simply held in order to have room to expand the chora when the opportunity arises. Petty conflicts between states often concern rival claims over such lands. Disputes over dominion land are not referable to the Emperor because no sacred customs, rules or boundaries are in question. It is possible to take a dispute to the Korantine League for arbitration; but in reality this is just a sign that someone feels very hard done by, as these conflicts are recognised as fine opportunities to practice martial skills and compete for honours.

Boundary Changes

As a city-state's population rises and falls with the generations, the possible extent of the city limits does also. From time to time a city may be re-founded in order to bring its sacred and secular boundaries back into line. The rites of consecration only last as long as the current high priestess of the City Goddess maintains it by way of the Extension Miracle. As a result, the consecration must, in any event, be renewed upon the investiture of a new high priestess, and this presents the opportunity for the city authorities to decide whether to revise the boundaries at the same time. If, for some reason, it is decided that the primary settlement must be moved, then the city cults can

be transferred to a new place, and the rites of consecration to establish its boundaries conducted anew.

What a City-State Looks Like

The majority of Korantine cities have walls. It is considered ideal if the heart of it, the place where the city-goddess' own temple is located, is situated on an easily defensible terrain feature with its own fortifications – a citadel or refuge – since if this ever falls to an enemy then the state itself may be permanently destroyed. Additional circuits of walls are added over time as the urban area expands in size, in order to directly offer protection to the inhabitants or to ensure that strategically important bits of the surrounding terrain are secured from occupation by would-be attackers.

Inside the city walls, the Korantine preference is for orderly street plans, so far as is possible laid out on a grid; but the more ancient the city, the more likely its plan is to be rather more haphazard. Within the consecrated areas of the city are found all the grandest buildings, and often residential buildings built to several stories in order to accommodate as many people as possible on the most desirable real estate. The streets and public spaces are cobbled or flagged, and since beasts of burden are generally kept off the main thoroughfares, are mercifully free of the quantities of ordure that can be encountered in foreign cities.

Every city has a space where citizens meet to conduct the business of law or politics, and this is closely connected with areas set aside for temple precincts that double up as civic administration areas. The most magnificent temple in a city, with rare exceptions, is that to its own eponymous goddess.

While peasant buildings may be roofed in thatch or turf, most urban dwellings and all public buildings are roofed with tiles.

Fine saw-cut masonry is the preferred building material for high-status buildings, but the majority of homes and businesses are actually made of brick or irregular masonry coated in a render and often painted in bright colours. The arch is known but its use is often no more than decorative – few buildings are on a scale to require it, and there are magical means to replicate the structural benefits that arches provide while retaining the classical look.

Population

Korantine cities have a combined population of some 2.5 million people. The nature of city-state life means that they have a much higher proportion of city-dwellers than most cultures, as many farmers live in the city and go out to their fields in the surrounding countryside each day. The tables on the following pages give more detail on the propulation numbers for the leading city-states and the small cities.

Economic self-sufficiency and political self-determination are regarded as the essential requirements of a city-state, which means there must be enough people to provide all of the city's basic needs and defend it from others. Five hundred citizens is regarded as the absolute minimum size, and if the number falls below that and remains so at the end of the calendar year, the city will cease to exist. If some disaster befalls a small city, such as the loss of a large proportion of its citizens to war or famine, the survivors have to take drastic action to restore the citizen body, often by freeing slaves or inviting settlers from elsewhere

How big a city may be is much debated. Once it becomes so large that it is no longer practical for its citizens to all be directly involved in state ritual, including the political process; or the population outstrips the available land to feed them and there is no room for expansion; or simply the population becomes so large that there is an increase in factionalism and internal strife as the fraternal bonds of citizenship are loosened, then it is common to send some of the citizens away to found a new city somewhere else.

The urban population includes those living inside the walls of the city – but also anyone inhabiting a suburb within one hour's walk of the city centre, and anyone living in a municipal town, which is a satellite town or colony with its own local magistrates and regulations; in effect, a suburb located some distance from the city.

The Rural Population comprises all those who live in small towns (typically less that 1,000 inhabitants), villages, hamlets and in individual farmsteads or on the country estates of the wealthy.

The demographic profile of a city-state is generally as follows:

Male Citizens	Female Citizens	Freeborn Children (16 and under)	Metics, All Ages	Slaves, All Ages
20%	20%	35%	10%	15%

In many cities the number of metics (resident foreigners) is considerably higher due to the presence of a large pagan community. In these cases, the proportion of slaves may be correspondingly lower, since these people provide an alternative source of labour to a slave population. In others, particularly important ports like Sarestra, Masia and Kipsipsindra, there is a significant transient population. Slavery is at its highest in the more democratic states where the rich cannot keep the poor in a state of economic dependence, and need an alternative supply of compliant labour. If the state has significant additional territory to exploit beyond its chora, than slavery is often required to exploit it properly.

Pagan Korantia

Pagans are not all marginalised and exploited by their Korantine neighbours. Some occupy good land, in pockets that are too remote from a city to have been properly incorporated into its chora. They may have the blessings offered by their ancient gods and spirits of the earth, and are frequently called upon to harness or propitiate them for the benefit of the Korantine community. Nobody actually counts them, but it is possible they number up to half a million all told. Yet, for the most part, they are too restricted and enclosed to genuinely thrive. Throughout Korantia and the Ozyrian mountains, the pagans are doomed to economic stagnation and are regarded as backwoodsmen and simpletons, an opinion often echoed among even their cousins in neighbouring Thennalt lands such as Camtri and Marangia.

Korantine Culture

Being Korantine

Are you a Korantine or a foreigner? Are you of my city, or are you an outsider? Are you a citizen, or do you just live here? Are you rich or poor?

To be considered Korantine is a matter of language. If you speak the language as a native, it is assumed you also understand the basic principles of behaving in a civilised manner. This is not enough to ensure another Korantine will think well of you – attention is next paid to whether you come from the same

Korantia

Leading City-State Populations

City	Urban Population	Rural Population	Total
Agissene	60,000	190,000	250,000
Aspallian Tetrapolis	38,000	98,000	136,000
Borissa	40,000	160,000	200,000
Bosippa	8,000	12,000	20,000
Hilanistra	9,000	33,000	42,000
Himela	75,000	180,000	255,000
Keba	25,000	42,000	67,000
Kipsipsindra	14,000	44,000	58,000
Mersin	17,000	48,000	65,000
Nysil	18,000	48,000	66,000
Sarestra	62,000	95,000	157,000
Tysil	35,000	120,000	155,000
Yaristra	80,000	160,000	240,000
The Small Cities (combined total)	187,200	608,300	795,500
Total	**668,200**	**1,838,300**	**2,506,500**

city, or a friendly one; perhaps their city is traditionally hostile to your own because of some ancient land dispute or recent spate of cattle rustling; or indeed you are from some place they have never actually heard of.

Within a city, the difference between citizen and non-citizen is usually very clear. Everyone shares the basic assumption that all citizens are equal under the law, but this only loosely applies to people of citizen rank from other cities; does not extend to non-citizens with whom they live and work day by day but who lack the citizenship; and it certainly doesn't extend to slaves.

Social class is not an obsession, but it is very important when it comes to deciding who from among the citizenry should exercise power on behalf of all the rest. Most (but not all) Korantines are happy to acknowledge that fortune allots wealth to some by birth, others by deeds and a few by sheer chance. Wealth is measured in property, and the benchmark for all property ownership is how much farmland you have. If your wealth is tied up in other things, it only counts if those things can generate an income from produce or rents just as a farm does.

It is commonly believed that those who have property are more heavily invested in society, and rich people who have the luxury of not having to get up for work in the morning can and should busy themselves with contributing to the public good. This is the theory, and, of course, some rich people are better at it than others; and then there are those who think that the public good and their own best interests are one and the same.

Among citizens, the rank an individual holds within one of the state cults is very important, especially since cult ranks are the means through which political power is exercised. Achieving status within a cult is all part and parcel of the Korantine love of showing prowess, whether in the city's politics, the law courts, athletic competition, warfare or literacy.

Korantines can be very conservative about gender roles. It is fine for a strange foreign woman to mix freely with men and pursue a male-dominated career, as is common in Tarsenia and among other barbarians – but they would not want their own womenfolk getting any such funny ideas. For this reason, female courtesans who make a living from mixing with male society are almost exclusively foreigners, admittedly often women from other Korantine cities. Gender roles are clearly defined, and only the peculiarities of some of the more unusual cults and customs permit the rules to be bent.

Korantine Language and Literacy

Korantines all speak the same language, and if there are regional variations in dialect, classical Korantine – the dialect of the elite used for official and diplomatic purposes and for high class literature – is the same wherever you go and is relatively stable through time. The Korantine script is alphabetic, with some differences between regions in letter forms, particularly in how vowel sounds are rendered.

Small City Populations

City	Urban Population	Rural Population	Total
Aranela	4,000	14,000	18,000
Asbera	5,500	11,000	16,500
Avella	7,000	18,000	25,000
Boletta	6,000	3,000	9,000
Enkiste	1,500	4,000	5,500
Erakle	2,800	8,000	10,800
Hatrya	3,600	8,000	11,600
Heba	4,500	11,500	16,000
Hispola	6,500	32,000	38,500
Karkendra	8,000	27,000	35,000
Lanissa	9,500	34,000	43,500
Lukestra	4,700	18,000	22,700
Masia	11,000	34,000	45,000
Nolestra	3,900	7,000	10,900
Orissa	5,700	25,000	30,700
Pelostra	6,000	16,000	22,000
Poestra	14,000	8,000	22,000
Remoria	2,000	8,000	10,000
Sarsinaya	2,900	6,700	9,600
Sustra	9,000	21,000	30,000
Suthria	7,500	45,000	52,500
Tanyes	6,000	38,000	44,000
Tersippa	4,400	22,500	26,900
Thoria	9,000	35,000	44,000
Tugara	10,000	44,000	54,000
Velathela	1,200	8,600	9,800
Velthurisa	9,400	41,000	50,400
Vestrikina	6,200	24,000	30,200
Yolsos	3,800	15,000	18,800
Yustrum	3,600	17,000	20,600
Zarendra	8,000	4,000	12,000
Total	**187,200**	**608,300**	**795,500**

Korantines are a highly literate people, and even folk of quite low station may have a basic grasp of letters. Intellectual pursuits are prized among the rich, although a young man should take care to also show an interest in physical pursuits or be branded a bookish weakling.

The major forms of literature include sophisticated poetry, history, geography and philosophy.

Games Master Note: Any character of Propertied status and above is expected to have Literacy as a skill. In many cases those who have limited Literacy will be excluded from high office or indeed any cult rank higher than Initiate. Since the elite use their education to set themselves apart, a skill level in excess of 50% is required to be taken seriously.

Korantia

Poetry

The classic works are epic cycles retelling the stories of the exodus from Methelea and the subsequent generations of heroes who stand behind the foundation of all the early cities. The nearest thing to a national epic is that of Holenyo the Fool, a man who founded many cities but never found a home and died without issue. Holenyo's tale features many of the other heroes of Korantine lore as minor characters, and is appreciated above all for its mixture of magical adventure, comedy and pathos. Holenyo's epic is an anonymous tale that in fact exists in several versions.

Epic is now a lost art, and new works in the genre are generally literary exercises for the amusement of an intellectual elite that never catch on. Modern poetry is all short, florid and pithy verse in which the chief demand upon the writer is the clever juxtaposition of words and the innovative use of metre. The most celebrated poets of this style hail from Yaristra, of whom the prolific Klanthros of Pthoria is the most famous, if not the best.

History and Geography

Writing histories does not carry much weight among Korantine scholars; however, geographies are a fine way to demonstrate prowess as a traveller or explorer combined with skill as a writer, and the Korantines are second to none in writing about distant lands and peoples. Much of the best work dates from before the Cataclysm, when more of the world was accessible to Korantine scholars than is the case today. The overall assumption is that things probably haven't changed much since then – but this may be very mistaken.

The historians of note with whom well-educated people are supposed to be familiar are Retorios of Kelso (a city that no longer exists) who was a court historian to Emperor Enkilos II; and Dabaratus of Himela, who wrote histories for Enkilos' great-nephew, Emperor Antekos, which are very different in character, being a collection of historically inspired moral lessons for a young Emperor with no Empire left to rule.

Philosophy and Magic

Korantine philosophers differ markedly from Assabian philosophers in being very circumspect about the practical application of their insights, and will have nothing to do with sorcery. Instead, they concentrate on how the divine order should properly be reflected in the way a city is organised and the way in which an individual should conduct himself in public life. Baristates of Velathela is regarded as the pinnacle of advice on living the life of the good citizen. A quirkier contemporary, Sostrum of Sustra, was the founder of a movement that still exists today, a movement where its members believe that all life can be expressed through mathematical codes and harmonics, but are more famous for the fact they tend to insist on going about their cerebral business entirely naked, even in the public places.

Even in those places where sorcery is not strictly illegal, every so often there is a purge of anyone practising anything that looks like sorcery. Atheism is considered treasonous on the grounds that it represents apostasy from society and state, so its adherents are regarded with suspicion and often hounded out of town.

Those who practice Animism are regarded as bizarre and dangerous folk, especially since spirits are considered to be an especially dangerous phenomenon.

Mathematics

Given how city states are constituted and consecrated, the requirements of land surveying and measurement have resulted in significant advances in mathematics. Yaristra is considered the seat of learning, but the father of Korantine numbers was Mentho of Sustra, who was, incidentally, mentor to the famously undressed Sostrum of Sustra. The city still has a school founded in his name that accepts aspirational number-crunchers from other Korantine cities.

Sports and Entertainment

Korantines love sports, and physical education is regarded as a key part of a child's upbringing. The pinnacle of sporting action is horse racing, and every state worth its salt has a course that takes its riders across open country where all the riding skills expected of a young man accomplished in the hunt or in war are put to the test. In the biggest cities, the racing can be more formalised, and wealthy owners who keep whole stables of racehorses sponsor professional jockeys to race each other around circuits on the flat. In Agissene there is a famous 'intramural' race, where the course is all set within the sacred boundaries of the city, passing by each of the major temples on their route.

Combat sports are for educational purposes and not for public entertainment, other than a form of wrestling where two oiled fighters test their skills in an event that ladies are not permitted to watch, let alone participate in. This wrestling is called

Assabian Style, despite the fact that nothing very much like it takes place in that land.

Water sports are essentially taboo, although Korantines do learn to swim. The nearest thing is a race between rival rowing teams on sleek military galleys that takes place at an annual review of the Sarestran fleet, and to which vessels from other cities are sometimes invited.

Athletics are very much encouraged, and the suite of running, jumping, throwing and endurance events is considered a fine demonstration of manly skills (and rarely, of womanly virtues). The greatest prizes are for those who show all-round prowess – being good at only one thing smells of professionalism, and in athletics professionalism is frowned upon. For the same reason, trophies and prizes are symbolic, rather than valuable, in nature.

The Law

Among Korantines, custom and law are essentially the same thing. Being rather conservative folk, the way things were done in the past is regarded as the best way, and only when that proves inadequate for some reason is custom changed. Customs are not rules that need to be written down as everyone knows what they are, and, in any event, they can benefit from the process of subtle change over the generations to remain relevant. However, if customs are to be decisively altered, a law must be made and set up as an inscription in a public place so nobody can have any doubts about it. The new law becomes part of the Customs of the Korantines, a body of lore that dictates how people are expected to conduct themselves both in public and in private from city to city.

Games Master Note: Familiarity with the customs and laws is reflected in the Custom skill. In a character's home city the skill does not normally need to be rolled against unless seeking to exploit some inconsistent or ill-defined feature of the law, or recall some obscure or rarely used tradition. When abroad in other Korantine cities it is a useful skill to know or to guess what is likely to be different, even if it does not reveal precise information, but the skill roll will be at least one grade harder.

Going to Court

In Korantine legal cases it is normal for one citizen to bring a case of law against another to seek redress for a slight or injury, or accuse them of some crime. Minor cases and anything to do with foreigners is dealt with by an individual magistrate appointed to look into the matter, but in most major cases where a citizen is involved, there is recourse to adversarial justice in front of a citizen jury. In democratic Himela that jury is made up of whoever happens to be there on the day rather than a representative selection, and can be quite chaotic.

Slavery

Slavery is very common, but Korantine slaves are generally protected, by law, from serious mistreatment and are permitted some dignity as human beings. Condemned criminals and foreign prisoners of war are an exception, and will be routinely worked to death in the mines or other hazardous places of work. Otherwise, slaves are regarded as members of their owner's extended family, albeit ones who cannot fully participate in public life any more than children because they are under the legal authority of another.

Organisations such as cults (including those cults that encompass an arm of state) can also own slaves, and frequently do. Such slaves may be educated and often have real status derived from the work they are given.

Debt Bondage

In most Korantine cities, it is illegal for a citizen to offer his own person, or that of any freeborn person in his power, as security for a debt. Therefore, those who fall into debt this way are mostly resident non-citizens to whom no such protection under the law is available, and the vast majority are impoverished members of Pagan communities. Debt slavery is all too common a plight for these people, and frequently the cause of unrest. Debt slaves usually have a better life than those who come into slavery through the market or as prisoners, but this is not always the case.

Buying Slaves

Slaves can be purchased from authorised dealers. Being a slave trader is regarded as a shameful (if necessary) business, a trade that is usually handled by non-citizens. Slave markets take place whenever a consignment arrives at a suitable location, and auction is the usual practice. Slaves can start from as little as 100SP and reach prices of 1,000SP and more.

Nesterin, the port of Bosippa on Valos, is the major clearing house for the slave trade, a role it has retained following the conquest and enslavement of many of its inhabitants by Kalacho of Agissene.

Enslaving a Defeated Enemy

One way to deal with a defeated enemy is to claim 'ownership' of them as a humane alternative to killing them out of hand. If the foe submits willingly and the state has no prior claim either because they are wanted for a crime against someone other than you, or because they are citizens of a state with whom some

Korantia

sort of treaty or prisoner swap arrangement is in place, then the defeated enemy becomes your property. On the whole a captured bandit, robber or murderer is not worth anything as a slave, being of demonstrably bad and unruly character. Consequently, the state is likely to pay a higher bounty than their slave value for the removal of such undesirables from society by being handed over for a brief interview with the acolytes of Kos in charge of law and order and subsequently to the executioner.

CITY-STATE CONSTITUTIONS

Each city's constitution is different, but they are all variations on a model that places the acolytes of one or more of the state cults at the head of a council made up of the city's leading citizens, to exercise their power on behalf of the sovereign people. The details in how the model is applied can produce immensely different results, with the most important difference being in how Social Class is used as a barrier to entry into the state cults.

Citizenship

The rules concerning who is eligible for citizenship – according to age, gender and parentage – may be very different according to which city you come from. Himela requires that you have a citizen parent on both sides and have reached 16 years of age. Sarestra requires that only one parent is a citizen, and Keba is content to allow those born elsewhere – and even freed slaves – to become citizens if an existing citizen of good standing sponsors the application. If you are citizen, you are expected to take part in public cult to the state gods, and have rights and obligations to take part in public life.

Government

There are three basic types of constitution and they are all defined by how they deal with the differences of social class.

Democratic constitutions grant all citizens the same access to its most influential cults, and thereby to the decision-making bodies of state, no matter what their financial means. This is in fact a rather poorly observed principle – actually allowing a poor man to stand for high office (become an acolyte of a state cult) is regarded as radical even in democracies, and only the Himelans do it. Democracies are nevertheless very suspicious of the power and influence wielded by its richest citizens, and the feeling is often mutual. Because of the universal privileges of citizenship and the fact that the rich have less opportunity to exploit the poor in the ways they would like, democracies tend to have the strictest rules for acquiring citizenship.

Mixed constitutions restrict senior positions of power to the wealthier citizens, and make sure all the important debates happen in council rather than in front of the whole citizenry, but grant some important rights of approval – including election of the top magistrates and the declaration of war – to the people's assembly. Most Korantine cities are in this category. The city of Vestrikina is, for many reasons, considered the gold standard of a mixed constitution.

Oligarchic constitutions restrict access to power to a narrow section of society – by birth, wealth or some other element that produces a very narrow pool of people to choose from who can arrange things amongst themselves. The diarchy (dual kingship) of Kipsipsindra is an extreme version. Acolyte roles in the key state cults are restricted to members of the ruling group, and the council is stuffed with oligarchs and their cronies. In some cases, the roles of acolyte and priest are merged. Oligarchies tend to be prone to revolution and internal strife, as inevitably there is dissent even amongst the rich and powerful over who is 'in' and who is 'out' of the club.

Constitutional Crisis

When it all goes wrong and the constitution is challenged by internal strife, the result is usually one of two outcomes: a tyranny, in which one man gathers enough popular support to suspend the normal laws and rule by decree; and anarchy, when nobody knows who is in control, only that the laws are suspended and that there are a lot of dead bodies in the street. Neither situation tends to last for very long; however, there have been several tyrannies that have survived to a second generation, because the tyrant in question (Zilathro of Yaristra, who was rumoured to be a woman in disguise, is the most famous example), turns out to be rather good and there is no appetite to get rid of him (or her).

MILITARY

The Korantine world has very little in the way of standing armies. The Emperor's Paladins are full-time warriors but they are not especially numerous nor automatically at the state's disposal, except in the case of external threat – if such a warrior joins a fight against another Korantine city, he does so as a private individual.

Shores of Korantia

Many Korantine city states are on, or near, the sea, and each maintains a certain number of warships and transport vessels at the expense of the state, although usually only the key crew members are permanently employed and the rest are levied when there is a need for action.

Military Manpower

In most states, only the freeborn male citizens of certain age are eligible or expected to serve in their city's army, namely those between 19 and 41 years old. Those younger or older, and capable of bearing arms, are usually kept back for garrison duty at home. This places the available citizen manpower with which to take to the field at approximately 15% of the total; hence, Agissene has a paper strength of 38,000 or so. It is rarely practical, prudent or desirable to call out every able-bodied citizen, and in any event, at least one third of those will not have the means to furnish themselves with even the bare minimum of equipment. When Kalacho marched the men of Agissene to join the invasion of Valos he took only 8,000 soldiers with him. If the state also has a navy, it must be fed from the manpower pool, although it is not unknown to use slaves to bolster the numbers. The navy is a good place to use your poorest citizens because they need no arms, just the power of their backs to pull an oar.

The Citizen Levy

The men eligible for service are only called to arms when there is some sort of emergency. It is a local matter, and also a question of how serious the situation, as to how far down the economic scale the call to arms can reach. The model citizen soldier turns up for duty equipped with a helmet, spear, shield and sidearm; and, if he is a man of means, perhaps with some armour too. The poorest classes may present themselves with no more than a sling or simple bow, and many might find themselves appointed to row in the fleet if their city has one. In some of the most conservative states, the poor are not called up but instead the need for lightly armed troops is filled by the servants, slaves and other dependants brought to the field by the wealthier citizen-soldiers.

For the citizen body, the chief war god is Torthil, who is both a farmer and a warrior, a defender and destroyer of homes and crops.

Patriotic Bands

'Patriotic Bands' of volunteers are a state's first line of defence – men who are ready to take up arms at a moments notice, before the citizen levy has been summoned. Their composition differs from state to state according to the balance of power sits between the elite and the masses. In some cities, these are aristocrats and their armed retainers; in others, they are a mob of lightly armed peasants. In peaceful times, Patriotic Bands can act as a constabulary or come together to form a posse. Their common feature throughout the Korantine world is that the members are all initiates and acolytes of a military cult, in most cases, in honour of Palaskil, Veltis, or even, in maritime states, Pyrolus.

A character who joins a Patriotic Band must be a citizen and is expected to bring his own armour and weapons, and in some cases, even a horse.

Games Master Note: The Combat Styles and traits for Patriotic Bands tend to be the same as for the local citizen levy. Band members may well be responsible for drilling the militia in basic combat skills.

Sacred Bands

Some cities have one highly elite Patriotic Band known as the Sacred Band, whose lot it is to fight to the last man in defence of the state. Their essential function is as the citadel guard, and to these people also falls the job of defending the city-cult's temple as last-ditch protectors. For some obscure traditional reason, a Sacred Band can never number more than 300 men – and is usually less. The Sacred Band Miracle is reserved for the use of these elite units.

The Sabatines

The merchant societies under the tutelage of Sabateus, the God of trade and travel, maintain their own standing forces used to guard depots, caravans and shipping and, if need be, support the state, classically as marines.

Traditionally uniformed in green, Sabatines can be hired from anywhere as long as they speak enough Korantine to follow the orders of their Korantine officers, and hence, the vast majority are not of citizen status. Their equipment is provided for them at state (cult) expense. Not all cities have a force of Sabatines as the smaller ones have neither need nor the resource, to maintain such a force.

Korantia

Foreign Mercenaries

Whole contingents of warriors from foreign parts may be hired in the case of an emergency or major campaign, especially if they have specialist skills to offer, such as archery or horsemanship. In these cases, the Syndics of the local Sabatean cult negotiate the deal on behalf of the state. Sometimes a city's Patriotic Bands might even offer themselves to another city as 'paid help' in conflicts between, or within, other states.

Armour and Weapons

Korantines tend to use leather, scale and plate armour. Bronze or gilded iron plate has aristocratic connotations, of course, and is favoured by the Paladins. Traditional weapons include shortsword, spear, a flat oval shield (Thureos, stats as per Scutum) or round hoplite shield (Clipeus), with a wicker Pelte carried by the most lightly armed or poorest. A variety of missile weapons including slings, bows and darts are used, amongst which javelins are counted as the most 'manly'.

City-State Religion

Every Korantine city-state has its own pantheon of deities that its citizens are expected to honour. These pantheons are essentially the same from one city to another with minor differences, comprising a selection from the Celestial Court of deities shared by all Korantines; however, the cults set up to worship the gods are specific to each city and exclude all but their own citizens. Each part of the machinery of state and every section of the community is operated as a cult of its respective tutelary deity. A cult's rules for membership and the obligations of membership are state-specific, so those of the cult of Himelan Anayo will, for example, differ from those of Anayo of Agissene. More information is provided in the Cults chapter.

The Civic Trinity

There are three key cults in any city, and these are to the City Goddess; to her husband Anayo, god of rulership and government, wisdom and knowledge; and to Torthil, who is a god of agriculture and war. The city-goddess is the chief cult for the city's women; Torthil is the chief deity for the city's menfolk, and Anayo is the chief deity for those who rule the community.

Sometimes a different deity replaces Torthil in this trinity, if it better reflects the concerns of the city's male citizens.

Several other deities have important state roles to play and either have dedicated cults in their honour or are represented as sub-cults to one of the trinity, lending perhaps a single Miracle to its worshippers. In such cases, one of the cult's acolytes or priests has the responsibility of representing the sub-cult and learning its Miracle. The various arrangements made to accommodate these minor deities is one of the things that can make the state religion of each city unique.

Religious Practices

Almost all religious observances are public business, even if some of them might be restricted to some particular elite or social group. Mystery religions that take place in secret and have membership that cuts across the traditional divisions of the community are frowned upon. Most rites take place indoors in specially constructed temples; however, if mass participation is involved the temple is sure to be set overlooking a big public space where worshippers can gather in numbers.

Korantines routinely bury their dead, although cremation is regarded as an expensive and glamorous way to go and is still practiced by the upper classes in some cities and by the Lanists. The dead are always disposed of outside the sacred limits of the city unless granted hero status; hence, when these limits are extended it may be necessary to move the location of entire cemeteries or else describe the new city limits in ways that avoid them.

Cult Hierarchies

The most important people in a cult are often the acolytes rather than the priests. An acolyte is likely fulfilling an important job as an officer of state with influence outside the cult's own hierarchy, and an acolyte's appointment is therefore not just in the gift of the cult itself but requires some form of approval from the wider community. Priests, on the other hand, are permanent appointments and their selection is an entirely cult-controlled process.

Worshipping in a Foreign City

Membership of a cult in one city gives no status with the equivalent cult in another city-state, unless this is arranged by a treaty between the two communities. Such a treaty can arrange that the citizens of one city can worship at the shrines and temples of another, thereby restoring their devotional pool or accelerating magic point recovery; however, the restrictions are many and a 'foreigner' may never gain greater benefits from worship than a local citizen of Initiate level.

The Sacred Year

Korantines measure the year as a Solar Cycle, and ignore the misalignment of the 13 months with the lunar phases and instead intercalate two days at the end of the lunar calendar in order to make 13 equal months of 28 days fit the scheme. Each month is punctuated by four weeks, a Korantine invention used to remove reliance on lunar phases by counting days instead, and there are usually several religious festivals in each month of varying importance.

The months of the year may have different names in different cities, but the old Imperial Calendar provides the most commonly used version, which goes as follows:

The Korantine Calendar

Month	Event	Season
Trigelso	Start of the year; opening of the roads	
Arribea	Spring wheat planting; opening of the seas	Spring
Lanthril	Shearing time	
Sheyloris	Winter wheat harvest	
Pyrlo	Campaigning season	
Lassica	Campaigning season	Summer
Torthil	Spring wheat harvest	
Sabatine	Grape harvest	
Plashkis	Harvest festivals, blessing stores	Autumn
Veltune	Winter wheat planting	
Zolestine	Olive harvest; closing of the seas	
Semordine	Midwinter festivals	Winter
Anyune	Elections and public appointments	
Orynsa	Heaven – 2 day intercalation	

THE WIDER WORLD

In this chapter, the lands accessible to travellers on the Ocean are briefly described. These include places where an overland route is technically possible, but the time, challenges and expense involved are so great that journeying by sea is always preferable. Each of the areas described constitute a Locale skill that can be learned by the well-travelled adventurer.

THE SHORES OF KORANTIA

The Shores are Korantia-outside-Korantia; that is, where the Korantine way of life prevails beyond the heartland on the Western coast of Taygus. Some of these places were colonised over the long millennium of the Empire, some of them really quite recently. The Shores Of Korantia are connected and held together only because the sea-lanes between them are open. Should they be interdicted by foreign powers, divine anger or natural disaster, then the Korantine community would itself be fractured again just as when the Cataclysm sundered the Empire 160 years ago.

Old Korantis

The site of the lost capital of the Empire is now no more than a collection of small islands, each being an upland peak of the sunken land of Korantis. The islands are uninhabited and shunned by all except the occasional treasure hunter searching for valuable relics beneath the waves. Sometimes there is a spectacular find, such as when some of the Emperor's Paladins successfully located and raised the Sapphire Throne and carried it off to Hilanistra.

Valos

Valos was settled by several different peoples over the centuries. For a while, it was home to a Korantine colony founded from Tysil, but this was destroyed by Kapolan invaders shortly after the destruction of Korantis. Marangians settled there some time later and in concert with the Kapolans made it the base of operations for wide-ranging acts of piracy and plunder. When Kalacho of Agissene finally conquered the island in order to put a stop to the inhabitants' predatory ways, Valos was settled with colonists drawn from right across the Korantine world. One of these is the capital of the Korantine League inaugurated under the Emperor's auspices in 1210.

Valos is about 40 miles long and 20 wide, with a chain of steep mountains that drop abruptly to the sea to the north, but which shelter a plain to the south. The Korantine settlements are all to be found in its south-west corner, but the eastern parts are still inhabited by the descendants of the earlier Kapolans and Marangians, and there a composite language known as Valot is spoken.

At the north-east end of the island are the remaining settlements of the Corsairs, now much diminished, pacified and robbed of their charismatic leader, Korsaddin (a Guyuntar from Tapropiscur). It is said that Korsaddin's son Korsaris escaped the siege of Mount Nester with some followers and fled to Marangia – certainly the more optimistic of the Valots predict a victorious return at the head of a liberating army.

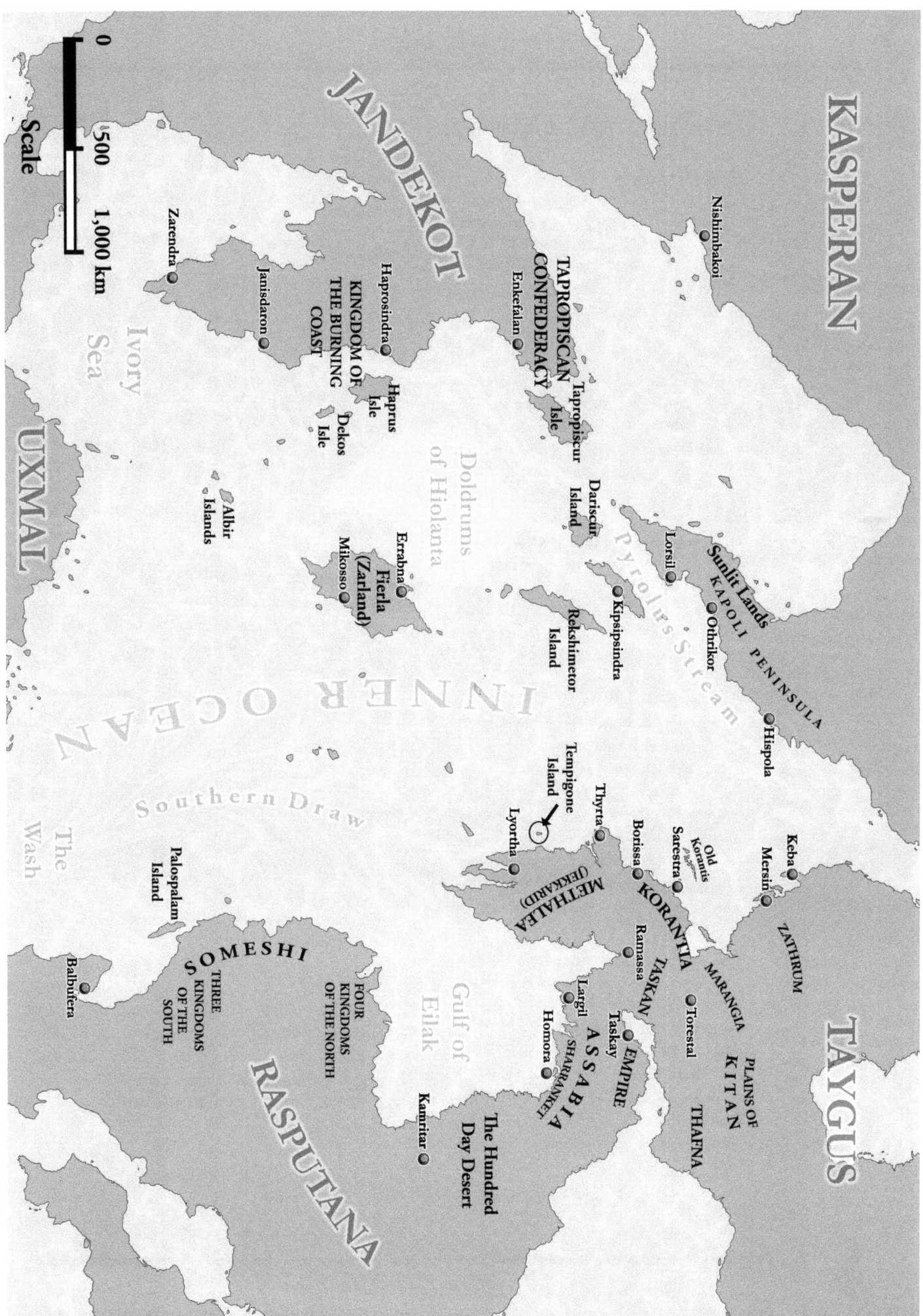

Shores of Korantia

Searching for Anathaym?

If you want to locate Anathaym and her city of Meeros in the world of Thennla, look to the city of Mersin, a Korantine colony of some antiquity located on the shores of the Thennalt land of Zathrum. The people of Mersin long ago absorbed many Thennalt customs, including worship of the bull-headed god Myceras as an aspect of the Korantine/Thennalt deity known elsewhere as Torthil. When first the King of Zathis granted the lands to found the colony, he asked that as part of the deal the Korantine settlers would relieve him of a loyal but rather troublesome all-female warrior society, a sisterhood that recognized no husband but Myceras. The Korantines were sorely in need of wives, but perhaps had not envisaged taking wives like these; and the Sisters of Myceras themselves had no intention of becoming subordinate to Korantine husbands. Nevertheless a deal was struck, by which the women would marry the settlers but in their new land would become equal to their husbands as citizens with a vote in public affairs so long as they retained their habit of training at arms.

While the women of Mersin are not eligible for the citizen levy, and these days most 'Meerish' women are no different to those of other Korantine cities, its Patriotic Band must allow the inclusion of women and those who take up arms in this way sit alongside the men in all public rights and duties.

Colonies and Outposts

Aspala
A peninsula upon which are situated the northernmost colonies of Korantia. Here is found Keba, and also Tetrapolis, an aggregation of four small states that have merged in order to resist the power of Keba, which has for a long time claimed hegemony over the whole region.

Hispola
A Korantine colony on the Kapoli peninsula, which is a stopping place for some of the seaborne traffic between Korantia and Kipsipisindra. The settlement was a combined enterprise by several smaller states and sponsored by Sarestra. Hispola has a wide territory for its size, as its citizens have fanned out to where good land or pastures can best be found in what is a rather wild and rocky region. The outlying villages are sometimes plagued by the depredations of Thurian Centaurs, who are an aggressive folk from the interior. Hispola's constitution is moderately democratic, and the citizens have friendship treaties with Himela.

Kipsipsindra
Kipsipsindra is thought to be the largest city west of Himela, although that assumes you can discount the frightening rumours that the orcish city of Nishimbakoi holds more than 150,000 people. It dominates the island of Kipsiperan, and owes its success to having been an important outpost of the Korantine Empire in ancient times. The city still has many monuments of that era, including sturdy city walls and a naval harbour big enough to hold 100 ships of war.

The people of Kipsipsindra are proud of their Korantine history and claim the right to hegemony over nearby islands on the strength of it, an attitude with which their neighbours are quick to take issue. The coming together of Korantines and Archipelagans of predominantly Kapolan stock in the makeup of Kipsipsindrans has created a vibrant culture. Its most noteworthy feature is a dual monarchy; one royal house currently headed by King Pathes represents the sun god Lanis as ruler of the sky, the other, headed by King Mollo, represents the storm god Palaskil as ruler over the ocean waves.

Kipsipsindrans have themselves founded colonies: Haprosindra to the west, and several in Fierla, of which only Errabna remains. Both are now fully independent from their mother city, and no longer Korantine in character.

Mersin
A Korantine colony founded on territory acquired by purchase from the king of Zathis, which prospers from the grain and timber that it can ship to Korantia proper. It is also a good place from which to access the Pyrolus Stream, the important current that helps convey ships towards the West. Mersin is famous for its inclusion of women in some traditionally male roles within society, something that has its origins in the deal done with the Thennalt king when it was founded. King Uskil was plagued by a warrior society comprised of female warriors that had many times caused him and his retinue humiliation. So he found a way to betray these women to a force of Korantine mercenaries, and they were made wives instead of slaves to the founders of Mersin. To this day, some women of the city claim the privilege of standing alongside the menfolk in the city militia.

Tempigone
An island dominion of the state of Himela that lies closer to the Jekkarid than it does to Korantia. Ruled by an exiled duke and with a population that is mostly non-Korantine, its importance lies in the rich deposits of iron ore and other minerals found on Mount Tempiger, which is its main geographical feature.

Thyrta
A colony founded by the state of Borissa on the coast of Brotomagia and expected to achieve independent city status within the next few years. This place is described in detail and is the starting point for the adventures provided in this book.

The Wider World

Zarendra

This far-flung colony was planted long ago on the coast of Jandekot and now there is hardly anyone who has ever been or met anyone who has. Nevertheless, this is a thriving community sticking to the old Korantine ways and worthy of being considered a Korantine city.

Zarendra was settled during the final years of the Old Empire by colonists from Kipsipsindra. Its location near the mouth of the mighty Saa River was a daring attempt to exploit the potentially boundless resources of this immense, sparsely populated and largely uncharted continent.

When the Korantine Empire collapsed this isolated city managed to keep going against the odds, but has frequently fallen victim to foreign conquerors. In recent times, Zarendra was held by Halerik of Haprosindra against his brother Valerik, with whom he fought over the succession to the Kingdom of the Burning Coast. Halerik was murdered by his own mercenary captain, Hemerik of Ishkeleb, because he was late with his payments, and Hemerik took over control of the city. After 16 years of tyranny, he was deposed, in turn by his idealistic son, Redanger, who brought the people into his faction by promising a return to constitutional law. Redanger then proceeded all the way to Korantia to announce his city's loyalty to a rather surprised Emperor Koibos XXIV, who had no idea that the city still existed. Redanger declared himself to be regent of the Dominion of Zarendra on the Emperor's behalf, which neatly absolved him of the need to step down from his position of power in order to preserve the ancient constitution. He even took the name Koibion to demonstrate his sincerity.

The Civilised East

At the edge of Korantine territory, there are few well-travelled routes into neighbouring lands. The most important passes over the Ozyrian mountains via Hilanistra and ultimately arrives in Taskan territory, passing through Camtri and on to the Taskan heartland of Tarsenia. While there may be many obscure trails offering alternative passage over the mountains, any mounted or wheeled traffic is forced to go around them to the north east through the territory of Tysil or Nysil into Marangia or else to pass round them to the south-west via Vestrikina and Tersippa to Brotomagia.

Brotomagia

A land famed for its beauty, the wooded hills and green valleys of Brotomagia are home to many a local chieftain of Thennalt stock who can sport a Korantine education, fluency in several languages and sophisticated tastes. Some even have a nymph for a wife. However, as Brotomagia is a buffer zone between the Jekkarenes, Taskans and Korantines, there is always a feeling that the good life may one day come to a disastrous end.

Camtri

Camtri is a Thennalt land that has now embraced Taskan rule and is beginning to embrace Taskan customs. There are still a few people around who dream of independence or who resent that they are now drawn into the orbit of the Taskan Empire. Such people increasingly find it convenient to keep their ideas to themselves. Camtri is administered from Torestal and is a key strategic region for the Taskan army.

The ancient kingship of Camtri is now a ritual post only, and a number of prominent families now administer the territory though controlling the major priesthoods of the local Taskan Emperor-Cult. Taskan culture and customs are taking over and those who do not embrace the process generally up sticks and look for hospitality in Marangia or look for work in Korantia.

Marangia

The Marangians are famously warlike and considered even by other Thennalts to be venal and untrustworthy. The Marangians have a royal seat at Timolay, but this is now under Taskan control and King Arkenson the Portly made their puppet and supplied with advisors sent from Taskay itself. The presence in the area of opportunistic Taskan grave robbers, drawn by rumours of fabulously wealthy tombs and cemeteries, increases tensions between the occupiers and the natives and makes life more dangerous for everyone.

The Marangians generally feel very much oppressed even if outside direct Taskan control; with Timolay under foreign occupation the ancient cultic centre at Oster is now regarded as their capital, and it is generally not a welcoming place to foreigners.

Zathrum

Beyond Marangia to the north is Zathrum, a Thennalt land inhabited by folk regarded as either very old fashioned or in touch with their traditions, depending on your point of view. The most powerful ruler is Radabus the King of Zathis, as a result of his inheriting a Korantine colony on his doorstep at

Mersin – sited on lands granted by an ancestor in return for trade monopolies and a regular tribute. Malstrom, the King of Gort, has control of much of the rest of the territory but has no such easy access to the outside world and prides himself as the great and manly upholder of ancient traditions, a posture appreciated by the wild mountain men of Gumathena to the east (considered barbaric even by Marangian standards) whom he can call on for support when he needs to.

Methalea

Methalea is a huge peninsula dominated by what is considered to be the oldest civilisation still in existence, the Theocracy of the Jekkarenes. The northern part is a wilderness region known as the Forest of Sard, and the eastern part of the peninsula is a rough, almost barren region known simply as the Methalean Badlands. The rest of the peninsula – and indeed sometimes by extension the whole peninsula – is known as The Jekkarid after the secretive and matriarchal society devoted to the night-goddess Jekkara. This goddess manifests as the Moon, usually visible by day but at night the biggest and brightest planet visible in the heavens. The moon hangs stationary in the sky above the capital city, Parlasos.

The Jekkarenes' capital, and indeed the only city of any size, is Parlasos. The city is situated in an area known as the Vale of Shadow, because it is the centre of a shadow cast over Methalea as the sun passes above the moon in a daily eclipse. At its heart is a temple of breathtaking size that is the centre of worship, as well as the palace of Queen Semankore, chief priestess and ruler of the Jekkarene Theocracy. The city is surrounded by a rural hinterland where famous corn known as silver barley is cultivated, which can draw its nourishment from the moon rather than the sun. Its grains are sought after by foreign alchemists, but there is an outright ban on their export and only temple estates are allowed to cultivate the crop.

Very few foreigners ever go to Parlasos, as the Jekkarenes restrict the vast majority of their dealings with foreigners to the two cities created for the purpose. When they do they are given fine hospitality but it usually comes with close escort and surveillance.

Lyortha

Lyortha is a port on one of the southern fingers of the peninsula that acts as an entrepôt for trade arriving or leaving the Jekkarid. This is the only place where foreign vessels may land or load goods, and all goods being transported further into Jekkarene territory may only be carried by Jekkarene shippers. The town is ruled over by the notorious Baron Solfernoy – albeit under the supervision of a trio of priestesses from the capital. Solfernoy is not only a very rich man, as a result of the perquisites and bribes he takes along the way, but also an extremely influential one, with ambitions to exercise power as well as influence beyond the borders of the Theocracy.

One of only two places in the Jekkarid where foreigners are welcome, Lyortha is also home to a small flotilla of five warships built and maintained for the Taskan navy and, in fact, the only ocean-going navy the Taskans have. Above all, though, Lyortha is a trading town where the Jekkarenes attempt to gather in goods from the oceanic trade routes and export some of their own.

Ramassa

Solfernoy's counterpart in the north-east of the country is Baron Lankermost, who controls the other entrepôt, Ramassa. Most Taskans who enter the Jekkarid do so here. Lankermost is no maverick like Solfernoy, being instead a trusted and deeply conservative patrician who is the right man to handle the sensitive commercial, diplomatic and religious traffic between Taskay or Ashkor and Parlasos, all of which passes under his nose. Ramassa is situated near the sea and at a great river mouth but the waterways here are shallow, shifting and choked with silt; in fact, Ramassa is useless as a port other than for flat-bottomed boats used in and around the delta.

The Badlands of Methalea

The whole eastern side of the peninsula is a lawless region dotted with small communities attempting to scratch a living from the soil through a mixture of agriculture and pastoralism. Where possible, banditry and piracy provides additional income. These people are mostly of Jekkarene origin, but they or their forebears were cast-out of society for some misdemeanour or other, and are living in exile. Despite its generally grim reputation the area attracts some voluntary exiles as well as escaped slaves and the occasional religious or social apostate from further afield. One or two notorious wizards have made their homes here in order to practise their researches away from the eyes of civilisation. Less appealing is the fact that lycanthropy is rife. The Jekkarenes have long used lycanthropy as a traditional curse upon their outcasts, as they are of the opinion that it will keep the exiles' attentions focussed on survival and fear of one another rather than getting organised and causing a nuisance.

The Forest of Sard

This extensive wilderness region is in fact a mix of hills, valleys and wetlands some 150 kilometres miles from north to south and more than 350 kilometres east to west, of which half the total area is forested. Through the middle runs the Quickwater River, in places cutting deep ravines, in others fanning out over a flooded landscape. South of the river is a favourite hunting ground for Jekkarene nobility. North of the river is a playground for the Thennalt lords of Brotomagia. Very few people actually live in the forest and those who do are mostly on the fringes. The north west of Sard is increasingly cut into by the Borissan colony at Thyrta, so you might encounter Thyrtan prospectors there. Deeper into the wilderness there may be a few bands of outlaws and the occasional hermit but by and large the land is given over to nature and in the great expanse of the forest any number of exotic creatures may lay hidden.

The Taskan Empire

The Taskan Empire is the most powerful political entity in the world at present. Two hundred and fifty years ago an exiled Jekkarene warlord by the name of Zygas Taga intervened in the endemic wars between rival city-states in the land of Tarsenia, and, ultimately, unified them choosing one, Taskay, to be his capital. Since that time the Taskan Empire has grown in size and power, and has brought many neighbouring lands under its rule. However, the Emperor himself was declared a god and has shut himself away in his palace to prepare for his ascension to the heavens. In his place, he left a magically animated statue to be his chief officer of state and manage the Empire's affairs, supported by colleges of priests who run the Emperor cult in each city and province. First came the Marble Simulacrum, which was destroyed in a disastrous battle over 100 years ago, then the Iron Simulacrum, which still rules the Empire today.

The heartland of the empire is Tarsenia, a heavily cultivated and densely populated region comprising the cities of Taskay, Tarsang, Pryjarna, Ashkor, Felsang, Merat and Zarina. The empire has grown to incorporate the Kingdom of Yegusai to the east, the Thennalt land of Camtri to the west, and a region now known as Further Tarsenia to the north where the city of Ralmyra has been founded. Morkesh and the Jekkarene theocracy are its protectorates.

Sorantia

A little kingdom surrounded on all sides by the Taskan Empire yet nominally independent. Sorantia is also a failed kingdom, and much of its lands are now returning to wilderness or at the mercy of bandits and outlaws. However, its capital, the city of Sorandib, is still a place of wonder, for here is the seat of a famous sorcery school known as the Artificers. These people are thought to have fashioned the magically animated statue, The Iron Simulacrum, which rules the Taskan Empire. Sorantia is known as the origin of a drug called Fengo that can be refined for a variety of purposes, as well as the source of gunpowder used by an elite regiment in the Taskan army, The Unconquerable Heroes of Taskay.

Assabia

Assabia forms the intersection of two continents – Taygus and Rasputana. Much of the region is desert. Its most populated areas comprise of the lands of Djesmirket, Sharranket and Morkesh. Rich and varied magical traditions, access to the wider world across the Gulf of Eilak and the Inner Ocean and a constantly shifting political landscape make Assabia a place where there are many adventures are to be found.

Djesmirket

Djesmir is a huge city that is regarded with a reverence in the region as home to the most ancient and important temples and of the most skilled and powerful sorcerers. In reality, it is in a state of decadence and decline – Sharranketan merchants no longer consider the place to be the most prized market for their goods and the Taskan Empire has always been cool towards the Djesmiris since they participated in a war against the Taskans 80 years ago. Djesmirket was once synonymous with the whole region of Assabia but is now simply the territory directly to the south of the Korazoon including the cities of Djesmir, Ankwar, Perlak and Khorala. These cities are Sultanates, independent monarchies that share the same cultural traditions as one another and both recognise and uphold each others' rights of sovereignty. Sometimes Jelhai to the east is considered among their number, but the religious and magical ways of that place are regarded as particularly dangerous and unsavoury and its ruler is snubbed by his peers.

Gulf of Eilak

This little sea is a busy stretch of water, with trading ships of all sizes criss-crossing between the ports of Assabia and those of the nothern kingdoms of Rasputana. It is, of course, dominated by the Sharranketans, whose fleet of well armed and magically augmented galleys keeps the sea lanes clear for the comings and goings of its merchant galleons.

Morkesh

Sitting astride the Briga River, Morkesh is a powerful kingdom currently ruled by a feisty Queen, Tursiba the Lioness, but is also a protectorate of the Taskan Empire. While considered Assabian in culture, its inhabitants speak a dialect sufficiently different to the Djesmiri of their neighbours to be classed as a language in its own right. The royal dynasty that rules Morkesh was founded by a pirate from across the ocean called Tark the Reaver, and rules from Morkar. The city of Largil on the coast is the biggest and most important port for oceanic trade and travel outside of Sharranket, and is the site of Tursiba's impressive Summer Palace, surrounded by a broad dry moat inhabited by her pet lions.

Sharranket

Sharranket is a small but very wealthy nation famous for its position as the hub of many of the world's most important trade routes, and for being the only nation to have an economy almost exclusively based on trade. The territory consists of two off-shore islands and a small stretch of mainland bordered to the north by Djesmirket. Each of the islands has a city, one the capital of Homora, the other a smaller city named Ronispur; the third and smallest city, Shimir, being on the mainland. Formerly a sultanate, Sharranket is now ruled by a council drawn from five families of merchant princes who plant trading enclaves along the major trade routes they operate, which stretch right across the Ocean and far as distant Jandekot, and are serviced by the most advanced fleet of ships in the world.

Rasputana and the South

Rasputana is a land everyone knows of, but very few outsiders have visited. Of those that have, the vast majority are traders and merchants from Assabia, among them those of Sharranket who monopolise the trade in pepper, spices and exotic materials out of Balbufera in the south. The land route from Taygus via Kamritar is not for the faint hearted, and it involves crossing a corner of the vast and mostly uninhabitable desert that occupies much of the continent's interior before arriving at the Kingdom of Menkh. Civilisation as represented by the Four Kingdoms of the North and the Three Kingdoms of the South seems compressed between the desert of the interior and the highlands of Someja. The barbarian inhabitants of Someja, the Someshi, are peaceful enough if left alone but are quite aware that they control the choke point between north and south, known as the Usarwi Plain.

Southern Draw

This current is a surge towards the outflow from the Inner Ocean into the Outer Ocean. It picks up more power on its way until it runs into the inflow current coming the other way, and the battle between these huge volumes of water creates an area of turbulent seas that makes navigation of the straits between Rasputana and Uxmal impossible.

The Four Kingdoms of the North

These coastal kingdoms – Eilak, Menkh, Shuja and Rastush – are hardly known to Korantines but represent important trading partners for merchantmen from Assabia.

The Three Kingdoms of the South

These three landlocked kingdoms – Zibud, Kessum and Jal – tend to be rather more warlike than their northern neighbours, but expend most of their aggression in fighting each other over petty disputes or stirring up trouble with the Someshi.

The Wider World

Pandospalam

The Sharranketans like to keep their trading bases on easily defended islands, and Pandospalam is one of those, situated just off the coast of Rasputana where it is a key stopover point on the long voyage to Balbufera. Pandospalam has a small native population, but the Sharranketan port is its main centre. The island is a domain of the Hirambil family, and Rais Hirambil, a cousin of the family's patriarch, is the Factor of Pandospalam.

Balbufera

The southernmost city, a place where Sharranketan merchants load with pepper and spices in return for silver. Balbufera is a remarkably peaceful place that relies on its distance from other human settlements for its security. In its long centuries of peaceful existence it has spawned many strains of mysticism, and many exotic arts.

Someja

Home to the Someshi 'barbarians', this region of rugged coast has no proper ports, but there are places to put in with a small vessel and the welcome can be quite warm if the visitor brings a desirable cargo. The Someshi themselves have little to do with the sea and seem rather frightened of it.

Cannibal Coast

This stretch of coast is aptly named. The people of Uxmal are indeed cannibals, and while the ruling caste keeps many lesser folk in thrall and treats them as livestock, foreigners washed up on their shores make for an exotic alternative.

The West

Albulo

The capital of the Albirs, situated on the largest of the three main Albir Islands, and home also to a permanent trading post of the Zamada merchant family from Sharranket. Albulo is compose- mostly of circular huts whitewashed and roofed in thatch, with a few larger stone and mud-brick buildings housing the royal and cult centres. Famously within some of the simple structures are said to be enormous riches, elaborate cult and votive objects fashioned out of gold. It is said that one of the reasons the Sharranketans made friends with the inhabitants (aside from their political interference in dynastic struggles) was that they came to the Albirs offering to bring them gold in exchange for goods and services rather than to steal it by force. Albulo is ruled by Barraby, a bloated 50 year-old man who can hardly rise from his stool yet was once a warrior famed for his energy, prowess and beauty.

Dariscur

Here, the locals are said to build the finest, unsinkable, boats found on any ocean, from a timber called *floatwood*. While this is an exaggeration, Dariscur-built boats have an automatic +10% bonus to their Seaworthiness (see page 111). Export of this timber is strictly forbidden, which means that the local shipwrights are assured a steady stream of orders from wealthy patrons from across the Inner Ocean. The island has no overall ruler, and the locals are prone to raiding one another and fighting over control of farmland, sacred sites and, of course, forestry.

Doldrums of Hiolanta

An expanse of ocean where the winds are always light and often at a dead calm – except, that is, when a violent but very localised storm brews up. These storms behave very oddly, are completely static, and can occur when the weather all around is bright and clear. The Doldrums are haunted by the souls of those who have died of exposure on a becalmed ship, and the wraiths made of those swept up in its supernatural storms. Yet they are also home to the Dagomils, who live on artificial islands created by the accumulation of flotsam and jetsam and surface seaweed that gathers here.

Dekos

An inhabited island with a famous shrine to the Ocean Father, a great sea-cave to which Dagomar's priest Hettrik the Drowner summons monsters of the deep and sends them to do his bidding. Dekos is part of the Kingdom of the Burning Coast ruled from Haprosindra.

Enkefalan

This bustling little port town is part of the Tapropiscan Confederacy, and the largest settlement within it. Ruled over by an old one-eyed trader called Damaric, Enkefalan is remarkable for having a settled and more or less integrated population of orcs. These are not an outpost from one of the Orcish lands in Kasperan, but an accumulation of those who have left their native culture behind and embraced life among the archipelagan peoples. Damaric uses them to be go-betweens in his trade with the orcs of Nishimbakoi to whom he unloads as many slaves as

he can. Damaric also happily trades in the proceeds of plunder, and it has become common practice that once a pirate or raider had sold on his booty to Damaric, there is no case for restitution to those it was taken from, only for revenge.

Haprosindra

The seat of power of Valorik Blueface, who pretends to the title of King and calls his domain The Kingdom of the Burning Coast. Apart from a small area around Haprosindra itself, his kingdom comprises mostly of the large, but thinly inhabited, island of Haprus and the more densely settled island of Dekos.

Ivory Sea

The stretch of water takes its name from the main commodity that is shipped from its shores. Mammoths are found in Uxmal and elephants in Jandekot, and for the Sharranketan trading colony at Janisdaron gathering tusks to ship back to the East is a mainstay of its business.

Janisdaron

A trading settlement established on the coast of Jandekot by the Zamada family from Sharranket. Once per year a galleon arrives to collect a cargo of ivory and other exotica harvested from the locale. The Sharranketans have brought a contingent of Albir mercenaries and settled them close by to serve as protection – partly against the natives but mostly against foreign raiders in the long months between each sailing as the valuable stockpile of goods accumulates.

Kapoli

A long peninsula that is home to the Kapolan race, who tend to be clustered in settlements strung along the southern side facing the Inner Ocean of which Othrikor is the largest. On the north, facing the Spawning Sea, is The Sunlit Land of the Essanzerai, a kingdom that has been ruled by the same dynasty for seven generations, which is regarded as a remarkable and slightly eccentric degree of stability among archipelagan folk. It is a land that is blessed in its climate and fertility but cursed by orcish slave-raids. The Korantine colony of Hispola occupies territory facing Korantia itself, and is so positioned as to be a useful layover for traffic passing between the northern Korantine states and Kipsipsindra.

Lorsil

The second largest town of the Kapolans (after Othrikor), Lorsil is the cult centre of their race. Every year there is an immense gathering of people arriving by boat to celebrate the festival of Dagomar and Diotima, Father and Mother Ocean. This is an event from which all those of Korantine stock are barred by taboo, which includes most people of Kipsipsindra even though they no longer all identify themselves as Korantine. Lorsil is ruled by a council of priests, and the council appoints a strong man to run the town's affairs on a day to day basis. The current Sealord of Lorsil is Rukkos the Slight. In a ritual peculiar to Lorsil, the priests appoint Rukkos' successor in secret, and the would-be successor must devote himself to the archipelagan god Orchang who supports revenge and feud (i.e, socially sanctioned murder), and then attempt to assassinate the incumbent. The more underhand methods of killing are not allowed – no poisoning, hired assassins and the like. Rukkos has been Sealord now for seven years, and nobody has succeeded in removing him.

Mikosso

The Sharranketan port on the southern coats of Fierla. As is the case with most Sharranketan settlements, the main town – perhaps a few hundred inhabitants at most – is situated on an island just off the shore for security, and close at hand is a natural deep water harbour. While this is a staging post for traffic to and from Janisdaron, the Factor of Mikosso (the Zamada family's local chief) does send people into the interior to prospect and to seek out exotic goods and materials for trade. The current Factor of Mikosso is called Subursh.

Othrikor

The largest town of Kapoli, Othrikor is a rough port city built mostly of timber with a few stone buildings between. It has four times been all but destroyed by fire and rebuilt, and now there is a permanent shrine to the Ocean Father down by the docks, entirely dedicated to calling up Undines to put out the fires should disaster strike again. Othrikor is mostly inhabited by Kapolans; however, you may expect to find many transients there too. It is a good place to hire sailing crew and said to be an excellent place to gamble, carouse and drink if you are willing to brave the rough and ready character of its mud-filled streets and its drink-filled inhabitants. Othrikor is run by a strongman called Jaskar the Bronze, but he needs to be an accomplished diplomat and free with bribes and gifts to ensure that nobody deposes him. Support from the kings of Kipsipsindra is a great help.

The Wider World

Pyrolus Stream

This current is born in the gulf where Kasperan, Thurina and Taygus meet, and sweeps south and west, passing between Kipsiperan and Rekshimetor, skirting the Doldrums of Hiolanta where it is joined by the spawning currents, then turning south along the coast of Jandekot until its power is spent. It is a boon to Korantine sailors travelling westwards, and its path has played an essential role in the establishment of trade routes and the placement of settlements.

Rekshimetor

Home to the turtle-folk, a Guyuntar people who jealously guard access to the giant turtles that come to their shores on the same day every year to lay their eggs. The Rekshmetans worship the turtle god, and make a fine stew from the flesh of his creatures and armour from their shells.

Tapropiscur

A large island with many settlements, and the source of aggressive raiders (Reavers) famed for their willingness to travel the breadth of the ocean in search of adventure and plunder. Tark the Reaver, founder of the royal house of Morkesh, and Korsaddin the Reaver who was crushed by Kalacho of Agissene in the attack on Valos, were natives of Tapropiscur. The islanders are part of a loose confederacy ruled over by a single strongman, which is currently Mororsi the True; who despite his name is one of the most untrustworthy, ruthless, brutal and successful pirate captains of the last 20 years.

Fierla

This huge island has been little explored since before the Cataclysm, and most of the earlier settlements have been abandoned or destroyed over the last two centuries. One persists on the north coast; Errabna is an old Kipsipsindran colony that is now a free port where local Sealord Torrik the Greedy makes a point of welcoming anyone who comes to his town, but relieves them of as much wealth as he can while they are there. In the south is Mikosso, a natural deepwater harbour that is simply a stopover on the route to and from the far west. The interior is said to contain many monsters, including dinosaurs and Slargr, who may be dumb brutes or intelligent dinosaur herders, hunters or worshippers – nobody seems quite sure. What is very clear is that these Slargr are very dangerous and best left alone.

CHARACTERS

You can create a character for play by making use of the MYTHRAS Basic Character Creation chapter with no adjustments. There are some additional notes you may want to be aware of, however, you should feel free to treat these things as optional.

CHARACTERISTICS

In Thennla, all characteristics generated on 3d6 or on 2d6+6 have a maximum score in of 21, and if this is ever exceeded, it denotes that the character concerned has undergone some sort of change in their nature – becoming god-like, or freakish, depending on your point of view. This should have an effect in on the way that character is perceived, and perhaps, provides some additional trait. For example, a human being who achieves a SIZ of 22 or greater (which is true of some remote tribes in Jandekot) may effectively be giants and capable of using oversized weapons. Likewise, a character with a Characteristic less than 3 suffers from a serious affliction or disability that should have an effect in play, while a score of zero is a cause (or consequence) of death.

Games Master Note: When generating characteristics that use different die combinations, each additional d6 or +6 used in generating a characteristic increases the Maximum score for the Characteristic by 7 and the minimum by 1 or 6.

> ### Skill Progression Limits
> In the Thennla setting there is a default cap on skills progression of five times a character's Basic Percentage. This represents the limitations of humanity, and is one of the reasons people pursue magical augmentation.

CULTURE AND COMMUNITY

The default background culture for a player character is Korantine – however, there are a host of alternatives provided later in this chapter. The Korantines are a civilisized people, but they uphold ancient traditions that celebrate prowess in physical pursuits, as well as the social skills required to fully participate in city-state life.

Korantine Cultural Skill Points

Standard Skills
Athletics, Conceal, Drive, Influence, Insight, Locale, Willpower

Example Combat Styles
Citizen Infantry, Equestrian Levy, Levy Archer, Levy Skirmisher, Levy Slinger

Characters

Professional Skills
Art (Any), Commerce, Craft (Any), Language (Any), Lore (Any), Musicianship, Rites (Korantine), Streetwise

Cultural Passions
Loyalty (Home City).

This passion is common to all citizens. Non-citizen characters may substitute another Passion; for example, a slave might have Loyalty (Master) instead.

Choosing a City

There are many different city-states that a character can choose as home. The Korantia chapter in this book contains a little information about the major city-states, and a complete listing of the smaller ones. Each can have its own unique traits, but not all are defined and it can be up to the Games Master and players to decide together what might be unique about the city they choose to be their character's point of origin, and how this might affect the character. For example, perhaps people from the city of Velthurisa are known for their greed, the Bolettans for their appreciation of food, Suthrians for their appreciation of obscure ideas and philosophies and Pelostrans for their love of gambling.

Background Events

Determine character background events as normal, using the MYTHRAS tables found on pages 18-20 of the main rules.

Korantine Social Class

A Korantine character is presumed to be a member of the citizenry of their home city. This is a broad category that consists of people from a variety of economic circumstances. Korantines cities routinely assess their citizens according to their wealth, both to see if they should be paying taxes and to determine whether they are on the electoral rolle or are expected to provide some community service like serving in the militia. A successful adventurer can use his hard-won spoils to improve his station in life, opening up new opportunities for the future (see the Korantine Wealth chapter in this book).

The Landless

Born to a citizen family but with no property to speak of and just their own labour with which to earn a living, these people cannot support any dependants and often go hungry themselves. Typically found looking for casual or seasonal work, they might drift from town to country and back again as hope or desperation takes them. When it comes to an empty belly, rags for clothes and a hovel for a home, someone of this class could be forgiven for envying a slave who is provided for by his master. While they can enjoy some pride in their citizenship rights, the destitute are rarely encouraged to cast a vote in public assemblies, and in most cases are not called up for military service either.

Democratic states attempt to remove this demographic altogether by redistributing land on a regular basis to those who have a legitimate claim to citizenship. Militaristic states do the same thing, only by taking the land by force from foreigners rather than inconveniencing their own rich. The poor regularly end up in debt to those better off than themselves, and such unfortunates are referred to as debt-bondsmen in order to avoid the use of the word slave, but they are no less in thrall to their creditor, unless the state steps in and cancels debts to bring relief to the poor.

Typical Professions:
Farmer, Fisher, Herder, Hunter, Miner, Sailor, Thief

1D100	Social Class	Typical Professions	Starting Money (SP)
01-05	Landless	Farmer, Fisher, Herder, Hunter, Miner, Sailor, Thief	d6SP (average 35CP)
06-55	Poor	As above, plus: Crafter, Entertainer, Merchant, Warrior	2d6x10SP (average 70SP)
56-85	Middling	Alchemist, Crafter, Farmer, Merchant, Official, Physician, Priest, Scholar, Warrior	2d6x25SP (average 175SP)
86-95	Propertied	Farmer, Merchant, Official, Paladin, Priest, Scholar, Warrior	4d6x75SP (average 1050SP)
96-99	Rich	Official, Priest, Scholar, Warrior	6d6x100SP (average 2100SP)
00	Aristocrat or Land Magnate	Official, Priest, Scholar, Warrior	2d6x1,000SP (average 7000SP)

The Poor

The largest group in any city are poor folk who can at least claim regular employment, whether in the fields or in some urban occupation or workshop. Some may have a small share in a business or own a little piece of land, but nowhere near enough to support themselves and a family – so they also rent land from richer folk and/or work for others for a wage to supplement their income. In democratic states they may even be paid to turn up to sit as jurors in the courts or vote in the citizen assembly, but that sort of thing requires that the state coffers are swollen with money from military campaigns or a publicly owned resource such as a silver mine.

Typical Professions:
Crafter, Entertainer, Farmer, Fisher, Herder, Hunter, Merchant, Miner, Sailor, Warrior

The Middling Sort

Regarded as the backbone of society, the middling sort are not really average, but rather a mid-point between the rich and poor, able to align their interests with one and their sympathies with the other. These people own enough land or other business interests to support themselves and their immediate family, and at the top of the scale perhaps to support some extended family, slaves and other dependants too. They are usually the core of the infantry fielded by the city, and are expected to keep some basic military equipment, enough that at least one adult male from the family can serve his country in times of war.

Typical Professions:
Alchemist, Crafter, Farmer, Merchant, Official, Physician, Priest, Scholar, Warrior

Using Social Class in Play

A player should not feel that differences in social class advantage one character over another in play unless the game has a particularly socio-political angle to it. To act with disrespect towards a citizen from a lower social class because of his class is at best ill-mannered and at worst politically dangerous. Aside from starting wealth, the main advantage of high status is ready access to people of influence, yet it may be difficult to pass unnoticed amongst common folk or resist the constant barrage of requests to use money and influence for the benefit of others. If people from different ends of the spectrum are treated differently, it is only because wealth brings with it influence and power over others, and poverty brings with it the threat of starvation or dependency. Going on adventures in search of wealth is one way to bypass the vagaries of fortune and improve one's station in life, or to escape the demands and rivalries inherent in domestic power-politics.

Characters

Men of Property

The propertied class are a sort of minor gentry, comprising families of sufficient wealth that they have money to spend on luxuries, and do so in order to show how they aspire to the status of those even richer than they. A typical family may have several dependants – extended family, paid workers, tenants and slaves. Men of property are regarded as the cream of the citizen infantry, being the best equipped to take the field, with full armour as well as spear and shield – and thereby are expected also to show their prowess in the front ranks.

Typical Professions:
Farmer, Merchant, Official, Orator, Paladin, Priest, Scholar, Warrior

The Rich

Freedom from physical labour, and possession of the time and resources to pursue leisure, is the de facto definition of being rich. The leisured classes are wealthy families with substantial landholdings or commercial interests in which the leading members probably shun any form of work, instead employing agents and even slaves to take care of their business. People of this class indulge in public service, hunting and other sports, intellectual pursuits and the amusements of drinking parties and banqueting. In many states, the rich are expected to furnish themselves with a horse for their militia service and provide a cavalry arm. In some cases, they can instead pay for professionals to take their place.

On the whole, the rich play-down how rich they are, pointing to their good taste and high achievements rather than their luxurious lifestyle, to assert their superiority. In fact, to do otherwise is a sign of bad manners or decadence. For a rich young man, the height of achievement is demonstrating physical prowess through athletic competition or warfare. For a rich old man, demonstrating intellectual prowess and wisdom through exercising public authority or producing scholarly works becomes the mark of greatness.

Characters from a Rich background should replace Conceal with Ride when determining their Cultural Skills.

They can take the Equestrian Levy combat style, which has the Skirmishing trait.

Typical Professions:
Athlete, Official, Priest, Scholar, Warrior

The Aristocracy

In the more conservative cities these people pretend to aristocratic status based on descent from ancient heroes and city founders. In reality, what usually sets them apart is their huge landholdings as compared to anyone else's. In all but the most radical democracies, people of this class repeatedly fill the highest offices of state, so forming a politically powerful elite – if only because they are famous and have a lot of tenants and other dependants who, they can pressurise to vote for them. The very rich actually shoulder a big part of the burden of public spending as they are expected to pay for major public works or meet the cost of religious festivals from their own resources. In Sarestra, they have to pay for the provision of ships for the fleet. For this reason, many of these people think that they are the city, and everyone else is a hanger-on.

Typical Professions:
As for Rich

Non-Citizen Characters

In any city-state, there are many people who are not of citizen status – in some cases, more than half the population is in this category. Non-citizen characters are still assumed to be an integral part of the Korantine milieu and the same Cultural Skills apply; however, a separate Social Class table is provided. Creating a non-citizen character should be a choice for the player unless all players are directed by the Games Master to do so.

If you roll Transient on the Social Class table, you can decide whether this character still carries the cultural heritage of an exotic homeland. If this is so, then select a different set of Cultural Skills using the Characters From Foreign Cultures section in this chapter (see page 44), substituting where necessary Korantine language and Korantine culture (and even Locale) to their Professional skill options to ensure they have at least a basic ability to navigate their way through life amongst Korantine folk.

Outlaws and Outcasts

This category is a perplexing mix of the mad, bad and deeply unfortunate – anyone, in fact, who falls into such hard times that they are forced outside of the boundaries of normal society. This might be an escaped slave, a condemned man on the run, a pagan rebel or someone who has become a bandit or robber. Also in this group are the least fortunate of all slaves:

Shores of Korantia

1D100	Social Class	Typical Professions	Starting Money (SP)
01-05	Outcast, Outlaw	Hunter, Miner, Thief	D6SP (average 35CP)
06-35	Agricultural Slave/	Crafter, Farmer, Fisher, Herder, Miner,	2d6x10SP (average 70SP)
36-55	Pagan Peasant Worker		
56-70	Household Slave	Crafter, Entertainer, Official	2d6 x 25SP (Average 175SP)
71-85	Transient	Crafter, Merchant, Sailor, Thief, Warrior, Scholar,	2d6x25SP (average 175SP)
86-98	Metic	Agent, Courtesan, Crafter, Merchant, Sailor, Scholar	4d6x75SP (average 1050SP)
99-00	Exiled foreign aristocrat	Agent, Courtesan, Scholar,	4d6 x 150SP (average 2100SP)

The Taskan in Korantia

When the Taskan delegation arrived in Hilanistra, there was some excitement over the identity of one of its leading figures, Count Balthus the Iron Companion. He was handsome and dashing, and tales of his exploits had reached even Korantine ears. The young Korantine Emperor loved to hear Balthus tell of his adventures, not least because this Taskan lord spoke such excellent Korantine. When he pressed Balthus for why this should be so, Balthus revealed that it was because he was born and raised in Korantia. This news caused some excitement, and the Emperor and his court all strained to hear from what city Balthus had come and why he had abandoned his homeland. To their surprise Balthus replied that while he was born and raised in Korantia, he was no Korantine; and while he was a proud Taskan, he was neither born nor raised there. Because in Korantia, said Balthus, he had been a slave; but in Tarsenia he was a free man. The Emperor was amused with this answer, and wondered whether perhaps all the slaves of Korantia were Taskans too? 'Not yet', said Balthus. 'But aye, one day may it be so'.

those who are consigned to work in mines where life expectancy can be very short and who are owned by the state rather than an individual. If not prisoners of war, mining slaves are probably condemned criminals.

Typical Professions:
Hunter, Miner, Thief

Agricultural and Industrial Slaves

Probably acquired on the market but also the offspring of slave parents, agricultural and industrial slaves might have a tough life of hard labour on the estate of a rich man. In some cases even those with quite modest landholdings or businesses expect a slave to do much of their heaviest work, or to endure the drudgery of the hardest or most distasteful industrial processes. Nevertheless these slaves usually work alongside free men, as there is no trade that is exclusively reserved for slave labour.

Typical Professions:
Crafter, Farmer, Fisher, Herder, Miner

Pagans

On the fringes of almost all Korantine cities, and in the gaps between their territory, can be found the people that Korantines call Pagans – a term which means 'country folk' and denotes rustic simplicity. These Pagans are often of different blood, being of Thennalt 'barbarian' heritage, and people who have been gradually pushed into marginal land, subservience and debt bondage as the Korantine cities have expanded in number, size and territorial control.

Typical Professions:
Farmer, Fisher, Hunter, Herder

Household Slaves

These slaves are usually born within the household, however, rich families may add to their staff with choice purchases from the market. Household slaves in Korantia are often considered to be integral family members and typically well treated. A household slave is likely to have a specific function, and while most of these involve drudgework, slaves with specialist skills are highly valued. The very biggest households might have a cook, a slave running the administration and doing the book keeping, a tutor for the children, or even a physician. Also in this category are the 'household slaves' owned by temples and cults, who may perform important secretarial roles. Sometimes slaves are set free by their owners, and freed slaves are in some cities allowed to apply for citizenship.

In order to go adventuring a slave needs either to run away, to acquire his freedom through legitimate means, or to be instructed by his master to do so. It is said the Taskan hero Count Balthus was originally a Korantine slave who escaped his master and absconded to Tarsenia.

Typical Professions:
Domestic, Physician, Scholar

Transients

Transients are people who are just passing though – currently rootless, separated from their homeland for some reason. In the biggest cities, especially those with a major port, transients can form a significant minority. In the landlocked and conservative cities of the hinterland, they are rare and stand out from the crowd. Some of these people are rootless Korantines, people who have left their home city but never permanently settled down elsewhere. Alternatively, the character could be from some foreign culture, even from some exotic land, as agreed with the Games Master, and their Cultural Skills devised accordingly.

Typical Professions:
Agent, Crafter, Entertainer, Merchant, Thief, Warrior

Metics

This class of foreigners is made up of people who are permanently settled on city-state territory – their name means 'co-habitants'. They are the well-to-do non-citizens, typically those acting as merchants and traders, especially if indulging in businesses (such as slave trading and moneylending) that are lucrative but regarded as inappropriate trades for respectable citizens. Metics are not entitled to own land within the city's territory, they cannot take part in politics, but they are expected to volunteer for service in the militia or pay for others to serve on their behalf. The majority of metics are Korantines from other cities and can be generated as characters using the same Cultural and Professional skills.

The metic class includes the Paladins – they are counted as foreigners even if their family has lived locally for generations because they answer to the Korantine Emperor and exclude themselves from citizenship. In a cheat to the custom that non-citizens may not own land, Paladins hold land in trust on behalf of the Emperor, who is accorded the privilege of honorary citizenship in every city.

Typical Professions:
Agent, Crafter, Merchant, Official, Paladin, Scholar

Exiles

The only respectable exiles are those who are so wealthy and important that they can expect a friendly reception from people in another city with whom they have ties of guest-friendship, marriage or mutual business and political interests. There are rather more of such people than you might expect, a consequence of the highly charged nature of Korantine politics. An exile may be temporarily ostracised from their home city, thrown out in a political coup, or on the run for some crime that people of their wealth and status expect to be able to get away with but occasionally fail to do so. They are probably a lot poorer than their aristocratic status suggests, having had to quit home with only as much wealth as they could carry.

Typical Professions:
Agent, Official, Scholar, Warrior

Starting Money

The Social Class tables in this chapter provide details of starting money appropriate to the setting. Bear in mind the Silver Pieces used in the setting have much more buying power than MYTHRAS Silver Pieces. When a new character is created their starting money is presumed to be portable wealth they can get their hands on – maybe they have saved up, been given it by relatives, or inherited it.

Families

If you want to spend more time exploring a character's social background, then using the MYTHRAS Parents table it is possible to determine if a character's parents are alive and if he or she stands to inherit their property – or perhaps already has! Actual status is usually derived from living parents, but once they are gone a character's own worth must be measured. Korantine families like to make sure at least one offspring will inherit as much as is needed to remain in the same Social Class into which he was born, in the interest of ensuring the future status of the family name. The remainder may be presented to siblings, used as dowry and so forth. Fleshing out the immediate and extended family background using the tables in MYTHRAS will help decide whether a character has a chance of coming into an inheritance, and in combination with the Background Events table, can determine whether there may be significant family politics in the way of claiming it.

Allies, Contacts, Rivals and Enemies

Determine these as normal.

Cults and Magic

A Korantine citizen character commits one magic point permanently to his city goddess and is a Lay Member of her cult, gaining the Loyalty (City) Passion and the ability to use it to augment tasks when three or more citizens are working together.

All characters can, if desired, start play as a Lay Member of one other cult, typically one relating to their career. If you choose to allow players to start as cult initiates, they will need to buy Devotion and Exhort skills with free skill points.

There are many places and means by which to learn a few handy cantrips, and non-citizen characters can know 1d3-1 Folk Magic spells at start of play.

Characters from Foreign Cultures

If your players would like to play more exotic characters from foreign civilisations and barbarous or far-flung lands, here is where you can find the information you need, together with some recommended careers for each culture.

Fill in the details using the normal MYTHRAS rules, including rolling for Social Class except where provided for here. For starting money, use the following in bullion Silver Pieces or equivalent, and apply the normal Social Class money modifiers:

- Y Barbarian: 4d6 x 15SP
- Y Civilised: 4d6 x 25SP
- Y Nomadic: 4d6 x 10SP
- Y Primitive: 4d6 x 5SP in trade goods

Taskans

Taskans are people who come from a powerful empire to the East of Korantia. Relations for now remain peaceful and some trade takes place, but many Korantines are convinced that the Taskan emperor has ambitions to seize their cities. These same people may express concern that the Taskans, who allow women equal status with men, and who do not practise slavery but bow to a god-emperor and the animated iron statue who is his factotum, threaten to replace Korantine traditions with monstrous foreign customs. Taskans are recognisable with their penchant for long-sleeved tunic and trousers, the men wear neatly trimmed beards and let their hair grow to their shoulders.

The Taskan heartland is known as Tarsenia and is a federation of formerly independent city-states: Taskay itself, Tarsang, Zarina, Ashkor, Felsang, Zarina, Merat, Ralmyra, Haran and Pryjarna. Provinces include Camtri, a Thennalt land; The Little Kitan, inhabited by the Escar horse-people and Yegusai, an ancient riverine kingdom which practices ancestor-worship. The Taskans are protectors of the Jekkarene Theocracy, the traditional enemy of the Korantine race, and also of Morkesh.

Culture Type
Civilised

Language:
Taskan

Customs
Taskan

Standard Skills
Conceal, Deceit, Drive, Influence, Insight, Locale, Willpower

Example Combat Styles
Taskan Citizen Infantry, Zarinian Equestrian Levy, Ralmyran Levy Archer, Tarsangan Levy Slinger, Ashkorite Pikeman

Professional Skills
Art (any), Commerce, Craft (any), Language (any), Literacy (Tarsenian), Lore (any), Musicianship, Rites (Taskan), Streetwise

Cultural Passions
Loyalty (Emperor); many will also have a loyalty towards (or love for) for their home city or province and there are times when these things are conflicting drives.

Magic Type

Folk Magic, Sorcery, Theism. Taskan citizens, like Korantine citizens, have one magic point permanently deducted from their total as a cost of their citizenship, in this case, put at the disposal of the divine emperor Zygas Taga.

Ordinary Taskans benefit from Folk Magic made publicly accessible by the authorities or public-spirited individuals, and gain 1d3 such spells at Character Creation – however, these are rarely, if ever, spells that have practical use outside domestic and civic community life, and the manner in which they are made available requires that a character is literate (Literacy 26%+) to actually learn them. Typical civic spells are Cleanse, Cool, Heal, Perfume, Light, Tidy and Polish. Citizens are expected to use them to keep public spaces, monuments and shrines in good order.

Some Taskan theist cults offer standard benefits to initiates, but the majority exist to provide moral and financial support to an individual's personal journey of devotion (see the Magic chapter for information on Personal Religion). Typical Taskan deities are Thesh, god of fire; Tarsen, god of civilisation and letters; Machank, god of war; Tethis, goddess of love; Samanse, goddess of the hearth and home; Basat, god of life and light, and Hoonvel, god of farming.

Social Class for Taskan Characters

The Taskan Empire has no slaves and the ruling class – aside from the emperor himself who has no progeny – refers to the powerful individuals and families who occupy positions of power in individual cities, provinces or in the army. For Taskan characters, a roll of 03-20 on the standard MYTHRAS table for Social Class is treated as a Freeman, and 00 is treated as Aristocracy. Taskan citizens are not assessed by wealth or status, and all citizens, male and female, have the right to vote for their local leaders and stand for public office… so long as they do so through the auspices of the emperor-cult.

Typical professions

Any

Thennalts

Almost ubiquitous in the northern parts of Taygus, the Thennalts are a matrix of many different peoples, speaking related languages and united by the recognition of the earth goddess Theyna as the paramount deity. Thennalts are spread across an enormous geographical area, and live in communities that operate at a variety of levels of development and cultural sophistication.

Thennalts can also be quite mobile; a bored young man stuck in an agricultural backwater in Zathrum may well go in search of fortune elsewhere and, for example, offer his services to a Marangian warlord if he thinks that will get him what he wants from life. Home is where you are born and where you hope to bring up your children and see your bones laid to rest; however, at any other time going off to see the world is considered a manly virtue.

Gender roles among Thennalts are clearly defined and traditional, but there is no particular dignity attached to one gender or the other. Thennalt men tend to wear a short tunic, often colorful, gathered at the waist with a broad girdle or belt, usually of leather and adorned with bronze. The sword is a status symbol; only married men who are heads of their own household are entitled to use one.

Culture Type
Barbarian

Language
Thennalt

Customs
Thennalt

Standard Skills
Athletics, Brawn, Endurance, First Aid, Locale, Perception; and either Boating, Drive or Ride.

Example Combat Styles
Chariot Fighter, Huntsman, Levy Spearman, Thennalt Levy Skirmisher

Professional Skills
Craft (Any), Language (Any), Lore (Any), Musicianship, Rites (Thennalt), Survival

Thennalts from Korantia must take Korantine Language as one of their professional skills; Thennalts from Camtri must likewise take Taskan.

Cultural Passions
Loyalty (Local Warlord, Head Man or Chieftain, or one of the Thennalt Kings)

Love (Friend, Sibling or Romantic Lover)

Hate (Rival Community, Enemy Lord)

Marangians tend to have a particular and violent hatred for Taskans.

Magic Type
Folk Magic, Theism. There are examples of Animism in Thennalt lands, generally referred to as Witchcraft. Typical Thennalt deities include Theyna, the all-mother; Thenn, the hunter and civilisation god; Palaskil the storm and sky god and Sheagu, goddess of death and burial.

Typical Professions
Crafter, Farmer, Herder, Fisher, Merchant, Scout, Warrior

JEKKARENES

The Jekkarene Theocracy is a closed nation where a land-tied peasantry lives in thrall to the matriarchal cult of the moon-goddess Jekkara. Head of state is Queen Semankore, who rules from the temple-city of Parlasos. A narrow caste of male 'patricians' are elevated to high office (baronies) to fulfil key administrative and military roles, but always subject to their local college of priestesses. The queen's position is not hereditary but a life-long appointment. Every Jekkarene queen is chosen by a college of senior priestesses from a pool of more than 100 young women and girls, all carefully selected and removed from their parents when only five years old and subjected to intensive training for a role that, likely as not, they will never have the chance to fulfil.

Ordinary Jekkarenes are extremely parochial and deeply conservative; the world they inhabit is overwhelmingly agricultural in nature. They have almost no experience and little knowledge of the world outside and live their lives in the fixed patterns ordained by the priestesses in the goddess' name. Those who find themselves dreaming about something different may find themselves driven out of their homes and cast out of society, or worse. Apparently those who particularly upset the priestesses are first cursed with lycanthropy, as a mark of how they have rejected civilised society, before being forced across the border so they can sow terror amongst the exile communities of the badlands.

Culture Type
Civilised

Language
Jekkarene

Culture
Jekkarene

Standard Skills
Deceit, Drive, Endurance, Influence, Insight, Locale, Willpower

Example Combat Styles
Huntsman, Peasant Levy, Noble Warrior

Professional Skills
Art (Any), Commerce, Craft (Any), Language (Any), Literacy, Lore (Any), Musicianship, Rites (Jekkarene), Streetwise

Cultural Passions

Loyalty (Jekkarene Theocracy (women and people of rank only))

Love (Friend, Sibling or Romantic Lover)

Hate (Local lord (for peasant), Korantines (anyone))

Magic Type

Folk Magic, Sorcery, Theism. Male Jekkarenes are barred from any form of higher magic unless they are members of the hero-cult of Zygas Taga, the Taskan eEmperor, which is generally restricted to the rich and powerful (Social Class roll of 96 or higher). Women are only entitled to practice Theism and Sorcery through the auspices of the Moon cult honouring the goddess Jekkara and her daughter Jezri. Both sexes may have Folk Magic though – roll 1d3-1 for male characters and 1d3+1 for female.

Typical Professions

Crafter, Farmer, Herder, Official, Priestess, Temple Dancer, Warrior

Social Class for Jekkarene Characters

Jekkarenes keep very few slaves as the peasantry is tied to the land and there is little need for additional subservient labour; however, they have a large outcast population living in the badlands of Eastern Methelea. Roll 1d100:

1D100	Social Class	Starting Money (SP)
01-15	Outcast	x0.25
16-75	Peasant Class	x0.25
76-95	Artisan Class	x0.5
96-99	Patrician Class	x5
00	Ruling class (female characters only)	x10

Jekkarenes are also poor in portable wealth – their traditional currency is in heavy iron bars, to prevent the emergence of a more liquid economy that would be harder for the theocratic state to control. Of course the highest echelons of society have ways to circumvent these limitations.

Archipelagans

Settled on several coasts and many islands, the Archipelagans, or Peoples of the Sea, range from peaceful farmers and fishers to fierce pirates who are the terror of the high seas. Two major tribes are known: the Guyuntars, who are dominant on most of the islands, and the Kapolans, who occupy the Kapoli peninsula and the large island of Kipsiperan. Adorned with tattoos and accoutered with seashell jewellery and turtleshell armour, bearing weapons of bronze and in sleek, open decked ships, the Archipelagans can be encountered almost anywhere across the wide ocean.

Culture Type

Barbarian

Language
Guyuntar, or Kapolan

Customs
Archipelagan

Standard Skills
Athletics, Boating, Deceit, Endurance, Perception, Locale (varies), Willpower

Example Combat Styles
Levy Spearman, Reaver (Sabre or Sidearm, Dagger, Buckler. Trait: Sure-Footed), Seahunter (Spear/Harpoon, Club, Dagger. Trait: Thrown Weapon (harpoon)).

Professional Skills
Art (Any), Commerce, Craft (Any), Language (Archipelagan), Lore (Any), Musicianship, Navigate, Rites (Archipelagan), Seamanship, Survival

Cultural Passions
Loyalty (Clan or Crew)

Love (Friend, Sibling or Romantic Lover)

Hate (Rival Clan or Faction)

Magic Type
Folk Magic, Theism. Archipelagan gods include Dagomar, father ocean; Diotimar, mother of fishes; Palaskil, storm, sailing and farming; Orchang, war and feuding; Koremchai, god of piracy and plunder; and Heder and Hember, twin brother gods of herdsmen and crafters.

Typical Professions
Farmer, Fisher, Herder, Sailor, Warrior

DAGOMILS

Round-eyed folk with partially webbed hands and feet, the Dagomils are nomads on the ocean. They are part of the cultural matrix of islander peoples, and yet different – distinguished by their physiognomy, language and lifestyle. The Dagomils are regarded as being sufficiently close to the gods and spirits of the ocean that they are somehow suspect of complicity in the Cataclysm that destroyed Korantis. For this reason, they are despised, reduced to beggary, and poorly treated in places like Kipsipsindra, and few wander the northern seas as a result.

Dagomils are said to have a floating refuge somewhere in the Doldrums of Hiolanta, built upon rafts made of seaweed and flotsam, and only they know how to navigate those dead seas or appease the wraiths that haunt them.

Culture Type
Nomad.

Language
Dagomish

Customs
Dagomil

Standard Skills
Athletics, Boating, Deceit, Endurance, Perception, Locale, (varies), Swim

Example Combat Styles
Seahunter

Professional Skills
Art (Any), Commerce, Craft (Any), Language (Any), Lore (Any), Musicianship, Navigate, Rites (Archipelagan), Seamanship, Survival

Cultural Passions
Loyalty (Clan)

Love (Friend, Sibling or Romantic Lover)

Hate (Rival Clan or Faction)

Magic Type
Folk Magic, Animism, Theism. Dagomils worship the same pantheon of deities as their Archipelagan cousins, but with emphasis on different divinities. Animism is practised by Dagomil witches, who essentially are there to mediate with the sea-wraiths that lurk around their home waters.

Typical Professions
Fisher, Hunter, Sailor, Scout, Shaman, Warrior

Special
Swimming is a natural talent for a Dagomil. All skill tests are one grade easier.

Assabians

The teeming cities of Assabia are not for the faint hearted. Humanity in its all its glory and monstrosity is to be found on open display and nowhere else in the civilised world are such extremes of wealth and poverty to be experienced in such close proximity. This is a land where children are sold into slavery by their own parents; where slave owners enjoy complete discretion in how they treat their chattels and brutality is routine; where the pampered wives of rich merchants, hidden from the eyes of men beneath swathes of cloth, are carried to the shops on litters past near-naked prostitutes who ply their trade on the open street. Everything has a price and everyone dreams of one day making their fortune; if anyone should be lucky enough to rise from rags to riches, they are sure to be celebrated in story and song no matter how it was done. Assabia is made up of several sultanates (Ankwar, Djesmir, Jelhai, Khorala, Perlak), the Kingdom of Morkesh (actually ruled by a queen, who is said to be descended from foreign pirates) and Sharranket, a former sultanate, now a plutocracy ruled by five ludicrously rich and powerful merchant families.

The Assabians met within foreign lands are often merchants from Sharranket or sailors from Morkesh. Sharranket's merchant galleys are the most massive ships upon the ocean. But it is also a land known for its sorcerers, and is thought to be the wellspring of their art.

Culture Type
Civilised

Language
Djesmiri or Morkeshite

Customs
Assabian

Standard Skills
Conceal, Deceit, Drive, Influence, Insight, Locale, Willpower

Example Combat Styles
Duelist, Levy Spearman, Crossbowman, Levy Archer

Professional Skills
Art (Any), Commerce, Craft (Any), Language (Any), Literacy (Djesmiri), Lore (Any), Musicianship, Rites (Assabian), Streetwise

Cultural Passions
Loyalty (Sultanate, Merchant House (Sharranket) or Kingdom (Morkesh))

Love (Friend, Sibling or Romantic Lover)

Hate (Rival People, Faction or Gang)

Magic Type
Theism, Sorcery. Deities such as Basat, Shomat (a local sun god), Haliset (water and fertility god variously described as a toad, cat or hoopoe-bird) and Tolat (earth goddess) are the most popular deities, and their worship is supported by many localised cults. Temmush is also very popular as the bringer of wealth and maker of deals. In Sharranket most people are lay worshippers of the national goddess, Shara Peshwan. However, Assabians are atheists at heart, believing that the gods do not deserve to be worshipped, and ironically, the Holy City of Djesmir (as it is often called) is the spiritual home of the movement. Perhaps the reason for this is that the religious practices of the region are grossly venal, conducted in whatever way an individual feels will benefit them most. Many visitors would be shocked at the extent to which, in Djesmirket in particular, relations with the gods are looked on as business transactions in which both parties negotiate a mutually beneficial deal. Assabians are famous for their pacts with demons and deities.

Typical Professions
Sharranketan Merchant, Djesmiri Sorcerer, Morkeshite Sailor

Albirs

These formidable black-skinned barbarians inhabit the Albir Islands in the southern part of the ocean. Although they say they are made from the soil, it has been said they originally migrated or were transported there from Jandekot. Of all the islander peoples, they alone appear to lack a seafaring tradition. The islands have limited resources, and in Albir history there are periods during which violence is at levels that interrupts or even reverses population growth. Since the Sharranketan merchants set up a trading post on the island of Albulong, more and more Albirs have been seen in Sharranketan service as mercenaries and bodyguards. Albirs are famed for their stature and physical prowess. Some of them find their way to the cities of the East, because some of those who hire-on are hired as mercenaries inevitably decide never to return home.

Orcs

I once saw an Orcish man come ashore from his boat at Haprosindra. Many of the locals were angry at his arrival and threatened to kill him. This grossly ugly but magnificently built brute with his sallow skin and hairless body stood his ground and introduced a dirty looking Dagomil woman who translated for him. He said he was here for the slave market, but not even the slavers would deal with him, and so he sat down and quietly waited while the auction went on, all the while cradling a large pot, and didn't bid for anybody. When the auction was all over he simply approached the auctioneer and took the cover off his pot to reveal a pile of electrum scraps (he called it 'dirty silver'), then proceeded to weigh out quantities until the slaver agreed to hand over the weak and feeble individuals that nobody else had bought. When the Orcish man had loaded his purchases onto his boat everyone hissed and spat at the auctioneer, as they knew what fate awaited those wretched people. The auctioneer shrugged and pointed out that now he had a lot of money, and people would soon want to be his friend again.

To generate Characteristics for an Albir character, roll STR on 4d6 and SIZ on 3d6+6 and drop the lowest scoring die in each case.

Culture Type
Barbarian

Language
Albish

Customs
Archipelagan

Standard Skills
Athletics, Boating, Brawn, Endurance, First Aid, Locale (Albir Islands), Perception

Example Combat Styles
Mercenary

Professional Skills
Craft (Wood, Leather or Iron), Healing, Language (Archipelagan or Djesmiri), Lore (Animal Husbandry), Survival, Track

Cultural Passions
Loyalty (Chieftain)

Love (Gold, Glory)

Hate (Personal enemy)

Magic Type
Folk Magic, Theism. Albirs honour Zondonza, a version or aspect of the sun god represented as a bull and said to support the sun's disc between his horns. An initiate of this god can only fuel his devotional pool by sacrificing cattle. While this is expensive, the god is happy for his worshippers to consume most of the body. Each 3 STR of bull sacrificed provides or restores one point to the devotional pool, and the presiding priest can decide who eats which organs and thereby gains all or some of the available points.

Typical Professions
Crafter, Herder, Mercenary Warrior

Orcs

The tribes of Kasperan are another group displaying characteristics affected by ancient pacts. Orcs come in several strains, often reflected in significant physical variations, and operate a caste system both within tribes and between them. Skin colour ranges from chalky white to slate grey. Orcs tend to be disliked by most others; they propitiate rather aggressive and dangerous gods and regard anyone who does not as being fair game. They are not entirely evil but it has to be admitted that their biggest city of Nishimbakoi is the scene of human sacrifice on an almost industrial scale.

Orc Piracy
Orcs have successfully taken to the sea and are very much feared; for whilst their black ships sometimes come for peaceful trade, just as often they are looking to fill their holds with captives to be taken home for sacrifice to their gods. They have also colonised islands across the Inner Ocean but this has been a haphazard and sometimes accidental venture resulting in a scattering of settlements, some of which have not had contact with other human beings for decades.

Orc Characteristics are normally generated according to the standard rules for human characters, however, high caste Orcs (Social Status 96-00) usually sport increased STR, CON, and POW as god-given gifts received in return for the human sacrifices that take place when they are born. These characters can be expected to have +1d6 in one of these Characteristics.

Those Orcs who inhabit the town of Enkefalan and its environs are more or less integrated with the Guyuntar population they share the settlement with. They desist from their human sacrifices, but this does not stop either them or their neighbours from profiting from the slave trade.

Culture Type
Barbarian

Language
Orken

Customs
Nishimba or Archipelagan (Orcs from Enkefalan)

Standard Skills
Athletics, Brawn, Endurance, First Aid, Locale, Perception; and either *Boating* or *Drive*.

Example Combat Styles
Huntsman, Tribal Warrior, Lizard Rider

Professional Skills
Craft (Any), Language (Archipelagan, Jande), Lore (Any), Musicianship, Rites (Orken), Survival

Cultural Passions
Loyalty (Local Warlord, Head Man or Chieftain)

Love (Friend, Sibling or Romantic Lover)

Hate (Orlocks, a related tribe of headhunters found in the Jandekot forests; Centaurs, a ferocious race found in the open plains of Kasperan)

Magic Type
Folk Magic, Sorcery. Orcs can weave sorcery spells through the memorisation and recombination of a rich store of poetic verse. The deities they worship are collectively known as The Hungry Gods, but they work no Miracles, merely accept sacrifices and allow the Orc sorcerer-priests to gain some margin on the deal.

Typical Professions
Beast Handler, Crafter, Farmer, Herder, Fisher, Merchant, Sailor, Scout, Slaver, Sorcerer-Priest, Thief, Warrior

TRIBES OF JANDEKOT

The great and largely wilderness continent of Jandekot is where you can find more extreme environments, greater concentrations of magical effects and more isolated populations than anywhere else. Physical types range from pygmies to giants and skin colours include mottled green, red and hues of blue. The slightly-built (SIZ 2d6+4), brown-skinned Warong are the most numerous population group but they share the jungle with some bizarre neighbours – from red-skinned Mandiko (STR 4d6, SIZ 3d6+6) to shy and reclusive tribes of pygmies (STR 2d6+2, SIZ 1d6+6). The forest folk have a close relationship to the spirits that share their environment with them, providing advantages that go a long way to make up for their primitive technologies.

Tribes of Jandekot are widely scattered and there are many different cultures and languages. The common tongue of the jungle continent is Jande, a combination of sounds and signs used for interactions between tribes, but not everyone can manage it. The mere fact such a language exists suggests that Jandekot may not have had more internal trade and diplomatic connections in times past than exist now.

Culture Type
Primitive

Language and Customs
Varies by tribe. For example, Nothern Warong, Mandiko

Standard Skills
Brawn, Endurance, Evade, Locale, Perception, Stealth and either *Athletics, Boating* or *Swim*

Example Combat Styles
Forest Hunter, Mandiko Warrior, Orlock Headhunter, Yshpato Spirit Warrior

Professional Skills
Craft (Any), Language (Jande), Lore (Any), Navigate, Rites (Tribal Tradition), Survival, Track

New Skills: Conditioning, Puissance and Forensics

Conditioning (POW+CON)

This is the equivalent of the Meditation skill, and is the ability to maintain a regime of mental discipline, exercise and diet that keeps the body in top physical condition, so long as the athlete is living at a standard which is no less than Propertied.

Just as with the Meditation skill, the total intensity of enhancements that can be applied to the athlete's skills and attributes at any one time is 10% of the athlete's Conditioning skill.

The benefits of Conditioning are not triggered by spending Magic Points and cannot be turned on or off or changed at will, but are always active. They typically take a whole month of dedicated work to set up, and the process is conducted using the extended task rules with a task round of 1 week. Reconfiguring the regime, or revitalizing it to apply a new intensity when his Conditioning and Puissance skills have increased, similarly takes a month, should the athlete want to refocus his talents and redistribute the available intensity. At every standard of living below Propertied the task to build and maintain a regime is one grade harder.

If the character is unable or unwilling to stick to his regime for more than one month he must make an Endurance test or lose the benefit until he has the opportunity to re-establish it.

Puissance (DEX+CON)

Puissance is the non-magical equivalent of the Mysticism skill. The athlete can enhance selected skills and attributes by an intensity that is 20% of his Puissance skill. A Korantine athlete can apply his enhancements to the following skills and attributes: Acrobatics, Athletics, Brawn, Drive, Endurance, Swim and Unarmed. Attributes that can be enhanced are Fatigue and Healing Rate. He can alternatively allocate to a new trait, Buff, which boosts his STR, CON and DEX, dividing the Intensity between them. No single Characteristic can be boosted by more than one third of its original value.

Forensics (INT x2)

The trade secret of the professional Orator, Forensics is the art of making an argument based on pure reasoning. It designed both to deconstruct an opponent's position by undermining the actual evidence and the logical inferences made from it, and to enable the skilled debater to make their own argument appear more convincing. Or as some say, it is the art of making the wrong seem right and the right seem wrong. For every 20% in this skill the user can make any Oratory roll one grade easier. In debates with opposed rolls, the Forensic advantage of each participant is compared and only the difference applied. Forensics is also routinely used to augment Influence and Deceit rolls – but only when the character skilled in Forensics has the time and opportunity to make a proper argument in speech or writing.

Cultural Passions

Loyalty (Headman or Headwoman)

Hate (Rival clan or tribe)

Magic Type

Folk Magic, Animism. Every tribe has its own set of Traditional Spirits that they can call upon or summon and expect a compliant and friendly response. Some favour Nature Spirits, some favour Ancestors; others, such as the Orlocks, take the spirits of enemy tribesmen they have slain and make them subservient to their own clan.

Typical Professions

Beast Handler, Fisher, Hunter, Scout, Shaman, Warrior

Careers

In most cases, the careers provided in Mythras are used as given. However, note that the Courtesy skill has little use in the setting, and an alternative choice of Professional Skill should be offered. Also, where Folk Magic is a skill option, it is replaced with the Rites skill.

Some examples are provided here of careers that are unique to the setting or have some specific differences to those presented in Mythras.

Assabian Sorcerer

The home of sorcery is Assabia, and for many, the language of Djesmirket is the language of magic itself, since all the great works on the subject are written in it. The Assabian Rites skill can be used to augment Sorcery skill rolls. Assabian sorcerers may be artisans or even slaves, but the most highly skilled practitioners are usually members of a philosophical school or tradition. Mavericks and loners may end up as dangerous wizards wielding powers to selfish and sometimes highly unsavoury ends.

Standard Skills
Customs, Deceit, Influence, Insight, Perception, Willpower

Professional Skills
Craft (Any) Invocation (Grimoire or Philosophical School), Language (Any), Literacy, Lore (Any), Rites (Assabian), Shaping

Sorcery Lores

Assabian Sorcerers study the Three Realities (see Magic chapter) as an essential aspect of arcane knowledge and arts. The knowledge they acquire is an essential part of understanding and dealing with supernatural phenomena, beings and artefacts. When these lores are put to use, it is quite possible the object of study is deliberately trying to avoid detection or confound analysis – for example, a spirit that covertly possesses a human victim, a demon that is taking steps to prevent the revelation of its true name, or a magical item whose creator has obscured its function and purpose. In these cases, the Sorcerer's lore skill should be opposed by a relevant skill of the target or its creator. The Games Master should also take care to ensure appropriate difficulty levels are set for a task.

Lore: The Mundane Arcana
This Lore is used to study and interpret the operation of magic within the material world. It combines physics and metaphysics and an understanding of the way in which the other realities impinge upon and influence mundane existence. All Assabian schools of sorcery can, and should, learn this skill. With this skill a sorcerer can:

- Detect the action or presence of magic, or of a supernatural entity connected to the material world.
- Determine the type of magic at work (Sorcery, Theism, Animism, etc.)
- Estimate the strength of the magic or entity at work
- Analyse a magical item or enchantment to determine its function and purpose
- Research the necessary means to conjure a specific ethereal entity (Jinn) using the Evoke spell.

Lore: Spirit World
This skill is the specialist field of certain schools of sorcery whose main interest is in summoning and dealing with spirits and other entities who inhabit the Second Reality, the Spirit World. Sorcerers do not have means of discorporation and astral projection, so are limited to dealing with those spirits normally capable of manifesting and interacting with mundane existence. Given that this can involve haunts, wraiths and other souls of the dead, this lore is often regarded as equivalent to necromancy.

With this skill a sorcerer can:

- Detect the action or presence of a spirit, including those bound to a physical object
- Determine the nature of a spirit and its capabilities
- Estimate the strength or intensity of the spirit
- Work out a means to Evoke the spirit, forcing it to materialise or manifest so it can be communicated with, dominated, banished or combatted

Lore: The Many Hells
This lore is rather more restricted and exotic than the others; few sorcerers study the Third Reality in great depth because of the dangers and difficulties inherent in putting this lore into practice. The Many Hells are also far more varied and extensive than the other two realities, so even those who have learned everything mankind can know are aware they are merely scratching the surface.

With this skill a sorcerer can:

- Detect the action or presence of a demon
- Determine the nature of a demon and its capabilities
- Estimate the strength, duration or cause of a demon's presence in the mundane world
- Work out the means and probable cost to evoke a certain type of demon
- Research the true name of a specific demon if it is known to humanity

Domestic

Domestics spend their whole time doing household chores, although the range of skills required in a household may be broad or narrow, depending on how big and wealthy it is. Cooking, cleaning, minor repairs, serving at table, shopping, running messages and errands, even entertaining the master of the house and his family, may all come into a day's work. Slaves are often given at least basic education so they can understand written instructions and deal with shopping bills and accounts.

Standard Skills
Endurance, Deceit, Drive, Insight, Locale, Perception, Willpower

Professional Skills
Commerce, Craft (domestic skill, e.g. cooking, sewing), Craft (Secondary), Literacy, Musicianship, Sleight, Streetwise

Jekkarene Temple Dancer

The girls chosen as temple dancers are separated from their parents at a young age and brought up in a convent. Each must have a CHA score of no less than 14. Those who remain with the moon-goddess' cult beyond the age of 17 may well become temple guardians, the female warriors who act as both temple guards and secret police. Those who do not, if given no role to fulfill in the priesthood, may be married off to a deserving noblemen as a gift for his loyalty and service, and so some run away to avoid having their fate decided for them.

Standard Skills
Athletics, Combat Style (Guardian), Conceal, Customs, Dance, Insight, Willpower

Professional Skills
Acrobatics, Acting, Devotion, Exhort, Oratory, Musicianship, Sleight

Korantine Athlete

Some of the wealthy dedicate themselves to athletic competition, and travel Korantia to take part in all of the sporting festivals where there are glory and prizes to be had. A prospective athlete must have an average of STR, CON and DEX of 13 or more.

Korantines take athletic competition so seriously and it is such an important profession that it has its own kind of mysticism attached to it – the skills of Conditioning and Puissance (see page 52). These specialist skills are only taught by a cadre of very high-rent coaches, former athletes themselves, who get to pick and choose who they work with.

Standard Skills
Athletics, Drive, Evade, First Aid, Willpower, Ride, Unarmed

Professional Skills
Acrobatics, Conditioning*, Gambling, Literacy, Puissance*, Rites, Teach

Korantine Orator

Oratory is a classic education for a Korantine boy from a wealthy family, and from the earliest age, they are taught to learn and recite speeches, then to compose their own, to know the laws of their city and to debate. A young orator cuts his teeth making speeches at weddings and funerals, then progresses into

Characters

the law courts where he can practice his skills in cases involving poor people before progressing to more noteworthy matters. Practising law is regarded as excellent preparation for politics both for the skills developed and the public visibility, so these people often have easy entry into the cult of Anayo and the city council.

Standard Skills
Custom, Deceit, Influence, Insight, Locale, Native Tongue, Willpower

Professional Skills
Bureaucracy, Commerce, Forensics*, Literacy, Lore (Korantine Philosophy), Oratory, Rites

Orc Slaver

Orc slavers are in the business of buying or seizing captives on behalf of their sorcerer-priests who have a regular demand for sentient sacrifices. The northern jungles of Jandekot were hunted out long ago, and this has been one of the reasons they have taken to the sea.

Standard Skills
Boating, Brawn, Conceal, Deceit, Perception, Stealth; Combat Style: Slave Taker

Professional Skills
Commerce, Language (any), Navigation, Seamanship, Survival, Track

Orcish Sorcerer-Priest (Lapith)

These fellows are the spiritual hub of the community, who inform, educate and entertain through the use of magic poetry, memorised or extemporised at enormous length. Revered and feared in equal measure, the Sorcerer-Priests also lead the community in worship of The Hungry Gods, personally entering into demonic pacts that provide the wellspring of orcish religion. The great city of Nishimbakoi is effectively run by their order. Sorcerer-Priests also oversee the trade in sourcing, grading, shaping and distributing obsidian, which is the preferred cutting edge of orcish weapons; hence their name of Lapiths.

Standard Skills
Conceal, Custom, Deceit, Influence, Insight, Sing, Willpower

Professional Skills
Commerce, Craft (Enchanting), Craft (Obsidian), Poetics (Orcish Sorcery), Lore (Mundane Arcana), Rites, Shaping

An Orcish Sorcerer-Priest is illiterate, but stores the knowledge of his spells in the huge well of poetic verse that they commit to memory and out of which they can compose new songs on the fly. Such a person knows no more than one sorcery spell for every 10% of their Lore (Poetics) skill.

Orcs fuel their magic through sacrificing others – and power magical enchantments and divine gifts the same way. The Evoke (Hungry Gods) spell brings one or more of the entities they worship to feed on sacrifices, and must be cast with a range that reaches to the volcanic portals from which they seep into the mundane world from the Many Hells. When a sentient victim is sacrificed, the Lapith transfers its life force to the Hungry Gods using the Tap spell. Every 5 Characteristic points tapped provides one Magic Point that is retained by the Sorcerer for his own use. By combining the Tap spell with the Enchant ritual, this can be made permanent. Lapiths are denied the ability to permanently augment their own Characteristics, as the benefit of such enhancement is reserved to the nobility. If one does, he is declared outlaw and hunted down.

On the other hand Orcs are prolific manufacturers of magic items so long as they have a ready supply of captives for sacrifice. Orc artefacts are spurned (at least in public) by most other people as blood magic.

Typical Sorcery Spells:
Enchant, Enslave (Humans), Evoke (Hungry Gods), Hinder, Imprison, Palsy, Sculpt (Obsidian), Revivify, Store Manna, Tap (STR, CON or POW)

Paladin

The Paladins are highly trained Korantine warriors, brought up from childhood by the cult of Lanis the sun-god in the service of the Korantine Emperor. Once graduated to adulthood, the Paladins are maintained on land grants sufficient that they are freed from all other obligations than to practise their martial skills. Across Korantia there are some 2,200 such Paladins, of whom a little under half are based in and around Hilanistra itself, the remainder being settled upon lands within various Korantine city-states where they live as metics.

Standard Skills
Athletics, Endurance, Evade, Combat Styles x2 (Paladin, Archery), Ride, Unarmed

Professional Skills
Devotion (Lanis), Exhort, Literacy, Lore (Battles), Lore (Strategy and Tactics), Oratory, Rites (Korantine)

A Paladin character starts play as an initiate of Lanis the Adventurer, unless for some reason he has fallen out of the cult before reaching the necessary age. He will also have 1d3 Folk Magic spells taught by the cult.

Sabatine Mercenary

These men can come from anywhere, but are employed as mercenaries by the Korantine trade cults, and so are known as Sabatines. Their training will vary according to whether they are expected to serve at sea or on overland trade routes

Standard Skills

Athletics, Boating, Combat Style (Sabatine), Conceal, Drive, First Aid, Perception

Professional Skills

Bureaucracy, Commerce, Culture (any*), Language (Any), Navigation, Seamanship, Streetwise

* *For Sabatines of foreign stock, this should be spent on Korantine Culture. If they take citizenship on mustering out of the unit, this is converted to be their Custom skill.*

Combat Styles

The world of Thennla is an ancient-style milieu, and the available weapons and combat styles reflect that.

Combat Styles come in various different types:

Monster Styles

This is a Games Master's shorthand, a combat style that covers all of a creature's attacks, whether ranged weapons, close combat weapons or natural weapons. NPCs that do not require detailed statistics can be given a 'monster style'. Whenever the creature or NPC picks up an impromptu or inappropriate

weapon, their skill will revert to Basic STR+DEX or half their Monster Style, whichever is higher.

Militia Styles

These are basic forms of military training as provided to the levy of able-bodied citizens or tribesmen. They are generally limited in scope, with just a main weapon and shield, perhaps a thrown weapon as well. They may have a simple Trait, or none at all.

Military Styles

The preserve of professional training as part of a formed unit, Military Styles tend to have a more comprehensive combination of weapons, and, possibly, a more complex Trait.

Civilian Styles

Whether urban streetfighter, aristocratic duellist or irregular barbarian warrior, Civilian Styles are either self-studied or conveyed by individual weapon masters. This group can include styles such as Archery or Slinger that have clear military uses.

Militia Styles

Equestrian Levy, Levy Spearman, Levy Archer, Levy Slinger

The simplest combat training is applied to get the locals to line up in some semblance of order and present a threat to an enemy. The leading element of these styles is usually the shield itself, and this is paired with whatever is the most effective or readily available cultural weapon – typically a spear. Levy and militia are expected to bring their own weapons and armour to fight with. Hence poorer citizens may instead be called up to fight as missile troops.

Militia Styles do not usually provide training in more that one or two weapons, so if a character resorts to a back-up weapon with a shield his skill is reduced by one third (or to his basic Combat Style percentage, whichever is higher).

Mounted militia often do not get enough training to gain the Mounted Combat trait, but are instead treated as skirmishers.

Games Master Note: References to Sidearm are to any one-handed, short-reach hafted weapon (Club, Hatchet, Mace); or bladed weapons with short reach (Dagger, Shortsword).

Levy Skirmisher

(e.g, Borissan Horde, Barbarian Levy)

- Y Typical Weapons: Javelin or Dart; Spear or Sidearm; Shield (Pelte or Target)
- Y Traits: Skirmishing

Levy Spearman

(e.g, Korantine Citizen Militia, Barbarian Levy Spearman)

- Y Typical Weapons: Spear and Shield (Thureos* or Hoplite Shield)
- Y Traits: Shield Wall

A large oval shield, usually flat with a central grip. Use statistics for Scutum.

Equestrian Levy

(e.g, Korantine Citizen Cavalry)

- Y Typical Weapons: Javelin or Dart, Spear, Shield (Pelta or Target)
- Y Traits: Skirmishing

Military Styles

These styles tend to provide a more comprehensive range of weapons.

Ashkorite Pikeman

From the military capital of the Taskan Empire, the evolved phalanx style of the Taskan infantry involves a 2-handed pike, with a large buckler slung over the left arm on a strap providing a passive parrying device.

- Y Typical Weapons: Pike, Sidearm and Buckler
- Y Traits: Formation Fighting; Phalanx. In phalanx formation the unit's hedged spears and/or shields combine to provide some protection for the group against missiles. The unit's average Lore (Tactics and Drill) is used to oppose incoming missile fire, which prevents the automatic award of a Special Effect if ranged attacks are not actively parried.

Korantine Citizen Infantry

A more evolved form of the militia style, with additional training provided for members of the local Patriotic Bands or for those in the higher property qualifications who are expected to take the lead in military service to the state. In any case those who have this style are likely to be in the foremost ranks when the militia is drawn up for battle.

- Y Typical Weapons: Spear and Shield, Javelin OR Sidearm
- Y Traits: Shield Wall, Formation Fighting or Phalanx. A Korantine hoplite phalanx is able to extend its cover to other troops in its midst – up to one for every two hoplites.

Targeteer

(e.g. Taskan Imperial Light Infantry, Korantine Peltast)

A professional combination of a light (small or medium) shield used to ward off enemy missiles, a light spear, sidearm and thrown weapons such as javelins and darts. This is one of the classic weapon combinations. Targeteer is also used as the main Combat Style of some cavalry units, particularly in Korantia.

- Y Typical Weapons: Buckler, Target or Pelte; Darts or Javelins, Shortspear, Sidearm (Club, Hatchet, Mace or Shortsword)
- Y Trait: Skirmishing

Paladin

Professional warriors in the service of the Korantine Emperor, they are the most highly trained in all Korantia. Most Paladins have a second style in addition to this one, such as Archery.

- Y Typical Weapons: Javelin, Sword, Spear, Shield (Hoplite or Thureos)
- Y Trait: Choose One of Mounted Combat or Formation Fighting

Shortsword and Large Shield

(Agissene Infantry Style)

A Korantine Combat Style in which a soldier is taught to effectively use a short cut and thrust sword in combination with a large shield.

- Y Typical Weapons: Shortsword, Javelin, Shield (Hoplite or Scutum)
- Y Trait: Flurry. Any active shield parry can immediately be followed up by a sword blow at the cost of a further Action Point

Polearm/Poleaxe Infantry

A single Combat Style that covers two-handed hafted and bladed weapons capable of cutting and impaling, as often seen amongst the royal units of Assabia or among some Thennalt warrior societies. The use of a spear is included when learning this style.

- Y Typical Weapons: Halberd/Poleaxe, Shortspear, Longspear
- Y Trait: Formation Fighting

Civilian Styles

Cloak and Dagger

The duelling style of Taskan nobility; but sometimes a handy means of self-defence that makes use of things commonly worn in civilian dress. In days of old, Tarsenian noblemen were taught how to fight each other in the street armed with a dagger or the traditional Tarsenian dirk and a cloak or tunic wrapped around the left arm to provide a parrying device.

This form of fighting is still practised and no longer just by noblemen. The parrying cloak can be just about any large piece of heavy cloth or soft leather but if properly made can also produce the Entangle Special Effect. Depending on what it is made of, it will also provide an additional 1-3 Armour Points to the left arm; but bears the obvious risk that if an opponent chooses the 'Damage Weapon' Special Effect the weapon in question is the fighter's arm, not the cloak.

- Y Typical Weapons: Dagger, Shortsword, Cloak
- Y Traits: Unarmed Prowess when using cloak

Characters

Duellist

In Assabia there is a tradition of duelling styles with which people work out their differences in a violent but elegant manner, with the use of beautifully made and sometimes highly ornate weapons. A variety of blades form the canon of weapons that are considered appropriate for use with the style. The rapier is an elongated leaf-bladed narrow sword. The Assabian main gauche is curve-bladed.

- Typical Weapons: Scimitar, Main Gauche, Rapier, Dagger, Buckler
- Traits: Choose One of Excellent Footwork or Thrown Weapon

Knife Fighting

While this Combat Style is rarely actually taught outside illegal fight clubs, it is something those who inhabit the darker recesses of the big cities find themselves developing as a skill. Knife Fighting makes use of a claw*, knife, dagger or dirk, along with very fast footwork. The knife fighter needs to be nimble enough to get out of the way of a big weapon that he cannot hope to parry with a small blade and be ready to get a quick stab or slash back at the attacker.

- Typical Weapons: Claw, Dagger, Knife
- Trait: Dodge. This Combat Style can be used to dodge incoming blows with the effectiveness of a parry (Size S), without going prone as when Evading.

Hunter

A hunter is one who goes to work with a missile weapon such as a bow and can take the Archery style, but some, particularly those who chase large game for sport, may opt for spears and javelins, ready to get close or to withstand a charging beast using a set spear.

- Typical Weapons: Javelin and Shortspear, or Bow (any)
- Trait: On the Fly. Reduce ranged attack penalties for a fast moving target by one grade

Archery

This Combat Style covers the use of any kind of bow, apart from crossbows. Different arrowheads can be used to produce special effects. The basic bows such as the short bow do not have enough draw strength for the archer to apply a positive Damage Modifier, if any, although a negative modifier will still apply.

- Typical Weapons: Long Bow, Recurve Bow, Short Bow
- Trait: Rapid Fire. The archer can reload and fire prepared ammunition as a single Action up to three times, however, each shot is at one grade of difficulty higher than the last (Hard, Formidable, Herculean)

Marksman

This Combat Style is a rare one outside of Assabia. It applies to crossbows of any type, including stonebows. Such weapons are sometimes acquired from master bowyers in Assabia but they are regarded by Korantines and Taskans as unmanly for use in battle, and usually only employed for hunting.

- Typical Weapons: Heavy Crossbow, Light Crossbow
- Trait: Hawkeye. Penalties for shooting smaller than man-size targets are reduced by one grade.

Slinger

Although this Combat Style does not give access to a whole range of weapons, it is one of the most widely practised forms of ranged combat, and the necessary equipment is dirt cheap and easy to acquire. Pebbles of the right size and shape will deal 1d8 damage and a properly cast lead slingshot is capable of 1d8+1 damage; but even a lump of soft clay, when that is all there is on hand to make use of, might inflict 1d4 and 1d6 if baked hard. Staff slings are not known in the Eastern continents.

- Typical Weapons: Sling
- Trait: Windage. Reduce the difficulty imposed by wind strength by one grade

Maul

A single Combat Style covering two-handed hafted weapons, all of which are typically ENC 2 or 3 and Size H. These weapons are uncommon, and most likely to be seen in the hands of barbarous Marangian warriors.

- Typical Weapons: Great Axe, Great Club, Great Hammer, Quarterstaff
- Trait: Intimidating

Sidearm

The use of any basic one-handed weapon without specialist functions or techniques is covered by the Sidearm Combat Style. This skill can be used for any ENC 1 battleaxe (1H), club, falchion, hatchet, light mace or shortsword. Sidearm training is not widely available – it is sometimes provided in a military context but most civilians generally have to work on improving their techniques through practice. Sidearms remain distinct from weapons such as a dagger or dirk, which many soldiers carry but are last ditch 'hold out' weapons in battle or else for civilian use.

- Y Typical Weapons: Choose Battleaxe, Mace, Hatchet and Shield OR Shortsword, Falchion and Shield
- Y Traits: Versatile. Any ENC 1 single handed weapon can be used with only one grade of difficulty harder

Swordsman

Korantines do not have a tradition of swordsmanship, and tend to use just a short sword or falchion (single edged blade) as sidearm or as a backup weapon. A longer sword is used by some professional warriors such as Paladins to give them the reach they need when fighting from horseback. This sword type is based on the broadsword used by Thennalt men of status (those who are head of a family). Both Tarsenians and Assabians have a more developed sword culture; in those lands master swordsmen still run schools where the art of swordsmanship is taught, and there are written treatises on the subject that can be consulted in the libraries. Other schools of swordsmanship exist, dealing in archaic weapons such as the rapier, foreign weapons such as the scimitar and tulwar, or specialist weapons such as the sabre used from horseback.

- Y Typical Weapons: Broadsword, Falchion, Longsword, Sabre
- Y Traits: Varies by master or culture

MAGIC

Thennla is magic-rich; many people have access to low-level spells and cantrips so long as they are respectable members of their society, and, thereby, not excluded from the skills and knowledge their local traditions have to offer. Higher magic is frequently encountered and its effects and possibilities are built into the fabric of most societies.

The Nature of Magic

Thennla appears on the surface to be much like our own world. For the most part, it behaves in a predictable fashion and in accordance with rules that can be discerned through direct observation and experiment. However, the presence of gods and other supernatural entities, and the proximity of the Material World to other dimensions, can produce unexpected and surprising phenomena. As a result, natural laws are provisional and can be interrupted, adapted or suspended; and the mechanisms by which that happens are generally described as 'magic'.

Magic Point Recovery

In Thennla, a character's Magic Points are recovered at the character's Healing Rate per day, assuming adequate rest. In normal circumstances the day's Magic Point recovery is achieved by a decent night's sleep. Recovery may be accelerated or hindered by the magical nature of a location, at the Games Master's discretion. It may also be prevented by interrupted sleep, inadequate rest, illness or chronic fatigue.

In the Spirit World, a spirit that is native to that world recovers Magic Points at its Healing Rate every hour. As spirit entities lack CON, use their CHA to establish their Healing Rate instead.

Entities that are outside their normal realm – spirits manifest or bound in the Material World, discorporated mortals in the Spirit World – are unable to recover Magic Points except from external sources (veneration, sacrifice and so forth).

How Magic Works

Magical effects are the product of energy generated through the interaction of the parallel dimensions that comprise the Three Realities of the cosmos, shaped and directed by those with the knowledge to do so. In game terms, this energy is represented by Magic Points. Harnessing and deploying this energy may come easily to supernatural entities that can move between the realities or states of being, but for humans it is quite a feat. Getting the help of the gods in the form of Miracles is the most efficient, and often the most efficacious, way of doing so. Working magic with only the abilities with which a human being is endowed is much more difficult – sorcerers and shamans spend lifetimes learning to master their professions.

Most Korantines believe that humans should leave magic well alone unless it is fully socialised (Folk Magic) or divinely sanctioned (Theist Miracles). The gods can be relied upon to maintain the balance and harmony of the cosmos, and so they know best what magical interventions are acceptable. Sorcery involves too much human agency and its very creativity encourages dangerous meddling.

Many foreigners take an entirely different view – the Materialist Movement philosophers in the Sultanate of Perlak in Assabia would argue that magic is essential to the fabric of existence, and as much responsible for maintenance of the ordinary as it is for producing the extraordinary. They are less inclined to trust in divine wisdom and more than happy to explore where the magical arts can take them.

What Magic Is For

Magic is encountered day-to-day, used in ways that enforce and support a culture's traditions and economy. When deployed to support a community's efforts to grow food, reduce the chance of a merchant ship sinking, or provide defences for a unit of soldiers, it can make the difference between feast and famine, life and death, victory or defeat. Magic can both diminish and magnify the world's destructive forces. Like any other resource, it is usually more readily accessible to those with wealth and status, and so in some societies, access to it serves to deepen class divisions. There are even whole cultures that are magic-poor because they have few resources and no infrastructure to develop the magical potential of their people.

There are also many self-centred and ambitious individuals who see magic as a way to escape their limitations – whether that is to give them extraordinary mental or physical capabilities, immunity from diseases or eternal life. The simple fact that magic offers these hopes is one of the reasons for the inevitable pursuit of magical enhancements, even when society frowns upon them. Spells, enchantments, potions, divine gifts and spirit possession all have a part to play in the search to be more than nature alone would allow. Eventually those who augment themselves to extremes enter territory where they perhaps have passed beyond being human and become something else. That 'something' may be as wonderful as achieving godhood, or as terrible as becoming some cursed abomination such as a Vampire.

THE THREE REALITIES

The earth, sky and oceans of Thennla all belong to the material, or mundane, realm; which is itself just one of the three realities that are known to exist. The philosopher Atrivaskos of Masia was the first to demonstrate through reasoning alone that these realities must constitute the entirety of existence. Besides which, he observed, since nothing appears able to escape the realms and nothing new to enter them, even if it were not true it would make no difference to anyone or anything. While Atrivaskos' Proof is yet to be challenged, there is in fact no reason why there could not be some portal between one of the realities of Thennla and some other dimension in which one or more inhabited worlds are found.

The Material World

Everything in the Material World is expressed in some physical form. There are five recognised Natures of which physical things are made, which are Earth, Fire, Air, Water and Flesh. Everything in the Material World partakes of one or more of these natures.

In the Material World, a soul can only persist so long as it is combined with, or cloaked in, a physical form. The most suitable housing for a soul is flesh, a type of matter that is defined by being in a constant state of change and known to be transitory. It is for this reason that a living creature's lifespan is limited, unless magic is deployed to prolong it artificially.

Creatures and entities that are native to the other realities cannot enter the Material World without the aid of magic – in most cases through some form of summons or conjuring spell. Unless subsequently imprisoned or bound in a physical form or object, the visit is always a temporary one.

The Spirit World

Just beyond mortal perception is the strange and abstract world of the spirits. This dimension touches on the Material World at almost every point, and sometimes spirit beings intrude into it or directly influence its inhabitants. The Spirit World is described by some scholars and mystics as like an ocean; one that both divides the Material World from the Many Hells and, for those who know how to navigate it, connects them. When a mortal dies, his soul is parted from the flesh and has to pass through the Spirit World to its final destination in the Many Hells where it will assume a new form.

A living person can only enter the Spirit World if his soul can be Discorporated, or temporarily separated from the body. To do this requires a rare ability practiced by some shamans, powerful drugs, or a theist Miracle.

An entity of any kind can only have INT, POW and CHA characteristics when present in the Spirit World.

The Many Hells

Beneath the surface of the earth, in a vast subterranean world that dwarfs the upper world of the living, are the Many Hells. These are the lands of the dead, with their own complex geography and their own kingdoms and empires. Those who are native to the Many Hells are commonly called *demons*. They

cannot enter the Material World without the intervention of powerful magic, because they must generate or bring with them a physical form to do so. Even the insubstantial souls of the dead that have made it to the Many Hells to take up permanent residence there cannot be permanently returned to the Material World again without divine intervention or reincarnation.

A soul that descends to the Many Hells faces many dangers, not least of which is the bleak prospect of an eternity of misery and mindless boredom. Fortunately, the newly deceased should carry with them the help and protection of the gods they worshipped in life – and perhaps even enjoy the rewards of a special place reserved for the gods' favourites. If not, they may find themselves enslaved and put to eternal servitude on the estates of some demon lord.

In the Many Hells, only creatures who are entirely native to the place can recover Magic Points at all and, unless allowed access to one of the few locations where Magic Points are known to accumulate and can be harvested, its denizens rely on the offerings made by the relatives of the dead to their loved ones. These tend to dry up after they have been dead a few years and have passed from living memory.

Games Master Note: In the Many Hells, it is possible to encounter inhabitants who have different or variant versions of the characteristics possessed by creatures in the Material and Spirit Worlds. One such example are Shades, creatures formed from the spirits of the dead and cloaked in substance produced from no more than shadows – for only in the Many Hells can darkness be a substance (nature) in its own right rather simply an absence of light.

SUPERNATURAL BEINGS

Even in the Material World it is possible to encounter magical, ethereal or demonic entities.

Ethereals

Ethereals are magical beings that are able to materialise or dematerialise a physical form at will. These entities are not the same as spirits as they actually possess a material body, one that can suffer hurt and which can be subject to the ravages of time. Even when dematerialised, they retain a presence in the Material World. If they can be detected, for example, by a Soul Sight Miracle or Mystic Vision, they can be targeted with spells.

Ethereals can readily be summoned or evoked, but the summoner must use a spell or Miracle with sufficient Range to reach wherever they are, or be present at the right time and in a place where such beings are known to be lurking. Ethereal beings can be banished if the appropriate spell or Miracle is known, but the effect is only temporary and prevents the ethereal from assuming physical form for the duration.

While in material form these beings can suffer injury and the effects of ageing, but cannot recover Magic Points. When in ethereal form they are immune to the ravages of time, can recover Magic Points but usually very slowly – at their healing rate per month, season or even per year, according to type, but cannot heal their physical bodies.

The many types of ethereal include the ifrit, a tribe of elemental giants who wield sorcery; elves, goblins, trolls and fairie races such as kobolds and pixies.

Some ethereal beings are familiar to Korantines – nymphs and satyrs, in particular. But Korantines otherwise fail to distinguish between ethereal denizens of the Material World, and spirits and demons intruding from one of the other realities. Any and all of them might be called 'daemons'.

Elementals

These more-or-less dumb spirits only have any meaning or purpose when they combine with some aspect of the Material World. Yet they live outside it, and must be summoned or evoked. Summoning an elemental through sorcery requires one point of Magnitude per cubic metre of elemental, and enough of their natural substance with which they can cloak themselves to form a physical body.

Spirits

Creatures in the Material World cannot normally see spirits, engage them in spirit combat or target them with spells, and vice versa. However, there are some spirits that retain a psychic connection to the Material World and can Manifest, making themselves visible, causing physical phenomena or even making psychic attacks on unsuspecting humans. Of these by far the most common are haunts and wraiths. In all cases there are conditions on when, or to whom, a spirit can manifest. An ancestor spirit, for example, may only be able to manifest itself to someone of the same lineage. The Games Master may rule Manifestation a skill, with a basic percentage of POW+CHA, and with a typical skill for a spirit that possesses the trait of five times this number. A sorcerer can only Evoke a spirit that possesses the Manifestation trait, whereas a shaman or witch with access to the spirit world by Discorporation can force other types of spirits into the Material World too.

Almost any spirit can be bound to a place, object or person in the Material World by an act of will or magic. A place to which a spirit is bound, such as the area to which a haunt is confined, is usually called a locus. A binding object is referred to as a fetish, and binding to a person or creature is usually seen in the form of possession or the control exerted over a spirit by a shaman. These bindings limit a spirit's normal access to its Spirit World home, or cut it off completely.

Demons

Demons are creatures from the Many Hells, and have a physical substance very different to that of the Material World. They do not and cannot exist as discorporated spirits, and so to engage with the Material World, must have a physical presence. This can only be accomplished by a significant expenditure of Magic Points, provided by whoever seeks to summon them. When a demon's physical form is destroyed, its soul is destroyed with it, and vice versa.

Demons can be unique entities or belong to a tribe or race. Many of them are bizarre and shocking to behold for human eyes, and have highly unusual powers and abilities. When designing a demon, feel free to make use of the Chaos Features provided in MYTHRAS pages 275-276 in order to represent this.

There are no known theist Miracles by which a demon can be summoned to the Material World. The evocations of sorcerers are the only known means to achieve it. For a sorcerer to summon a demon, he must commit one point of Magnitude per Intensity of the target, but also must commit one Magic Point for every point of SIZ possessed by the demon in order for its physical form to be forced into the Material World.

Learning Magic

Magical arts can be acquired in a number of different ways. Simple Folk Magic may be passed down within a family or a trade, and those cults which have an integral role to play within a society usually ensure that magical traditions are preserved and passed on to each new generation. As you would expect, the more powerful abilities and arcane skills are reserved to those who prove themselves worthy in some way. However, there are many supernatural entities in the cosmos which can be a source of magical knowledge to those who seek them out and strike whatever deal suits both parties, so there are ways to bypass the straight-jacket of cult rules and hierarchies.

The Rites Skill (INT+CHA)

The Rites skill represents the basic magical and religious knowledge a character learns and absorbs from their cultural background. This skill replaces the Folk Magic skill, but has wider uses too.

Every culture has its own traditions and philosophies for dealing with magic and the supernatural, and hence there are separate skills that can be learned for Korantine Rites, Taskan Rites, Assabian Rites and so forth. The Rites skill can be used to accomplish basic magical tasks learned within that culture, including casting Folk Magic, making the proper observances in a religious ritual, perhaps even using a fetish containing a spirit that is friendly to the character's native traditions.

Games Master Note: In some instances, the Rites skill can be used to augment other compatible casting rolls. A Korantine priestess exhorting her deity to provide a Miracle may, for example, take her time over it and augment the Exhort roll with up to 20% of her Korantine Rites skill. You may also allow that the augment can be divided between her Devotion and Exhort skills. Only Assabian Rites can be used to augment sorcery. The Rites skill therefore defines the benefit to be gained by using Ritualistic Casting Times (see MYTHRAS Page 115). To gain the advantage of Ritualised Casting requires increasing the casting time to Minutes for Folk Magic and Hours for Theism and Sorcery.

Types of Magic

Folk Magic

Folk Magic is not a discrete category of magic in the setting, but a general term for forms of low-powered magical cantrips and blessings that are in the grain of a culture or tradition, and that provide some resource for those starved of the more potent forms of magic.

The most frequently encountered form of Folk Magic is a blessing provided by a deity or spirit, and accessible though its cult. Folk Magic is usually cast or invoked using the character's Rites skill, depending on where and how it is learned, rather than with a separate Folk Magic skill, but otherwise behaves as per the rules in MYTHRAS.

Mysticism

Mysticism is an isolated practice, studied and transmitted within extremely narrow communities. Outside of Rasputana the only traditions that conform to the Mysticism model are the Korantine Sibyls, who are no more than a dozen female seers scattered across the whole of Korantia and their apprentices;

Magic

and the Black Hand of Jelhai, an unsavoury body of fanatics that enforce the rule of Jelhai's Sultan. A number of traditions are known to exist in Rasputana, and even there Mysticism is a rather exotic practice. Rarely, a foreigner may travel there to learn from the mystics, and even more rarely such an individual returns to their native land laden with the esoteric knowledge they have gained.

Sorcery

Sorcery is distinguished by being a body of magical lore entirely created through human endeavour. It is the major magic system for several important cultures but its true home is Assabia. It can even provide the framework for religious practices, as sorcery incorporates sophisticated language and protocols for dealing with supernatural entities. Knowledge of a few spells from a widely distributed grimoire may be quite common amongst educated people; however, to be considered a professional sorcerer requires not only that you know a handful of spells but also that you are adept at manipulating them. The Shaping skill (sometimes referred to as Spellcraft) is generally only taught to those serving as apprentices to a sorcerer, or through an order or guild. The same can be said for certain spells such as Charm, Enchant and Evoke.

Sorcerers are distinguished from other kinds of magic users by the importance of the written word through which their knowledge is recorded, compiled and passed on. Spell books, glyphs, runes, grimoires, arcane signs and lost languages – these are all the stock in trade of a sorcerer, hence you usually only find sorcerers in literate societies. Nevertheless, it is also the favoured magic system of the barbarian Orcs of Kasperan, who have only a syllabic script that is not up to the job of communicating the complexities of spell casting and whose grimoires are epic songs running into thousands of lines that the sorcerer needs to commit to memory.

A sorcerer who gets consumed by his trade, and goes about it in ways that puts him beyond the pale of regular society, is referred to as a wizard. He may be forced to retreat to some lawless border region such as the Badlands of Methalea, where a wizard can continue his work without intrusions in some lonely and likely enchanted stronghold.

Charms (Temporary Enchantment)

A charm is created by combining Enchant with one or more other sorcery spells creating what is sometimes referred to as a Temporary Enchantment. Such a spell is no longer dependent for its duration on a multiple of the caster's POW, but becomes part of the fabric of the world, and its duration is measured according to natural divisions of time. In some cases the enchanter must ensure he conducts the casting ritual at a specific time in order to benefit from the full duration available.

A charm cannot have a Duration longer than a year and a day. Unlike other spells, the caster can no longer end it at will; once set, the enchanter must possess or have access to the enchanted person or thing to lift the spell, and he must make an appropriate Invocation roll to do it.

Games Master Note: Where spell durations are concerned, a year is always the old 364-day lunar year, hence a year and a day is a duration of 365 days.

Charm Shaping Costs Table

Game World Time	Shaping Cost
1 hour	1
2 hours	2
3 hours	3
Until Sunset (Or Sunrise)	4
One Day (24 hours)	5
One Week (7 days)	6
Waxing or Waning Moon (14 Days)	7
One Month (28 days)	8
One Season (3-4 months)	9
A Year and a Day (365 days)	10

Limits on Charm Duration and Magic Point Recovery

A sorcerer capable of producing temporary enchantments has a balance to strike – the Magic Points used are dedicated to the charm and they cannot begin to regain them until such time as the enchantment expires, or it is unmade by the enchanter. A sorcerer may thus be vulnerable immediately following the expiry of a protective charm if he awaits Magic Point recovery before renewing it. He may decide to do so immediately but then will find himself temporarily very low on magical energy.

Enchanting Concentration Spells

With an extended time within which the Sorcerer can choose to let a Concentration spell fall idle, and then resume concentration at a moment of his choosing, spells such as Wrack become effective curses and tools with which to force a prisoner or minion to obedience – after all, the sorcerer may be in a position to kill the spell's target at any time for up to a year. Many other spells such as Fly, Intuition or Mystic Vision may be maintained in constant readiness to be activated, depending on whether the sorcerer's player considers the advantage of not having to make a Skill Test or spend an Action Point to focus concentration, worth the Magic Points being set aside and not released for recovery.

Smother is treated as a Concentration spell, and can be used to kill. Other spells, such as Palsy, may have variants with the Concentration trait, allowing the sorcerer to turn it on and off at will.

Permanent Enchantments

To create something that acquires permanence is a debilitating process, wherein the sorcerer sacrifices some part of his own, or someone else's, being and transfers it to the enchantment. The simplest (but by no means only) way to do this involves combining Enchant with the Tap (Characteristic) spell and whatever other magic is to be applied. The loss of characteristic points to generate these magic points is permanent and irrevocable. Enchant is always cast as a ritual, with a casting time measured in Hours, not Actions.

Enchanting Conditions

In addition to using a different scale for spell duration, a charm may have one or more Conditions applied. Conditions can be used to define or limit who the enchanted item works for, who it can target, and when it works. Each Condition costs the Enchanter an additional point of Shaping to effect.

Enchanting Autonomous Spells

A sorcerer or his paying client typically enjoys the facility of a charm for defensive magic such as Damage Resistance, Spell Resistance and Spirit Resistance. However, spells such as Sculpt (Substance), Holdfast, Haste and Phantom (Sense) may also be set up for more creative purposes – such as to protect or decorate a sorcerer's mansion.

Theism

Seeking the help of the gods is the most effective way to channel magical energy from beyond the material world, because there are supernatural entities on the other end of it that define the effects of the magic and ensure that it works. The cosmos is littered with deities big and small who can offer Miracles, Gifts and more. Some supernatural entities that are not really regarded as deities can also be dealt with in ways that are similar to the rules of theism.

Magic

Deities

The gods do not all live in one place but are scattered about the Three Realities; it is almost a definition of a god that it is a being that exists in more than one reality at once. However, many gods are still geographically fixed, and while able to move freely along the axis between types of existence, cannot range beyond a particular locale in any one of them, or are limited to a specific pathway or element.

Gods have power to intervene in or interfere with the world, and, consequently, every human culture interacts with them in some way. While most gods are supernatural beings, not all of them started out as such, and history records several human beings who have achieved this status in their lifetimes. Any entity that is capable of accepting prayers, dedications and sacrifices from a mortal, and providing some sort of favour in return, could be considered a god. However, many daemons and spirits have this trait, and at the same time are not regarded as properly divine.

Gods cannot be compelled to do anything by the use of sorcery, but must be petitioned, propitiated or bargained with, and this is what religions are set up to do. A true deity can only be requested to appear to its worshippers, typically through the Miracles provided to the worshippers for that purpose. A god that answers the call makes an 'epiphany' and is present in a real sense; however, all the more powerful ones manifest a version or aspect of themselves rather than reveal their full glory, which can be disturbing to mere mortals.

Types of Deity

Gods come in many shapes and sizes. The greatest are the Titans, those that you will know about even if you do not worship them. They have been fixtures in the make-up of the world since it began. In fact, the Titans may be so high and mighty that in many cultures they attract a rather exclusive following or none at all, because they are so beyond the human condition that people cannot relate to them. Nor can any single human culture grasp the entirety of their natures, so it is normal that the way in which they are worshipped in one place bears little relation to how they are worshipped in other lands. Mother Earth, Emperor Sun, Father Ocean and Queen of Heaven are examples of Titans. Lesser Titans are of the same generation but of more limited power and aspect. The Moon, the Planets and the key Natures – Fire, Water, Flesh, Air and Stone – lead this group. The Titans are more or less immutable and can afford a measure of indifference about their popularity as objects of worship.

The remaining arrays of gods are very specific – they are attached to a particular place or field of activity but they may, through their lineage, combine powers and natures inherited or borrowed from the Titans. They have a more precarious existence and are motivated to recruit worshippers in order to maintain and grow their power. They fit themselves closely to the needs and social structures of human beings, because this is what wins them followers and enhances their power through worship. Most gods are described in terms of gender, however, this can be quite confused and of course is not always a relevant term of reference for so complex an entity as a deity.

Likewise, there are the demigods, ancestors and heroes; formerly mortal creatures who have ascended to a state of godhood thanks to their actions in their mortal lives, who despite their junior ranking among deities are often the most enthusiastically worshipped because they are closer to humanity.

Pantheons

For the purpose of worship gods are gathered into pantheons, which simply means an array of gods who are receptive to the same rites. These pantheons are therefore human constructs and may not actually reflect a cosmic reality. They may be rigidly defined, as is the case with the Korantine Pantheon, or they may be in a continual state of creation through a gradual process of selection, assimilation and accretion, as the Tarsenian pantheon. Some gods may happily belong to more than one pantheon but perhaps show a different side of themselves to worshippers in each one, and are consequently known by many different names. There are gods who do not belong to any pantheon, or who currently have no worshippers.

Man-Made Divinities

Some gods are actually created by mankind, called into existence in a form that is relevant and accessible to human minds, fashioned from the essence of some more impersonal or abstract force by an act of human will. The City-Goddesses of the Korantines are just such an example. The POW of an entity of this kind is generated entirely by the prayers of its worshippers, as it has none of its own. Its consciousness is usually some fragment or aspect of a greater entity.

Types of Worship

In many cases, the relationship between an individual and a deity is managed by a cult, and, in these cases, promotion within the god's cult and access to Miracles is handled in accordance with the Mythras rules. However, there are many other types of theist relationship available; every culture has its own ideas about the best way to manage them and new ones are being invented all the time. Some examples of how these are represented are given here.

Personal Religion

Not all access to divine power is conducted through the medium of a cult. In many cases, and in the Taskan Empire in particular, an individual strikes up a direct relationship with a supernatural being, becoming a devotee. In these situations, the worshipper does not hold a cult rank by which to determine which Miracles and spells he is eligible to access, and so the Devotion skill is used as a measure of worthiness both for access to Miracles and as a guide to the maximum size of the worshipper's Devotional Pool.

Devotion Requirements

Mythras Cult Rank Required	Minimum Devotion Skill Required
Initiate	51%
Acolyte	71%
Priest	91%

Improvement rolls for the Devotion skill are usually gained through pilgrimage, service and making dedications to the deity concerned, and not from the Improvement Rolls awarded through normal play.

Gaining Miracles still requires access to the entity that provides them via some sort of sacred connection – either a face to face confrontation, or through a temple, shrine, relic, holy person or holy place. Such access is often controlled by a cult that attempts to restrict access to its own members, or by some other local power or ruler who charges handsomely for the privilege. Without community support, it may also be difficult to gain access to the place where the devotional pool can be replenished as required.

In lands such as Tarsenia where personal religion is the norm, the role of a cult is more like that of a Brotherhood, and can be simply a mutual support organisation to prepare devotees to undergo the personal pilgrimages and other observances required to establish and grow their relationship with the god. It is quite common for a shrine, artefact or holy man to offer only a single Miracle, and the devotee who wants to develop his range of divinely-inspired powers may have to spend a great deal of time, energy and cash to do so as he makes the rounds of the shrines and religious festivals to be found across the Empire.

A character can have many such devotions so long as they are not mutually exclusive because of the hostility of one deity to another.

Multiple Cults to the same Deity

A deity may have many cults devoted to its worship, and not all are of equal status. Each cult will have its own rules and ranks, and it is entirely possible these cults are hostile to one another, competing for the god's favour and for access to sacred sites and artefacts that add to the cult's influence, prestige and magical power. Some of those cults may not provide the god's full range of Miracles, and some may have access to unique Miracles that even bigger and more potent rival cults cannot reproduce.

Pacts

There are gods who receive no organised worship, and there are many creatures who are god-like or who aspire to being gods, and there are entities that are a fragment or aspect of a true deity that does not merit full worship. All these entities might seek bargains with mortal creatures that provide them with Magic Points to use as their own, and offer any number of benefits, favours, and gifts in return. Such a relationship is known as a Pact.

Pacts are often sought out by sorcerers who spend lifetimes researching what entity can provide them with the benefit they need, how the entity can be summoned or contacted, and what are the tactics to use when negotiating the terms of the deal. In Assabia, Pacts are the norm for how business is conducted between man and gods, since Assabians make little distinction between deities and demons, treating them all much the same way.

In contrast to the devotional pools of Theism, a Pact actually places part of the dedicator's soul at the entity's disposal, and so reduces the dedicator's personal Magic Points until such time as the Pact is terminated. The minimum Magic Point dedication is 1 and, if the entity accepts donations of Magic Points from sources other than the individual's own personal resources, there is no maximum. The points allocated to the devotional pool are not used for calling upon Miracles, but traded for benefits referred to as *boons*.

Boons

A boon is a favour granted by an entity as its side of the deal in a Pact. This is something that directly enhances the dedicator in some way. The cost of a boon in dedicated Magic Points is provided in the table; however, as Pacts are always negotiated agreements the Games Master is free to adjust these costs as appropriate to each situation.

Boons are permanent effects and continue for as long as the Pact is in place.

Magic

Boons

Boon	Effect	Pact Dedication Cost
Talented	All skill tests in the chosen talent are one grade easier than normal	Standard Skills: 1 Magic Point Professional Skills: 2 Magic Points Magical Skills: 3 Magic Points
Touched by Genius	Boost the Critical Range of one skill by 1d4+1	2 Magic Points
Characteristic Boost	+1d3 per Characteristic (except POW), up to species maximum.	If Characteristic is at or below average prior to taking the Gift: 1 Magic Point; if Characteristic is above average: 2 Magic Points; if Characteristic is 18+: 3 Magic Points
Folk Magic Effect	Bestows a permanent effect taken from the Folk Magic section of MYTHRAS. As for the Curse Folk Magic Spell, but the effects can also be benign	1 Magic Point
Mastery	+25% or an increase to 90% (whichever is higher) in a skill relevant to the deity's nature	1 Magic Point If the skill is already 50% or higher. 2 Magic Points otherwise.
Possession	Covert possession by a cult spirit	1 Magic Point per Intensity

The examples provided here are not exhaustive, and you should feel free to use the sample Gifts provided on page 202 of MYTHRAS as alternative boons. Instead of a magical enhancement there may be some other benefit provided to the dedicator. It is said that certain schools of sorcery have been founded on magical knowledge imparted as part of a Pact. Demons have given service, magical artefacts acquired, religions founded and disasters averted. There are no hard restrictions on what is possible to achieve through a Pact. Even the destruction of Kor antis may have been the result of a Pact between the Jekkarene queen and Father Ocean.

Games Master Note: When assessing the cost of a boon, bear in mind that a greedy demon or godling will charge as much as it thinks it can get, and a canny one may discount the cost, at least to start with, to encourage mortals to enter into the deal in the first place. It should always feel like a genuine sacrifice – so if a character who seeks a boon has an abundant supply of Magic Points, this is an opportunity for the entity they are bargaining with to demand more!

Pact Terms

Unlike normal Theist practise a Pact is not expected to be a permanent devotion, but is a bargain or contract that lasts a limited period of time. It is true that some Pacts are concluded that are 'until death shall part us' and some even extend into the afterlife; however, many have a fixed term, with a year and a day being standard.

Pacts usually have other contractual terms that dictate when the Pact expires and the devotional pool ceases to exist, but can include all sorts of provisos, obligations, geasa, quid pro quos and conditions that are to be adhered to, which may include providing additional Magic Points to the entity through sacrificing (or Tapping) others. Someone who breaches the terms may find themselves paying dearly for doing so. It is not unusual for an entity to take permanent possession of their dedicated Magic Points if a Pact is breached, permanently reducing the transgressor's Magic Points Attribute.

Animist Traditions

Animists recognise that anything that has life – is animated – has a spirit, and as spirits can persist independently of the Material World and transitory flesh, the Spirit World therefore represents a higher form of reality. Hence animists study the pathways between the Material and Spirit Worlds and seek to travel them to connect with the greater cosmos. Their traditions sometimes involve or include the worship of gods, but may rather treat certain spirits as friends, family and allies. Animism is often said to be a primitive practice; however, it is not confined to primitive cultures, and the Shaman-Priests of Yegusai and Zagre are famous examples of animists who are the religious leaders of a sophisticated civilisation.

Shamans

A shaman is a serious practitioner of Animism, someone who knows Binding, a skill that allows him to negotiate with, combat and bind spirits. These spirits are then under his control and will submit to his commands, performing a service or perhaps augmenting his power with their own through spell-like effects.

A very few people are able to project their souls into the Spirit World. This ability, the Trance skill, is usually unlocked through a rare talent or divine gift, a form of mysticism, or is replicated through recourse to a Miracle or powerful drugs.

Games Master Note: When entering a Trance entirely through the use of drugs, the Shaman's Trance skill is equal to the Potency of the drugs used.

Traditional Spirits

Each animist culture or cult has certain types of spirits to which it is allied, referred to as Traditional Spirits. These allied spirits can be summoned using the Binding skill and will usually negotiate the terms on which they grant favours or provide service, rather than require the animist to force them to submit to his power and bind them. Followers of an animist tradition who acquire or are given control of a Traditional Spirit to use can do so using their Rites (Own) skill rather than Binding.

Alternative Magical Systems

In Thennla magic is used through a variety of arts that operate according to a variety of principles – but they are all simply alternative techniques for accessing and manipulating the same forces and are not exhaustive. It is quite possible for new approaches to magic to be discovered, encountered or invented. Like great artistic movements, schools of sorcery may flourish then disappear, spawn some avant-garde and revolutionary new approach, or find themselves the subject of a revivalist movement long after their original aims and purpose have been forgotten. They may dominate a whole culture, or be the product of a single insane genius. As Games Master you should feel completely free to borrow alternative systems of magic that are compatible with the MYTHRAS system or invent new ones, if it adds colour and excitement to your interpretation of the setting.

The Runes

Runes of one sort or another are used by most of the world's cultures. These are just a part and parcel of the tool kit of any magician, the written or inscribed form or magical words, thoughts and actions. Some people maintain that there are higher forms of such symbols that have universal significance and potency and from which the marks made by human hand draw their power. A true grasp of runes is revealed to humanity only through a lifetime of study, or through the agency of some supernatural entity.

KORANTINE WEALTH

In this chapter, you will find information on your characters' living costs as well as prices provided in Korantine Silver Pieces for some common items of equipment, goods and services.

Currency

The Korantine Silver Piece (SP) has higher purchasing power than the standard MYTHRAS equivalent. This is because it is a bullion coin, one that contains substantial silver content – around 4.5-5g. It represents a decent day's wage for a skilled worker, and is rather more than is needed for an individual to get by on if living a frugal lifestyle.

A Korantine SP is equivalent to:

- 2 State Silvers (SS), coins issued by the mints of individual city states
- 1 day's wage for a skilled worker
- The daily cost of living for a man of property
- The daily cost of living for a poor family (2 adults and their children)
- A Peck (6.67kg) of grain, enough to grind flour for up to 20 loaves of bread

There are two other bullion silver coins in circulation that have equivalent value to the Korantine SP: these are the Sharranketan Dinar and the Gleam, a rarely-seen coin minted in Sorandib.

State Silver

Silver coins are minted by individual Korantine cities in varying degrees of purity. Irrespective of their actual size and weight, the silver content is much lower than for a Silver Piece – either a small coin of high purity or a larger coin containing a proportion of base metal. These coins now form a de-facto second rank of silver coin, typically called Small Silver (SS), trading at two to the bullion Silver Piece.

One SS is equivalent to:

- 2 Bronze Pieces (BP) or 5 Copper Pieces (CP)
- 1 day's wages for an unskilled worker or for a citizen on militia duty
- The daily bread for a family (2 adults and their children)
- 1kg of good quality meat
- A round of drinks at a tavern (2 bottles of basic wine or 2.5l/5 pints of ale)

Small Silvers are very common currency, and are equivalent to the Taskeen issued in the Taskan Empire and the common Dinars issued from Morkesh and the Sultanates of Djesmirket. They are much less useful than Silver Pieces for international travel and exchange outside Korantia, because everyone knows the silver content can vary wildly, as can the ability of the issuing city to guarantee them.

Some states issue bronze coins (BP) at 4 to the SP instead, which saves depletion of silver reserves.

Gold Coins

Gold coins are hardly ever seen and even more rarely used. The most common are the Imperials minted by the Korantine Emperor; and, being larger than SPs, they trade at 20SP for one Gold Imperial. However, Imperials minted prior to the catastrophe that destroyed the ancient capital of the Korantines often carry a higher value than recent issues.

Silver Piece minted in Vestrikina. The coin depicts the god Arribeus on both sides and is known as a 'Four Header'. It is common practice for any Silver Piece being used in a coin toss to be checked that it is not of Vestrikinan origin...

One GP is equivalent to:

- Y 20SP, 40SS, 80BP or 200CP
- Y The weekly living cost of a rich man
- Y The monthly wage of a lowly henchman
- Y The price of a hoplite shield, or a sheep
- Y The cost of a smart banquet for 5 people including high quality wines, a variety of meat and fish, serving staff and entertainment

Copper Pieces

Smaller copper pieces (pennies) are issued that generally trade at 10 to the SP. These CP have retained the same notional value over the centuries, so there are many very old, worn coins still in circulation. You can purchase a loaf of bread using a single

Korantine Wealth

CP, and two loaves of bread is enough to provide the necessary calories for an adult human to get through the day.

Currency Exchange Rates

Money changers take the first coin and every 20th coin thereafter to change money into a local currency, and rather more to convert to bullion. The usual equivalences are as shown.

Coin	Foreign Coins of Equivalent Value	Value (SP)
Gold Imperial	Thafneving Royal	20
Silver Piece	Sharranketan Dinar, Sorandine Gleam	1
State Silver	Taskeen, Morkeshite Dinar, Djesmiri Dinar	0.5SP
Bronze Piece	-	0.25
Copper Piece	Jekkarene Iron Bar, Taskan Penny	0.1

Lifestyle and Cost of Living

The Cost of Living table on page 74 shows what a character needs to spend to keep himself in a lifestyle appropriate to each Social Class. There will be occasions where an adventurer might spend a lot of money for a short period of time to give the impression he is richer than he is, and of course penny-pinching and miserly characters can lead a rather meaner existence than is expected of them.

Supporting a Family

To quickly find the additional cost of supporting a family, multiply the Cost of Living by 1.5. Hence, the daily Lifestyle cost for a Middling character and his family is 6+(6x 1.5) = 15 CP, or 1SP and 1SS. This will account for a spouse and up to three juvenile or elderly dependents and assumes the head of the household consumes a disproportionate share of its resources. Other members of the household may be economically active too, and, in poorer homes, this is frequently a necessity just to make ends meet.

Minimum Income Qualification

When it is time for a census, the state will want to know what is the reliable income of the head of the family. Usually nobody with a living father needs to prove their own Social Class – the spouse and offspring (even if grown up) of the head of the family are assumed to share in his status and will only be separately assessed when he is dead.

Assessment is made of the minimum dependable income from assets – land, business, property and other tangible things that can be counted. It is possible to pretend to a certain status by spending cash to live the lifestyle, but when it comes to deciding who is entitled to enjoy certain privileges (such as access to higher cult rank), the assessor wants to know that you have real property that generates this wealth, so it is referred to as a property qualification. Cash and treasure, while pleasing and useful, don't count.

When a property owner dies, it may be that his estate is divided up in ways that leave the next generation in a lower Social Class. Some families like to keep the estate together and disinherit all but one of the children. Others divide it up unfairly, and a minority split it up and leave the next generation to make their own fortunes.

Earning a Living

Being in paid employment is often an uncertain situation, with job security being a reward for loyalty rather than an expectation. Most jobs pay enough to keep the employee in an acceptable standard of living, but if the employee has others to support it is frequently not enough. For this reason it can be necessary for anyone who is old enough to contribute to the household income in some way.

The sample jobs found in the Sample Careers table on page 74 provide some guidelines for rates of pay a character may expect to recieve when in employment. Those marked with an asterisk typically have basic maintenance covered, so the payment represents take home pay. Militia soldiers only receive maintenance when in the field, mercenaries have to be maintained full time. If they are mounted troops and provide their own horses, double pay is usual.

Monthly and annual income is in many cases less than the daily wage would suggest – this is because people don't work every day, and only soldiers get paid for days they don't work. Workers generally put in an absolute maximum of 312 days per year and often less – the remainder being one sort of holiday or festival or another. This even applies to slaves, who are (at least in theory) way too expensive and valuable to kill through overwork.

Cost of Living

Social Class	Daily Cost of Living	Weekly Cost of Living	Monthly Cost of Living	Annual Cost of Living	Minimum Income Qualification
Landless	2 CP	1.5SP	6SP	75SP	None
Poor	4CP	3SP	12SP	150SP	100SP
Middling	6CP	4SP	17SP	220SP	500SP
Propertied	1SP, 2CP	9SP	35SP	440SP	1,200SP
Rich	3SP	20SP	85SP	1,100SP	3,000SP
Aristocrat or Land Magnate	12SP	85SP	340SP	4,400SP	N/A

Sample Careers

Job	Daily	Monthly	Annual
Slave's Pocket Money*	1BP	6SP	78SP
Low-Skilled Craftsman or Labourer	1SS	12SP	156SP
Craftsman/Skilled Worker	1SP	24SP	312SP
Elite Artisan	4SP	92SP	1196SP
Secretary	1SP, 1CP	26SP	338SP
Mercenary*	1SP	28SP	366SP
Soldier (Militia)*	1SS	14SP	N/A
Senior military or civilian officer of state	N/A	440SP	5720SP

Price Lists

The typical costs of useful and important items and equipment are fully listed on page 77. If an item found in MYTHRAS is not listed in this book and you think it should be available, dividing the MYTHRAS price by five is a reasonable rule of thumb. Otherwise put, one MYTHRAS Silver Piece is worth 2CP in Korantia – but the overriding rule here is common sense.

Each item has an availability rating:

Common: Available even in backwater towns

Uncommon: Most likely available only in cities although a small city should suffice and even smaller towns may have some of these things available if a tradesman happens to reside there

Rare: Available only in a city, and probably a large city at that.

Special Order: Not generally available, and to acquire it you must go to a specialist supplier; probably only in the largest cities and then one that sits close to the point of origin or is on the right trade route.

Clothing

Some basic items can cost a considerable proportion of your earnings. Clothing, in particular, is an expensive necessity; hence, the poorest folk and slaves might have no more than a simple shift of unbleached wool to their name, or even something sewn together from scraps. The destitute might still get hold of animal skins, which are cheaper than woven cloth.

Good clothes truly mark out an individual as someone of means. The quality of the cloth, the use of dyes and additional embellishments such as embroidery, fringes or even little metal adornments sewn into the cloth are all clues to the status of the wearer.

Korantine clothes don't have pockets. It's common to keep a couple of coins tucked inside a cheek, but anything more needs a purse (or a servant) to hold your cash for you.

Foods

The staple food in Korantia is wheat. Barley is used for fodder or as a cheap alternative. Honey is the standard sweetener.

Korantia is a land of wine-drinkers, and in its diluted state, wine might be taken at any time of day.

Meats are rarely consumed by the poor except on feast days. Game is hard to come by around the coastal plain of central Korantia, but the inland cities and particularly those nearer the mountains are famed for their hunting grounds that provide sport for some and free meat to others. The prices here are

for flesh, with no particular distinction about what part of the animal the flesh comes from.

Livestock

Korantines make use of a wide variety of animals, and like any other society do so at all stages of the lifecycle. Once a food animal reaches its optimum weight, or when a beast of burden passes the point at which its value as a carcass is greater than its value as a working animal, every part that can be is used or consumed. Young animals are always less expensive as they have to be cared for and fed, and possibly trained, until they can be put to use. Prices here are for adult animals, ready for exploitation.

Tools

These basic tools are manufactured by blacksmiths and carpenters and do not usually require the work of a specialist. Prices given here are for tools with metal fittings. Significantly cheaper, if less effective, versions can often be made without the benefit of metal parts, and may cost no more than a few CP.

Arms and Armour

A basic panoply for militia service is relatively inexpensive and typically costs about a month's wages. The minimum equipment required is a large shield of the hoplite type or a flat shield (thureos) similar in size to a scutum; a spear; a simple helmet, and perhaps a sidearm such as a shortsword. Preferred armours are padded and quilted cloth, typically linen stuffed with wool; scale armour made from leather, horn or metal, or some composite combination thereof.

Land and Property

Owning land brings respectability and an annual income so long as you work it, rent it out or pay someone else to do so.

Korantine writers on such things agree that the right size plot to support an average family is about 5 hectares. You need a bit more than this if you practice fallowing and crop rotation or if not all your land is good for grain, adding up to 10-15 hectares of arable, pasture, orchard and garden.

The prices given are for good arable land. The best pasturage, suitable for horses and fine cattle, costs much the same. For marginal land suitable for olive trees and grazing goats, multiply price by 0.4; for forestry or uncleared land, multiply by 0.25. For unproductive land multiply by 0.01. Proximity to a temple or sacred site that provides reliable divine blessings to agriculture will increase land prices, because Miracles may be available that restore fertility to tired soil without leaving a field fallow.

The cost of dwellings is for something built to order or already standing. In the countryside, most people build their own simple houses at minimal cost and pass them onto future generations, who then fight to keep them standing until it reaches the point when it is easier to plunder the ruins for building materials and start over.

A hectare of good arable land requires 20SP's worth of seed corn and will deliver a yield of six times the seed sown, generating a net return worth 100SP (0.67 tons of grain). In particularly good soils or with generous magical support it is possible to as much as double that return.

Transport and Shipping

Transporting goods by land is vastly more expensive than doing so by sea. Cities of any size are almost always on or close to the sea in order to make shipping commodities and other goods in and out a viable process. The following costs give an idea of how much it costs to ship a big load from one place to another – or alternatively, the sort of money a character can charge for doing so himself. These costs include all hands required to do the job, as well as the use of the ship, wagon or beast of burden. Guidelines are also provided here for acquiring watercraft and wheeled vehicles.

Metals

The key metals in regular use all occur naturally and do not need alloying. Bronze is a yellow metal found all over but particularly used in the West and by the Oceanic races. It is favoured by some because it does not readily corrode (hence its popularity among seafaring people) and is very showy when polished up to a shine. In the East, the grey metal iron is more common for everyday purposes but though it has similar practical qualities to bronze, it is particularly prone to corrosion if not well looked after. On the plus side, it can be turned into steel, in which case it is more durable and can hold a better edge.

Trade Goods

The largest volumes and values of trade are conducted in commodities such as grain, timber, metals and slaves, much of which arrives in Korantia from the northern colonies such as Mersin and Keba. Foreign goods and exotic luxuries reach Korantia's coastal cities from as far afield as Kipsipsindra or Assabia, but the landward trade with the Taskan Empire is rather limited in volume, given the difficulties of overland travel and the intervening mountains and barbarian peoples. There is very little trade with the Jekkarid to speak of due to traditional enmities, but Jekkarene goods, when they appear, consequently have a cachet among the wealthy classes and command a high price.

The Trade Goods table provides a variety of trade goods available in Korantia that are brought in from foreign lands. All items should be considered Rare or Special Order.

KORANTINE WEALTH

KORANTINE PRICES

Clothing

Item	Availability	Cost
Basic tunic or shift of unbleached wool, for a slave or peasant	Common	2SP
Simple Tunic	Common	3SP
Tailored and Dyed Tunic	Uncommon	9SP
Tailored, Dyed and Decorated Tunic	Uncommon	15-50SP
Basic Cloak	Common	1SP, 2CP
Fancy Cloak	Uncommon	5-10SP
Basic Shoes or Sandals	Common	8CP
High Status Shoes	Rare	1SP, 5CP
Straw Hat	Common	2CP
Leather Hat	Common	1SP
Military or Working Boots	Uncommon	1SP, 2CP
Fine Wool, 1m wide	Uncommon	1SP per metre
Cotton, 1m wide	Rare	1.5-2SP per metre

Food Staples

Item	Availability	Cost
Loaf of bread	Common	1CP
Barley	Common	1CP per kg
Wheat	Common	1.5CP per kg
Rye	Common	1CP per kg
Honey	Common	1SP, 2CP per litre
Barley Flour	Common	2CP per kg
Wheat Flour	Common	2.5CP per kg
Salt	Common	1CP per kg
Olive Oil	Common	1SP per litre

Meat

Item	Availability	Cost
Pork	Common	5CP per kg
Mutton	Common	1SP per kg
Goat	Common	4CP per kg
Beef	Uncommon	6CP per kg
Game bird, e.g duck, partridge, pheasant	Common	1.5SP per bird
Poultry, domesticated fowl e.g duck or chicken	Common	1SP per bird
Venison	Uncommon	5CP per kg
Crustaceans and Premium Saltwater Fish	Rare	8CP per kg
Other Saltwater Fish	Rare	5CP per kg
Freshwater Fish	Uncommon	3CP per kg
Preserved (salted) Fish	Uncommon	2CP per kg

Drink

Drink	Notes	Availability	Cost
Wine, Fine	Morado from Agissene and Solarnian from Himela are the most widely celebrated wines	Rare	2SP per litre
Wine, Good	The hill country between Hatrya, Nolestra and Remoria is the largest producing region	Uncommon	1SP per litre
Wine, Basic	locally produced and blended, and slightly diluted before it is sold to the market.	Common	2CP-4CP per litre
Ale, Premium	Considered a barbarian drink, but consumed as a refreshment. The poorer sort may be available at 1CP for a large 2L pitcher, or free with food, and is often provided to slaves.	Common	2CP per litre

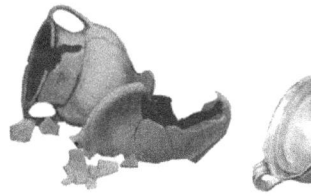

SHORES OF KORANTIA

Livestock

Animal	Notes	Availability	Cost
Ass/Donkey		Common	35SP
Bull	Usually kept to be rented to other famers. A Camtric Bull is the gold standard, but rarely seen except on the estates of the wealthy.	Common	80SP
Draft Ox	Oxen are a vital resource for pulling both wagon and plough.	Common	65SP
Milk Cow		Common	45SP
Mule	Favoured for beasts of burden; a good compromise between strength and speed	Common	100SP
Pig	A young pig may reach 60kg but fully grown they can reach twice that weight.	Common	25-60SP
Pony or Pack Horse		Common	130SP
Racing Horse	Careful selection and care produces a premium animal. Spirited, but probably not a patch on an Assabian thoroughbred	Rare	400-600SP
Riding Horse	Korantine horses are all of the same basic type whether used for riding, hunting or war.	Common	275SP
Sheep	Korantine wool is well regarded, and flocks are often kept close to home rather than out on the hills where exposed to raiders	Common	10-20SP

Tools

Item	Availability	Cost
Adze or Hoe	Common	1SP
Axe, Hatchet	Common	2SP
Axe, Tree Felling	Common	3SP
Pick	Common	3SP
Ploughshare and Board	Common	7SP
Scythe	Common	1SP
Shovel	Common	1.5SP
Work Maul	Common	1SP
Yoke for Oxen*	Common	10SP

*Complete with tracers and harness. Can also be hired at a rate of 4 SP per month

Armour

Armour	Notes	Availability	Cost
Stiffened Or Padded Cloth Or Leather Cap, Helmet Or Hood, 1AP, 1 Enc		Uncommon	6SP
Simple Metal Or Composite Helmet, 3 AP 2 Enc		Uncommon	12SP
Fancy Metal Helm With Crest 5 AP, 4 Enc		Rare	30SP
Metal Helmet, Premium, Full Face 6 Ap, 5 Enc		Rare	50SP
Scale Armour, Leather Or Horn 2AP, 2 Enc Per Location		Rare	15SP per Location
Scale Armour, Composite 3AP, 3 Enc Per Location		Rare	20 SP per location
Scale Armour, Bronze Or Iron, 4 AP, 3 Enc Per Location	Some linothorax armour incorporates scale into the chest or abdomen area	Rare	25SP per Location
Padded Cloth Or Leather Armour, 2AP, 1 Enc Per Location		Uncommon	5 SP per location
Laminated Linen Linothorax Cuirass 3AP, 2 Enc Per Location	A single armour piece protecting chest and abdomen	Rare	24SP per location
Half Plate Armour, Bronze Or Iron 5AP, 4 Enc Per Location	A Korantine warrior usually only has plate armour on selected locations rather than full body	Rare	60SP per location

Korantine Wealth

Bows and Accoutrements

Bows, Etc	Notes	Availability	Cost
Hunting (flat) bow		Common	2SP
"Kitanian" (composite) bow. Statistics as for recurve bow	Most examples in Korantia are imported from Assabia or, more rarely, from Kitan	Special Order	40SP
Arrows		Common	1CP each
War or specialist Arrows, each		Uncommon	2CP each
Simple quiver		Common	1SP
Case and quiver for recurve bow		Rare	5SP

Shields

Shields	Notes	Availability	Cost
Buckler	Carried by some swordsmen and missile troops	Uncommon	15SP
Hoplite Shield/ Clipeus	Preferred by some militias and patriotic bands	Uncommon	20SP
Militia shield/ Thureos	A large oval shield with central grip, covers up to 5 locations	Common	18SP
Skirmisher Shield/Pelte	Standard light shield for skirmishers and marines	Common	8SP

Weapons

Weapon	Notes	Availability	Cost
Club	The most basic weapon, but capable of being customised to provide +1 damage for an extra 1SP	Common	5CP
Dagger		Uncommon	10SP
Dart	A small javelin, or shorter dart with lead weight	Uncommon	1SP
Falchion	Korantine examples are usually S rather than M length, with a straight back and curved, single cutting edge	Uncommon	35SP
Horseman's Sword	A longer weapon providing sufficient reach to strike from horseback. Use the Broadsword statistics from Mythras.	Rare	50SP
Javelin Or Hunting Spear		Common	4SP
Mace Or Battleaxe	Rarely used as military weapons	Uncommon	6SP
Militia Spear	Short Spear	Common	3SP
Shortsword	The standard sidearm, a short leaf or straight-bladed double edge sword	Uncommon	30SP

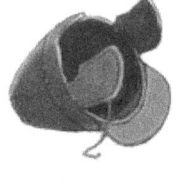

Shores of Korantia

Transport and Shipping

Transport	Notes	Cost
Cost of moving goods by open sea	Typically by merchantman between major ports, each vessel carrying 75-100 tons, but some capable of carrying 250 tons or more	2SP per ton per 100KM
Cost of moving goods overland	Typically by ox cart, each cart moving circa half a ton per ox, and some carts are so massive as to have 16 animals to draw them. Cost includes pay for driver and boy, fodder, etc. A ton of goods might need a string of 8 or more pack animals to carry it, depending on whether you are using donkeys, horses, mules or camels and how heavily you are prepared to load them.	50SP per ton per 100KM
Cost of moving goods by river or by short coastal routes	Typically by small boat, barge or lighter; often an oared vessel. Capacity of 5-20 tons is typical	10SP per ton per 100 KM
Construction of merchant ship	To build and outfit a merchant ship, not including magical enhancements.	200SP per ton of capacity
Construction of oared warship	To build and outfit an oared galley, not including magical enhancements. Korantine examples from before the Cataclysm are said to have sometimes had multiple banks with up to 300 men at the benches.	200SP per rower's station
Fishing Boat	Small boat suitable for river, lake and coastal fishing, with a crew of up to 3 men	150SP
Ox Wagon or Cart	A big vehicle with four solid wheels capable of hauling a ton or more of bulk goods, drawn by teams of oxen.	24SP per half ton of bulk capacity
Litter	Used by people of rank in city streets where mounts and carriages are neither permitted or not practical	20SP

Metals

Item	Notes	Availability	Cost
Bronze	Bronze is more expensive than iron as it is less common and also has useful properties such as being resistant to corrosion and able to be polished to a shine.	Uncommon	5SP per kg
Copper	Copper's chief use is for cheap utensils and minting low value coins that have no real bullion value	Common	3.5SP per kg
Iron	Desirable as the standard metal for practical use in tools, weapons and construction, iron is abundant and relatively cheap	Common	3SP per kg
Silver	Bullion value. 1 kg of silver can make 160 bullion coins (Sharranketan Dinars), and this provides the benchmark market price for the precious metal	Uncommon	200SP per kg
1 Korantine Talent	1.875kg of gold, enough to strike 180 GP		4,500SP
1 Taskan Talent	Bullion value of 1 kg of gold, traditionally 12 times the same weight of silver		2,400SP per kg

Land and Property

Region/Property Type	Notes	Availability	Cost
House	An urban house suitable for a family. Probably 2-4 rooms at most, flat or tile-roofed. It may have a very small yard or kitchen garden, and if in the country, space for domestic animals	Common	3,000-6,000
Fine House	A house that includes separated rooms for entertaining, cooking and sleeping, a servants' area and possibly even plumbing	Uncommon	15,000-40,000
Grand House or Palace	Capable of impressing any visitor, and home to a whole establishment of slaves as well as the owner and his family. On the whole, showing off in this way is frowned upon – it is the mark of a tyrant.	Special Order	100,000-250,000

Korantine Wealth

Land and Property

Region/Property Type	Notes	Availability	Cost
Northern Korantia and colonies	Good arable land is cheaper the further away you go from the crowded coastal plain of central Korantia.	Common	300-400SP per hectare
Central Korantia	Land near Agissene, Sarestra and Yaristra is the most prized due to the huge size of the markets there which pay high prices for grain, and so may be at an additional premium	Common	1,000SP per hectare
Mountainside	Choral land in the more isolated cities in the shadow of the Ozyrian mountains is rarely on the market, but local magnates may buy up arable hectares in dominion territory, and these are usually situated in valleys up in the hills.	Common	500SP per hectare
Mature Vineyard	Planting a vineyard costs 2,500SP per hectare, and takes a year to prepare and plant and up to 3 more to be ready for cropping. A mature vineyard is therefore at a premium. Each hectare should generate 1500-3000 litres of wine per year	Common	6,000-10,000SP per hectare
Small Farm	A 4 hectare farm of which half is arable, the rest being marginal land with a little garden and space for pigs and goats. Includes a cottage and rudimentary shelter for livestock	Common	1,500SP – 3,000SP
Medium Farm	A 12 hectare farm suitable for a citizen family of the 'Middling' sort, of which a half is arable, and with enough room to pasture a small herd of cows or a flock of sheep. Includes a cottage and a barn or byre.	Common	3,500SP-7,500SP
Large Farm	A 20 hectare farm suitable for a family of the 'Propertied' class, of which at least half is arable but which may specialise with orchards, additional pasturage, grain, market garden and other resources. Includes a small house and additional cottages, outbuildings and shelters, granary etc	Common	10,000SP-18,000SP
Business Investment	Creation or acquisition of a manufactory, inn or other establishment that will generate an annual return	Uncommon	1,000SP per 50SP return per year.

Shores of Korantia

Trade Goods

Item	Availability	Cost
Books	For a typical collection of verse, or a short treatise on a historical, geographical or philosophical topic	10SP-20SP
Brotomagian Hunting Dogs	Elegant, sleek hunting dogs, prized by Solarists in particular; the Emperor is said to keep a collection of 40 of them.	125SP each
Carved ivory	Sharranket has a monopoly on the raw material, which is worked into plaques, boxes and furniture decorations before selling on	250SP per kg
Dariskan Boat Keel	A keel cut from Floatwood, and usually intricately carved and painted prior to export. These keels are thought to bring good luck to any vessel built upon them (an additional Group Luck Point for use on a voyage), and be the best thing to which to bind an undine.	300SP per Metre
Dinosaur Hides from Fierla	Due to their possible size, these are typically assessed by the square metre. The hides can have a variety of textures and colours, and are used for the most exotic armours	300SP per Metre
Feathers, exotic	Some exotic feathers are highly prized for costume and even to decorate war gear. This is for a single large feather plucked from the tail, crest or wing of an exotic bird or creature:	1-10SP each
Fengo Hash	The drug is rare enough in Korantia not to attract any official notice or control.	60SP per kg
Jekkarene Fineware	Beautifully decorated pottery from the old enemy appeals to the big-city rich. Price for a cup or other small item approximately 1-2SP, here for a large wine mixing bowl	30SP-50SP
Marangian War Dogs	Sometimes used for hunting, but mostly for guard duty or kept by a Patriotic Band for use in bringing down thieves and bandits	75SP each
Silk of Jelhai	Only ever seen from Assabian merchants, a tiny quantity arrives per year in Korantia as the Sultans of Djesmirket buy as much of it up as they can	250SP per square metre
Slave, child or elderly		25-100SP
Slave, youth or adult		100SP+
Slave, specialist or exotic		200SP-400SP
Turtleshell from Rekshimetur	In raw form and ready for the production of combs, plaques, boxes, etc	60SP per kg
Wyrmstones	Extremely rare and valued items retrieved from the skull of one of these fearsome monsters. Hardly any ever appear on the market	1,000SP x square of the Magic Point capacity.

CULTS

Korantines worship a Celestial Court of gods, each of whom is responsible for an aspect of life relevant to the day-to-day workings of a well-ordered society. Lanis the sun god is the head of state; his prime minister is Anayo, whose wife Orayna is Queen of Heaven and Mother of the Nations. They are assisted by Estrigel, the court's herald, and Kos, its guardian and enforcer. Around them are at least a dozen important deities and scores of lesser ones, each with its own part of human society and state for which they take responsibility.

Mythology

For the Korantines, as for most people, myth plays a rather minor role in their conception of the divine and of the nature of the gods. The fact the gods demonstrably exist, and their power is visibly at work through their mortal followers, means there is no particular role for myth to play in determining beliefs and practice. Myths are simply a corpus of moral, romantic or amusing stories that are learned as children and told around the family hearth. They serve to illustrate the nature of the gods, but in doing so make them appear more human and approachable than they really are. They also teach some of the essential dynamics of the roles each deity may play in the cosmology, in relation to humanity and to one another. Myths do not have a magical role, and do not convey any particular esoteric meaning.

Human action can change the cosmos and, in so far as deities are more or less immutable entities, it is their representation by mortals and the extent of worship they receive that changes their nature by regulating the power they enjoy and their capacity for action.

The Legendary Past

Legends and traditional narratives of the past are more functional and important than myths about the gods. Human history, and the role played in it by gods and the cults that honour them, reinforces many attitudes and behaviours that are reflected in religious practices. The legendary narrative of past events is the one that is familiar to most people, whether or not it accords with the existing annals, and is relied upon where historical records fail completely – and many annals and histories were lost when Korantis was destroyed by the Ocean. Legend is also regarded as a perfectly adequate record, even to the point that it can be cited in court as evidence. Scholars are of course aware of the potential divergence from what really happened, or the existence of competing legendary traditions. While both legend and recorded history tend to describe past events and their causes as driven by human and divine actors, legendary tales will emphasise the role of character and motivation, and produce a more satisfying drama. As a result the legendary narrative is the one deployed in poetry and song, and in dramatic performances – and ultimately in the religious rites of the community.

Gods of Korantia

The most commonly worshipped deities in the Korantine pantheon are as follows:

Anayo, The Ruler
Anyone playing a role in public political life worships this deity. His initiates form the bulk of a city's council.

Orayna – Queen of Heaven
Anyone who is a citizen of a Korantine city-state must have dedicated 1 Magic Point to their local city goddess, each of which represents an aspect of Orayna.

Kos – The Guardian
Death god, celestial court enforcer. His worshippers are those who protect the civil state, and those who enforce and implement its decisions.

Sabateus – God of Trade
His cult in each city maintains relations with its counterparts in other cities, and regulates trade and exchange between them.

Estrigel – The Herald
God of language, oratory and poetry. Estrigel appears to be an old Thennalt divinity, adopted into the Korantine pantheon as herald to the sun god. His cults are generally very small, perhaps a specific family who are responsible for the duties of town crier. However, he is also worshipped by those who make a living through public speaking and recitals.

Lanthrus – The Toiler
God of labour and suffering. A minor deity except in times of social unrest, in which he acts as a rallying point for the oppressed poor.

Pyrolus – The Sailor
God of navigation and sailors. Ships are consecrated as shrines to this deity. His power is only over travel on the surface of the ocean, not the waters themselves.

Torthil – The Stout-hearted
God of agriculture, smithing and war. The most widely followed deity by the men of Korantia.

Veltis – The Destroyer
Goddess of war and discord. Represented as a fearsome hound, she is kept in chains, ready to unleash on an enemy state.

Lasca Veltis – The All-Seeing.
Goddess of wisdom and divination. Her followers are mystics, but her name is called upon by any who pray for some insight into their future.

Tarankis – The Maker
Goddess of crafts and building.

Semordis – The Saviour
God of healing and protection from evil spirits.

Arribeus – The Singer
God of performance, song, spring and the birds of the air.

Sheylo – The Warm Earth
Goddess of wheat crops, fertility, and the soil.

Zolesta – The Cold Earth
Goddess of burials, mourning and the underground.

Diotima – The Ocean-Mother
Goddess of fishes and fishermen.

Dagomar – Father Ocean
God of the deep water and lord of both Inner and Outer Oceans. Considered a hostile deity who must be propitiated, not a core Korantine divinity.

Palaskil – Lord of Storm
Ruler over the waves, storm and rain clouds. Palaskil sometimes replaces Torthil as the most popular deity for male citizenry.

Cult Structures

Korantine cults operate largely in accordance with the standard form set out in MYTHRAS.

Common (Lay) Members

The common members of a cult are those who attend worship because the cult's role in the city's life is one that directly affects them. Hence if the militia is summoned, all those who present themselves for service are considered lay members of Torthil's cult until they once again lay down their arms and return to their civilian occupations. Some cults accept lay members who are not citizens due to their involvement in its sphere of interest and so engage children, slaves and resident foreigners in the religious community.

Cults

LANTHRUS

Initiates

Initiation in any state cult is only allowed to those who also qualify as citizens. In most cases, this means they have already become citizens but there are some instances where a cult admits those who have not yet reached their age of majority and so are not yet enrolled. Some cults have restricted numbers of active initiates, and in these cases, a candidate will be automatically rejected if there is not room or requirement for additional members, irrespective of their credentials.

Restrictions by Social Class

Initiation in a Korantine cult is often restricted according to the applicant's social class, because their cult rank and their status among the citizenry are directly related. Wherever this occurs the applicant's social class is measured according to their property qualification, which conforms to the divisions given in the Character Creation chapter. For most purposes ,the Aristocracy is merely a sub-set of the Rich; however, in rare cases, a particular priesthood or office may be restricted to a member of a specific family. A democracy like Himela places no such restrictions on membership, as a matter of principle.

Sometimes social class brings with it compulsory cult membership. For example, the militaristic state of Tugara insists that all its property-owning male citizens between 17 and 46 years old maintain themselves as initiates of a military cult unless given a specific exemption or found unfit for service.

Gender Roles

Korantines observe carefully drawn boundaries for gender roles. In the state religion that regulates so much of daily life, deities are identified as male or female. While lay members of each deity's cult can in most cases be of either gender, for initiate rank and above it is normal that only women may serve a goddess and only men may serve a god. An interesting exception is the worship of Arribeus, where it appears that so long as his worshippers remain adolescents their gender does not matter. Even here, the adult supervisors of the cult are all male.

Acolytes

Acolytes are people of status who are set up to perform a specific role for the community such as army general, governing magistrate, judge in the law courts, merchant syndic and so forth. Achieving this rank may be a result of election by the whole citizenry, co-option from the existing acolytes, or appointment by the priests. Eligibility is subject to a host of conditions that are more stringent versions of those applied to citizenship. These often feature a minimum or maximum age limit.

The appointment of any person to an acolyte position that fulfils a key office of state is in some way subject to approval by the citizenry. Failure to do so is the hallmark of tyranny.

An acolyte has access to the cult's Folk Magic and Miracles, and in many cases will benefit from a divine Gift. In addition, acolytes in one of the state cults may be able to access an Extension spell, although in most cases it does not have the open-ended duration of the priestly version, but is limited to their tenure of office. He will have very specific duties and obligations to fulfill

SEMORDIS

that leaves very little free time. For an acolyte, adventuring is usually something he can do only if it is part of his duties for the state.

Restriction by Time

Many cult positions are held for a fixed period of time in order to prevent individuals from monopolising the power that goes with them. This is routinely the case with senior cult ranks represented by acolyte status, but some initiations and even some priesthoods are restricted to a fixed term. Cult appointments, for example, into the ranks of a militia unit as a junior officer, may only last for the duration of a campaign or war, and likewise initiate and acolyte positions that bring with them a government post tend to be for a period of 1-5 years.

Priests

The chief purpose of a priest is ensuring the proper performance of the state rituals that the cult is responsible for, maintaining the magical resources, temples and sacred objects of the cult, and imparting their knowledge to the cult's members. Priests act as advisors to the acolytes, but in most cases are themselves restricted from public office or placed under taboos that prevent direct participation in the affairs of state.

Cult Magic

Korantines access blessings from their civic deities as normal. Those of initiate rank or higher in a cult have a devotional pool and can exhort their deity to send them Miracles.

City-Goddess Cults

A Korantine city is a goddess, one that is created solely by and for its citizens to represent a fragment of Orayna, Queen of Heaven, that is exclusively theirs and is known by the name of the city.

Creating the Goddess

The goddess of a city is born at the founding of a new community, when the citizens-to-be create a pact that binds them together as the community. The goddess embodies the identity, the laws and customs, and the community's well-being.

At the foundation of the city, every new citizen, both men and women, dedicates a personal Magic Point to the goddess under a Folk Magic rite Loyal Oath. The Magic Point dedicated by each citizen is not available for the character's Devotional Pool, nor can it be recovered until or unless the citizen is excommunicated or formally renounces his citizenship. Instead, it contributes to maintaining the existence of the goddess and acts as the glue that binds the city's relationship to other deities in the pantheon.

The accumulated dedications of all living citizens adds up to the power of their goddess. The bigger and more populous the city, the more powerful its goddess; if a city suffers calamity and disaster, its citizens killed or scattered to the winds, the goddess dies too.

Some of this power is available to provide for the magical protection and enhancement of the state. The First Matron, the woman chosen to be city-goddess' acolyte, can cast the Consecration Miracle with an area of effect of up to 0.3 hectares for every citizen who has submitted to the constitution. Certain Miracles, such as the city-goddess' own Fortify spell and even some provided by other deities in the pantheon, have as the area of effect the consecrated boundaries of the city, irrespective of the caster's POW. It may also be used to propitiate potentially hostile entities that could threaten the city, or to ward off supernatural attacks. Smaller states who do not have the requisite power may call upon the magical umbrella of larger states for protection by divinely sanctioned treaty.

Citizens (Lay Membership)

Every free and native-born person is expected to join the city cult as a lay member upon coming of age. Cities have differing views on what constitutes native-born, the more democratic the city, the more stringent its requirements.

SHEYLO

Cults

In most cities, it is enough to be resident and have a single citizen parent to automatically qualify; some states are much stricter and require that both parents are citizens.

If a character does not automatically qualify by birth, then their enrolment may take place at a later time when they meet the criteria imposed by the city's particular laws and customs to consider other applicants. In these cases, the candidate needs a sponsor; often this is a spouse or adoptive parent, a former master if a slave is given freedom, or a local host if a foreigner.

The rites of admission to the cult and to citizenship take place during the festival spanning the two intercalated days in the Korantine calendar that precede the New Year.

Once entered on the rolls, the new citizen partakes of the same rights and obligations as were settled upon by the original founders as the ancestral constitution. In particular, they will now meet the most basic qualification for joining other cults, which is to be a citizen. A citizen gains a Loyalty (Home City) passion at 30+CHA+POW%.

The new citizen can join one of the many other cults in their city that will give them access to a particular profession, and support a pursuit of it.

Obligations

Citizens are obliged to put themselves forward for public duties such as military and jury service and attend public meetings and cast their vote when required to do so.

Restrictions

The Restrictions of the cult are the laws of the city and its people.

City Matrons (Initiates)

City cult initiates are all women. Their role is to maintain the city's spiritual and social health and vitality. Their duties involve both formal ritual tasks, such as keeping the goddess' temple in good order and preparing for the main rituals of the year, to orchestrating the informal networks of wives and mothers who exert influence on the city's menfolk from behind the scenes

and determining who can make or break an application for citizenship or even a bid for public office.

The initiates look after the register of citizens, maintain the city's sacred boundaries and act as curators of the object that forms the centre of the cult, whether that is a statue of the goddess or some abstract representation such as a sacred flame.

Acceptance as an initiate requires the candidate is married and has had at least one living child that survived to the age of seven. In many cities, there is a minimum Social Class requirement. The candidate will also be tested for worthiness according to her command of cult skills, of which at least five must be at 50% or more. The test is abstracted to success in three out of five cult skill tests.

ZOLESTA

Cult Skills

Craft (usually weaving or spinning), Custom, Devotion (city goddess), Exhort, First Aid, Influence, Insight, Rites.

Magic

Female lay members may learn one or two of the cult's Folk Magic spells, which are all available to a worshipper of initiate level or higher: *Calm, Cleanse, Heal, Ignite, Loyal Oath*, Preserve, Repair.*

*The Loyal Oath spell is the rite by which a citizen is enrolled and is administered on behalf of the new citizen, who provides the Magic Point. The spell lasts until cancelled by a priestess of the cult, or the recipient formally renounces their citizenship or dies. Until that time the Magic Point spent to cast it remains reserved to the city-goddess to use.

Some city-goddesses have variant or additional spells available.

City-goddess cults typically offer the following Miracles:

Backlash, Consecrate, Excommunicate, Extension*, Fortify, Lay to Rest, Pacify

*The city-goddess' Extension spell operates only for Miracles cast within the city's consecrated area.

First Matron (Acolyte)

The role of acolyte is specifically granted to the wife of the city's leading man. Her role is honorific, but may bring a gift in the form of additional fecundity, enduring beauty, or the chance to return a critically ill loved one to good health.

Mothers of the City (Priestess)

Access to the priesthood is generally restricted to women who have passed 42 years of age and have at least one child grown to maturity and now a citizen. In practice, three children is regarded as the minimum qualification, and a mother's status is a highly dependent on the status and achievements of their children. The mother of a war hero, for example, is far more likely to be elected by her peers to the highest offices in the cult. The status of a woman's husband, whether he be living or dead, is supposed to be specifically excluded from consideration as the priestesshood is entirely bound to the character and status of the lady herself – something that the achievements of her children are said to signify and embody.

The Miracles produced by the City Mothers can have an area of effect equal to the sacred boundaries of the city.

Lanis: Sun God, Emperor, King

Korantia's sun god is a warrior, adventurer, hero and ruler, and his cult encompasses all the prowess that is so celebrated in Korantine Society. Lanist society is an education system all of itself, an exclusively male club where the kind of heroic warriors the cult celebrates are produced through a system that has lasted for centuries. His worshippers are organized into sub-cults comprised of age classes, and as they move through these sub-cults, they will play a role that is most suited to their time of life, skills and experience. These sub-cults also correspond to cult rank.

Mythos and History

Lanis is the ruler and lord of the heavens, and in his fiery journey across the sky each day he is the highest flier in the vault of heaven. He inspires his followers to follow in his path and make the world their own.

Until the Great Cataclysm of 1055, the cult of Lanis was a pre-eminent power in the world. But when Korantis sank beneath the waves its most ancient treasures and relics and its greatest temples were lost too. It is recorded that there were other Miracles that the cult provided in those days, now lost with the artefacts or sacred sites that generated them. In recent times, the Emperor's Paladins mounted an expedition to recover treasures from the sea-bed where the ancient capital once stood on Korantis, and returned the Sapphire Throne to the Emperor's court. This one act restored the Behold Miracle to the cult's armoury.

The cult is said to have once known the secrets to taming and riding the griffins that are an iconic heraldic device of the Emperor's court. Nobody has done this since the Cataclysm. Griffins themselves are thought no longer to exist, never having responded to breeding in captivity, and the wild population hunted to extinction by the wyrms that became common on the fringes of Korantia in the last 200 years. Much has been said about how the increase of these wyrms is the product of a Jekkarene plot.

In recent times, the cult has experienced the creation of an off-shoot Solar cult that rejects Imperial authority, in the form of the royal cult at Kipsipsindra. On the other hand, the recent arrival of Redanger of Zarendra at the Emperor's court, declaring the loyalty of his own Solar cult and the city he rules in distant Jandekot, has provided a new boost for the Emperor. Such an arrangement does not have precedent, and the Emperor's court does not yet have a plan as to how to accommodate it within its traditional structures.

The ancient marriage between sun and moon and the subsequent divorce and separation of their cults and the societies that embodied them has left its mark. The cult has a weakness; instead of being a beacon to illuminate the world at night while her husband the sun is gone from the sky, the moon is now its enemy. Lanist Miracles do not work between sunset and sunrise (although its Folk Magic does). Even Miracles to which Extension is applied fade away when the sun sets and are rekindled at sunrise.

The Solar cult was once also the source of fertility rites, but now it cannot create but only wield the Ripen Miracle, to accelerate the ripening of fruits that are already generated. Its other magic is largely to support its martial values, with the exception of Dismiss Magic, which owes its origin to the enmity between the sun god and his ex-wife, who is, among other things, the goddess of magic.

The Imperial Cult

The Imperial cult exists to direct its members in the service of the Emperor their whole lives through a hierarchy defined by age classes. The main power of the cult rests with the Paladins – and while the term of Paladin is often used for any of the cult's initiates, officially only the acolyte members, who are granted their own lands for maintenance and who are some 700 in number, are entitled to the name.

Cults

If a cult member reaches the age where he should progress to the next age class and yet fails to prove his worth in accordance with the normal requirements, he is usually given no more than one second chance that must be attempted within a year. If this too is failed, the applicant will be forced to retire from the cult and choose a different path in life. The Paladins are entitled to retain their status indefinitely and are not required to seek promotion to the priesthood. Nevertheless, if a Paladin reaches an age or condition where he is no longer able to meet the physical demands of his role, he is expected to hand his lot over to a younger and fitter successor who will support him in his dotage.

Lanis the Youth (Lay Membership, 9-19 Years of Age)

From the age of 9, boys begin their training to become a Paladin in the Emperor's service. Those whom the cult's priests think may not make the grade are ejected before they turn 17, as the last two years of training is the most intense. This includes a period allocated as a squire or understudy to an established Paladin, and those who go through it are almost sure to be inducted to the ranks of initiates. In some circumstances, a borderline case may be sent on some sort of mission to prove his worth

Lanis the Adventurer (Initiate Membership, 19-30 Years of Age)

At the age of 19, the youths undergo initiation into Lanis the Adventurer's cult. For now, they are still expected to live communally on temple property and are maintained by temple tithes and revenues, or more rarely with their families if they have living parents. Adventurer members are not allocated individual temple property from which to draw their maintenance, and are not allowed to marry. Adventurers are considered expendable and are the first to be sent out on missions that give them an opportunity to hone their skills, further the interests of their local cult leaders and to prove their valour.

Lanis the Warrior (Acolyte/Paladin Membership, 30+ Years of Age)

The cult's Paladins are experienced, veteran warriors with maturity and status behind their skills. If they do not have some hereditary claim on a specific patch of temple land one will now be allocated to them, in a lot of some 30 hectares. They are entitled – indeed expected – to now marry and raise children.

Warrior members are regarded as an elite, but also as a precious resource that needs to be carefully husbanded; the Emperor does not want to commit them in numbers to a situation where too many of them may get killed. Individual Paladins or small bands may be sent on extraordinary missions, accompanied by cult initiates and whatever retainers and hirelings they need for the job.

A small number of acolytes are appointed on an honorary basis. Honorary Paladins have not had the opportunity to pass through the cult's age classes but nevertheless have shown true devotion to the Emperor and proved valuable in his service. These acolytes are almost without exception foreigners of noble birth and standing, whose appointment increases the power and influence of the cult, and, thereby, of the Emperor himself. In most cases, they are already devotees of the sun god through a local or family cult (see Lanis the King).

Lanis the Wise (Priest Membership, 42+ Years of Age)

Many Paladins who reach the traditional Korantine age of seniority at the age of 42 will eventually step up to become priests of the cult. These men are teachers, administrators, ritual experts and courtiers to the Emperor. There is at least one priest in every state where the cult has lands, and dozens of them in Hilanistra.

Those Paladins who choose not to become priests in later life usually do so because they want to remain active warriors so long as is possible, and there are examples who have continued seeking danger right into their 70s. A Paladin who cannot keep up with the physical requirements of the job and yet for some reason does not become a priest is usually pensioned off.

Lanis the Ruler (High Priest Membership)

The Emperor's chief courtiers are the ruler-priests, whose job is to advise him on all serious matters of cult and state. There are only three of these roles at any one time, and filling a vacancy sometimes takes years of deliberation and politicking. Only those who are already priests of the cult are eligible.

Skills

Athletics, Combat Style, Command, Custom, Devotion (Lanis), Endurance, Exhort, Oratory, Perception, Ride, Rites (Korantine)

The cult has several combat styles, but the most common for Paladins comprises javelin, spear, sword and shield, and comes in a version that has the Formation Fighting trait and another that has the Mounted trait.

Magic

Folk Magic

Avert, Bladesharp, Firearrow, Heal, Light, Polish*, Warmth, Vigour.

*useable on yellow metals only

Miracles

Aegis, Behold, Clear Skies, Consecrate, Dismiss Magic, Excommunicate, Elemental Summoning (Salamander), Extension, Heal Wound, Lay to Rest, Rejuvenate, Ripen, Sacred Band, Sunspear, Truespear.

Gifts

Paladins of the cult often enjoy divine gifts, favours granted for notable acts in the Emperor's service. Perhaps one in ten Paladins benefit from a Gift, and perhaps one in 20 adventurer-initiates. Common examples include:

Abstinence, Alacrity, Healthy, Mighty, Resilience, Robust, Sagacity.

Cult Artefacts

Sunstones

Irregularly shaped lumps of yellow crystal, these cult artefacts used to be acquired from Sorantia where the material is mined. Trading links with Sorantia were lost during the Cataclysm and Sorandib, its capital, is now more or less surrounded by the Taskan Empire. The crystals called Sunstones by the Korantincs are now ground to dust to be the active ingredient in gunpowder for the Taskan army. If any of this material is recovered and returned to the cult, it will be acquired for significant cash or favours.

A sunstone can be used in a number of ways:

- Y If left out in direct sunlight, it will absorb energy, and will store that energy until exposed to the darkness, at which point it will radiate light bright enough to read by with a radius of 1m per 0.25kg in size for an equivalent period of time.
- Y If a sunstone is invested with Magic Points, it will act as a lantern. The scale of the effect is dependent on the size of the crystal, and bigger crystals require more Magic Points to power them. For every 0.25kg, the crystal can accept 1 Magic Point and illuminate an area of 3 metres in radius – enough to read by.
- Y A sunstone can be used to store a salamander as if it were bound, and it will find it quite pleasant and comfortable and be happy to be transported around that way. To have enough room to house a salamander a sunstone needs to be 250g for each 3 cubic metres of elemental contained therein.

The Sapphire Throne

The imperial throne, recently recovered from the waters that cover Korantis, enables the Emperor himself, while seated upon it, to view the world of his subjects in a way similar to the Behold Miracle. The throne itself is a chryselephantine (gold and ivory) construction, with griffins for arms and an eagle perched on each side of its high back; however, the magical potency is invested in the many sapphires that decorate it. The throne acts as a storage vessel for a devotional pool of 100 Magic Points accessible by the Emperor, and allows the Emperor, when seated in it, to use a Behold spell of unlimited range.

Lanis the King

This version of the Korantine solar cult is one that exists outside direct imperial control. It is practised among some Thennalt nobility, by one of the royal families of Kipsipsindra and by the Solarist rulers of Zarendra. Its origins lie in the aristocratic cults that existed in the early eras of Korantine history and which were crushed or absorbed in the creation of an all-powerful imperial cult by King Kribsion of Korantis and his son, Emperor Koibos I. The cult of Lanis the King is essentially one that supports aristocracy and monarchy, and the claims to sovereignty that it asserts on behalf of cult leaders makes for a difficult relationship with the modern republican city-states of Korantia in which sovereignty rests with the people.

While each instance of this cult is in effect an independent entity, the cult structures are more or less the same and each makes its own choice about whether or not it recognises the overall hegemony of the Imperial cult.

Lay Members

Lanis the King usually has worshippers made up of the family and retainers of the cult's leaders.

Initiate Membership

To become an initiate requires that the candidate is both a member of the ruling class or at least its key supporters, and can demonstrate prowess in the cult skills

Acolyte Membership

Acolytes of the cult are those who belong to the ruler's inner circle, including those chosen as the nominated successor and others who share the royal blood. An acolyte may be promoted to a priestly role, but only as the delegate or substitute for the cult's leader

Priest-King

The cult's head is the anointed ruler over his people, and in his person holds the power of both priest and hero. The king usually acquires a divine gift upon his ascension.

Skills

Athletics, Combat Style (any), Devotion (Lanis), Endurance, Exhort, Influence, Orate, Ride, Rites

Magic

There may be some variation in available magic from one instance of this cult to another. A typical version is given here.

Folk Magic

Firearrow, Glare*, Light, Pet**, Vigor, Voice

*This spell causes the target to shine with a fiery light, the glints and gleams of his equipment being dazzling to behold. It causes those who attack him in close combat to suffer a penalty of one grade of difficulty for a single combat round. It may also provide a bonus to efforts to intimidate, or to impress a crowd.

**Can be used on birds of prey and horses instead of small creatures. The target's INT (not its INS) must be no more than half the caster's CHA

Miracles

Aegis, Consecrate, Dismiss Magic, Excommunicate, Extension, Lay to Rest (Royal Burial), Rejuvenate, Sunspear, Truespear

Vestrikina – City Goddess

Vestrikina is a minor city that maintains laws and customs regarded as archaic by many of her neighbours and rivals. Her citizens, however, are proud of their heritage, and being a small city where close and personal connections still hold true, Vestrikina rarely sees internal strife between rival factions or social classes.

Mythos and History

As the locals tell it, the founders of the city were Dorasdi under the hero Akikalos. These settlers had followed divine guides sent to them in the shape of a magpie, a fox, a mountain lion and a snake, until they reached a tall hill on a spur of the Ozyrian mountains overlooking the swift-flowing stream of the nymph, Clazome. However, this hill was already the camp of a Thennalt king called Boretes (Bortz in Thennalt) who had taken Clazome as his wife.

Akikalos and his band fought a long and hard campaign to seize this land from Boretes and Akikalos eventually killed the Thennalt leader in single combat, taking Clazome for himself. When the city was founded, it took the name Vestrikina from the name Akikalos gave to the daughter born to him by Clazome. Some of Boretes' people, especially the war widows, were allowed to join with the Dorasdi to create the new city, above all because the settlers had few women with them. Many stories exist of the conflict between the genders as the Dorasdi attempted to subject their wives to the conservative values of their people, but were frustrated by the combative nature of these women when inspired by Clazome, and, subsequently, her daughter Vestrikina.

Vestrikina the historical personage is buried in the shadow of the citadel, and her tomb is an important cult shrine; however, she and the goddess are not directly identified with one another except in the sense that both goddess and woman are the progeny of Akikalos' deeds.

Once a year, the city's main festival is held in which new citizens are enrolled, serving magistrates lay down their offices, and elections are called. During the week of the festival the priests and priestesses of the state cults act as an interim government. The goddess is renewed in the process, and this is represented by a ceremony in which the new citizens refurbish the goddess' temple, clean and restore the robes and diadem that adorn her statue, and are guests of honour at her high holy day feast.

Lay Membership

Any free-born person of Vestrikina who has at least a citizen mother is expected to join the city's cult at the age of 17, and will be automatically accepted so long as there is no taint upon them resulting from an act of sacrilege or treason. Joining the cult as a lay member requires submission to the Loyal Oath and the commitment of a Magic Point indefinitely.

Each new citizen is allocated to a tribe according to Social Class: Lion (Rich and Aristocracy), Snake (Propertied Class), Magpie (The Middling Sort) or Fox (everyone else), which determines

how citizens are organised into voting blocks and who they will line up alongside if the citizen army has to take the field. Each tribe has the same number (five) of votes in public assemblies and elections, even though they are different sizes, so the richer you are the more your individual vote counts.

Every four years, the Matrons command a census be held, and if necessary the tribes are revised to take account of social mobility. In between each census, individuals can make a case to the Matrons to be awarded membership of a different tribe if their economic circumstances have changed.

Vestrikina rarely accepts outsiders into the citizen body. Whether native-born slave or free-born foreigner, the only route to acceptance is to enter into marriage with a citizen-woman of the city, and be declared free in the case of the slave or to renounce any rival claim upon one's loyalties in the case of the foreigner.

Benefits

A citizen enjoys the protection and privileges offered by the laws and customs of the city. For male citizens this includes attending the assembly of citizens and voting in elections and on proposals placed before the people by the magistrates and council. Female citizens are not entitled to vote but are allowed to be present, if only on the periphery of the meeting-place, and exert their influence by variously encouraging and ridiculing their menfolk, which is a peculiar custom among Korantines who generally prefer their women to keep a dignified quiet in public.

He or she can join other state cults restricted to citizens for which they meet the membership requirements.

A male citizen is entitled to vote in the appointment of senior positions within other state cults and on key matters of state such as whether to go to war.

Initiates

The rites of initiation are as standard. The Matrons of Vestrikina include an equal number of matrons from each of the tribes, so even if the decision is taken to increase the total size of the initiate body, the increase must be equally applied to each tribe.

Skills

The cult skills are as standard for a city cult

Magic

As a small city, Vestrikina cannot offer the entire suite of spells and Miracles that a city cult might otherwise provide. Women of the cult are taught Folk Magic, usually in secret and away from the eyes of men:

Avert, Calm, Cleanse, Heal, Ignite, Loyal Oath, Preserve, Repair, Voice

Miracles

Miracles are similarly only available to the women of the cult. Miracles offered are:

Consecrate, Excommunicate, Extension, Fortify, Lay to Rest, Pacify, Spirit Block

Acolytes

The cult may have acolytes chosen from Matrons of any age, and who are selected for their suitability for certain tasks within the cult, having at least 70% ability in five of the cult skills. Acolytes do a great deal of the cult's work, in particular playing the key roles required in public rituals.

Priestesses

The priestesses, the city's leading Matrons, are always mothers who are now regarded as being beyond child-bearing age, although it is not usually required that they demonstrate having more than one of the key cult skills at a level higher than 90%. It is rare indeed for any woman not of a Propertied family to be invited to join their number.

The cult's leader is an entirely honorary position, that of the city's most respected matron who chairs the meetings of the priestesses. Her selection and appointment for life may have more to do with having provided the city with fine sons and daughters who have had a distinguished career in the service of their country than with any skill level. There is a rule that the chief priestess can trace her ancestry back to Clazome via Akikalos' daughter Vestrikina; however, many families make this claim and none can truly prove it given the passage of a thousand years, so it is routinely ignored or taken as read.

The priestesses form a parallel government for the city. While they are excluded from direct involvement in politics, their opinion matters, their acts of praise or censure capable of stopping some ambitious politician in his tracks or propelling him to greatness. They can effectively direct the influence applied by wives on their husbands in public matters; as it happens the opinion of the Matrons is something formally agreed in meetings and communicated throughout the city by way of the social network provided by its womenfolk.

Allied Cults

Vestrikina is allied to Suthria and Pelostra. Citizens of these places are entitled to own property in Vestrikina, and to enjoy all other privileges of a citizen except to vote or stand for public office. The arrangements are reciprocal.

Anayo of Vestrikina

In a Korantine city advancement in the cult of Anayo provides the route to power as a member of the city's council, and, ultimately, as a magistrate wielding the authority of public office. Vestrikina is no different, and its particular arrangements are upheld as a model by many writers on politics.

Mythos and History

Anayo is the wise ruler, the great sage, the lawgiver. His planet burns brightly in the heavens, and appears to be surrounded by clusters of subordinate stars. Anayo is married to the Queen of Heaven, but she is such an all-powerful being that the marriage is celebrated in each city through his relationship with just one manifestation, the goddess of the city – in Vestrikina just as in all the others.

When Vestrikina was founded, the land was equally divided between Akikalos' followers. Thereby some 300 estates were created, each of them of sufficient size to support an extended family in some comfort so long as the labour could be found to exploit them. At first, the heads of each family were expected to convene regularly as a council, but later, as these estates were subdivided, fell into disuse or were added to by new settlements, ownership of a specific parcel of land was replaced with a simple property qualification for initiate membership. At the same time, the maximum size of the council was fixed at 300, to ensure that it would not swell to a point that the members

were strangers to one another. An age restriction was added as well as the provision that no man may be admitted into the cult ranks who has a living father already sitting as an initiate member. Up to a third of the members may hold their seats by virtue of holding or having held public office. This enables the occurrence of father and son sitting in council at the same time.

Nature

Anayo's cult oversees the proper functions of Vestrikina's government. It ensures the council meets on the appropriate days, its business is properly attended to, expert opinions sought, and decisions properly debated, voted and promulgated to the broader citizenry. It also provides the jury for legal cases involving citizens, 10 of its members who are chosen by lot.

Membership

Initiation in the cult of Anayo of Vestrikina is open to male citizens of the Propertied class and above, and who are over 30 years of age, by which point it is assumed a candidate will be married and have children. The candidate should also have at least 50% in three of the cult skills. Former magistrates, no matter what their cult, are automatically given the right to initiation. Initiation brings with it a seat on the city council.

Skills

Command, Customs, Devotion (City Goddess), Exhort, Influence, Literacy, Lore (any), Oratory, Rites, Willpower

Magic

The cult does not provide any Folk Magic. The worshipper's devotion to the city-goddess is used instead of devotion to Anayo himself to set the Intensity and Magnitude of cult Miracles. The following Miracles are available:

Backlash, Consecrate, Extension*, Inviolate, Mindlink, Ostracism**

*If cast by an acolyte rather than a priest, Anayo's Extension spell can last no longer than its caster holds their appointed office of state.

**A variant of the Excommunication spell that forces the target to leave their home city and go into exile until its expiry. The effects of excommunication only apply so long as the target remains within the chora of their home city.

Benefits

An initiate is entitled to sit on the city council, and to stand for election to public office.

ANAYO

Archons (Acolytes)

The cult's acolytes are the two annually elected archons it provides to preside over the city, alongside one other who is provided by the cult of Torthil; together these archons are known as the Board of Three. Their selection is via a public vote that canvasses all male citizens. In Vestrikina each tribe casts their votes in turn as a bloc and hence Fox, the lowest class tribe, may never need to be called, or their vote is simply a formal record of their opinion, because the election is already decided. The election is subsequently ratified by the priests unless they discover some irregularity – whether mundane or magical – that forces them to overturn the peoples' decision. The three archons are supported by other specialist officers of state chosen from candidates put forward by associated cults.

Priests

Priests are appointed from among those within the council who have served one or more terms as an acolyte, and are 42 years of age. Whenever a vacancy arises the priests co-opt a worthy candidate, then present their choice to the council for ratification. The priesthood generally consists of less than a dozen men, most of whom are heads of the city's most influential families. In Vestrikina the candidate is almost always from a rich family, and, in practice, the vast majority of priests have come from families who belong to the old aristocracy.

Cults

> ### New Miracle: Inviolate
> *Duration (Minutes), Rank Acolyte, Resist (Willpower)*
>
> This Miracle can be cast on any acoylte of the cult, or any acolyte or priestess of the city-goddess, or any sacred cult object relevant to the city's spiritual existence with a SIZ of no more than ten times the Miracle's Magnitude. Inviolate protects the recipient from harm so long as he or it is within the boundaries of the city. Hostile spells are automatically negated if they do not exceed the magnitude of the Miracle. Physical or supernatural attackers must commit an action point to attacking before making the resistance roll, but if they fail to resist the Miracle they lose the turn in which the attack was attempted. Successfully resisting the Miracle allows the attack to continue, but at one grade harder, and the spell negates any Special Effect gained by an attacker simply because the recipient is unable to parry or evade an attack.
>
> An attacker must resist the spell for every attack roll attempted.

Arribeus of Vestrikina

Arribeus' cult at Vestrikina is an example of a minor cult with an important role to play at major festivals and rites, but no power and influence within the state. Arribeus is the deity whose sphere is youth, spring and birdsong. The cult hierarchy is comprised of a small cadre of adults, its lay membership being comprised of adolescents, girls and boys who are taught the songs and dances performed at the major state festivals and rites.

Every year a competition is held in the spring to choose the leading chorister from amongst the children of citizen status, and for the next year this person is promoted to the rank of acolyte. He is then eligible to become initiated into the cult upon reaching adulthood and serve for the rest of his life as one of its functionaries. The lucky winner also receives a Gift from the deity with mastery of the Sing skill (raised to 100%). It is possible for the acolyte to retain his or her title in subsequent competitions, until achieving the age of majority, and thanks to the god's Gift, they usually do.

The initiates of the cult are choirmasters, teachers and ultimately the arrangers and promoters of performances. The cult has its own high holy day each spring, but is kept busy all year by its contribution to festivals for the other deities honoured by the state cults.

Since this cult is essentially a means of instructing the leading youth in the rites and service to their city, the Devotion skill used to determine the Intensity and Magnitude of its Miracles is that of the city-goddess. Nevertheless, the Exhort skill required for Arribeus' Miracles is his own.

Skills

Dance, Devotion (City Goddess), Exhort (Arribeus), Lore (Music and Song), Musicianship (lyre), Rites, Sing, Teach

Magic

Only initiates and the annual Acolyte may learn the cult's Folk Magic

Folk Magic

Tune, Ventriloquism, Voice

Miracles

Consecrate, Enthrall, Harmonise

Torthil of Vestrikina

Torthil is the god of the farmers of Vestrikina. During the agricultural year, he assists them in their labours, and during the campaigning season or at times of emergency, his cult organises the city militia. Torthil's cult is the most widely practised among the city's male citizens.

Membership

All the able-bodied citizen men of the city are likely to be lay members at some stage in their lives. For the farming community, it is a matter of course and the cult's major festivals and rites mark the agricultural year, but at key times, such as the harvest or mustering for war, this will also involve many people who are not directly involved in agriculture.

Initiate

Initiate members are blacksmiths, the headman in a small village or rural hamlet, members of Vestrikina's Patriotic Bands, and those who will serve as junior officers in the citizen militia. They are expected to acquire the Command skill if they are to progress to acolyte status, and must hone their knowledge of customs and rites if they have an eye for the priesthood.

Acolyte

Torthil's cult acolytes are military commanders. An acolyte must have at least 70% ability in five of the cult skills.

Torthil's acolytes are entitled to stand for election to the role of Military Archon (general), which both gives the winner command of Vestrikina's army and a seat on the Board of Three, the city's ruling magistrates.

Priesthood

The priests of Torthil play a significant role in the city, and are responsible for the day-to-day administration of each tribe. A priest's role is to see that the tribe to which he is appointed provides its share of men to the levy, plays its proper role in state rituals, performs its duties in elections and assemblies and so forth.

Skills

Athletics, Craft (Blacksmith), Combat Style: Citizen Infantry, Combat Style: Levy (type), Customs, Devotion (Torthil), Endurance, Exhort, Locale, Lore (Agriculture) Lore (Animal Husbandry), Lore (Tactics and Drill) Rites

Magic

The cult makes it possible for its lay members to learn up to three of its Folk Magic spells, and for Initiates and higher there is no restriction.

Alarm, Bladesharp, Bludgeon, Dry, Heat, Ignite, Ironhand, Might, Polish, Vigour

Miracles

Boundary, Burn Fields, Clear Skies, Consecrate, Extension*, Lay to Rest, Perseverance, Rain, Steadfast

*Torthil's Extension Miracle can last no more than one season

Associated Cults

Torthil's initiates, acolytes and priests gain the following Miracles from associated cults:

Anayo: Backlash

Kos: Dismiss Magic

Sabateus: Pacify

Special Cult Miracles

Boundary

Rank: Varies, Area of Effect: Special, Duration: Years

With this spell the worshipper sets the boundary of an area of land in a way that is endorsed by divine providence and fully recognised under the law. The land must be a single parcel of territory encompassed by an unbroken line that may pass through water only as deep as a man may wade through. The area is marked out with boundary stones by the caster, or perhaps by ploughing a furrow. The line of the boundary cannot intersect with a pre-existing boundary, although it can be contiguous.

The area of effect is measured in hectares for an initiate (1 Point Spell) so as to encompass a farm, and in square kilometres for an acolyte (2 Point Spell) so as to encompass the lands of a whole farming community. A priest (3 Point Spell) can affect an area of up to 3 square kilometres for every 100 citizens enrolled on the census and, in doing so, he marks out the whole chora claimed by his city.

The principle effect of this Miracle is to redefine the area of effect to which other magic can be applied. Only Miracles provided by Torthil himself or by allied cults may be affected. Bless Crops and Restore Earth* are compatible with this Miracle.

A Miracle provided by the goddess Sheylo, which restores the fields after harvest so there is no need for fallowing

Burn Fields

Rank Initiate, Area of Effect: Hectares

This Miracle can be used to clear land or burn stubble after the harvest. However, if used maliciously or as part of a scorched earth policy, it can also torch food-bearing plants within the area of effect, which is equal to one hectare per point of Magnitude, destroying any possible harvest this year. The crops affected must be in contiguous fields, as the area of effect flows out from the caster like a flood of fire and if it meets a gap of uncultivated land more than 3 metres wide it is stopped and must expend its energy in other directions. Living creatures within the burning zone are affected as if in contact with a small fire (1d6 damage per round, Evade test to avoid damage each round), and, if not burned, may find themselves suffering from asphyxiation by the smoke.

Cults of Sabateus

The various cults of Sabateus are the main agent of mediation and exchange between different Korantine cities. Sabateus is a god of merchants, and he also encompasses, protects and levies taxes from the non-citizen residents of a city – the metics. His cults issue currency that can be guaranteed in every state, and even maintain their own mercenary forces for the protection of goods in transit, depots and manufactories.

Mythos and History

Sabateus is a divinity who crosses boundaries – his planet seems to cut across the paths of the other gods in heaven with impunity, and he is said to whisper the business of one god to another as he passes by.

In the early era of Korantine history the Sabatines provided security for envoys and politicians when conducting business between cities or in foreign lands, often extending to conducting negotiations with the other party prior to official meetings between those holding genuine authority for the state. But the cult was soon looking after or facilitating all the run-of-the mill and less 'honourable' (for which read tainted with money) trades and transactions that go on alongside diplomatic missions. Whether brokering war reparation deals, fixing interest and exchange rates, collecting taxes or setting up trade deals, the Sabatines ultimately had a hand in everything and a man could make himself impressively rich if he could achieve status within the cult.

In some states, Estrigel the Herald, who is the chief announcer and messenger for the celestial court, is still represented as a sub-cult of Sabateus.

The cult of Sabateus conforms to a fairly standard pattern from city to city. It serves to perform the following services for the state and its citizens:

- Y To regulate trade and exchange, including the import and export of key commodities and natural resources.
- Y To raise taxes from import, export and market traders.
- Y To underwrite major enterprises, and act as bankers both for citizens and the city itself.
- Y To register resident aliens, regulate their business activities, and levy a poll tax on each.

Lay Members

Most lay worshippers are merchants, traders and businessmen who make up the rank and file of the cult, but also many minor officials, secretaries and accountants employed by the cult. Both citizens and non-citizens may take part in the cult as lay members.

The Sabatines

The Sabatines, which is the ancient name for all the cult's followers, now refers to a mercenary force of non-citizens who provide security for warehouses and banks and for major shipments of commodities and valuable goods. In addition to the usual pay and benefits on offer, if a Sabatine maintains lay membership during his service, the cult sponsors his application for citizenship after whatever passage of time is required in each city – a minimum of 5 years but, in some states, this can be 20 years or more.

Initiates: The Board of Trade

Initiation is only open to citizens. There are a limited number of initiate roles – in Vestrikina there are only 6, in Borissa 16, in Sarestra 27. These initiates who form a Board of Trade are essentially customs officials who assess the value of seaborne cargoes unloaded in port and overland caravans arrived in the territory for tax, and are responsible for collecting it. An initiate devotes significant time to the cult but is also paid for his work. This is actually rather small recompense for the fact that it is often necessary to hire someone to take care of private business affairs. The Board is nevertheless a necessary step on the way to one of the highly lucrative positions occupied by acolytes.

In order to secure a vacant post on the Board of Trade a member must have Literacy and Commerce skills of no less than 50%. Those of Aristocratic status are usually excluded from membership.

Acolytes: Trade Concessionaries

Acolytes of the cult are tax farmers, people who have been granted monopoly over a key trade route or type, and operators of key economic installations (mines, manufactories, etc). Their numbers are limited to the number of such concessions on offer, and they are generally a mere handful; but if a new opportunity arises or a new resource is discovered, a new acolyte position may be created to exploit it.

An acolyte must have Commerce as one of his cult skills at a minimum of 70%.

There is usually some sort of bidding process for acolyte status, whereby the prospective acolyte pledges a guarantee for how much money his concession will generate for the state in a year, and the process is overseen and bids chosen by the city's council. The acolyte will be bound to make good any shortfall, and can keep any excess. The support of the existing acolytes and the syndics (priests) is essential for a confident bid, as they will generally make good the shortfall rather than see their colleague ruined by having to do so from his own means, so to some extent this process is stitched up before it goes to tender. The rewards of membership are significant. Nevertheless the greatest rewards go to those who are already wealthy, as they can sink significant investment into the opportunities they are given rather than go begging for capital from others at punitive rates of interest or return.

Priests: Syndics, Corporation Heads

The priests of Sabateus are referred to as *syndics*, and these people are immensely influential. The government turns to them whenever there is a need for money to support a public programme, or indeed whenever an opportunity to make money for the whole state presents itself. A syndic automatically gains a permanent seat on the city's council. They regulate and control the activities of the acolytes and the board of trade, and watch out for any flagrant abuses that may cause other elements of society to attack their interests. One of the syndics is responsible for the mint, striking the cult's bullion coinage, and usually performs the same function for the city's own coinage as a service under contract. One of the syndics is put in charge of trade treaties with other Korantine states and another is made responsible for treaties with foreigners. The head syndic (high priest) bears ultimate responsibility for the cult's Sabatines, if it has any.

Skills

Commerce, Culture (Any), Custom, Devotion, Exhort, Influence, Insight, Language (Any), Literacy, Lore (Any), Locale (any)

Magic

Folk Magic

Appraise, Calculate, Lock, Polish, Translate

Miracles

Assay, Backlash, Consecrate, Excommunicate, Extension, Mindlink, Pacify

Assay

Rank Initiate

This Miracle gives the caster the ability to precisely establish the content of an alloyed metal, typically to assess or confirm the purity of bullion. For each Intensity of the Miracle the caster can analyze up to 3 kilos of a metal.

Cult of Kos

Kos is a god of justice and law who polices the proper order of things, ensures adherence to the commands and edicts of his 'brother' Anayo, and roots out those who are a threat to the quiet enjoyment of the rights and privileges of the gods. His cult does the same for the city-state. Any matter of justice and punishment that is not one to be dealt with as an open and public process is dealt with by a city's acolyte of Kos.

Membership

The cult of Kos usually operates as a subordinate cult to that of Anayo. One of the ruler god's initiates will be chosen to take the role of the state's enforcer, and be inducted into the god's rites as an acolyte. The cult has no lay membership of its own except during a civil emergency, when as the protector of the state the acolyte of Kos may demand all 'loyal' citizens participate in its rites as a sign of commitment to the status quo.

The cult's temple attendants and officials are usually slaves, owned by the cult and operating under a strict set of rules. There may be a single priest, possibly a former acolyte of the cult; a serving acolyte who is the main functionary, and a small number of initiates whom the acolyte has asked to join him in his work.

The acolyte's job is to investigate and pass judgement over cases involving violent criminal acts, sedition and treason. If the suspect is a citizen they may well be brought before an open court for judgement with the acolyte acting as accuser. In other cases, the acolyte has the ability to investigate, judge, torture and execute, a right that is extended even over the citizenry if a state of emergency has been declared. In addition, the acolyte is likely responsible for a constabulary made up of club-armed slaves, and has the right to call upon a Patriotic Band provided by one of the other state cults when he needs a posse.

Skills

Customs, Devotion, Exhort, Influence, Insight, Literacy, Rites

Magic

Folk Magic

Avert, Demoralise, Magnify, Tire

Miracles

Dismiss Magic, Extension, Obliterate, Thread of Life

Games Master Note: If you decide to introduce the notion of Chaos into the setting for your campaign, Kos should be its staunch enemy and provided with powerful spells to deal with it.

KOS

New Miracle: Thread of Life

Duration (Special), Rank Acolyte, Resist (Willpower)

Thread of Life prevents its target from dying. This spell has benign uses – amongst them rendering a Sever Spirit spell useless – or to keep someone alive until proper treatment can be applied; but its purpose is actually rather dark – it allows torture to be extended, or a prisoner to be prevented from suicide. The target's progress towards death is halted at the moment before he passes, and allows healing to be applied – or torture to be continued. When the spell expires so does the target, unless he has been given medical or magical treatment. It does nothing to reverse damage done – if the target is suffering from serious wounds or deadly fatigue, they remain incapacitated. But they also remain conscious.

Cult of Pyrolus

Pyrolus is the sailor-god of the Korantines. Ships are consecrated shrines to this god, and a ship's captain is an acolyte, sometimes even a priest, of his cult and the crew his congregation. Pyrolus' cult serves the same purpose at sea as Torthil's cult does on land; it supports the day to day labours of sailors, rowers and fishermen, and also supervises the call to arms for those who will serve in a city's fleet. In a maritime state Pyrolus might replace Torthil as the third deity in the trinity of chief gods of state.

Mythos and History

Pyrolus is one of the brightest planets in the heavens – so bright that it is the first to appear at night, before the sky is fully dark, and the last to fade from sight at dawn. His pathways across the night sky are also the most regular and constantly visible – by observing his position in relation to the moon and certain other heavenly bodies, it is possible to calculate bearings and heading with some precision – and if you know your bearing but do not know the date or even the hour, to calculate those too.

Pyrolus' worship was deeply affected by the Cataclysm. It remains limited in its interest to human endeavour upon the waves, not with the sea itself. The cult's Propitiation Miracle, originally used to calm the storms sent by the weather-god Palaskil, was put to use propitiating the Ocean, who at that point had become the Korantines' most dangerous enemy. The cult can summon sylphs and bind them to the sails or masts of their ships, but it is now taboo to bind an undine to a ship's hull as was done in ancient times, something that is now a significant disadvantage in maritime travel and warfare.

Lay Members

Anyone who spends time afloat is likely to be a lay member of the cult, and someone who is a professional sailor, deckhand, rower or marine is expected to be. The rank and file of the cult are often among the city's poorest citizens, being folk who are dependent on paid work when they can get it – and service at sea is regarded as significantly more dangerous than most jobs on land.

A lay member may be taught up to three of the cult's Folk Magic spells

Initiate (Captain)

Anyone who wishes to find employment as a key crew member, such as a helmsman, mate, navigator or ship's carpenter, must be an initiate of Pyrolus. This includes those who captain smaller vessels (Size M and below). Such an individual is referred to as 'captain' when at sea but not on shore.

Acolyte (Captain)

A Captain is someone who can captain a large vessel of the kind that has a significant crew. They can carry the title with them even when on shore.

Priesthood (Master of Ships)

Priests of Pyrolus are responsible for managing the god's rites on behalf of the whole city. A Pyrolus priest almost certainly holds a seat on his city's council.

Skills

Boating, Brawn, Combat Style: (any suitable to Marine*), Craft (any relevant, e.g, boat-building, carpentry, netmaking), Devotion, Endurance, Exhort, Locale (Ocean Quarter), Navigate, Seamanship, Survival, Swim

*Trait is Sure-Footed – no penalties for fighting on a heaving deck, and marines are even taught to hurl a javelin from a seated position without penalty.

Magic

Folk Magic

Beastcall (marine creature), Breath, Deflect, Dry, Glue, Heal, Might, Preserve, Repair, Sea Legs*, Shove, Vigor

*a cult special; allows the target to get past the worst effects of sea sickness, and reduces a skills difficulty modifier for activity on a heaving deck by one grade.

Miracles

Bless Ram*, Call Winds, Consecrate, Dismiss Undine, Extension, Excommunicate, Harmonise, Propitiate (Ocean), Elemental Summoning (Sylph), Lay to Rest (at Sea)

*Adds a Damage Modifier starting at 1d4 and increasing by 1 dice step per magnitude, when inflicting damage on an enemy vessel by ramming – whether or not the ship is equipped with a structural ram.

Cult of Lasca Veltis: The Korantine Sibyls (Mysticism Cult)

There are 7 Korantine Sibyls, although it has been said that in past ages their number may have been as high as 12. It is a great honour for any city to play host to these prophetesses, and consequently also a great dishonour should a Sibyl decide a city is not worthy of her presence and relocate somewhere more appropriate. Their order is deemed precious to all the gods but pays specific cult to the otherwise obscure Lasca Veltis.

Sibyls are mystics, who follow a tradition by which their ability to read human hearts and divine intentions in any individual is honed to an uncanny degree. A Sibyl's Meditiation ability often takes the form not of quiet contemplation but of exhausting frenzy.

Skills

Customs, Insight, Meditation, Mysticism, Perception, Rites

Magic And Talents

Typical Talents for a Sibyl include:

Augment Insight, Awareness, Indomitable, Life Sense, Magic Sense and Spirit Sense

LASCA VELTIS

The standard Gift, granted to any disciple who has achieved 90% or more in three cult skills including Meditation, is Oracle.

Foreign Cults

Cult of Theyna

The mother goddess of the Thennalt race, Theyna is one of the great goddesses of the world. She heads up a whole pantheon of chthonic deities and spirits, representing every aspect of her being. Someone who joins her cult is likely to encounter a specific instance of it that has its own idiosyncrasies and is largely ignorant of how her cult is celebrated in other locales. Theyna's shrines and temples are usually built around or incorporate a natural feature such as a cave, spring, sacred tree or rock. A shrine will have 1d3 Miracles available, a small temple 1d3+3, a medium temple 1d6+3 and a large temple 1d6+6. Only a great cult centre such as Oster might offer 2d6+6 Miracles, almost the whole range the goddess can provide.

Membership

All Thennalts are likely at some point in their lives to pay homage to this goddess as lay members of her cult, but her initiates are few in number, restricted to those who are actually being

groomed for the priesthood. Despite being thought of as a female deity, Theyna has both male and female priests, sometimes a married couple who run a temple or shrine together. The ethereal mistresses of the landscape – the nymphs – are often priestesses in her cult, and sometimes Thennalt lords marry them to confirm their claim to leadership of those who live in and around her domain.

The cult serves its local community, providing support for its agriculture; its relationship with local nature spirits, and fighting disease and injury that disrupts the natural order of things. A community with a shrine or temple of any size usually sets aside sacred herd animals, or even fields and orchards, from which the temple priests can draw a living.

Magic

Folk Magic

The cult is a common source of Folk Magic, and many different spells are available. A typical selection is:

Beastcall (Bovid), Bladesharp, Endurance, Heal, Pathway, Pet, Warmth

Miracles

Absorption, Backlash, Banish Satyr, Beast Form**, Bless Crops, Consecrate, Cure Malady, Earthquake, Entangle, Fecundity, Dismiss Elemental, Elemental Summoning, Extension, Heal Body, Lay to Rest, Rejuvenate, Ripen, Shield, Soul Sight.

There is no place known on earth where all of these Miracles are available. Her temples and shrines will have a small selection of these spells depending on the nature of the local environment and the character of its people.

Some unique Miracles may be available at particular sacred sites and the Games Master should feel free to introduce plenty of variety to the way the goddess' cult is presented across its vast reach.

> ### New Miracle: Banish Satyr
> *Duration (Hours), Rank Initiate, Resist (Willpower)*
>
> This spell simply serves to force a satyr to abandon its physical form. The Miracle only works on a target with no more than 3 POW per point of Intensity, who can resist using his Willpower. The banished satyr is prevented from manifesting for 1 hour per Intensity, but this can be extended.

*Specific shrines will offer different transformations.

Jekkara, Goddess Of Moon and Magic

The cult of Jekkara rules the nation named in her honour, and its chief priestess is their Queen. Girls of high status seek positions in the cult, and those who are successful are subjected to an intensive educational regime and are set demanding standards that many will fail to meet. Like the cult of Lanis, that of Jekkara is organised into age classes, and failure to meet the grade from promotion when the time is right will result in a shameful exit from its ranks.

Mythos and History

Jekkara was once worshipped through a cult that was intimately woven with that honouring the sun god Lanis. Over a thousand years ago, these cults severed ties with one another, and the Solarists abandoned the common homeland in Methalea and colonised the region now known as Korantia. The matriarchal cult of Jekkara remained as the paramount authority with those that remained in Methalea and quickly tightened its grip on society, ensuring things would stay that way. The divorce of sun and moon has never been forgotten, and the enmity between Jekkarene and Korantine that persists to this day is the result.

The Theocracy of the Jekkarenes is now the only known matriarchal society in the East, but it commands a vast region that supports a significant population.

Jezri the Virgin Daughter (Lay Membership, 7-17 Years of Age)

The daughters of people of quality are eligible to join; however, if the priestesses encounter a girl of lower station who clearly has abilities (DEX, POW and CHA all at 15 or above), they may forcibly take the girl from her family and bring her up as one of their order. From the age of 7, girls begin their training as a temple dancer under the sub-cult of Jezri, the goddess' daughter, who can be seen in the night sky as a small star that appears to orbit around her mother. Those the priestesses think may not make the grade are ejected before they turn 12 and returned to their parents. After that age, the cult assumes ownership of the girl, including the right to betroth her to one of the leading men of the nation as a reward for his services.

Cults

The cult sets about inculcating not only the skills needed to perform at cult ceremonies, but a sense of loyalty to the cult and the queen, which begins at 30+POW+CHA of the cultist.

The Guardians (Initiate Membership, 17-32 Years of Age)

At the age of 17, those lay worshippers deemed to be of continuing value to the cult undergo initiation into the ranks of the Guardians. They become fully fledged members of the cult, but for now are still expected to live communally on temple property and are maintained by temple tithes and revenues.

The Guardians comprise a regiment of 700 amazons who are well schooled in fighting techniques and wonderfully equipped – but the unit is dispersed around the temples, has never fought a proper battle and is completely untested militarily. Their main purpose is as a sort of Praetorian Guard and they provide security for the temples and priestesses so that no man needs to be admitted to sacred areas; they also serve as a secret police, and those who do so may learn the more wily arts of an assassin whose job is simply to effect the extra-judicial killing of those that the priestesses believe may be a present or future danger to the state.

Any initiate who begins to fall short of the cult's expectations and their oaths of faithfulness to its rules will be stripped of her initiate status and married off. For those who are found guilty of actually transgressing cult taboos, a far more severe punishment is applied – of which exile is perhaps the most lenient of the options available.

Devout Daughters (Acolyte Membership, 27+ Years of Age)

From among the ranks of the Guardians are chosen the Devout Daughters, who serve as officers or as enforcers of the cult's will. Those who have an INT and POW in excess of 15 each may be taught some of the cult's sorcerous secrets and the skills to use them.

Jekkarene Miracles

Lycanthropy
Duration (Hours), Rank Priest, Resist (Endurance)

The target of this Miracle is cursed to become a werewolf under the priestess' control for the Miracle's duration. In normal circumstances the victim is expelled from his community while under its effects, never to return. Even after the end of the Duration he (and it is only ever used on a male target), must resist the Miracle again every night of the full moon, or be shape-shifted until daybreak; but, this time, with no priestess to command him, he becomes an uncontrolled violent monster.

Moonbright
Duration Special, Rank Initiate

Moonbright is used as an Extension spell, affecting any form of magic except Miracles. The caster can extend the Duration of any non-instant spells of her own casting up to a combined Magnitude equal to the Magnitude of the Moonbright Miracle. The Miracle can only be called upon between sunset and sunrise. The extension lasts until sunrise the same night and no longer. If the spell being extended is an offensive spell, the target gets to resist that spell a second time at the expiry of its original Duration.

Synchronise
Duration (Minutes), Rank Initiate, Resist (Willpower)

With this Miracle, originally devised to precisely synchronise the movements of a troupe of dancers, the caster forces one target per point of Magnitude to exactly copy their movements. An unwilling target gets the chance to resist, and if the target is forced to behave in a way likely to result in death or serious injury, they get another chance to break the spell (assuming they can see the danger). Willing recipients being led in a dance or acrobatic routine have the difficulty of any associated skill roll made one grade easier

Mothers (Priestess Membership, 32+ Years of Age)

The priestesses of the cult are separated into eight colleges, each of which heads one of the eight provinces of the theocracy. The leading college is that quartered at the massive temple complex at the capital, Parlasos, and is headed by the queen herself. Semankore has reigned now for five years.

The Mothers are entitled to take a husband, and if necessary, set their cult duties aside long enough to bear a child. Any girl child will have the easiest of entries to the cult as a lay member when she turns seven.

The priestess of each college meet together every month to debate and set the strategy for their provinces, decide upon the appointment of administrators and generals who can enact their will, and decide who among them will be responsible for monitoring and reporting on progress.

Skills

Athletics, Combat Style: Assassin* or Guardian**, Dance, Deceit, Devotion (Jekkara), Exhort, Influence, Insight, Invocation (Jekkarene Grimoire), Lore (Any), Passion: Loyalty (Jekkarene Theocracy), Rites, Shaping.

*This style includes Dagger – the cult weapon is a curved moon-blade that is hard for the uninitiated to adapt their technique to – Knife and Mace or Club. Trait is Assassination

**This style includes Rapier, Dagger, Buckler and Morningstar Flail (Ball & Chain). Trait is Swashbuckling.

Magic

Folk Magic

Cantrips are made available to lay members, who can learn up to three spells. Initiates may learn up to six spells:

Alarm, Avert*, Babble, Befuddle, Cleanse, Coordination, Fanaticism, Find (Runaway Peasant, Trespasser on Temple Property), Glamour, Heal, Knock, Light, Tire.

*As Jekkara is goddess of magic, the Avert spell taught by her cult negates any Intensity 1 spell or spirit effect, not just Folk Magic.

Sorcery

Sorcery is taught to a minority of priestesses. The cult's grimoire is limited in scope and seems never to be added to; an ossified tradition.

Abjure Love, Bypass Armour, Eavesdrop*, Enchant, Intuition, Mystic Vision, Regenerate, Spirit Resistance, Summon, Transfer Wound

* Project Sense (Hearing)

Miracles

Jekkara's Miracles are powerful, but only work at night for worshippers of Initiate rank. Acolytes and priestesses can call upon Miracles in daylight hours, however, while Intensity is calculated normally they will have a default magnitude of 1 and are in any event one grade easier to resist.

Absorption, Behold, Bless Crops (Moon Barley), Chameleon, Consecrate, Enthrall, Excommunicate, Lay to Rest, Lycanthropy*, Moonbright,* Obliterate, Rejuvenate, Synchronise*

*See boxed text, page 103.

Koremchai (Demonic Pact)

This deity is a demon who encourages pillage and plunder by sea. Most acts of piracy are raids upon poorly defended coastal communities by sea-borne raiders, but ship-to-ship encounters are not unheard of. The Archipelagans are the most profligate pirates known, and Koremchai is the demon who supports them in their work.

Mythos and History

Koremchai is a water-demon, one who is born of the Ocean but was confined by Ocean himself to a watery region of the Many Hells, where he collects the souls of the drowned and the treasures of the shipwrecked. When Korantis sank beneath the waves, Koremchai was denied the vast glut of drowned souls the disaster created, as this would have upset all manner of deities whose worshippers had never even been to sea, let alone knowingly committed their lives to the whim of the ocean gods. In compensation, Koremchai was offered a cult, one which would guarantee an increased harvest year on year. Hence his cult is an off-shoot of the worship of Father Ocean (Dagomar), and each instance is instituted by a propitiatory rite provided by Dagomar's own cult.

Membership

Those who join this cult are usually the young bucks of a community, perhaps a few older hands who have nothing much else to do or to live for, or harbour a burning desire to gather some

Cults

loot to improve their lot. Being one of Koremchai's cultists is a dangerous existence, and it serves among other things to give work to idle hands that may otherwise cause mischief at home.

Koremchai is summoned to 'bless' the commitment of a ship and its crew to pillage upon the high seas, and receives a portion of the spoils in lives and plunder.

A prospective pirate captain must first be an initiate of Dagomar, and approach his priests with his proposal to raise a pirate crew. To have any chance of success, he must be someone of status. This means someone who possesses a suitable ship himself or has access to one provided by a wealthy kinsman, and who can also be sure enough of finding a crew to join him — perhaps indeed has one ready. A small Archipelagan war boat requires a crew of 20, most have a crew of 30, and the biggest have a crew of 50.

When the captain takes his vow, he assumes the role of acolyte-priest of his crew. He may nominate up to three others to be his initiate-lieutenants, the remainder will be lay members of the cult. When they swear their brotherhood in blood, each provides a single Magic Point to the crew's contract, which cannot be recovered until the Pact is ended by mutual agreement, or expires. The total of Magic Points dedicated in the Pact is the basis for the Devotional Pool at the disposal of the captain and his initiates. 1/4 of the dedicated Magic Points are made available; however, the captain and initiates cannot have a greater personal pool than allowed by their cult rank. This pool cannot be replenished, and next season the captain must seek renewal of his status and institute his cult following and its Devotional Pool from scratch.

Example – Hettric the Drowner assembles a pirate crew for a large warboat, and has a total complement of 52 men. Hettric has three 'mates' (initiates). Hettric can have a Devotional Pool up to half his POW, and each of the mates a quarter of theirs. This means Hettric's maximum Devotional Pool is 5, and his mates are entitled to 3,3,2 – for a total allowance of 13 points. This neatly absorbs the allowance of 13MP available to Hettric and his henchmen from the 50 Magic Points donated to Koremchai by the crew.

Koremchai demands some part of his followers' spoils be sacrificed by being cast into the ocean – and this includes human captives. Islander pirates routinely drown a proportion of those unfortunate enough to fall into their hands. Of the remainder, it is traditional that half is returned to the Dagomar temple where some at least should find its way to the local community. The rest is divided up amongst the crew, with five shares for the captain, three for each of the initiates, and one each for everybody else.

Skills

The cult does not teach skills, but expects its recruits to have following skills at 50% or greater:

Athletics, Boating, Brawn, Combat Style (any)

As well as two of the following at 50% or greater:

Deceit, Endurance, First Aid, Perception, Seamanship, Swim, Unarmed

Magic

The cult does not teach any Folk Magic.

The cult's Miracles are:

Bind Vessel, Breathe Water, Command Shark, Elemental Summoning (Undine), Wooden Walls

---

New Miracles

Bind Vessel
Duration (Hours), Ranged (Hundreds of Metres), Rank Acolyte

This Miracle reduces the speed of the target vessel, by 1m per point of Intensity. The size of vessel that can be affected is as follows:

Vessel Size Required Intensity: Small 2, Medium 4, Large 6, Huge 8, Enormous 10, Colossal 12

Wooden Walls
This Miracle is identical to the Fortify spell provided in MYTHRAS; however, it affects a wooden ship. The spell must have sufficient Intensity for the size of vessel being protected.

Travelling Korantia

Sea lanes and trade routes are the great highways of the Korantines, connecting those cities that are situated by the coast. So long as two cities are on friendly terms, it is likely that there is regular seaborne traffic between them, and ample opportunity to take passage on a merchant ship or, for the wealthy, to charter a vessel for private use. However, very many Korantine cities are situated inland, including the Emperor's capital. To reach any of these, or to explore the wildernesses between and beyond them, or to strike a path into one of the lands bordering Korantia, requires the more arduous business of overland travel.

Land Travel

Land travel is a slow, expensive and often dangerous undertaking. Travelling light or on a swift horse is preferable, but if you have baggage then you are likely to be limited to the movement rate of the ox-cart. Draught oxen cannot be pushed for long hours, and while they are the best available non-magical means of pulling a heavy load, they dictate a slow plodding pace for the journey.

Roads

There are few metalled roads in Korantia, and none beyond its borders until you reach the Taskan Empire. Those that do exist connect a city-state's capital with key outlying municipalities, ensuring easy transport and travel between them and acting as a bond that helps keep them politically connected. In past centuries, there were more, sponsored by the Emperor and used to move goods and troops across his Empire, and so connecting the city-states that owed him tribute. Stretches of these roads still exist, but often lead nowhere or end abruptly in a dirt track.

For the most part, traffic using well-travelled routes across Korantia relies on the most rudimentary of road surfaces. Lesser routes are simply well worn tracks following the path of least resistance through the landscape, avoiding where possible the steepest hills, thickest forests and the flood plains, and often taking significant detours in order to make use of the most convenient river crossings.

There has been talk at the Korantine League of building roads across city-state boundaries, particularly to create key routes connecting to Hilanistra or to a port from where a connecting boat can be taken to Valos; however, it does not look like there will be any agreement in the near future about what routes these roads will take and who will pay for them.

Inns

Inns are widely dispersed, generally situated just outside towns that are more or less a day apart by horse for a traveller unencumbered by baggage. Inns are all private establishments and have no set architectural plan, but usually have a common eating area, a mix of dormitory and private rooms for accommodation, and stabling for horses, mules and donkeys and a barn for other animals. Prices in Korantine inns are entirely at the landlord's discretion, those given here are average. During busy times, such as when there is a major market or festival in the area, they can be anything up to five times the price.

Travelling Korantia

Inn Rates

Room Type	Price (SP)
Dormitory room or camping space	0.2
Dormitory room and half board	0.5
Private room	2
Stabling per horse plus fodder	0.5
Other large livestock barn plus fodder	1
Bath	0.5

Travel Times

The length of an overland route is obviously greater than the straight-line distance. To quickly estimate the actual distance that needs to be travelled between two points on the map, refer to the Distance Modifier on the Travel Distances table. This provides a multiplier between 1.25 (Main Routes) and 2 (Trackless Wilderness) that is applied to the 'as the crow flies' distance between them.

The table also provides the distance that can normally be achieved in a day's travel for each terrain type, assuming reasonably favourable weather conditions and up to 10 hours of progress per day.

River Travel

Using a river involves travelling by water but meeting with land-based conditions and encounters. So long as a river is navigable for the type of craft being used, average travel distances over a 10-12 hour period are as follows:

River Travel Times (Korantine Miles per Day)

	Up Stream	Down Stream	Skill Test Grade
Weak/Slow Current	30	50	Hard
Medium Current	20	60	Standard
Strong/Fast Current	15	75	Easy
Roads	x1	45	30

Travel Conditions

Travelling by night is hazardous and difficult, and the achievable travel distance should be halved unless the travellers have recourse to special abilities or magic that allows them to operate as readily as in the day. There are also fixed obstacles that may prevent any movement – crossing a major mountain range may be an impossibility unless a known pass is used, or an expert guide can show the characters a way across by some trail known only to local shepherds. Rivers may be in full spate after heavy rains and even the usual fording places impassable.

Travel Times (Korantine Miles per Day)

	Distance Modifier	Hiking	Ox Cart	Mounted	Courier	Skill Test Grade
Wilderness	x2	20	N/A	20	N/A	Formidable
Open Country	x1.5	25	15	40	30	Hard
Main Routes	x1.25	30	20	45	60	Standard
Roads	x1	45	30	50	50	Easy

Distance Modifier: A multiplier to the straight-line distance between two points, to help the Games Master quickly determine the actual travel distance.

Hiking: Unencumbered travel on foot, including military units on the march without baggage, or mounted on slow animals such as a donkey.

Ox Cart: Encumbered travel on foot, baggage carried on a cart, a donkey or similar.

Mounted: Unencumbered travel on horseback or in a carriage.

Courier: Unencumbered travel on horseback with reduced rest periods and access to remounts.

Weather

Severe weather conditions reduce the rate of progress by 25% to 100% as determined by the Games Master.

Bad weather can cause serious problems on the road, or even bring all progress to a halt by placing obstacles in the travellers' path. Wind storms can throw trees across the route, torrential rain can spark flash floods; heavy snowdrifts, sandstorms, dense fogs and the like can also make travel difficult and dangerous. An extended period of rain may threaten to make the ground too soft for wheeled transport, or make rivers and streams break their banks, and even in civilised Korantia, there is little in the way of sophisticated engineering technology to manage the problem. In these circumstances, the action may need to move to combat rounds or local time to deal with the hazard.

Exceeding Typical Travel Distances

If in pursuit of a foe, hurrying to arrive somewhere in time to save the day or running from an enemy, it is necessary to try to cover the ground more quickly. This is a simple matter of expending fatigue to get you there quicker (see MYTHRAS page 69). In real terms, the travellers either continue on for longer or force a hurried pace. Once fatigue starts to build up, additional rest time must be taken and travelling hours cut to recover.

Skills rolls such as Boating, Drive, Ride, Locale and Survival may be called for on a regular basis. The Games Master should adjust the difficulty levels suggested if accounting for tougher than usual conditions. If travelling with baggage animals or wheeled transport, a Drive roll is required; if mounted or courier, a Ride roll is needed, or no extra distance can be gained. Fumbles in these rolls may result in a lame animal that needs to be properly treated or, if the party needs to keep moving, cut loose, or a broken wheel or axle that forces a stop for repairs.

SEA TRAVEL

Travelling by sea is the fastest, and usually one of the safest means to cover long distances and explore foreign lands, and is without doubt the cheapest and best means to move a cargo. Many ships can make their way for a full 24 hour period, so significant distances can be covered in a relatively short time.

On the other hand, sailing for extended periods of time in the open ocean and out of easy reach of a safe port or harbour is highly dangerous. If a ship gets into trouble with the weather, waves or wildlife it can be easily be fatal for everyone aboard.

Sailing in Strategic Time

When an adventure involves travel by sea it is often a good idea to stay in Strategic Time, and allow that the journey is completed as expected. As a rule of thumb, Strategic Time is used when the total time taken for the journey is what matters, and the voyage is an interlude in an adventure rather than part of it – something to be handled quickly before progressing with the action.

To work out roughly how long a voyage should take, assume that the typical ship under sail can travel 200km in 24 hours. When working around coasts and islands, the rate is a little slower, producing an average rate of more like 150km per day.

Oared vessels such as war galleys normally travel under sail anyway, using the rowing crew for bursts of speed, or to keep the boat moving in a calm. However, assuming a fresh crew and relatively good conditions, a galley may be able to sustain 130-150km in a 10-12 hour working day, meaning that in coastal waters the galley can make equivalent distance to a sailing ship and still be able to put in for the night.

Exceeding Travel Distances

Sailing speed cannot be increased unless the winds and weather make it so. For oared ships, the captain can gain extra distance either by pushing the pace or denying proper rest breaks to the crew, in either case gaining up to 50% additional distance at the expense of a level of fatigue per day. Of course, an undead crew can row indefinitely, being immune to fatigue.

Taking a Ship

There are no scheduled passenger services. Except for specialist military vessels, the main purpose of all ships travelling between ports is to transport a cargo. People who intend to travel by boat need to go to the docks and find out which vessels are sailing in the direction they want to go and see if they can negotiate passage. Of course those who have unlimited funds can charter a vessel for the journey and thereby dictate when it sails.

Passage on a ship is not necessarily very expensive. Assuming the passengers provide their own food and are prepared to sleep on deck – often the only option – assume a cost of 1-2SP per person per day, depending on the quality of the ship and the comforts it can afford. Large animals take up a lot of cargo space and care, which amounts to approximately 8SP per horse per day.

Travelling Korantia

Charters can be had from 15SP per day for a small vessel with a three-man crew, and can easily go up to 250SP per day for a larger vessel with an expert captain and a complement of 25 crew.

Sailing Distance

The sailing distance between two points at sea is almost never a straight line, due to the effect of wind and currents, and the actual speed of a ship is often different in each direction for the same reason, so the Games Master can use some discretion in deciding exactly how long a journey can take. Some typical travel distances and times are provided on the table below. Bear in mind that these are continuous days' sailing, and many of these journeys are routinely broken with layovers at ports along the route. The round trip for a Sharranketan galleon of the House of Zamada, from Homora to Janisdaron via Albulo, which averages 36 days at sea, usually takes a full three to four months once you take stops into account.

To achieve these times requires that the sailing conditions are good; if for any reason, the Games Master judges the conditions are not ideal – whether due to poor winds or a failed Navigation roll – the Adverse Conditions modifier is applied.

Sailing in Local Time

A great deal of fun can be had adventuring at sea rather than just treating the ocean as a thing to be crossed. In order to do that, it is necessary to go into a little more detail about ships and sailing. When sailing in local time the distance and route is plotted, and the time taken to reach a destination calculated according to the vessel's movement speed, the sailing conditions, and the captain's Navigation skill.

Navigation

The essential skill to get a vessel from one place to another is Navigation. If the journey is a short hop (less than three days) between locations well known to the captain of the ship, the roll should be Easy, or if it is a simple journey along a familiar coast on which land and landmarks are always in sight, then the roll should be Very Easy, or treated as an Automatic Success.

If the Navigation roll succeeds, then the ship will arrive at its destination at more or less the expected day, unless encounters or disasters of seamanship prevent it from doing so. Should it fail then a suitable delay is placed on the ship's arrival at its destination, perhaps resulting in more encounters; the skill is then rerolled, with each failure adding further delay. If the roll is fumbled than the Games Master should feel free to declare the ship has gone wildly astray and come up with a suitable bit of empty ocean, or an unknown shore, for the ship to find itself upon before the crew realise they have gone wrong.

Sailing Conditions

The weather is a fundamental consideration for anyone trusting their life and fortune to a sea-going vessel. While weather conditions may be capricious and unpredictable, the truth is that in most cases a sea captain waits for conditions to be favourable before setting out on a voyage and hopes that they may remain so. On the whole, people do not sail at all during the winter when the weather is both more unpredictable and capable of greater extremes. Thennla has a fixed set of seasons that occur more or less at the same time across the world, albeit with much variation in the range and variability of temperatures and precipitation that may occur according to local climate and conditions.

Fair Wind Sailing Table

Route	Days Voyage Out	Days Voyage Return	Sailings	Adverse Conditions Modifier (days)
Sarestra to Kipsipsindra	9	12	Weekly	+ 1d4
Mersin to Keba	3	3	Monthly	+ 1d2
Kipsipsindra to Haprosindra	10	12	Monthly	+ 1d6
Kipsipsindra to Errabna	7	10	Seasonal	+ 1d4
Sarestra to Thyrta	3	4	Seasonal	+ 1d2
Kipsipsindra to Zarendra	21	30	Seasonal	+ 2d8
Himela to Tempigone	4	4	Annual	+ 1d3
Keba to Hispola	5	6	Seasonal	+ 1d3
Homora to Mikosso	16	18	Annual	+ 2d6
Albulo to Janisdaron	5	5	Annual	+ 1d3

The Sailing Conditions Table table gives a general idea of what sort of conditions are encountered. In most cases, it is a matter of waiting in port until a good moment to set out to sea. Of course, sometimes there is no choice but to risk whatever the gods bring.

Changing Weather

The weather is quite capable of changing during a voyage. Rather than roll for weather conditions every day, assume that the rolled weather will remain the same for 1d4 days in winter, 1d8 days in summer, and 1d6 days in spring or autumn.

Wind Damage

Wind damage is inflicted daily if the weather is bad enough. The damage inflicted by the wind, during gales for instance, is calculated by taking the Wind Strength value and cross-referencing it against the Damage Modifier table on page 9 of the MYTHRAS rules. Thus damage only ensues when the STR reaches 26 or more. However, the Armour Points of the vessel reduce this damage.

Boating and Seamanship

When travelling in Local time, Boating and Seamanship become vital skills. Whoever is in charge of running an ocean-going ship must have the Seamanship skill. Boating is used for smaller craft, but at a minimum of one grade of difficulty harder if on the open ocean rather than on rivers, lakes or inshore. These skills are only tested when the ship encounters a hazard or there is a situation that requires a response from the captain and crew.

Ships and Galleys

Single-mast square-rigged vessels, sometimes supplemented by oars, are the standard maritime technology but without magical assistance, they are at the mercy of prevailing winds and currents to set their speed of progress. The biggest Korantine vessels are all merchantmen, of which the very largest are over 50 metres long with a capacity of 1,000 tons. Typical merchant ships are between 15 and 30 metres long carrying cargoes of 75–500 tons.

Sailing Conditions Table

Spring	Summer	Autumn	Winter	Wind Type	Distance Modifier	Seaworthiness Roll
01	01-02	01	-	Dead Calm	No movement unless under oar	Easy
02-04	03-05	02-03	01-02	Poor Wind	Reduce by One Third	Standard
05-07	06-08	04-05	03-07	Contrary Winds	Reduce by Half	Standard
08-12	09-14	06-09	07-08	Good	No Adjustment	Easy
13-15	15-16	10-12	09-11	Following Wind	Increase by Half Again	Standard
16-18	17-19	13-17	12-14	Heavy Seas, Violent Winds	Reduce by Half	Hard
19-20	20	18-20	15-20	No Sailing	Reduce to One Tenth	Formidable

Calm: Insufficient wind to provide impetus for the sails.

Poor Winds: The winds are weak; vessels under sail struggle to make enough speed. Wind STR is 2d8-1

Contrary Winds: The wind is blowing in the wrong direction, and requires tacking (a zig-zagging course). Wind Strength is 2d8+14

Good: A good wind blows from the right quarter. Wind Strength is 2d8+29

Following Wind: A powerful tail wind will give the vessel a fast ride across the ocean. Wind Strength is 2d8+44

Heavy Seas, Gale force conditions on the very edge of manageable. If the captain fails a Hard Seamanship roll the ship will go badly off course. Wind Strength is 4d8+57

No Sailing: Conditions are dangerous due to fierce storms, poor visibility or other problems. No captain will take his ship out on that day unless forced to or provided with dependable magic or divine help. Ships start stacking up in port waiting for better weather. If already at sea a vessel's Range (the frequency in days in which Seaworthiness must be rolled) is halved. The captain must make a Formidable Seamanship roll to hold his course. Prevailing Wind STR is 4d8+87.

Military ships and some private transport are galleys, of which the biggest examples are Korantine vessels with over 300 rowers. The disadvantage of a galley – in addition to paying all those rowers – is that they are crammed full of people. These vessels cannot carry much cargo nor sustain themselves at sea for very long and need to beach regularly to give the crew proper rest and space to prepare food and so forth. Ideally, this happens every night.

Ship Class

For game purposes, every waterborne craft is categorised as one of three basic classes according to its purpose, available tools and materials for construction, and the prevailing technology. The huge variety of circumstances, conditions and technologies that may be encountered mean that many variations and hybrid types exist, and frequent bouts of competitive escalation in vessel size and magical enhancement have also produced some interesting departures from the standard models.

Seaworthiness

The class is the primary factor in determining a vessel's Seaworthiness, a percentage score that acts like an Endurance skill to resist damage from wind, waves and other hazards. A good captain takes care with his ship – and can augment the Seaworthiness roll with his Seamanship skill. If the roll succeeds, then no harm is done. If the roll is failed the vessel takes on water, suffers stress to its timbers or sails – or simply suffers overall wear and tear that requires maintenance and repair.

The three basic classes of vessel are as follows:

Utility

The craft is designed for a very specific purpose or with restricted access to materials, and cannot be expected to stand up well to damage and punishment when in situations it was not designed for. On the other hand, a utility vessel may provide its crew with an easier grade skill roll when performing the task it is designed for, and to gain the same advantage itself if a Seaworthiness roll is called for.

The basic Seaworthiness for a Utility craft is 30%.

Galley

The ship is proportionally long for its width (beam), with a ratio of approximately 5 or 6:1, sometimes even more. A galley is built for speed and to accommodate plenty of rowing positions along its length, and with high sides if it is to accommodate more than one bank of oars. Galleys are shallow draft and can usually be beached (dragged onto the shore) as well as ride at anchor. A galley's specialist design results in some compromise to its stability, or perhaps makes it more fragile. Each vertical bank of oars after the first increases the ship's Size but can also reduce the vessel's seaworthiness.

Most galleys are either warships or private yachts. A war galley is typically 30-40m in length, and 5-6m across the beam. With a full crew at the oars it can produce sprint speeds, which increase ramming damage, but also allow it to overtake or outmanoeuvre a vessel dependent on sail alone.

Merchant galleys, with a smaller rowing crew manning perhaps 10 oars to the side and cargo capacity for between 100 and 200 tons, are commonly used for shipping goods up and down the the larger rivers, but are also used at sea. They are not capable of the sprint speeds that a war galley or sleek yacht can deliver, but have the same advantages when making a voyage in calm weather. Galleys cannot risk going out onto the water on a 'no sailing' day any more than a sailing ship can.

The basic Seaworthiness for a galley is 50%, however, the bigger it is, the less seaworthy. For every Size above Large, a galley's Seaworthiness is reduced by 10%. Archipelagan warboats are something of a hybrid between Galley and Transport, having some of the advantages of both, and have a Seaworthiness rating of 70%.

Transport

The vessel is optimised for carrying a cargo; hence, it typically has a lower length to width ratio (circa 4:1 but Sharranketan Galleons are more like 2.5:1), and deeper draught. Such vessels are usually the most resilient to heavy seas, but have to be anchored off shore or berthed in a harbour rather than beached.

The basic Seaworthiness of a Transport vessel is 70%.

Range

A vessel has a Range of one tenth of its Seaworthiness. The Range is the amount of time in days it can remain on the open sea – including riding at anchor outside a sheltered harbour, before it begins to suffer from the effects of the elements and general wear and tear. Whenever a ship is at sea for a period longer than its Range, it must make a Seaworthiness test. It must make a further test if it exceeds its Range x2, a third if it exceeds its Range x3 and so forth.

Ship Condition

Failed Seaworthiness tests always result in a reduction in the ship's Condition – similar to when a character suffers from fatigue – that requires measures such as drying out the hull, repairs, re-caulking, careening and so forth to reverse. If too much deterioration is allowed to accumulate, eventually the vessel ships too much water and begins to sink. A brand new vessel starts life as Ship-Shape, and once this has deteriorated, then it needs to undergo repairs and refitting to bring it back up to top condition. However, if it has suffered damage to its Hit Points, it can never be restored to full seaworthiness unless the Hit Point damage is repaired first.

Ship-to-Ship Combat

Much of the time a contest between two vessels is in reality a combat conducted between their crews, which can be run according to the rules provided in MYTHRAS. Nevertheless, the maneouvering that takes place to get into a position where one vessel can attack another – whether to grapple, or ram, or line up a shot for an on-board siege weapon – is most easily dealt with using opposed Seamanship rolls between the two captains. In these cases, it can be helpful to have a few further details on hand about the ships.

Ship Statistics

All ships have the following Attributes:

Movement Rate

All waterborne craft have a basic movement rate of 12m per combat round. Oared vessels can achieve higher speeds if all hands are at the oars.

Size

A rough measure of the relative bulk of a vessel. The Size tells you whether this vessel is vulnerable to attack from collisions with other vessels, or can shrug off damage; just as when comparing weapon sizes in a parried attack.

Vessels that are suitable for just one person have a size rating of P for Personal.

Hit Points

Size also determines how many dice are used to calculate the ship's Hit Points. Hit Points are an abstract measure of the ship's size and structure. This tells you how much damage the vessel can take before it is in danger of breaking up.

Each time a ship receives one third of its Hit Points in damage its Condition automatically deteriorates by one step. Thus once a ship reaches zero Hit Points it is either Swamped or Sinking.

Ship Condition Table

Condition	Speed	Skill Modifier	Repair And Refit Modifier	Range
Ship Shape	-	Standard	-	
Seaworthy	-	Standard	x1	-25%
Battered	-25%	Hard	x2	-50%
Swamped	-50%	Formidable	x3	-75%
Sinking	-100%	Herculean	x4	-100%

Condition: The vessel's state of repair.

Speed: The effect of the ship's condition on its movement rate.

Skill Modifier: The effect of the ship's condition on its handling, applied as a difficulty modifier to Seaworthiness, Seamanship or Boating rolls.

Repair and Refit Modifier: Whether dealing with Hit Point Damage or Condition, repairing a vessel requires the entire crew to undertake an extended task with a basic Task Round Unit of an hour for a Personal vessel, six hours for a Small vessel, a day for a Medium size vessel, two days for large, four days for Huge, and so on. The Repair and Refit Modifier acts as a multiplier to the duration of the Task Round Unit.

Range: Once a vessel starts taking on water, it needs regular bailing and other action by the crew to prevent deterioration. The result is a decrease in its Range.

If the vessel continues to take damage and reaches a negative score equal or greater than its starting Hit Points, it breaks up completely.

Armour Points

Like any inanimate object a vessel's armour points are a function of its construction materials:

Bark, Skins, Leather	1
Reeds	3
Wood Planking	4
Seasoned Timber	6
Heavy Timbers	8
Hull sheathing	+2 (each +2 reduces the vessel's Seaworthiness by 10%)

Damage

The damage a vessel inflicts on another ship or a creature when there is a collision, is dependent on its Size.

A vessel's damage dice are based on the damage it will inflict if moving at a normal speed and striking an object that is not fixed in place such as another ship or a creature in the water. If moving at ramming speed add 1d6, if moving at a slow speed reduce damage by half.

When two ships collide, their relative size is compared, and the damage inflicted adjusted accordingly in exactly the same way as when comparing parry damage.

If hitting rocks or a hidden reef, the ship's Size-based damage is used against itself – however, shallow draft vessels might gain a significant reduction in the right circumstances.

Crew

The minimum crew for a vessel is also a function of Size. Certain boats (Size P) are made to only require (or accommodate) a single crewman. A Small vessel has a minimum crew of 3, Medium of 5, Large of 10, Huge 15, Enormous 25, Colossal 40. A craft being handled by an undersize or skeleton crew makes Seamanship rolls at least one grade harder.

For larger oared vessels such as galleys, bear in mind that oars are not the basic propulsion but a substitute for sail or an adjunct. As a result it is the sailing crew that determines whether there are sufficient hands to manage the vessel. When the ship is in a situation where the oarsmen are required, then penalties for reduced rowing crew may apply.

Ship Quality

Seaworthiness and other attributes can be improved – or, indeed, reduced – by using the Manufacturing and Quality rules provided in MYTHRAS (see MYTHRAS page 65). Spells, enchantments and other factors may also make a difference.

AP: Add 1 per enhancement

HP: Add the minimum of the dice being rolled, counting each +6 as an additional die (so 4d6+60 becomes 4d6+74) per enhancement

For example, Enhancement provides +1 per dice (4), and +1 per +6 added to the dice (10). In this case 4d6+60 becomes when enhanced 4d6+60+14 = 4d6+74.

Seaworthiness: Increase by +5% per enhancement

If a boat builder or shipwright fails to properly complete the extended task project to build a vessel, the effect is usually to reduce the vessel's Seaworthiness.

Crew Quality

The quality of a ship's crew (their average skill) affects the difficulty of the captain's Seamanship rolls, with a skill of 26-50% delivering Hard rolls. A green crew with an average seamanship skill of less than 26% is at a Formidable grade. Professional crews of 51-75% has no effect on the Seamanship roll, while 76% and above make the roll Easy.

Other Features

There are many ways to augment or improve a ship – some examples are given here.

Ships with Personality

As a major construction and something that people place a great deal of faith in, it is common to invest a vessel with personal attributes – and in MYTHRAS this can of course mean actually binding a spirit into it to literally bring it to life. The Archipelagans use an Awaken Miracle to summon one or another deity to inhabit their ships – or even a part of the ship, such as the spur or ram.

Ships as Temples and Shrines

Larger vessels are routinely consecrated, and a sea captain may well act as a priest for his crew (at the very least being of acolyte status). Korantine ships are generally consecrated to Pyrolus.

Shores of Korantia

Vessel Types and Statistics

Vessel	Class	Size	Armour Points	Hit Points	Damage
Raft, Small	U	P	4	1d6+3	-
Kayak	U	P	1	1d6+6	-
Dugout	U	P	8	1d6+6	-
Rowing Boat	U	P	4	1d6+6	-
War Canoe	U	S	1	1d6+6	-
Small Fishing Boat or Skiff	U	S	4	1d6+9	-
Raft, Large	U	M	4	2d6+6	1d3
Reed Galley	U	M	3	2d6+12	1d4
River Transport	T	M	4	2d6+18	1d6
Archipelagan Warboat	G	M	4	2d6+18	2d6
Small Merchantman	T	L	4	2d6+30	2d6
Small Galley	G	H	6	3d6+24	3d6
Medium Merchantman	T	H	6	3d6+30	3d6
Trireme	G	E	6	4d6+60	4d6
Large Merchantman	T	E	6	4d6+72	4d6
Hexareme	G	C	6	5d6+90	5d6
Grain Transport	T	C	8	5d6+120	5d6
Sharranketan Galleon	G	BC	8	6d6+150	6d6

Ship's Weaponry

Ships can be fitted with weapons with which to hurl missiles at enemy vessels, or to give them an edge in ship to ship combat.

Rams

A galley can be augmented with a ram, which adds +1 Damage per dice it can inflict on an enemy vessel. Hence a Trireme at ramming speed will do 5d6+5 Damage when it strikes an enemy ship.

A ram enables the Sunder Special Effect and also enables the naval equivalent of the Bleed Special Effect. If the attacker's player gains Special Effects and chooses Breach Hull, the defender must make an immediate Opposed roll of the ship's Seaworthiness against the original attack (Seamanship) roll. If this fails, the defender is now holed below the waterline, and until some emergency measures or repairs are taken must make a further Seaworthiness roll every 15 minutes or the ship's Condition will deteriorate.

Siege Weapons

Sufficiently large ships may mount a single siege weapon. The size of the siege weapon carried cannot exceed the ship's own without causing stability problems; for every step by which this limit is exceeded, all Seamanship and Seaworthiness rolls are one grade harder. Conversely, mounting a siege weapon smaller than the maximum permitted, allows one extra weapon per step difference between the two. Thus a Small Galley permitted to mount a single mangonel, could install two ballistae instead.

Siege Weapons Table

Siege Weapon	Size
Scorpion	M
Ballista	L
Mangonel	H
Onager	E
Couillard	C
Trebuchet	BC

Elementals

Sylphs and undines are important resources when at sea. They assist in movement, and have many other uses – for example a large enough undine can be used to raise a ship above a reef, or swamp an enemy vessel; a sylph can fill the sails in a calm or shred an enemy's canvas. They can provide motive power to a ship that is becalmed or has lost its oars.

Ship Elementals Table

Vessel Size	Minimum Elemental Required	
	Spell Intensity	Spirit Intensity
Personal	2	1
Small	4	2
Medium	6	3
Large	8	4
Huge	10	5
Enormous	12	6
Colossal	14	7
Beyond Collosal	16	8

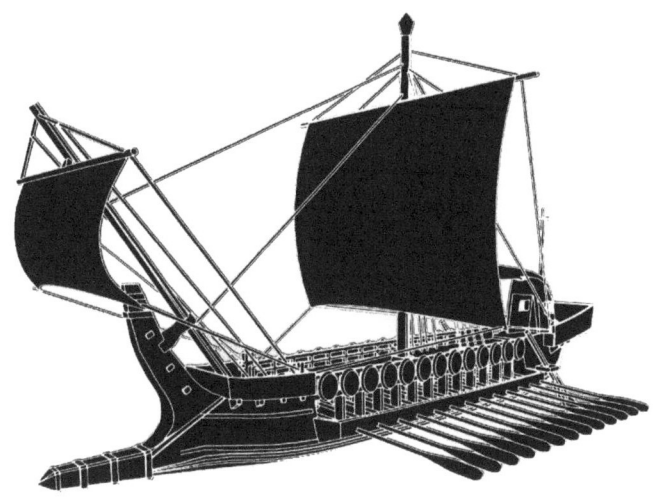

Summoned and Bound Elementals

The use of an Elemental Summoning miracle together with Extension – or an Evoke Elemental spell with sufficient Duration or Enchant applied – can enable a captain to make use of the power of an elemental for the full length of a voyage. So long as the Intensity of the Summoning or Evokation magic matches the minimum requirements (see the Ship Elementals table), then the conjured elemental will affect the vessel.

A Sylph filling the sails can make the winds blow stronger or safer, improving the ambient sailing conditions by one step (see page 110), depending on the caster's wishes. Every two Intensities the slyph is larger than the minimum (or one Intensity if using bound elemental spirits), this bonus in increased by an additional step

An Undine on the other hand can be used to float and propel a vessel, providing motive power equivalent to a Poor Wind enabling it to make progress without either sail or oar. It can also reduce a ship's draft whilst crossing shallows, refloat it if grounded, and prevent the ship from sinking if it is holed.

Smaller sylphs or undines can stack their strength together as a substitute for a sole larger one, but in this case the number of lesser intensity elementals must be equal to the square of 1 plus the shortfall in Intensity. For instance a Viking ship requiring a Summon Sylph miracle of minimum Intensity 8 to boost its sailing speed, could instead use four Intensity 7 sylphs to substitute, or nine Intensity 6 slyphs, and so on, all the way to sixty-four sylphs of Intensity 1.

In the case of Animism, bound elementals confer the same advantages as summoned ones, save that the effects are permanent until the binding is broken. See the Ship Elementals table for the alternate Intensity value required for binding spirits into a vessel.

Animist Binding

Animists tend to vest a vessel with an Animus – to bring it alive with an allied or awakened Fetch that gives it consciousness. Any spirit controlled by the fetch can apply its effects to the vessel itself. As with elementals the Intensity of the spirit should be in keeping with the size of the vessel for it to fully exert whatever powers it has; alternatively different parts of a ship – the sail, helm, prow or ram – might be invested with different spirits. Typical choices are Ancestor Spirits, Elemental Spirits and certain Nature Spirits. A suitable spirit should be able to grant enhancements to a vessel just as a Nature Spirit would do; this could be anything from increased Seaworthiness, Armour Points or Hit Points to additional Group Luck points to the passengers or personal Luck Points for the captain.

Flying Ships and Submarines

It is possible for a big enough sylph to hold a vessel aloft, enabling it to fly through the air, or for a big enough undine to wrap itself around the vessel, holding water at bay while it moves beneath the waves. The basic requirement for this is a single elemental of an Intensity three times that required to assist the vessel's movement. The last reported example of this was the warboat of Zikrik the Blue whose vessel, complete with a fighting crew of 20 men, attempted to travel through the clouds to the stronghold of Mororsi the True and rob him of his treasure in a surprise attack. Unfortunately for Zikrik, the wily Mororsi had a pet priest of Palaskil who got wind of the attack and robbed Zikrik and his crew of their Sylph, which brought them crashing down to an untimely end.

Archipelegan Pirate Captain. Note the fine Turtle Armour

ENCOUNTERS

Sometimes a journey is an adventure in itself, and either there is genuine jeopardy involved in getting from place to place in time and in safety, or the environment through which the characters travel presents its own challenges and opportunities.

Whenever characters travel somewhere, there is a good chance they will have encounters along the way. Even if an encounter is mundane – perhaps coming across fellow travellers, farmers in a field, some game animals – it should be given some significance. At the very least, it can provide the Games Master with some narrative ideas to help describe the journey before moving the action along to the next locale.

Encounter Chance

The Games Master should determine the probability of an encounter according to the needs of his game and the style of play of the group. The default is a 20% chance of a significant encounter, checked for in the morning, in the afternoon and at night. The frequency of checking for encounters should be increased if in a busy place where a lot is going on, and reduced if in a desolate wilderness or on the open ocean with no signs of life for miles around, to a minimum of one roll per day.

Special Encounters

There is always a chance for a 'Special' encounter, an unusual or exotic event, or an opportunity to stage a 'random' encounter that has a direct bearing on the character's chosen goals. In the following tables, a Special encounter occurs on a roll of 00; however, you may wish to increase the frequency in order to increase the pace of key events in the campaign, especially if you do not spend much time in play on the process of travelling. One simple approach is to allocate 99 and 00 to a Special encounter result, and another is to allocate all doubles (11, 22, 33 and so forth) to either a Games Master-dictated event or a Special encounter from the tables.

JOURNEYS IN KORANTIA

When travelling through Korantine lands, use the Roads Encounter Table (page 118) to generate random encounters, depending on the nature of the route taken. The Encounters are described below.

Abandoned Property

Tumbledown cottages or farm buildings, fields left to grow wild, empty pastures. For some reason this land has fallen out of use and its former occupants have been taken away or have moved on.

Beggars

1d10 destitute folk who beg the characters for coin, food or anything that can be of material help. Their condition may be the result of a natural disaster that has ruined their livelihoods; or perhaps they are the slaves of a neglectful master or the tenants of a greedy and inhumane landlord.

Hazard

Depending on the terrain and season, the way ahead has been washed away by a flood, blocked with trees brought down in a storm, made treacherous by a landslide, earthquake and so

Shores of Korantia

Roads Encounter Table

Well-Populated and Major Routes	Rural Backwaters and Minor Routes	Encounter
01-03	01-08	Abandoned property
04-07	09-12	Beggars
08-09	13-14	Hazard
10-14	15-16	Inn or Stopping Place
15-19	17-24	Inquisitive Locals
20-21	25-26	Lanthrus-Stones
22-23	27-30	Large Game
24-53	31-63	Locals about their business
54-55	64	Merchants
56-58	65	Messengers
59-61	66-67	Official and Retinue
62-69	68-72	Peddlers
70-71	73	People of Status
72-74	74	Pilgrims
75-76	75-80	Robbers
77-79	81-82	Rustic Shrine
80-86	83-93	Small Game
87-90	94-96	Soldiers
91-93	97	Thieves
94-99	98-99	Travellers
00	00	Special

forth. Going forward requires skills rolls to negotiate safely. There is a 30% chance of another encounter caught up in, dealing with, or taking advantage of, the hazard.

Inn or Stopping Place

A place with facilities for passing traffic, including shelter for livestock, access to food and water, possibly just a house, hamlet or farm situated by the roadside equipped for the purpose as a sideline, but a 30% chance there is actually an inn where travellers can get proper board and bed, even perhaps a bath. If an Inn, roll 1d3 times on the Encounter Table to determine who else might be there.

Inquisitive Locals

Some locals who have a reason to take an interest in the characters – to sell them something, ask for their help, plague them for information or news, or find out if there is reason to be suspicious of them.

Lanthrus-Stones

These cairns are good luck for weary travellers. All that is asked is that you add a stone to the pile, or restore some that have fallen down, if you stop there to rest. Performing this rite (making a Rites (Korantine) roll) and giving 1 Magic Point reduces the recovery period for fatigue by one level.

Large Game

The characters are lucky enough to come across a wild pig or deer – game that is of substantial value if brought down and butchered, either directly as meat and skins, etc, or taken to market for sale (countryside only).

Locals about their Business

Farmers in their fields or driving carts of produce or equipment from one part of their land to another; woodsmen at work coppicing or cutting timber; perhaps, a gardener with a donkey-load of produce heading to market; a band of local men out hunting; women fetching water, washing clothes or working in the fields; or citizens on their way to town for market, or to attend a religious rite, including participating in elections and jury service.

Encounters

Merchants

Each merchant with 1d3 assistants or slaves and, if (70% chance) carrying significant goods or cash to a value of 1d4 x 1,000SP, one or more guards or bodyguards (assume 1 guard per 1,000SP of value or fraction thereof). Roll 1d6 for type:

1d6	Merchant Type
1-3	Commodities such as metals, bulk foodstuffs, cloth, dyes, hides or livestock in a large caravan of up to 50 draft or pack animals, wagons, and substantial numbers of wagonners and wranglers.
4	Specialist and luxury or imported goods such as fine finished metalwork, fine wines, premium textiles, spices, slaves; in a small caravan with 1d4 vehicles or strings of pack animals
5	Exotica such as ivory, precious or semi-precious stones, objets d'art, ritual and magical equipment, books and texts, specialist slaves, rare or exotic animals, rare examples of mundane goods; probably a single wagon or string of pack animals plus mounts for the merchant and his guards.
6	A large caravan of several merchants (roll 3 times and add together to determine the extent of the caravan). Road or settlement only, otherwise re-roll.

Messengers

1d3 messengers on foot or, if out in open country, on horseback. They are likely carrying a private communication between people of high status, conveying something of value (add 2d4 guards), or could be an official delegation (add 1d4 slave attendants and 1d3 guards).

Official and Retinue

Most likely a member of the local syndics: a tax-farmer surveying land, a market inspector checking on goods being offered for sale, or a revenue official intercepting inbound merchant traffic. The official is accompanied by 1d3 free or slave servants, a clerk and assistant, and there is a 30% chance that he has a bodyguard.

Peddlers

Itinerant traders with a cart that contains their wares or serves as a mobile workshop. Roll 1d6:

1d6	Peddler Type
1-3	Peddlers in goods such as clothing, pottery, useful items for the household, metalwork, leatherwork. Usually with a small cart pulled by mules or a donkey.
4-5	Itinerant craftsman offering both finished goods for sale and to perform simple work to order – repairs and so forth. Probably with a more substantial cart or wagon pulled by mules or oxen.
6	Specialist services such as a travelling band of musicians or prostitutes, a healer or apothecary.

People of Status

Some high-class folk going about their private business. If in rough territory, they are most likely a group of 1d4 men out hunting, accompanied by up to four times their number in attendants, slaves and beaters, as well as a brace of hunting dogs. There is a 60% chance the huntsmen are mounted. If in a more settled area or near to town, they are probably 1d4 members of the same family visiting their estates, holdings and tenantry, either on horseback or, if there are women and children, in wagons or coaches. There is a 30% chance they have armed protection, otherwise the men of the family and their attendants and slaves defend themselves.

Pilgrims

A group of people on their way to a religious site or festival. Since most religion in Korantia is organised for the citizens of a specific city-state, pilgrims are usually travelling to a healing shrine with a sick relative; or to seek an audience with a Sybil, one of them being perplexed by a question of great importance; or to a sporting festival, perhaps one of them being a competitor. They may be very serious about religious matters or little more than tourists. Roll 1d6:

1d6	Pilgrim Type
1-2	A single traveller or small group of pilgrims, possibly a family, 1d6 people in total
3-4	A small group travelling together, 1d4x10 in number
5-6	A large group numbering 1d10x10 and including people from many walks of life, including sub-groups, perhaps from different cities, who may not know or trust each other.

Robbers

While anyone may turn opportunistic robber if they encounter weaker folk than themselves on a lonely road, these people set out with the intent to rob, approaching the matter though open threats and violence. They only attack if they outnumber the number of victims who bear arms and expect to be successful. Robber gangs usually number 2d6+2 individuals.

Rustic Shrine

A little outdoor religious site to one of the local deities, probably Torthil or Sheylo if anywhere close to the city, a Pagan shrine if out in the boonies. The shrine consists of an altar decorated with flowers and set with carvings in stone or wood.

Small Game

An opportunity to take something worthwhile for the pot, perhaps wildfowl, rabbit or hare. They may be difficult to catch without some specialist techniques or knowledge.

Soldiers

If on home territory, they are patrolling, on guard or a posse in pursuit of criminals, bandits and raiders. Outside of their home territory, they are likely to be raiders, and will be happy to bully and rob folk who are not known to be friendly to their home city or community.

Thieves

1d6 thieves who will generally try to steal without threatening or using deadly violence unless this is needed to make an escape. They use stealth or deceit or a bit of both by distracting attention while pilfering. Probably posing as travellers, interested locals or anything else that sounds plausible (or roll again on this table to see what their disguise is), they will attempt to grab property and make off with it.

Travellers

A small group of people (1d10) passing through the region on the way to somewhere that is several days' journey distant, most likely heading to visit family to attend some event such as a wedding or funeral, to take care of a business matter, or perhaps to attend to a court case in which they have an interest in the outcome or are to provide testimony. May be very wary of strangers or, alternatively, are seeking companionship on the road, directions or help.

Special

Roll on the *Special Encounters* Table (page 122).

WILDERNESS ENCOUNTERS

A wilderness is a region with no (or at least negligible) permanent human settlement. There is usually a reason for this, involving inhospitable terrain, lack of resources for human survival, or the danger posed by mundane or supernatural inhabitants. Any people who are found there are outlaws, loners, hermits, hunters, woodsmen and explorers who have a compelling reason to venture beyond the edge of civilisation.

For most Korantines, the wilderness means the Ozryian Mountains, and patches of more or less sparsely populated backwaters that persist between some of the city-state territories. Those Korantines who live in colonies situated in less densely populated lands are rather more familiar with how extensive and desolate a true wilderness can be.

Sometimes, it is necessary to enter a wilderness area or to cross one to reach a foreign land, but almost by definition the wilderness is trackless, and so without an experienced guide or some form of magical assistance, it is very easy to get lost and into trouble. The best daily movement rate possible on land is that for open country. While those with horses may be able to use mounted movement where there are open plains, in all other circumstances the Hiking movement rate is used. If forced to pass through forest, wetlands, hills and mountain passes this rate is halved, and the Games Master can decide that an even greater penalty to movement is appropriate. In rough country wheeled vehicles are useless, and in some cases, mounted and courier travel is also impossible as horses have to be led. The best way to get through a wilderness is usually by river.

Whenever characters stray far from settled areas into hills, mountains and deep forests, use the Wilderness Encounter Table (page 121). The encounters are described below.

Feral Beast-Man

A beast-man such as a minotaur, boar-kin or faun that lives wild and feral amongst a group of its natural creature cousins. If in open country, perhaps a minotaur among a herd of wild ox; in the forest, a boar-kin accompanied by a herd of wild boar; in the mountains, a faun amongst mountain goats or perhaps even a panthotaur amongst mountain lions. The beast-man behaves as the alpha male of the group and can be aggressive in defence of mates, young or territory.

Hazard

Depending on the terrain and season, the way ahead has been washed away by a flood, blocked with trees brought down in a storm, made treacherous by a landslide, earthquake and so

Encounters

Wilderness Encounter Table

1D100	Encounter
01-02	Feral Beast-Man
03-10	Hazard
11-22	Hunters
23-27	Isolated Community
28-41	Large Game
42	Nymph
43-46	Outlaws
47-50	Predator
51-52	Raiders
53-55	Ruin
56-57	Satyr
58-82	Small Game
83-84	Wild Shrine
85-99	Woodsmen
00	Special

forth. Going forward requires skills rolls to negotiate safely. There is a 30% chance of another encounter caught up in, dealing with, or taking advantage of, the hazard.

Hunters
These are outsiders who come to the wilderness for the greater hunting opportunities presented, being 1d3 rich and/or noble characters from a nearby land and 1d4+2 companions, beaters and other followers for each of them.

Isolated Community
A tiny hamlet made up of simple log cabins or turf dwellings, and holding a community of 1d4+1 adults and 1d4+5 children and adolescents. These people have somehow chosen or been forced to make their home out in the middle of nowhere. They have survived by forming a close bond with some of the entities and intelligent creatures also found in the vicinity. Most likely they will avoid or hide from intruders, because they are generally very distrustful of people they don't know – which is practically everyone. While apparently fairly weak and harmless they can call on some very dangerous friends to defend them or to take revenge for a wrongdoing.

Large Game
The characters are lucky enough to come across a large wild herbivore such as boar, deer, goat or wild ox. Some of these are capable of turning the tables on a hunter, others are simply expert at flight and evasion in their home terrain.

Nymph
The characters have strayed into the home territory of a nymph. A standard Perception roll is enough to detect that there is some magical quality to the locale. A nymph will often manifest to, and be friendly towards, a group containing a male character with a CHA of 16 or higher. It will seek to harm or destroy those who cause damage or defile its home, or who are in some way a danger to those it likes.

Outlaws
1d6 outlaws, condemned men who are at risk of summary execution if caught in the vicinity of their home city, so are hiding out in the wilderness. Outlaws are desperate folk and will kill to secure their subsistence or to avoid being captured. They will generally have simple weapons and limited armour, if any.

Predator
Bears and wolves are the most common; however, there are still lions roaming below the tree line of the Ozyrian Mountains.

Raiders
There are slim pickings in the wilderness, but nevertheless these parts can be the ideal route through which to approach a settlement undetected. 1d10+10 Raiders may be on the way to their target, returning home with booty, fleeing from an unsuccessful attack or simply lost. These raiders are from a city or settlement not far from the edge of the wilderness, and their chief concern is livestock or human captives and readily portable wealth, although causing damage to property they cannot carry away may also feature in their plans.

Ruin
These ruins are very ancient and have been eroded or overgrown in such a way that they have merged with the landscape. Nevertheless, a little examination shows that they were once extensive in scale, and impressively built. They may be hundreds of years old – perhaps relics of the glory days of the Korantine Empire that nature has now reclaimed, or more ancient still, harking back to an era that is lost to human record. Ruins make an ideal lair for a creature, outlaw hangout or something supernatural; there is a 30% chance they are now inhabited by something potentially dangerous.

Satyr
Satyrs cannot help interfering with human travellers in lonely places, and enjoy sowing confusion – finding ways to lead people to danger, get them lost or spoil their supplies. Sometimes a satyr will manifest physically and directly interact with

characters, particularly if there are high (16+) CHA females in the party.

Small Game
An opportunity to take something worthwhile for the pot, perhaps wild fowl, rabbit or hare. Difficult to catch without some specialist techniques or knowledge

Wild Shrine
Whether a place of beauty or dread, this is a numinous spot where creatures and daemons of the wild – even the nymphs and satyrs – gather to honour a powerful local presence. The flora and fauna may behave in bizarre ways; intruders who fail to realise they are on hallowed ground may be first warned, then attacked if they fail to take heed. It is possible to locate Nature Spirits appropriate to the local deities or environment here.

Woodsmen
1d6 Hunters, trappers or wood cutters, almost certainly of pagan Thennalt origin, they have high Locale skills and are often hired as guides and beaters by outsiders who enter their world. These fellows exploit the wilderness for its resources and are a good source of information about it that can be useful for navigation and survival within it.

Special
Roll on the *Special Encounters* Table.

Special Encounters

These encounters represent stumbling into a situation that can be a mini-scenario or a campaign seed in its own right, and the examples provided here should be added to as required, or replaced once used.

Abandoned Shrine
A shrine that has fallen out of use, and, for some reason, is shunned or forgotten by the locals. Nevertheless, it has a spirit, and the spirit, whose name is Sontalos, wants to be restored to its glory days when it was given respect and offerings as the venerated representative of a god. Sontalos will manifest to anyone he deems an appropriate champion – someone who can help him find a home as part of a cult to a more powerful deity, resurrect some forgotten rite or even establish one for himself. Sontalos's powers are appropriate to the type of deity he is (or was) connected with and can include extensive Folk Magic as well as a unique Miracle he can teach to those who agree to

Special Encounters Table

1D100	Encounter
01-05	Abandoned Shrine
06-10	A Challenge
11-15	A Cry For Help
16-28	Airborne Predator
29-30	Army on the move
31-35	Beast-Man Gang
36-40	Desecrated Graveyard
41-50	Divine Portent
51-56	Foreign Raiders
57-61	Haunting
62-66	Important Non Player Character
66-72	Monstrous Predator
73-79	Old Tomb
80-84	Scene of a Fight
85-93	Supernatural Being
94-00	Supernatural Predator

worship or venerate him. He could be benign or evil, a useful allied spirit, or a constant irritation.

A Challenge
Arrithus of Agissene is an athlete who is making penance for cheating at a competition by challenging passers-by to come and match themselves against him in Brawn, Athletics or Unarmed skills (their choice). Arrithus attempts to tone down his prowess, and always competes with a skill no more than 20% higher than the character who accepts the challenge. If he loses, he repeats the challenge, offering the money he has accumulated over the years betting on his own victories if the character wins, but not holding back at all (Athletics 130%, Brawn 122%, Unarmed 115%). If beaten, he offers a pound (0.5kg) of gold to the victor.

A Cry for Help
A cry for help from a terrified woman, being pursued by one or more assailants seemingly intent on robbery or worse. If rescued, she is able to provide a substantial reward for her safety, whether in money, information relevant to the characters' quest, magical help or a magical charm that provides protection from spirits or sorcery. However, the 'victim' is actually a horror such as a lycanthrope, lamia, or someone possessed by a bad spirit that leads her to behave in an evil fashion as soon as the opportunity presents itself. It is possible that her pursuers had discovered the fact and that this accounts for their murderous intent.

Airborne Predator

A wyrm hunting far from its eyrie decides the characters or their animals are a tasty opportunity. Swooping down from above, the wyrm will attempt to make one or more passes from the air before landing to finish the job. If the wyrm is killed, the act may bring the characters wide recognition, as well as the bonus of the wyrmstone embedded in its skull that can be used to store 1d6+6 Magic Points.

Army on the Move

The first encounter is probably with outlying scouts or foragers, 1d6+6 skirmishers (rough terrain) or horsemen (open country), moving d6 km out from the main force, which consists of 2d6x500 troops and a baggage train incorporating one pack animal per 10 soldiers or one wagon per 100 soldiers. Within and close by Korantia, most such forces encountered will be the citizen army of one of the local city-states, going about the business of war with a rival or neighbour. Even if the army is that of a friendly power, these soldiers will be quick to 'requisition' supplies, mounts and equipment from the characters, or even try to press them into service. Roll 1d6:

1D6	Army Type
1	An army on its way to campaign in the territory of an enemy city
2	An army manoeuvring to intercept an enemy force (which may or may not materialise)
3	An army returning from campaign beaten and bedraggled, having lost a quarter of their number
4	Army returning from a campaign in good shape and laden with plunder and prisoners
5	An army en route to join with an allied force, perhaps for an exercise or to meet some serious threat requiring cooperative action (see 6, below)
6	A foreign army – Barbarians, Taskans or Jekkarenes, depending on which border is nearest, staging an attack. An invading force may not intend to occupy territory; in most cases it will be in search of victory and plunder before withdrawing.

Beast-Man Gang

Beast-men are all assumed to be magical creations in origin, but sometimes form successful breeding colonies or create gangs of mutant outcasts who cleave together for survival and companionship. This group is highly organised and well led. They may include both INS and INT-driven individuals within the same gang, always led by an INT-driven 'alpha'; or else are under the direction of a sorcerer or supernatural entity. The gang is made up of 1d6+4 beast-men. Humanity tends to persecute and hunt down such creatures, so they are invariably suspicious and hostile.

Desecrated Graveyard

This area or stretch of road is lined with cemeteries and tombs where funerary monuments to famous individuals and family mausoleums abound. Yet not far behind are the grave pits where the Pagan poor are buried in the earth without a stout stone tomb, and this has become the feeding place for a nest of ghouls. Since neither Korantines nor Thennalts normally cremate their dead, once a ghoul epidemic takes hold, it can get very serious before it is identified and dealt with. At present, there are 1d4+1 ghouls lurking in the vicinity. These ghouls are undead horrors created from individuals from an influential local Korantine family. The family's matriarch, one Drusima, has tried to keep the matter secret, and even knowingly sheltered the monsters in the family mausoleum. She has pressured her tenants to keep quiet or face eviction. Clearing out these horrors will win the enduring gratitude and respect of the local peasants, and expose Drusima and her family to shame and punishment for their wrongdoing.

Divine Portent

An eagle drops an object into a character's arms; or some immense apparition appears striding across the sky; or blood falls as rain; the sky turns dark as if night, or night appears as bright as day; the moon hides her face, or is eclipsed by the sun. Whatever the manifestation, a character or the whole party have experienced something that makes an important statement about their purpose or destiny, and consultation with someone such as a Sibyl may shed light on what it all means. A temporary bonus or penalty to the team's Group Luck Points is one way to describe an immediate change in fortune; or have each character roll their highest Devotion skill and remove or renew their Luck Points accordingly.

Foreign Raiders

A gang of foreign raiders intent on loot and pillage who have come from far afield. These 1d6+6 warriors under a fierce and cunning leader may be a small war band or the outliers for a much larger force. Encountering the characters is unexpected, and the raiders most likely want to deal with them quickly and prevent news of their presence being spread around. These raiders are not from the same culture as the characters but from

a hostile foreign power – perhaps Jekkarenes or Taskans – or from barbarian lands. Sheng horse-nomad war parties have been encountered on the fringes of Korantia, and barbarian Thennalts are inveterate raiders and looters.

Haunting

This place or stretch of road is the locus of a wraith, one that can generate a manifestation that appears physical to those whom it overcomes in a contest of the wraith's Willpower against the Insight of the target. He is – or was – Anselo, a robber, and can appear day or night. He will demand that a passing traveller leave a 'toll' of 1SP and one more for every beast, and may not harm anyone who complies. If someone tries to fight him, they may be in for a deadly surprise. Anselo's collected tolls are found in a hole under an ancient tree close by and amount to over 300SP. If Anselo kills someone with a higher POW than is own (14), that person will take his place as a wraith unless given a proper funeral using the Lay to Rest Miracle. Anselo's locus restricts him to a radius of 14m from the roadside tree at which he met his death at the end of a rope.

Important Non-Player Character

This encounter is a chance to meet a major Non-Player Character from the campaign setting by sheer coincidence. The meeting should be memorable to both sides, resulting in enmity, friendship or perhaps employment.

Monstrous Predator

Something big and dangerous has strayed into settled lands, probably in search of food, or perhaps driven out of its usual habitat. A pack of 1d6 giant spiders or a giant snake are the most likely candidates, for such creatures still lurk in the most out of the way places bordering Korantia. On the other hand, it could be much more ghastly or unexpected – a giant wolf (increase STR and SIZ to 1d6+18, bite Size L damage 1d8, skin/fur for 3 AP), or a pack of dire wolves, for example; but, if so, some god, sorcerer or whatever has probably caused it to be there.

Old Tomb

An ancient tomb, mostly overgrown. The fragmentary inscription in Korantine names the occupants as Mithralvos, his daughter Sulvi, and two others whose names are no longer legible. The entrance has been broken into, and within are scattered fragments of bone, pieces of coffin, broken drinking cups and other debris. If the characters take the trouble to clear the tomb, find broken fragments and put them back in the right place and clear away the undergrowth, an apparition will appear of a young girl with garlands in her hair who will give them a silent blessing. This blessing acts as a one-off bonus Luck Point (personal or group at the Games Master's discretion).

Scene of a Fight

The characters stumble upon the aftermath of a deadly combat. There are corpses left lying on the ground; their assailants are nowhere to be found, but have left tracks. Hidden in the undergrowth by one of his servants (Conceal 40%) is a survivor, an aristocrat called Hasimandias of Velthurisa. Hasimandias will try to stay hidden (Stealth 35%) and, if discovered, to hide his high status (Deceit 65%), terrified the party may also be a threat and add to his misfortunes. He is badly wounded and unless given immediate magical or medical help will soon succumb. He is in fact immensely rich, and a man of honour who will reward someone who rescues him with money, employment or the use of his influence in their favour.

Supernatural Being

An elf called Hepikokuni approaches the characters and attempts to open a dialogue with them. If he feels necessary he will swathe himself in a tatty cloak and try to disguise his nature (Conceal 45%). But beneath he is richly dressed in cloth that seems to be alive with intricate and abstract patterns that somehow reflect the environment around him and shimmer as he moves.

Hepikokuni offers to provide one or more of the characters with a boon or service – in exchange for performing a task of the Games Master's own choosing that may be routine (for a human) or grossly distasteful, such as a kidnapping a child that the elf then disappears with through a magical portal. Alternatively, the elf simply demands a Magic Point dedication and the observance of an obscure geas for a year and a day.

Use Characteristics for an elf from MYTHRAS, provided with Sorcery spells such as Phantom Sense, Shapechange, Switch Body and Portal, plus one or two spells suitable for attack and defence. Hepikokuni can dematerialise at the cost of one action point and 1 Magic Point, but cannot heal or recover Magic Points while in an ethereal state.

Supernatural Predator

Something evil stalks this place, and is intent on causing harm and plundering dead bodies for useful items and body parts. Denoladze is a hag, a nymph that has changed into some twisted abomination of life that is hostile to any human wishing to exploit her home territory. She has a penchant for stealing children and seeing them transformed into something she finds useful or amusing, and has access to her own Miracle to do just that. Like a nymph, she can control INS-driven creatures in her

ENCOUNTERS

domain and transform to an elemental – undines and gnomes are the most likely – and will depend on where this encounter takes place. Her locus is the roots of a twisted dead tree, a blasted stretch of moorland, or a stinking marsh.

CREATURES

Some of the encounter descriptions involve creatures not found in the bestiary provided in MYTHRAS, or ascribe nature and origins to the creatures there that have a twist unique to the setting. Details for those creatures are given here.

Beast-Men

These creatures do not share a common origin – some are sorcerer-made, some fashioned by spirits or gods. What they have in common is that some have found the ability to procreate through union with either the human or animal half of their nature. The result can be a feral, animal-natured progeny, or a creature with human-like intelligence and consciousness. Beast-men are almost always male, and capable of producing live young both with humans and with the animals they are related to. Reported beast-men include:

Boar-Kin

Very rare, and encountered only in the Forest of Sard and sometimes in remote areas nearby. Their origin is obscure, and thought to be either satyr-born like the goat-kin, sorcery-made or born of a powerful nature spirit living somewhere in Sard. Boar-kin do not form part of a gang, and are only encountered individually or accompanied by wild boar.

Centaurs

Centaurs are one of the most successful strains of beast-man. They claim to be god-made, thereby asserting a status akin to that of humans. Centaurs may be part of a developed culture of nomadic horse-herders (used for breeding mares) living by forage and hunting that roam in the north, found in Thurina and parts of Taygus and as far west as Kasperan. Centaurs are fierce and usually aggressive, antisocial and rather monstrous to look at, with a CHA of 2d6.

Fauns (Goat-Kin)

Whether related to some sort of deer or to a goat, these beast-men are the offspring of satyrs and human women. Despite being every bit as lecherous as their satyr progenitors, fauns cannot breed true, but they can sometimes produce degenerate (SIZ 1d6+6, STR 2d6+3) and feral (INS-driven) versions of themselves; a faun may be accompanied by a pack of such offspring. Fauns are also highly clubbable, and often consort with other beast-men, or with their satyr father. Use statistics provided in MYTHRAS for Chaos Hybrid with the chaotic and disease-bearing features removed. A faun has intrinsic knowledge of Folk Magic, 1d3+1 spells, cast at POW x3%.

Minotaurs

Minotaurs are usually solitary creatures, and thought incapable of breeding. Their origin is in Thennalt rituals involving earth magic, sacred cattle and ecstatic priestesses, and their appearance is deemed a blessing or a curse according to the circumstances of the conception. Minotaurs are considered sacrosanct by Thennalts, who will not generally admit them into their society and drive them away, but will not suffer a minotaur to be killed either.

Panthotaurs

A rare type of beast-man, found only in the wild hills and forests where mountain lions are also known to roam. Panthotaurs are assumed a sorcerous creation, and are always INT rather than INS-driven

Other Beast-Men

There are other types of man-beast monstrosity in the world that have not been encountered in or around Korantia. Lizardmen appear to be entirely sorcerous in conception, and do not breed but can be hatched by a wizard who knows the necessary rites and who will subsequently control them. Their purpose is essentially to provide minions to a sorcerer whose behaviour so beyond the pale, or whose lair is so far from civilisation, that he cannot assemble a coterie of human followers. Lizardmen have never yet been seen in Korantia, and are exotica of the South. Stories are told of Ophidians who inhabit some of the wild locales of the exotic West, but these may be no more than folklore; the notion of a race of such creatures who have culture and magic of their own inhabiting desert islands in the vast ocean is unsettling.

Nymphs

A nymph is a supernatural entity that is bound to a locus in the Material World, in almost all cases a natural feature such as a pool or spring, woodland grove, mountain, meadow or stream. When a nymph materialises (manifests in physical; form) she appears as a beautiful human woman, but there will always be tell-tale signs that she is somehow supernatural as her inhuman level of POW and CHA shines through.

Nymphs have a long history of interaction with humans, and even celebrate marriage with mortal men. The children of such unions are generally mortal, but often have at least one enhanced Characteristic, and perhaps a Gift or exceptional talent. A nymph is not always friendly, and will use her power against those who she considers to be a threat to natural features and creatures in her care – or even just towards those who offend her personally.

The exact type and boundaries of her territory depend on the landscape or feature concerned. A nymph can exercise her powers – using Folk Magic and controlling the creatures who live there – within a range of POW metres from the central point of her locus without manifesting physically. Beyond this limit, and up to the extent of her territory at POW x10m from her locus, she must materialise to act. If a nymph ever travels beyond this limit, she will begin to fade, losing 1 Magic Point per hour and unable to regain Magic Points until she returns home. When her Magic Points reach 1, she automatically dematerialises and returns to her locus. The only way the nymph can be taken away from her locus in spirit form is if she is bound.

Nymphs are powerful in their home environment, can manifest at will and can use Beastcall and Pet on any INS-driven creature that lives there no matter what its SIZ. Some nymphs are capable of turning themselves into an elemental, usually an undine or Gnome, with a SIZ of 1 cubic metre per Magic Point spent.

A nymph knows Folk Magic and as these are inherent abilities she casts these spells at her POW x4%. It can take an entire year for a nymph to recover spent Magic Points, and in most cases the process can only happen during a certain season.

Powerful Nymphs, Weaker Nymphs

Nymphs can have a greater POW depending on their type and natural habitat. Some common examples:

Species	Home	POW
Hamadryad	A Tree	1d6 up to 1d6+6
Hydriad	A pool	1d6 up to 1d6+6
Alseid	A grove	1d6+12
Leimoniad	A meadow	1d6+12
Dryad	A forest	1d6+18
Naiad	A spring or river	1d6+12 up to 1d6+30
Nereid	A coast, shore or cove	1d6+18
Oread	A mountain	1d6+24
Oceanid	The open sea	1d6+30

It is possible that a nymph's POW may rise or fall depending on the health and vitality of its home; a dryad whose forest has been mostly felled by woodcutters may, for example, suffer a reduction in Intensity with a consequent loss of 6 or more POW.

Evil Nymphs: Hags

One way a nymph divorces her own power from the state of health of her locus is by evolving into a hag. Hags are thankfully rare, corrupted and evil nymphs who generally have a bad attitude towards humans and many other forms of life. Hags have similar Characteristics to their more benign sisters, but may have claws, a venomous bite, a set of offensive spells and curses, and sometimes even control over undead creatures rather than the local wildlife.

Plague Demons

The most hated sort of ethereal entity, one that is the wellspring of diseases that can carry off thousands of victims. Although a plague demon has a material form it is in reality a miasma that can only really be seen with use of magic; however, the Lore (Medicine) skill can detect its presence. Due to its lack of substance to attack, the demon is immune to almost all physical damage, increasing the terror with which it is regarded. Most victims never even know they are under attack.

Encounters

Nymph

Characteristics (Ave)	Attributes		1D20	Location	AP/HP
STR: 3d6 (11)	Action Points	3	1–3	Right Leg	0/4
CON: 3d6+6 (17)	Damage Modifier	0	4–6	Left Leg	0/4
SIZ: 3d6 (11)	Magic Points	22	7–9	Abdomen	0/5
DEX: 2d6+6 (13)	Movement	8m	10–12	Chest	0/6
INT: 2d6+12 (19)	Initiative Bonus	16	13–15	Right Arm	0/3
POW: 1d6+18 (22)*	Armour	None	16–18	Left Arm	0/3
CHA: 3d6+6 (17)	Abilities	Physical Manifestation	19–20	Head	0/4

Typical POW for Dryads and Nereids. See Nymph POW table for POW for different species.

Magic Folk Magic (88%): Avert, Beastcall, Breath, Curse, Darkness, Extinguish, Heal, Incognito, Countermagic, Fate, Heal, Light, Mindspeech, Pathway, Pet, Phantasm, Protection, Witchsight

A nymph will know a number of Folk Magic spells equal to half her INT

Skills: Athletics 65%, Endurance 68%, Locale 152%, Perception 76%, Seduction 85%, Stealth 55%, Willpower 110%

Combat Style: Unarmed 45%

Plague demons have SIZ <1, INS 2d6+6, POW d6+18 and CHA 1d6. They have no physical attacks other than its ability to inflict disease upon a target. Its chance of doing so is equal to its Virulence, which is its POWx5. A plague demon can attack any victim within its CHA in metres for a cost of 1 Magic Point. This attack causes no damage but if not evaded or warded against triggers a Special Effect of Transfer Infection. The attack is normally unopposed, and so the Special Effect is usually automatic.

Once the Transfer Infection Special Effect is activated the target must make an opposed roll of his Endurance against the original attack roll, or be infected with whatever disease it propagates; if he succeeds, the target is immune to that particular demon.

A plague demon's victim is contagious and anyone who comes into contact with him in ways likely to allow infection (according to the specific application mechanic of the disease) is attacked with a virulence equal to the plague demon's POWx4; if they are infected they are also contagious, with a virulence of POWx3 and so on.

Illnesses caused by plague demons are mundane, and must be treated accordingly.

A plague demon cannot regenerate Magic Points while physically manifested, and when these are reduced to zero its force is spent and it dematerialises. Although eventually it will be able to regain its magic points and subsequently be able to manifest again, the conditions that allow it to do so are usually rather specific. A plague demon cannot move independently but can ride on air currents or in liquids, or attach itself to some person or object it has come into contact with – the carrier.

Sickness spirits are a form of Haunt often created from the souls of victims and bound to the material plane – a plague demon is actually following a natural instinct to procreate.

Roc

These immense birds of prey make their nests close to the ocean and each has a range that encompasses thousands of square kilometres over both sea and land. Humans are generally too small to bother with as prey except perhaps to carry back to a nest to feed a chick, but a horse or ox is a tasty morsel, and a vessel full of humans may make a worthwhile snackbox that the roc can return to over and again, swooping down and snatching a victim in its talons – indeed it is capable of catching up a human-sized target in each talon at the same time.

If a roc is in range of a source of handy missiles, it is quite capable of targeting a vessel with a dropped rock. The starting difficulty for this attack is Hard, adjusted for Size of target and range (vertical height) using the Size and Distance Difficulty Adjustment Table. A large rock dropped from a height can be a devastating weapon if it strikes the deck of a ship.

For statistics, see overleaf.

Satyr

A satyr is the male equivalent of a nymph, an ethereal creature that takes on humanoid form – if always betrayed by bestial features such as excessive hair, shaggy or even goat-like legs

Roc

Characteristics (Ave)	Attributes		1D20	Location	AP/HP
STR: 3d6+40 (51)	Action Points	3	1–3	Right Leg	6/13
CON: 2d6+6 (13)	Damage Modifier	+2d10	4–6	Left Leg	6/13
SIZ: 3d6+40 (51)	Magic Points	11	7–9	Abdomen	6/14
DEX: 2d6+6 (13)	Movement	3m, 20m (Flying)	10–12	Chest	6/15
INS: 2d6+6 (13)	Initiative Bonus	13	13–15	Right Wing	6/12
POW: 3d6 (11)	Armour	Feathers	16–18	Left Wing	6/12
	Abilities	Diving Strike, Flyer, Grappler	19–20	Head	6/13
	Magic	None			

Skills: Athletics 64%, Brawn 90%, Endurance 78%, Evade 52%, Fly 96%, Perception 72%, Stealth 40%, Willpower 65%

Combat Style: Lord of the Skies (Claw, Peck, Wing, Dropped Rock)

Weapon	Size/Force	Reach	Damage	AP/HP
Peck	C	L	2d6+2d10	As for head
Claw	C	VL	2d6+2d10	As for leg
Wing Buffet	C	VL	1d12+2d10	As for wing
Dropped Rock	C	N/A	3d6+1d6 per 5m dropped	

and animal-like genitalia and horns. Like nymphs, there are different types of satyrs, and some may have special traits and characteristics. Satyrs are rightly feared by mortals – they are capricious, lustful and dangerous entities. Usually a single individual is encountered, but there are times and places when satyrs gather together to feast and fornicate, and anything up to a dozen may be met with. Satyrs have strange, chaotic natures and without the direction of a more powerful spirit are as likely to start fighting amongst themselves as to band together and act in a co-ordinated fashion.

A satyr can form a body at will at the cost of 1 Magic Point, but only if it is in a wild place – and away from human sight. A satyr can roam the land, and is not restricted to an area or feature in the way that a nymph is. However, they represent the untamed and unfettered rule of nature, and will never come closer than within 1km of human habitation – which is sometimes a frustration, for their one weakness for human civilisation is a love of beer and wine. Offerings of fine alcoholic beverages are a good way for a traveller to ensure the satyrs leave him alone when crossing some lonely wilderness. It is similarly not unheard of to leave a condemned woman or a slave girl as an offering to the satyrs. Satyrs prize relations with human women, whom they regard as low-grade substitutes for the nymphs who so rarely favour satyrs with their attentions, but as far more interesting than satisfying their prodigious sexual drives with the local flora and fauna.

Many satyrs have some kind of horn or flute, with which they can create both music and a bizarre range of unsettling and affecting sounds with magical effects. Each such effect takes a full round to activate, costs 1MP and requires a successful Play Instrument skill test, opposed by the target's Willpower. As he continues to play, he can force a new target to resist the power of his music at the end of each subsequent round. Some people actively seek the effects of Satyrical Music, and attempt to summon a satyr to play for them.

Satyrical Music Effects

A satyr can use his instrument to perform one of the following miraculous effects: Beast Form, Berserk, Corruption, Enthrall, Fear, Madness. The Magnitude and Intensity of the Miracle is equal to half the satyr's POW.

Satyrs have access to Folk Magic and may know a number of cantrips up to half their POW. Satyrs recover spent Magic Points at their healing rate per year and must remain ethereal to do so.

Sea Satyrs (Tritons)

Known as tritons, these are the aquatic equivalent of the land-bound satyr. A triton is similarly part-human in appearance but with rough shark-like skin below the waist, gills set below the ears and hair like matted kelp. It uses a conch shell instead of a horn or pipes, and a blast upon the shell can produce miraculous effects – a version of the Earthquake Miracle that can toss

Encounters

Satyr

Characteristics (Ave)	Attributes		1D20	Location	AP/HP
STR: 4d6+6 (20)	Action Points	3	1–3	Right Leg	2/7
CON: 3d6+6 (17)	Damage Modifier	+1d4	4–6	Left Leg	2/7
SIZ: 4d6 (14)	Magic Points	14	7–9	Abdomen	0/8
DEX: 3d6+6 (17)	Movement	6m	10–12	Chest	0/9
INT: 2d6+3 (10)	Initiative Bonus	17	13–15	Right Arm	0/6
POW: 4d6 (14)	Armour	Fur on Legs, Horned Head	16–18	Left Arm	0/6
CHA: 2d6	Abilities	Physical Manifestation; Animal Instinct (satyrs have an INS score equal to their INT+6 that is used to calculate SR and Actions); Passions (Overindulgence, Lechery at 50+INS% each), which can be a satyr's undoing	19–20	Head	2/7
	Magic	Folk Magic (POW x3%): Befuddle, Bludgeon, Demoralise, Glamour, Might, Pathway, Tune, Ventriloquism, Vigour			

Skills: Athletics 65%, Endurance 85%, Language (nearest human population) 35%, Locale 80%, Play Instrument 95%, Stealth 55%, Survival 125%, Track 80%, Willpower 30%

Combat Style: Unarmed 65%, Club 55%

a vessel about upon the waves, Call Winds to stir up the waves, or Cloud Call to summon a sea fog. Instead of a club, a triton is usually armed with a trident of magically shaped and hardened coral, and may be riding a sea creature of suitable size.

A triton has legs terminating in fins, but when it emerges from the sea these can transform to serviceable feet. Nevertheless a triton cannot voluntarily dematerialise when out of water, and if he travels more than his POW in metres from the ocean he will lose 1 Magic Point per hour and begins to suffer the effects of dehydration after only CON x1 hours, with a dehydration rate of Hourly (see MYTHRAS page 82). There is a sea captain called Settrik the Diver from Othrikor who is rumoured to be a triton in human guise, but nobody has ever managed to learn the truth of these rumours from Settrik or his crew.

ENCOUNTERS AT SEA

When at sea, a high proportion of the encounters a vessel can run into are likely to be natural phenomena that are nevertheless the most common source of peril and disaster. Check once per day; there is a 20% chance of an encounter.

Change in the Weather

An immediate re-roll to the Sailing Conditions, that takes effect within 1d3 hours.

Dangerous Current

An unexpected but powerful current pulls the vessel from its course. It may be natural in origin – but it is just as likely that some supernatural forces are at work beneath the waves and this current is a by-product. The captain must make a Seamanship roll to compensate or to escape the current: Roll 1d6 to determine the level of challenge:

1 Easy; 2-4 Standard; 5 Hard; 6 Formidable. For every failure until a successful roll is made the vessel is pushed off course by 1d6 x10 km, or six hours' sailing.

Fishing Fleet

If close to land these are a collection of 1d10+4 little fishing boats from the nearest coastal settlement with a handful of crew, or a team of vessels working together to hunt a large shoal. Further out to sea, they may be bigger vessels after bigger fish.

Flying Predator

Wyrms, harpies and, even more rarely, griffins, can be found roosting on remote islands or desolate shores and spreading

Sea Encounter Table

Coastal Waters	Trade Routes	Deep Ocean and Wilderness	Encounter
01-15	01-17	01-19	Change in the weather
16-19	18-21	20-23	Dangerous Current
20-33	22-31	24	Fishing Fleet
34-36	32	25	Flying Predator
37-41	33-37	26-30	Fog
42-50	38-39	31-33	Grounded
-	40-44	34-43	Island
51-55	45-51	44	Pirates
56-60	52-54	45-49	Reef or submerged rocks
61-70	55-76	50-75	Sea life
-	78	76-79	Sea Monster
71-73	79-80	80	Shipwreck
74-80	81-85	81-89	Storm
81-86	86-92	90-93	Trade Ship
87-92	93-94	94	War Ship
93-94	-	-	Wreckers
95-00	95-00	95-00	SPECIAL

Encounters

their hunting territory over the sea. Few such creatures are able to take off again if they hit water, but they are more than capable of taking someone from the deck of a ship. The roc a giant bird capable of carrying away even large animals in its talons, has been encountered off the coasts of Rasputana, Uxmal and Jandekot, and there may be more than one species. Some think these giant birds are so smart they are thinking creatures with an INT characteristic.

Fog
All visibility beyond 50m is lost. The fog lasts for 1d6 hours before clearing, in which time the vessel may become lost unless it has non-visual means of navigation. A Navigate roll is required not to stray from course.

Grounded
The vessel runs aground in shallows or a sandbank, causing an immediate Seaworthiness test. The captain and crew have to find a way to get free by jettisoning cargo, being dragged or towed to deeper water or reducing draft through other means. If a vessel runs aground it gets stuck and needs a feat of Seamanship and 1d3 hours of work to get free. Running aground results in an instant Seaworthiness test, which is Hard for deeper drafted (Type T) vessels.

Island
A small and uninhabited island less than 10km across. There is a 40% chance (or the Games Master may allow use of a Luck Point) that there is fresh water to be had, and, if so, there is also likely to be interesting or edible flora and fauna. Quite possibly inhabited by a creature, such places being ideal basking or nesting sites for monsters.

Pirates
A warboat from one of the islands, with a crew of d4+2 x10 warriors and sailors. They will always attack if they have the odds very much in their favour – but pirates will not choose to get into a fight they don't think they can win.

Reef or Submerged Rocks
A ship that is driven onto a reef or rocks inflicts its own damage on itself, adjusted for speed. A ship can continue to take damage as the wind and waves pound it against the rocks over and again until it eventually breaks up. In each subsequent 15 minute period, until such time as the ship gets free of the rocks, it must succeed in a Seaworthiness roll, or the Wind inflicts its Damage Modifier. Many times, there are no opportunities to escape the hazard without recourse to magic, and it is a matter of time before the ship is torn apart. The beleaguered crew simply have to attempt to save themselves and anything else they can before they too are lost.

Sea Life
Sharks or dolphins, flying fish, a swarm of poisonous jellyfish, a huge shoal of tunny, a pod of whales – something delightful, useful, or simply frightening, offered up by the Ocean Mother.

Sea Monster
Offshore a giant crab or octopus is a likely encounter, in deeper water, a sea serpent. These creatures are big enough to take on a Small or Medium vessel, but otherwise will target individual characters they might grab from the deck, or contrive to see knocked into the water to more easily be dragged beneath and devoured.

Shipwreck
One or more shipwrecked sailors marooned on a coast and signalling for help, or adrift in a small boat, or even clinging to a piece of wreckage in the sea. Deeply grateful for rescue, they will reward as best they can for safe delivery to a port. Coastal shipwrecks may throw salvageable goods onto the shore.

Storm
A storm rips at the sails and whips up the sea to dangerous heights. A storm has the potential to cause damage to a ship's structure. For every hour a storm lasts, the captain must make a Seamanship roll to get his ship through undamaged. If a roll is failed, test the wind strength as a percentage against the vessel's Seaworthiness in an opposed roll. If it succeeds, the wind will inflict its Damage Modifier direct to the vessel's Hit Points, bypassing its Armour Points, in addition to the usual effects of a failed Seaworthiness roll.

Storms vary in duration and ferocity according to the season:

Season	Storm Duration (hours)	Storm Ferocity (STR)
Summer	1d4	1d20+75
Spring, Autumn	1d8	1d20+90
Winter	1d12	1d20+105

The Storm's Ferocity is used as its combined STR+SIZ on the Damage Modifier table to determine how much damage it can do to a ship when the captain fails to manage the ship through the storm's fury.

Shores of Korantia

Trade Ship

Choose or roll 1d6:

1D6	Encounter
1-3	A small trader from the nearest port that normally plies coastal routes
4-5	A large ship carrying bulk commodities
6	A merchant ship from a distant land, possibly carrying a cargo of exotic goods. Larger vessels may be a joint venture in which several merchants have placed their hopes of making a fortune

War Ship

A large vessel with an armed crew from a nearby civilised port, who could be on exercise, or on patrol, carrying dispatches, escorting a dignitary or on a raiding mission.

Wreckers

Wreckers are people who live on a coast where there are treacherous rocks and sandbars, and are skilled at luring unsuspecting ships into difficulties. Once a vessel is foundering on their shore they proceed to loot and pillage rather than rescue – perhaps killing or enslaving the crew, perhaps just leaving them to their fate.

Special

Roll on the Special Encounters Table

Special Encounter Table

1D100	Encounter
01-15	Cataclysmic Storm
16-18	Colossal Sea Monster
19-22	Deadly Swarm
23-30	Divine Portent
31-55	Fleet
56-65	Loathsome Fog
66-77	Mysterious Island
78-85	The Lonely Nereid
86-93	Triton Hellraisers
99-00	Zombie Ship

Cataclysmic Storm

This is a storm of such terrible ferocity, with black skies and inky seas, awesome waves of terrifying height and winds impossible to withstand – that there is no hope of survival except that offered by providence, and all that is certain is that even the survivors can expect a major change of fortune. The characters' ship is certain to be lost beneath the waves or dashed to matchwood upon the rocks; its occupants' lives depend on magic, divine intervention, or sufficient luck points to secure success in a Herculean Endurance, Survival or Swim test to ride out the storm until washed up on a strange shore or left clinging to a piece of wreckage in the ocean when the fury finally passes.

Colossal Sea Monster

One of the terrible predators of the deep decides the characters' ship is interesting prey. Use the stats for giant octopus or sea serpent, but increase SIZ and STR by +30 (or even more) and increase the Size/Force and basic damage of its attacks accordingly; or allow for a unique monster such as a jellyfish 100m across capable of sending electric shocks through its prey. Such creatures are capable of taking on and sinking even the largest ocean-going vessels. A monster of this size may be the instrument of some god's, sorcerer's or arch-priest's power.

Deadly Swarm

A bizarre swarm of tiny flying creatures bursts from the water and attacks the characters. This swarm is of terrible size (40+), with 6 Combat actions and inflicting 1d8 damage with its bites from the creatures' tiny, razor-sharp teeth. The swarm can divide into three smaller swarms, each with three actions and inflicting 1d3 damage, in order to chase different victims around a ship. It is as potent and as hungry below the water as above it, so there is no escape by plunging into the sea.

Divine Portent

See under Land Encounters, above. These portents may have a particularly maritime character – a great wave within which are seen a whole troupe of supernatural sea creatures: nereids and mermaids, tritons (sea satyrs), sea horses and the like; the sea turns the colour of blood, or seems to become as clear as glass revealing some mystery beneath the surface; a pod of dolphins appears to signal to the characters to change course or away from some danger or towards some new objective.

Fleet

A fleet of ships appears, signaling some momentous events are in train. Roll 1d6 or choose:

Encounters

1D6	Fleet Type
1-2	Migration Fleet: This is a whole community at sea – perhaps a tribe of nomadic Dagomils aboard their great ocean rafts; or a small fleet of Archipelagans searching for a new land in which to settle; or even a party of Korantine colonists, perhaps seeking to refound one of the cities lost before the Cataclysm. The fleet comprises d6x100 souls, and includes women and children.
3-4	War Fleet: Whether it has set out to mount an invasion of a foreign shore or is set to engage an enemy in a battle at sea, a war fleet is a terrific sight; the largest number more than 100 ships of war and occupy several square kilometres of ocean – it is said that, before the Cataclysm, the Korantines could sometimes put a fleet of 300 galleys to sea. The fleet is accompanied by a great number of transports carrying troops and supplies. A fleet will have fast, light ships detailed as scouts, and to intercept any vessel that might be a threat or could give its position away. It will also have significant magical capabilities, enhancements and other supernatural help.
5	Sharranketan Merchant fleet: Sharranketan fleets can comprise three of their enormous galleons, probably all belonging to the Zamada family of Homora, or possibly including a galleon of the Hirambils, but all anyway under the command of Gruzul Beloshi, a famous Zamada merchant-admiral.
6	Pirate Fleet: It is extremely rare for pirate captains to cooperate in a venture, but this gathering of seaborne villains and other hangers-on has created a short-lived alliance of d6+4 warboats. Their objective is no doubt some ambitious enterprise, to seize a Sharranketan galleon or attack a harbour or town.

Loathsome Fog

A thick fog bank rolls in; once it covers the characters' ship it has an oppressive feel to it and reeks with the stench of dead things thrown up on the sea shore. Within the confines of the fog lurk terrifying sea-wraiths, evil spirits well known to anyone steeped in the lore of the sea. The wraiths are described in MYTHRAS, page 153. 1d6+3 in number, they have the appearance of spectral sailors, some bloated in death, others draped in seaweed or crawling with sea life or with bits of their flesh nibbled away by the fishes. They may be costumed as contemporary crewmen, or in the archaic garb of a long lost era. Sea-wraiths are able to operate beneath the water as well as on the surface – and can appear to walk upon the waves, and to try and climb aboard any vessel that is not Consecrated to get at the crew. They cannot follow a victim onto dry land.

If becalmed in the Doldrums of Hiolanta, wraiths are a known hazard that accompanies 30% of any fog encounter. Elsewhere upon the ocean, these wraiths are a rare but no less terrifying phenomenon.

Mysterious Islands

An unexpected landfall; a tiny island less than 1km across, with a remarkable feature as created by the Games Master or picked from the following:

Y A scatter of bones and random treasures; there are jewels, coins and gems worth 1d10 x 1,000SP to be gathered up, but the task will take some time. Before it is complete, a monstrous creature that nests here will return. This should not come as a complete surprise – if the island is the nesting site of a giant roc there may be fragments of eggshells and immense feathers littered about. If it is the basking site of some sea monster, there may be huge faeces and perhaps ominous drag marks where it hauls itself in and out of the water.

Y An outcrop of rock containing a rare blue mineral that negates magical effects on contact. It is relatively soft and can be harvested as a grit or powder with minimal tools and effort. This substance can be used to render an item or person to which it is applied immune to spells for up to 12 hours or until removed; it can also be used to neutralise magic if applied to an object or person that is already under the effect of a spell. A weapon covered in the stuff will pass right through magical protection spells. One dose (50g) is sufficient to cover a medium-sized weapon, a piece of armour, or a human-sized hit location. It is possible to gather 1d10 doses for every hour of scraping and collecting; however, the island itself is contaminated. For every ten minutes a character spends on it, there is a 10% cumulative chance that any active spell or magical effect is blasted away, or that any enchantment temporarily ceases to work (permanent effects and enchantments returning within 1d3 days of leaving the island); and for every hour spent on it, there is a 10% cumulative chance that any enchantment carried by those ashore will be permanently neutralised or broken. The mineral is capable of being refined by an alchemist, but even in its raw state is worth perhaps 500 SP per dose.

Y A single tree bearing a single small fruit, and at its base is a terrifying creature – perhaps a chimera or an immense

serpent that must be overcome to reach the tree and take its fruit. Whoever eats the fruit immediately receives a combined Cure Malady, Heal Body, Heal Mind and Rejuvenate Miracle with a Magnitude and Intensity of 15. The tree will take 1d6+20 years to grow another fruit. The island is a fabled and sought-after location, and many kings have sent expeditions to try to find it. Aside from a random encounter it can only be found with directions from a supernatural source – an ocean deity or a demon who might divulge its location as a boon granted in return for a Pact.

The Lonely Nereid

The characters encounter Selemasse, an Oceanid who is on the hunt for a human suitable to provide company to Belaishe, her nereid 'little sister' who craves human company. Selemasse will attempt to kidnap or take as ransom a male crew member with a CHA of 17 or greater, turning herself to undine form and carrying him away to Belaishe's remote island, ocean cave or shore from which she is sure there will be no escape.

When the unfortunate prisoner arrives at the chosen place he may discover the sun-bleached bones of her previous lovers, as Belaishe is somewhat negligent in taking care of her guests' basic human needs; even so it is a place where he can, at least for a while, live like a king, as Belaishe tries very hard to keep him happy with the trinkets and treasures she has been told humans covet so greatly.

Triton Hellraisers

If several tritons coordinate their powers, the effect on a ship at sea can be devastating. This gang of ocean trouble-makers is led by Hezerumzee, who rides upon the back of a sea serpent. He and his gang of fellow tritons (1d4+3 of them) are often belligerent and spoiling for a fight just for the sake of it – but they may well demand some sort of payment or service in return for leaving a ship unmolested. These fellows can make themselves very unwelcome guests aboard a ship, taking anything they want for themselves – they are attracted to precious stones in particular, but also meat (beef being a favourite), which is very hard for them to come by, and alcoholic beverages, being unable to go on land for any amount of time. They may hold a cargo or crew to ransom until their demands are satisfied, possibly requiring the characters to run some land-based errand for them to fetch appropriate treasures.

Zombie Ship

Anywhere outside the southern shores of the ocean this vessel is simply lost or adrift. A reed galley, hardly suitable for the open ocean, rowed by tireless zombies, crewed by barbarous, cannibal Uxmali. The crew includes a captain, a priestess (shaman) and a master at arms, all Greater Uxmali; a rowing crew of 30 Lesser Uxmali zombies; a gang of six Slargr mercenary overseers and warriors; and a number of Lesser Uxmali deck hands, who are also food on the hoof.

For encounters in the northern half of the ocean (north of Fierla), substitute an orcish trading and raiding ship, carrying a handful of slaves already destined for sacrifice, some rowing crew revivified by the sorcerer-master of the vessel and almost certainly some Blood Magic enchantments intended to be traded for more slaves.

THYRTA

Thyrta is a town at the southern edge of the Korantine world. It is a prime location from which to search for adventure or for a new beginning – to reinvent yourself, or prove your worth. Thyrta stands on the edge of the ocean, at a point where the southern trade routes that are dominated by foreigners from the lands of Assabia meet the northern ones where Korantines still command the seas. It has a hinterland of largely untapped resources, occupied only by what appears to be a declining population of indigenous Thennalts who are easily pushed into marginal land or made tenants to an energetic settler. It even has one of the last great wildernesses of southern Taygus close at hand, the Forest of Sard. This great expanse of woodlands and wetlands sprawling on either side of the Quickwater river is said to harbour monsters and fabulous creatures unknown anywhere else. Sard is also the final barrier between the Korantines and their original homeland to the south in Methelea, where now is found their ancient enemy, the Theocracy of the Jekkarenes.

Getting There

Most people arrive in Thyrta by ship, and most ships heading to Thyrta arrive from Borissa carrying goods, supplies and colonists. It is possible to work a passage, but the price of a little space on deck is not very great, typically 5-6SP per head, unless you have a quantity of baggage to bring with you or plan to ship livestock as well. Some vessels arrive from further afield: The Celestial Queen is a grain ship that often makes the run to Thyrta from Sarestra, and there are a few traders from Assabia, mostly from Morkesh, who sometimes call there. One of these, the slaver Hiram Hiram, is the only one who touches at Thyrta before or after a trip out to the exotic West.

Overland the main route runs from Borissa and passes through the territory of Tersippa, a small Korantine city occupying a stretch of coastal plain where Korantia proper meets Brotomagia. Relations between Borissa and its tiny neighbour are rather cool, and it is often suspected that Tersippa encourages the natives around Thyrta to make trouble for the growing colony.

An alternative route from central Korantia avoids Borissa by passing through Vestrikina and on to Tersippa, thence to Thyrta. There are very few roads and almost no inns on the overland route, so travellers going this way should be prepared to rough it. Some of the locals can be dangerous and if you get lost the woods and hills are known to still harbour spirits and creatures that can be hazardous encounters. Few people approach Thyrta from the East, and those that do are usually taking the quickest but more challenging route from Hilanistra.

The Colony

Thyrta is an outpost of Borissa, one of the more bellicose and acquisitive of the Korantine city states. Its first foundations were laid as a trading post at a good natural harbour over 50 years ago, with the formal charter, under which Borissan colonists could settle permanently in the area without losing their citizenship, following some time after in 1178. The colony is a key expression of Borissa's expansionist ambitions and already the settlers here are pushing into the Forest of Sard or encroaching on land that Thennalt peasant farmers have been enjoying more or less peacefully for generations. Not yet a

city-state in its own right, Thyrta's progression to independent status has now reached a point when the time it should cut its dependency on the mother city draws near. Its foundation will involve the creation of a new goddess, a new name for the settlement, and a new nation.

The colony's urban area is unconsecrated as it is not yet a city-state with its own laws and constitution. Its temple precincts are consecrated to Borissa's gods, and have to be renewed annually.

Thyrta is ruled by appointees from among the ruling magistrates of its mother city. The governor is Rikalsos of Vimaylo; his right-hand man is Kortano, a Syndic of the Borissan cult of Sabateus and his enforcer is Aparinaon, priest of Kos and Torthil Acolyte.

Thyrta Town

Thyrta is right by the sea, on high bluffs with twisting ramps leading down to the water's edge. Its earliest settlers earmarked a patch of flat open ground to form the heart of the city, and this is where its main public buildings and temples are situated. The streets fanning out from the city centre are peculiar for being laid out in curving, sweeping patterns, which is due to a rather duplicitous deal done by the original settlers who had promised the natives that 'no straight-avenued Korantine city' would ever be built in their lands. These streets are dominated by well-spaced houses all standing in their own plots – some of them simple buildings with no more than three or four rooms around a courtyard and thatched roofs, others are impressive villas with tiled roofs. A few streets contain run-down or modest buildings where Thyrta's poorest inhabitants can be found, many living three or more to a room. A few of these are citizens fallen on hard times – but the majority are either landless Thennalts from the indigenous population of the region, or exile refugees from the Jekkarid.

Thyrta has no need for a wall on the seaward side, although her first stone fortification is a tower overlooking the harbour entrance. To the land side, there is a long ditch, rampart and palisade enclosing the settlement, inside which are the foundations for a dressed stone wall. The plan is to have wall and temple completed together in time for Thyrta's formal establishment as a city-state.

The whole city and its environs accommodates some 800 male citizens and their families. There is something of an over-supply of single male settlers, but once you add metics, slaves and transients to the total, Thyrta has a population of some 4,500 souls living in and around the town.

People of Importance

Statistics are provided at the end of the chapter, starting on page 153.

Rikalsos of Vimaylo

Rikalsos is a Borissan aristocrat who is leader of the colony under a lifelong appointment – an elective monarchy that is supposed to help see it through its formative years. This appointment brings with it acolyte membership in the cult of Anayo of Borissa, the city-state's ruler god. Once the monarchy has been in place for 30 years, the colony's founding charter expects the subsequent succession to effect a transfer to a system of rotating magistrates (cult acolytes) holding restricted tenure of office. Rikalsos was elected only 4 years before this 30 year period expired, so is to be the last "king" of Thyrta. He has been in place now for 12 years, is in rather robust health, and torn between voluntary retirement and the pressure from certain quarters not to do anything to hurry along a political upheaval that could be inconvenient to some influential people.

Simbale, wife of Rikalsos

Simbale is a mother of two and a devoted wife who will do anything to further her husband's career. She is more than a little disappointed in him – Simbale would rather see him in high office back in Borissa, but he blew his chances with some populist political gestures that saw his own class gang up on him and make leadership of the Thyrtan colony sound like a sensible next step. His consequent loss of confidence and streak of paranoia means that Rikalsos is not quite the man that Simbale would wish him be – but she has to work with the materials at hand. In a crisis she is likely to provide the steel Rikalsos needs to deal with things properly and decisively.

Kortano the Syndic

Kortano is the Syndic (priest) of the local branch of the Borissan cult-guild of Sabateus. As a result, he controls all official trade passing through or changing hands in the city. He has a hand in almost everything – except law and order and defence – and is constantly in and out of governor Rikalsos' presence. Many believe he has the power to make or break Rikalsos' stewardship of the colony. He even farms Thyrta's land taxes under contract, generating some 100,000SP per annum, which leaves the local branch of the Borissan Syndics with a massive 20,000SP profit on the price he paid for the rights.

Kortano is tall, slim, approaching fifty years of age, and has a haughty demeanour.

Aparinaon

Aparinaon is in charge of law and order and of the local militia. This means he is a priest of Kos, the deity who enforces the divine laws, and an acolyte of the Korantine war god Torthil. He has charge of a small force of 30 publicly-owned slaves who act as a night watch and constabulary, but he also commands Thyrta's Patriotic Band, membership of which is a fast track to receiving the best available land grants in the area. Sixty or so Thyrtans are members, and a further 300 more are liable for service if a full levy is raised. In reality, there are several thousand warriors back in Borissa ready to defend their city's colony if it comes to it, and the local forces just need to be enough to deal with any situation until such forces can muster.

Aparinaon is short and stocky, his balding head compensated for by thick hair on his arms, chest and back. Despite the gravity of the power he can wield, Aparinaon has a casual, even off-hand manner, and deals with life and death matters with little ceremony.

Volsenna

Volsenna is "mother" of the city, a widow of 39 who appears much younger. She is a recent appointment to the priestesshood, her promotion fast-tracked when no other matron could be found who would relocate to Thyrta. For now she is a priestess of Borissa's own city cult, but at the point Rikalsos steps down and the city's proper constitution is established she will be responsible for founding the cult of Orayna of Thyrta (or whatever the new city is then called), which will define the boundaries of citizenship. At that juncture she should also be wed, however, this strikingly beautiful woman has no interest as yet in again subjecting herself to the limitations of a claustrophobic patriarchal household. In any event, she has a very close relationship with Yezereus, the city's celebrated explorer. Volsenna is extremely popular, and even the roughest frontiersmen in town show her a dewy-eyed respect and will suffer no-one to speak ill of her.

Despite her privileged station, Volsenna has suffered her share of tragedy, having always suffered from a weak constitution. When sent to Thyrta she prayed mightily to her goddess to sustain her in the mission to civilise this colony, and has been granted the Robust and Resilience Gifts. She has a son of 19 years who remains in Borissa – a rather arrogant young aristocrat supported by a significant inheritance – and this separation is a cause of great sadness to her. Her love for Yezereus is unrequited solely because she fears it will estrange her from her son even further. Volsenna's mother, Volsenna the Elder, lives with her, and is a bilious old woman with disdain for Yezereus and the ear of the governor's wife Simbale.

Lord Skelfus

This man is the local Thennalt chieftain, grandson of the man who made the Korantine settlers welcome in the first place, and fully integrated into Korantine society. He has even been a paladin in the service of a Korantine Emperor (Koibos' father Baleus). His family have, over the course of 40 years, connived in divesting their own people of pretty much everything they had while retaining title to substantial lands and resources for themselves. Lord Skelfus is treated with some distaste by the other chieftains in the region, but cares very little for that. A keen hunter, despite his advancing years, he still takes to the saddle in pursuit of any dangerous creature that he hears about, and failing that spends his time in fruitless pursuit of a bandit chief called Varoteg in a contest of wills that has become almost a ritualised sport. His younger son, Ormsfil, is lodged in Thyrta and a student under the tutelage of the sage Medanthros. His eldest son Timellion, his pride and joy, is at Hilanistra in service to Emperor Koibos. Skelfus hopes that Timellion will be invited to the ranks of the Emperor's paladins, and has offered to make a portion of his estates over to provide the necessary financial support for the new paladin if this comes to pass. He would then effectively control the establishment of the imperial enclave in Thyrta upon its independence.

Places of Interest

The Peoples' Plaza

A broad paved court some 80m across is the main gathering place for citizens and residents and where all public business is done. On the west side is the public temple complex incorporating shrines to Anayo and Kos where business of law and state take place. On the north side, there are major construction works for the future temple of the city-goddess and in the shadow of those works is a little shrine to Borissa who for now remains the tutelary goddess of the place. To the east is the shrine to Pyrolus and the temple-offices of the Sabateus cult.

Who Hangs Out There

During the day, except in the hottest hours, there are always gangs of craftsmen and labourers working on construction. Kosimus of Pelostra, the celebrated architect-builder, is often on the scene. In the mornings, there are knots of poorer folk hoping for a day's employment on a work gang. The plaza is used for markets at least two days per week, more if there are

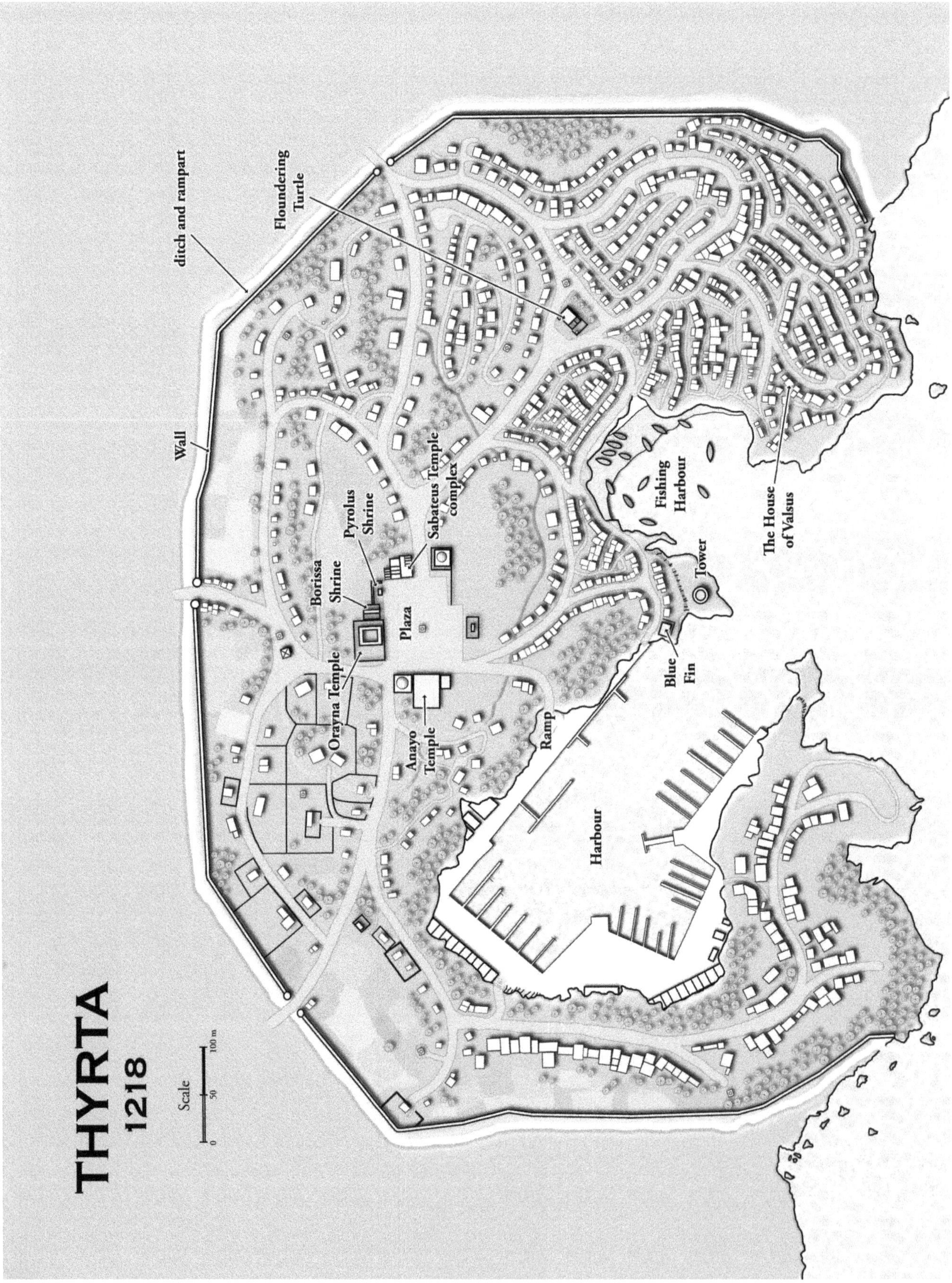

THYRTA
1218

Labels on map:
- ditch and rampart
- Floundering Turtle
- Wall
- Borissa Shrine
- Pyrolus Shrine
- Sabateus Temple complex
- Oravna Temple
- Plaza
- Anayo Temple
- Ramp
- Blue Fin
- Tower
- Fishing Harbour
- The House of Valsus
- Harbour

Scale: 0 – 50 – 100 m

festivals, and you will then also find dignitaries and minor officials from the Borissan Syndics – some of these being slaves – around the market, making their inspections of the goods on offer and ensuring those who are selling are paying over their duties. Kortano the Syndic is himself often in the square, if only to regularly cross back and forth between his own office and Rikalsos' on the opposite side. The governor often holds open air meetings here on non-market days, and the plaza also serves as an overspill for court cases and for public assemblies and votes.

The Docks

Thyrta's docks are set up for the loading and unloading of bulk cargoes, the harbour having a depth of over 6m, adequate for most forms of shipping. Around the docks and backing onto the steep slopes between the dock and the town above are a collection of warehouses and workshops, and a couple of eateries including At Salty Mari's.

Who Hangs Out There

As a small port, the dockside can be sleepy and quiet except when the fishing fleet is landing its catch, which is gutted, cleaned and sold right by the water. Sometimes there will be labourers and deck hands hanging around looking for work on one of the bigger ships, but most activity comes from the workshops where sailmakers, ropemakers, netmakers, carpenters and the like typically operate out of a large space open onto the dockside during the day and can be seen at their craft. On the rare occasions a foreign ship calls, there may be a whole throng of curious people coming down to the docks to take a look.

Inns and Taverns

Upon arrival in Thyrta, it is common to find some open space and pitch a tent or make a shelter until something more permanent can be found. The cheapest way to get a roof over your head is space at a doss house packed in with other hopeful settlers and fortune seekers for 2CP per night. However, those who have the means might take room at the Floundering Turtle, Thyrta's only inn, which costs a lot more – 2-3SP per room and a further 1SP per occupant for board.

The city's taverns are lively, and good places to meet the locals or fellow travellers. Since few people cook for themselves there are many establishments where you can get a cheap meal washed down with cheap wine.

Thalvi's Place (Street Bar and Eatery)

A little street corner tavern with some indoor space and seating, wine bowls sunk into a counter, a decent bakery next door. Reasonable grub, good bread from the bakery (where you can also bake your own dough), and reasonably priced, so very popular.

Thalvi is a mature woman whose husband died even before their Thyrtan land grant had yielded its first fruits. So she sold it off for the best she could get – which was very little – and set up this place. She's welcoming to foreigners. They often actually bring business rather than just hang out without buying anything like many of the dirt-poor no-hopers off the boat from Borissa...and frankly, they have much more interesting stories to tell.

Who Hangs Out There?

Thalvi's Place is popular with those in the know, so transients and sailors from ships that call regularly – like Jorelso of Sarestra and his partners Marrakon and Vitholas who own the Celestial Queen – can often be found here if in port. The local urchin gang hover about the place because the clients tend to be good humoured and generous, and it's next door to a bakery, after all. Ormsfil, son of Skelfus and student to Medanthros, spends the meager cash his father allows him at Thalvi's Place

At Salty Mari's (Downbeat Dockside Tavern)

Thyrta has plenty of doss houses and taverns where sailors can be found. In the sailing season they hit port with money in their pockets and a thirst to blow off some steam. In the winter they have little else to do but hang out awaiting work in the spring and by the end of it are properly poor again as sailors tend to only get paid when contracted to a ship and most ships don't sail in the winter months.

At Salty Mari's is the most established sailor hangout. It is downbeat, sometimes rough, often rowdy, sometimes just sparsely populated by lonely bored men in their cups. Salty Mari herself is long dead but much celebrated, and the current owner, a man called Jaxo, claims to be a nephew. Jaxo has a side business in running a book on anything anyone cares to bet on. The weather is a favourite, but those who are setting out to sea call in to have a last drink and lay a bet on their safe return.

Shores of Korantia

Less common knowledge is that Jaxo is also a fence for low-value pilfered goods and trinkets (anything over 30SP is rather beyond his appetite).

Who Hangs Out There?

The dockside crowd, joined by people who don't want to be noticed, and people who get off a ship and find themselves in the first available watering hole – typically crewmen of some of the higher-ups who own or captain the vessels. Hiram Hiram's crew use this place, and when they do many others avoid it.

The Blue Finn (Up-Market Tavern)

A bright and airy tavern right at the edge of the bluffs over the harbour, and offering panoramic views from the terrace out the back. A rather shabby man by the name of Zolatos runs the place on behalf of a well-to-do owner who lives most of the year in Borissa. The owner is an aristocrat, Toroson of Agme, a former athlete.

Who Hangs Out There?

Rilados the Navigator is a regular, and can spend much of the day holding court there. Yezereus often uses it as a meeting place when he is in town, and has been seen having trysts with Volsenna, albeit surrounded by a gang of her other admirers. Toroson comes to Thyrta once per year, stays at the Turtle but hangs out at The Blue Finn in between extended hunting expeditions into Sard.

The Floundering Turtle (High Class Inn)

The city has a few taverns (wine shops) and eateries but only has one inn: The Floundering Turtle. This is a large villa and garden turned to use as a hotel, and some of the guests there are long-term residents. It is the only place that can offer a level of comfort suitable to the better class of traveller. The innkeeper is a man called Melcro, the freed slave of a Borissan merchant who founded the place but died some years ago. Melcro officially manages the establishment on behalf of his former master's family who are absentee landlords, but is left alone to do so and the locals consider him to be the master of the house and treat him accordingly. Melcro has a very pretty daughter, Melsina, who is determined to catch herself a rich man and currently has designs on Melosson of Thrigos, whom her father considers a wastrel.

Who Hangs Out There?

Melosson of Thrigos and his drinking buddy Bazagar spend a lot of time in the social areas. Aparinaon has been known to use the yard as an impromptu courtroom, and it is in fact the only such place where you may sometimes find local dignitaries, as important visitors are often billeted here.

The Billet

Originally just a boarding house, this place has been converted to a club house by Ivanthus of Tysil and his mercenary gang, who buy in quantities of cheap wine and provide it to their friends and guests for free. Entry is by invitation only, or else an Influence or Deceit roll to persuade the gang your company is worth their time and attention. Regular visitors are expected to make contributions of food, wine or women.

Who Hangs Out There?

Ivanthus and his men, and whoever they are friendly with or have as hangers-on this season, which tends to change.

Law and Order

Governor Rikalsos spends considerable time dealing with complaints over property or violence brought by one settler against another. Where some sort of crime has been committed and punishment has to be meted out, or whenever non-citizens are involved, Aparinaon takes over. A Borissan citizen always has the right of appeal to the courts in Borissa itself in major cases, but this is a rare occurrence due to the costs involved. Minor public disorder and fracas is dealt with by Aparinaon's slave-constables, and serious threats to life and property may result in summoning the town's Patriotic Band, who may also form a posse to pursue felons or hunt down bandits.

Constables

These publicly owned slaves are mostly imported from Borissa, and are generally well looked after if despised by many of Thyrta's population. Each wears a simple homespun tunic and a large metal disc on a thong round the neck, proclaiming he or she is state property, and carries a wooden club with metal strips wound about it.

The Floundering Turtle at Thyrta

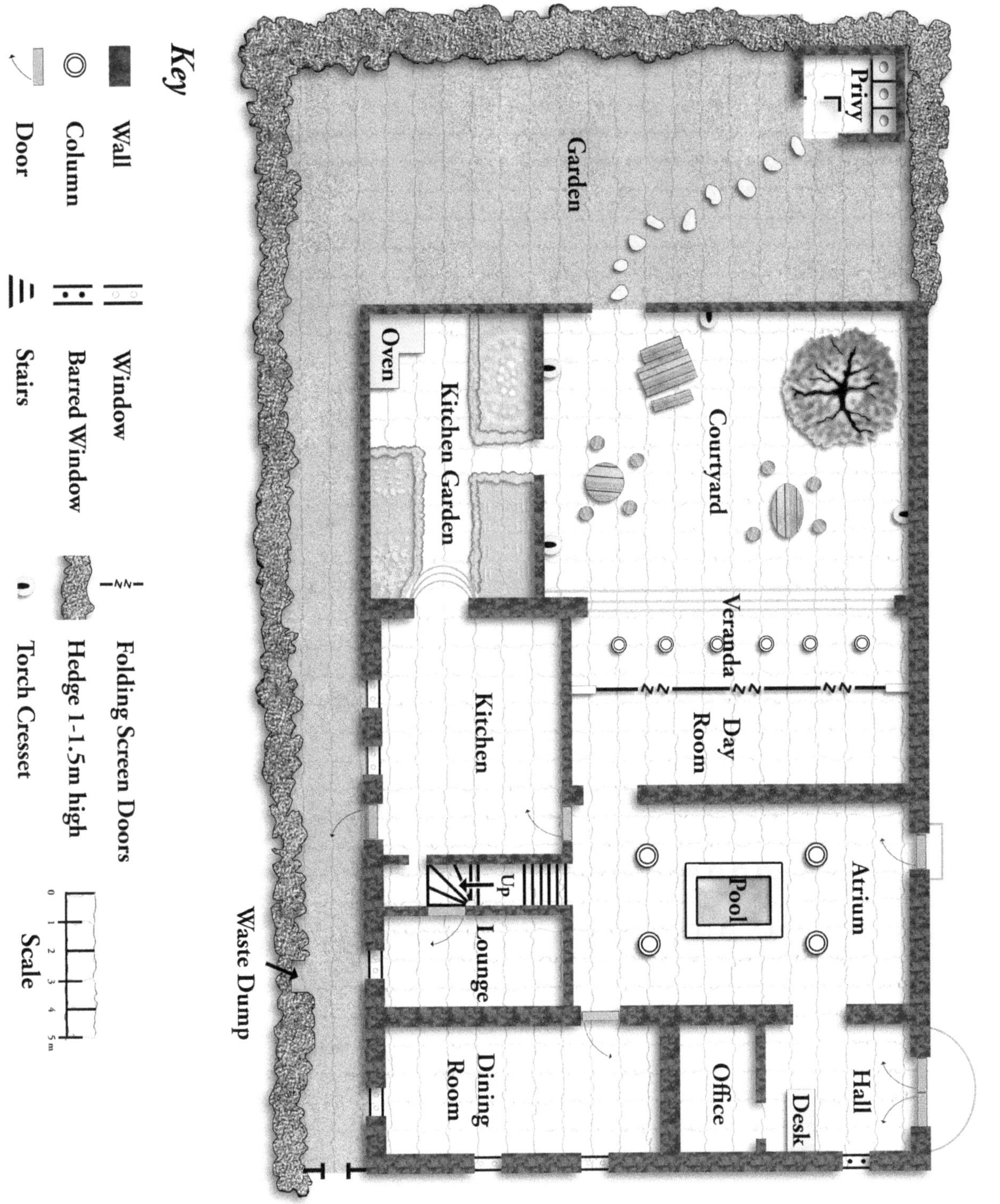

Key

- Wall
- Column
- Door
- Window
- Barred Window
- Stairs
- Folding Screen Doors
- Hedge 1-1.5m high
- Torch Cresset

Rooms shown: Privy, Garden, Oven, Kitchen Garden, Courtyard, Veranda, Day Room, Kitchen, Lounge, Dining Room, Atrium, Pool, Office, Hall, Desk, Waste Dump

Scale: 0 1 2 3 4 5m

Settlers

Thyrta has a potentially fertile hinterland; however, much of the territory is still untamed. Those who have taken grants of land have frequently been astonished at their good fortune in how much territory they have been awarded, only to discover that it will take years of back-breaking labour to clear all their land and bring it into production. They are however, a hardy and acquisitive lot – almost all of them have both farming and some military service to their name. Some specialists have also come to Thyrta to make their fortune, and these folk usually have no intention of breaking the soil through their own sweat and labour. Instead they attempt to make a business in the town with the intention of buying good land and subsequently populate it with tenants so they can live off the rent. These include both colonists from Borissa and metics – people from other cities who have put down roots and who presumably will acquire citizenship of the new state if they are successful.

Valsus of Kela (Metic)

Valsus is a merchant based at Thyrta who trades regularly with the Jekkarenes, and, in doing so, he has acquired an unhealthy reputation, as if simply by his regular dealings with them he is tainted by association. However, there is a market for Jekkarene goods – the complex and often beautiful styles applied to metalwork and cloth, and some unique fragrances used in oils and perfumes command high prices. Valsus appears to perform a useful service by being an outsider. He is not from Borissa but is a lapsed citizen of Himela, and can take care of business that respectable channels cannot. As a result, Valsus has become involved in a variety of distasteful business, handling deals with the slave merchant Hiram Hiram, or buying goods from freebooting adventurers arriving in Thyrta with loot from some private expedition. His trade is not in raw materials, foodstuffs or other bulk commodities as might form some substantial trade pattern, but of trinkets and objets d'art, curios, books, finished garments, perfumed oils and the like. It has made Valsus rich enough, but certainly not beyond his wildest dreams.

Valsus expects to be granted citizenship when Thyrta gains independence, and to have amassed sufficient wealth to become a leading citizen and landholder. To this end, he intends to save up a fortune of 20,000SP and he is well on the way towards his goal.

Valsus' statistics are provided on page 184.

Yezereus the Explorer (Colonist)

Yezereus is an acolyte of the Sabatean guild, and one who deals in breaking new ground beyond the Malthe river to find resources to be exploited, paces out new routes that might serve to move goods and people, and makes contacts with communities who present opportunities for trade and exchange. While his fellow Thyrtans are somewhat belligerent, Yezereus is a man who keeps his hand and his mind open when dealing with outsiders. He makes an annual circuit of the larger Thennalt settlements of Brotomagia with a small caravan of pack animals capable of negotiating the region's tracks and pathways. Yezereus is already a wealthy man, but this is not at all obvious by his dress or demeanour. He has the right to take a cut on the revenues generated by the commercial opportunities he opens up on his travels. Among these are direct overland trade with Hilanistra, and travelling with Yezereus in the late spring is the safest way to get there via the shortest route. Yezereus is personally tough, a former Sabatine who mustered out with Borissan citizenship. That is many years behind him now (Yezereus is in his mid 40s) but his outdoor pathfinding existence keeps him fit and active.

Medanthros the Educator (Colonist)

Medanthros is a sage and scholar, and such men are hard to find in Thyrta. He runs a small scriptorium close by the main square, staffed by Medanthros himself, an assistant and two educated slaves. He has a kindly nature and a burning desire to share all manner of useful or useless information with anyone he can engage in conversation. He has a command of many languages and scripts, and is willing to teach Literacy, Languages and Lores, with a Teaching skill of 68%. One of his pupils is Ormsfil, the younger son of Thennalt magnate Lord Skelfus.

Rilados the Navigator (Colonist)

Rilados is the leading light of Thyrta's maritime community, and an acolyte of Borissan Pyrolus, the national god of seafarers. A famous sailor, who keeps a small private merchantman of his own called Arribeus' Song – allegedly purchased with the proceeds of his adventures – but rarely puts to sea. Rilados is mostly famous for having ventured across the ocean via the dangerous southern route touching at Zarland (Fierla) and Haprosindra, which is dotted with many islands but almost devoid of civilisation, and where the natives you do encounter are as dangerous as the monsters that lurk beneath the waves. He is native born, a flashy dresser and smooth talker, and it seems he is not pressed for money but instead takes on only the voyages, cargoes and challenges that interest him, and it has been quite some time since something did. The truth to it is that

Thyrta

Rilados' adventures are some years behind him now, and while he cuts a swagger he is not overly interested in risking a life that is going so well.

Rilados appears to be in his late 30s with a weathered face – but still handsome and sporting a thick mane of dark hair that he wears longer than is usual. He is typically dressed in a tunic of deep blue embellished with patches of embroidery in orange – clearly expensive – and girt with a belt into which is thrust a large dagger with an ivory handle and a scabbard covered in embossed silver. Rilados does his carousing sporting his own silver cup, which is worth some 100SP as bullion. He keeps it with him at all times, and it hangs from his belt when not in use. He is full of stories and anecdotes, such as the one where he was adrift at sea on a raft with nothing but three turnips and a jar of stale beer, and only a webbed-handed Dagomil lady for company…

Games Master Note: Rilados drives a hard bargain for his services, but is a reliable sea captain and if presented with enough money can be paid to carry a band of adventurers across the ocean to destinations not on the route of most merchant captains. He is also a good source of information and, for a price that allows him to sit around in taverns spinning stories of his exploits, can provide the bearings to many obscure places and useful snippets of information about them.

Ivanthus of Tysil (Metic)

Ivanthus is a sell-sword, leader of a foreign Patriotic Band of 20 warriors from Tysil. Once off their home turf such people are essentially mercenaries dressing up their business in the nice language of concerned allies. These fellows have had little excitement since the expedition to Valos under Kalacho of Agissene some years ago and are hoping to find work in Thyrta in return for being resettled as citizens of the colony with land grants. He has a reputation, even in a place full of former soldiers, for being a hard and skilled warrior, and Ivanthus and his men often train with, and provide training for, the local militia. As they do not come from Borissa, they may have a long wait to secure a good stretch of land – unless they go carve it out of the wilds for themselves. For the time being Ivanthus and his gang drift in and out of employment; however, they are regularly called upon by the Thennalt magnate, Lord Skelfus, for their services.

Games Master Note: Ivanthus and his gang are likely rivals to the PCs, and maybe even enemies. If there's a job going for sell-swords, Ivanthus and his boys want it, and will use underhand tactics if necessary to see off competitors.

Urchins (colonists)

The Native Born is a gang of urchins who have been orphaned or abandoned, usually by those who have failed to make a success of coming here. They buzz around people who hang out at the taverns and eateries, looking for handouts, scraps or opportunities for employment on errands. By sticking together and making themselves known, it seems less likely any of them will be seized by an adult and forced into slavery or worse. So it is their job to be smart, entertaining and, if necessary, endearing in the hope people will look out for them and take an interest if they are physically abused.

Settler Land Grabs

The territory of Thyrta currently extends out to a day's march (typically 15 kilometres) from the city centre. Any viable arable land or pasture within this area has been assessed and divided into lots for distribution to citizens, in plots large enough to sustain a family and generate surplus – in effect, to guarantee the recipient the minimum requirement for a Social Class of Middling. This should mean a minimum of 4 hectares (10 acres) of good arable land per family, and comes with whatever additional marginal land lies between and among the fields, which may be the majority of its total area. Back in Korantia proper, a farm that size is worth up to 4,000SP as a going concern, well beyond the reach of most. In reality, of course, some plots are better than others. The authorities have tried to take that into account, issuing larger plots where the land is less easily cultivated.

Land is given out to settlers from the parent city of Borissa first, and to everyone else there is usually a price to be paid, or service to be rendered, to prove that they are suitable recruits to the city-state that will be created here.

Territory beyond one day from the city that is not already claimed by someone is essentially free to take and exploit. Some of this land is still used by indigenous Thennalts who may object, some has been settled by those who were for some reason denied a land grant, and some of it has been taken by those who decided their allocated plot was not sufficient for their needs and ambitions. In many cases the new landowners need more than their own sweat and toil to turn the territory into productive farmland. Dispossessed Thennalts and immigrants or settlers awaiting land allocation may provide casual labour, but Thyrta still has a need for slave labour.

Shores of Korantia

When Thyrta achieves independent statehood the city's total dominion is likely to be extended to a day's ride (circa 40km), which will take it right up to the edge of the Forest of Sard to the East, and to the coast to the West, encompassing some 3,000 square kilometers – including 100,000 hectares (a quarter of a million acres) of good agricultural land, enough for Thyrta to grow into a major city. Those who are in possession of land and find themselves in official Thyrtan territory are likely to be confirmed in their holdings, so long as they are (or become) citizens.

The acquisition of land here is a very hot issue, and lives as well as livelihoods are at stake.

TRANSIENTS

Many people find Thyrta a temporary place to stay – either they discover they are not cut out for the rigours of colonisation or they are content to enjoy the frontier feel of the town for a while, do a little business or even lay low – then move on.

Kosimus of Pelostra (Itinerant Craftsman)

Kosimus is a builder and architect who has turned down lucrative work at Bosippa in order to have a more or less free hand in the design and construction of Thyrta's new temple to its city-goddess. Kosimus follows a highly evolved classical plan, in which he applies the principles of aesthetic harmony through form, proportion, perspective and even acoustics with great sophistication. He has yet to move on to the surface decoration of friezes, statuary, painting and terracottas as he is yet to understand what will be the character and the ethos of the new city-state for which this will be the central public temple. Kosimus is arrogant but very talented, and he combines his artistic and professional skills with physical prowess. He prides himself in being able to match any of his brute labourers for strength and stamina, and is apparently an accomplished boxer. The temple is a 3 year project, with at least a year to go. Kosimus is then likely to return home and take a break until he returns to complete the decorative plan.

Melosson of Thrigos (Exiled Wastrel)

Melosson is a long way from home, an exile who fell victim to a purge of sorcerers from the state of Agissene. A rich father sends him funds from time to time, together with letters reassuring Melosson that his unjust exile is a temporary setback and will be reversed before too long. Melosson keeps rooms at the Floundering Turtle where he is a regular fixture in the tavern who loves mixing with the broad minded crowd often found in ports, and particularly in frontier places like this one. He has no pretensions to grandeur and finds it easy enough to tone down his education and aristocratic upbringing to fit in with the crowd. He keeps quiet about his sorcery – which is, in fact, an eclectic gathering of information and lore from the books that were the love of his life back home. Melosson's spells are scattered across grimoires with only one or two spells in each, and he does not know the enchanting ritual that would allow him to combine them. For this reason, he has four different Invoke skills and consequently none of them are very impressive. He does, however, keep a familiar, a hooded crow he calls Gewgaw. Melosson is very bright and, even though his magic is mainly self-taught from books, he is effectively an Adept (76%+ in Shaping). Melosson is up for adventure if the opportunity arises. His usual companion in wine and adventures is Bazagar, a stout and hairy prospector of Thennalt stock who knows the wilder parts of the region well.

Jorelso of Sarestra (Sea Captain)

Joreslo is captain of the Celestial Queen, a merchant ship running between Thyrta, its mother city of Borissa and onwards to Himela and Sarestra, his home port, mostly transporting grain. This provides a steady source of income, but not enough to prevent Jorelso and his crew being always on the lookout for other ways to turn a profit – anything short of piracy would be acceptable work, and they are not afraid of danger if the

The Celestial Queen, a Large Merchant Ship	
Power	Sail (2 masts, square rigged)
Crew	29
Dimensions	Length 37m, Beam 7.5m, Freeboard 2.5m
Capacity	250 Tons
Size	H
Hull Type	T
Hit Points	87
Armour Points	6
Seaworthiness	80%
Armaments	None; Damage 4d6
Notes	

Like most Korantine ships of her size, the Celestial Queen is a temple to the Korantine sailor god, Pyrolus, and the entire deck is consecrated. In front of the helm is a wooden statue of Pyrolus, 4' tall, that screams if anyone boards the vessel with intent to steal or do harm to the boat or crew.

Thyrta

rewards on offer are good enough. The Celestial Queen once plied the route between Sarestra and Kipsipsindra, but she now rarely ventures beyond coastal waters. Their ship is still seaworthy and much loved, but tatty sails and flaking paint suggest it is in need of a good refit. As befits the master of a good sized vessel like the Celestial Queen, Jorelso is an acolyte of the Korantine sea god, Pyrolus. Jorelso is good natured and likeable. He and his two partners Vitholas and Marrakon, each of whom own a third share of the ship, are firm friends and their crew are very loyal to them.

Games Master Note: The crew of the Celestial Queen are a band who can join your player-characters on a high seas adventure. Their vessel is ludicrously oversized for such work, but that will not stop them. Nevertheless Vitholas has reached the point where he wants to sell off his one-third share in the ship, and find an easier living – he is looking for 3000SP, but might take less.

Hiram Hiram (Morkeshite Slaver)

Hiram Hiram is a slave trader from Largil in Morkesh, and well known around the ports of Djesmirket. His vessel is the only one known that specialises in human cargo, although carrying and trading in slaves is not in itself uncommon. Hiram's interest in Thyrta is pretty limited, but there is a market there for labour to work the new land holdings being created both within and without the city's limits. Hiram does not generally deal in bulk slave labour as prices and margins can be low, however, if he has such stock to offload he stops at Thyrta, makes some sales, and occasionally buys individuals who have been condemned to slavery or those who have fallen into debt bondage, a highly divisive practice that Borissa is one of the last Korantine states to uphold.

Hiram is one of those captains who is familiar with the open ocean – every 2-3 years he actually takes his ship to Zarland, and even as far as Haprosindra on the coast of Jandekot, looking for exotic human specimens he can sell at a massive premium back in Djesmirket. The round trip takes five months at the very least, assuming favourable winds and no major repairs or refitting. His brutal-looking crew are not to be messed with, for good reason.

Games Master Note: Characters might meet Hiram Hiram to sell him their own captives – or find themselves confined to his slave cage – or perhaps need to purchase or attempt the rescue some unfortunate who has befallen such a fate. The local authorities are fully supportive of slavery as an institution, and will no more condone attempts to rob Hiram Hiram of his slaves than they would attempts to rob him of his purse.

Aromvelos of Tysil (Transient)

Aromvelos has long left his Korantine roots behind and become a wondering freebooter. Having started life as a marine in the service of the local Sabateus guild, more of his life has now been spent away from Korantia than in it, and he is an apostate (lapsed citizen). In the course of his adventuring career, he has plundered a famous royal tomb at Timolay, cleared out a nest of wyrms near Thyrta, and battled pirates off the coast of Haprosindra. These days he is liable to lay down roots and put his winnings into some venture or business for a couple of years – until the adventuring bug, or perhaps some cause he has taken a shine to – bites him again and he moves on.

Being of unremarkable appearance, Aromvelos has a liking for flashy gear that advertises his prowess. His helm and sword are of exquisite craftsmanship, his armour is made from the scales of a wyrm.

Games Master Note: There is a wizard in the Forest of Sard (Eashaddir) who would give near anything to get his hands on Aromvelos of Tysil. This wizard is wont to spend much of his life in shapeshifted form, and that of a wyrm is his favourite. So much so that he once had a female Wyrm as a mate, and there was even an offspring of their union...Aromvelos has no idea this wizard even exists.

Indeed wyrms are also regarded with reverence by Jekkarenes, and they would also take unkindly to the trophies he carries.

The Seaslaver, a Small Merchant Ship	
Power	Sail (1 mast, lateen rigged)
Crew	8
Dimensions	Length 22m, Beam 4.5m, Freeboard 2m
Capacity	80 Tons
Hull Type	T
Size	M
Hit Points	40
Armour Points	4
Seaworthiness	70%, Damage 2d6
Armaments	Large crossbow (arbalest) mounted on the rails
Notes	

Thanks to space devoted to keeping human captives under lock and key the Seaslaver usually only has a capacity of about 20 tons for regular cargo. However, she can hold some 40 captives, and more if Hiram is willing to risk a higher chance of damage to his stock, or simply chains them up on deck. Slaves typically sell for between 100 and 1,000 SP depending on age, health and skills, but the more exotic types that Hiram sources from the far west might achieve four times the upper end at auction in a major city.

Belisar of Mersin (Transient)

Belisar is a towering warrior from Mersin, a Korantine city-state located on the shores of the barbarian land of Zathrum. His family have for generations been warriors in the service of the distant Korantine Emperor, a convenient way to set themselves aloof from their neighbours. Being none too bright and at the time still naive, Belisar allowed himself to be caught up in a venture that seriously compromised his family's standing and rather upset the king of Zathis. As a result, he was refused his place as one of the local Lanist warriors, and was sent away with the instruction to return home with glory enough to set aside the shame he had brought on his family or not at all. Early in his travels, Belisar fell in with the much more more worldy-wise Aromvelos of Tysil, and, with him, has travelled widely on Korantine shores and beyond. Belisar is now in his prime; skilled, battle-hardened, magically supported, and with tales to tell of derring-do. He is rich enough to consider himself a success and to add to the family lands. He could continue to pursue the life of the freebooter, but his story draws him back towards Mersin.

Belisar is not one of life's tacticians. He has a gung-ho attitude, expects things to go his way if he just bellows a war cry and throws himself into the fray, behaving as if every fight is just another chance to show his prowess and earn a reputation. In this, he betrays his lack of smarts, as he frequently puts his life at risk in situations where his death may well go unnoticed by history, or he is the only witness to his triumph. His nine biggest scars are testament enough, in his mind.

Surrounding Lands

Bilinthus

An ancient Thennalt settlement, once the most important of the region, but now mostly in ruins. Its decline coincided with the arrival of the Korantines, hence the willingness of many Thennalts to welcome the settlers in the hope they would provide opportunities for commerce.

Bilinthus is a hill fort, its palisade is now gone and it is surrounded only by ditches and ramparts, which are in places overgrown with thickets. It never held a great number of dwellings, its main purpose was as a political and cult centre, and as a refuge. The political centre is no more, its chthonic cult functions struggle along, and the place has some inhabitants occupying ancient homes that they keep in serviceable repair and otherwise is mostly used for pasture. It is still the most important earth temple west of the Malthe river, but the temple at Simblay is now a rival.

Shrinking Hills

Rocky hills fill the north-west corner of the territory that drop precipitously to the sea. They take their name from the regular landslips that sacrifice ever more territory to the ocean, and for that reason are regarded as cursed by the Thennalts.

Bear Woods

Bear Woods were once part of the Forest of Sard. The forest here is thick with holm oak, and at its heart, is a great tree known as Bear Oak, which is the site of a dryad, Gallimee, who has, for years, been wife to the Thennalt Lord Skelfus.

Lakeside

A Thennalt settlement, part of which is built on stilts over the Sharpwater Lake. The inhabitants maintain a close relationship with nymph of the lake and are careful to maintain fish stocks. They take badly to intruders fishing in their waters.

Skelfus Fields

This large area is the demesne of Lord Skelfus, and everyone who lives within it is regarded as his tenant. Large areas are deliberately left uncultivated, in order to allow Skelfus the very best recreational hunting opportunities on his doorstep.

Odi's Fort

Just on the southern side of the Quickwater river, this fort was established by the Jekkarenes as a watch station for illicit traffic moving up and down the river valley that might wander into Jekkarene territory. It is manned by a band of 80 mercenaries, rotated every year or two, and currently under the command of Baron Osmestry. It occasionally receives high profile visitors in the form of Jekkarene noblemen on hunting expeditions into the Sard.

Tersippa

A small Korantine city that lies athwart the overland route between Borissa and its colony at Thyrta. There is no love lost between the people of Tersippa and their Borissan neighbours; however, they rely on an alliance with the powerful state of Himela, with whom they share democratic ideals, for protection. It is thought that Varoteg is covertly supported by Tersippa – certainly its people enjoy the discomfort his activities cause to Borissan interests.

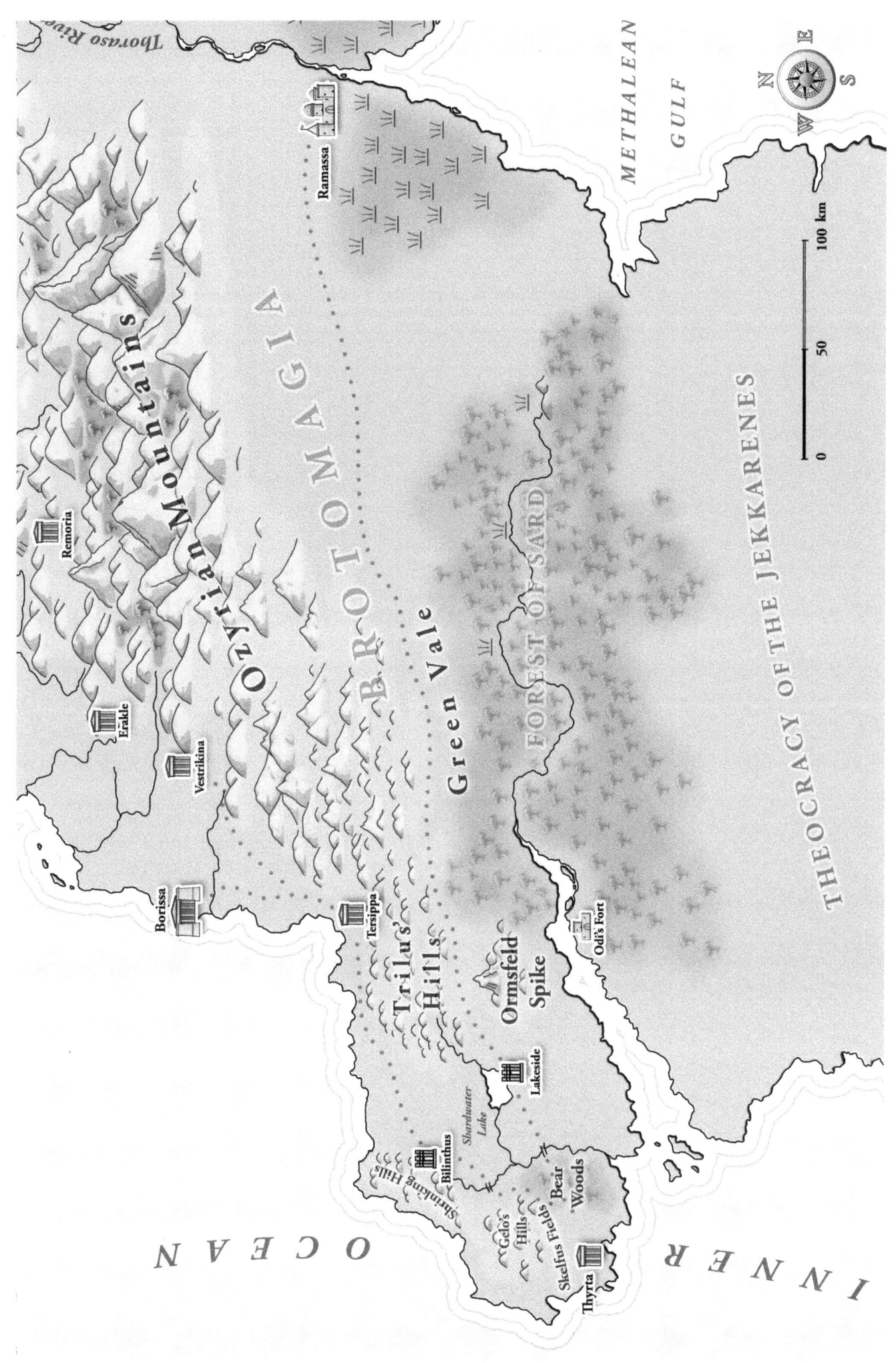

Trilus' Hills

Generally regarded as the most promising area for prospectors, nevertheless already one mine has been started and quickly closed as the results failed to meet the costs of the venture. New ventures await those with the capital to invest in digging deeper to access the minerals. The locals here are surly Thennalts, and the bandit Varoteg is popular among them – he frequently hides out here.

Oleg's Hills

This forested upland is the prime source of timber for the building and shipping trades, and Korantine loggers have been cutting into it with abandon now for two generations. Locals have become resigned to the fact, and take paid work from the loggers so long as they leave certain areas alone where they have sacred sites. Timbers are hauled a few miles overland to where they are dumped into the Malthe and floated to the coast. As the forests are pushed back, the prospectors move in to explore the hills for mineral wealth.

Malthe River

A convenient barrier between the territory that Thyrta intends to claim and the rest of Brotomagia, where the Thannalts expect to remain free.

Ornfeld Spike

A rocky crag close by Sard, said to be the lair of dragons. In recent times, a wandering adventurer from Tysil (see Aromvelos, above) slew a wyrm here. Lord Skelfus maintains he is too old now to scramble up to its highest reaches to hunt the monsters; however, rumours from his people suggest the last attempt proved that the wyrms' nest is somehow protected by powerful magic, and Skelfus has no stomach for wizardry.

Locals, Outsiders and Enemies

Varoteg

Varoteg is a bandit who represents the anger and desperation of those Thennalt communities who have been dispossessed by the land-grab conducted by the aggressive Korantine settlers from Borissa. His core following is only a dozen or so at any one time, but he could perhaps raise a force numbering in the hundreds if he summoned all his partisans to his side for some great deed or danger. Sixty years ago, the local Thennalt lord allowed the Korantines to settle, granting them certain lands and rights and subsequently selling them more until gradually the Thennalt peasantry found themselves dependent on working for the Korantines for wages, or even selling themselves into slavery. Varoteg uses that history to recruit warriors, informants and allies. His image is rather tarnished by his complete lack of ideology when it comes to whom he makes friends with and what he is willing to do to increase his wealth or notoriety. Nevertheless, his ongoing struggle to rob, outwit and humiliate Lord Skelfus has kept his popularity intact. Varoteg is not much of a threat to the territory of Thyrta, but for those colonists who have planted themselves beyond its official territory, his bandits are a frequent cause for concern.

Eashaddir

This wizard has made his home in the Forest of Sard. He specialises in shapeshifting, and many tales – dating back even to before the founding of Thyrta – about legendary monsters in the wild lands are actually stories about Eashaddir in one of the monstrous forms he enjoys adopting. He may spend months on end as a wyrm or some immense dire wolf. The wizard has been the doom of a quite a few adventurers who have set out to exterminate some poor bloody creature for their own personal glory only to discover the truth is rather more deadly even than the quarry they hoped to find. Eashaddir is completely adapted to the wilderness of Sard, and feels a duty of care towards the forest and its inhabitants. He has long forgotten what it is like to be a member of normal human society. However, Eashaddir currently lacks an apprentice; the last one got scared away some years ago by his master's erratic behaviour, which includes insisting that a would-be apprentice proves their worth by spending a year in beast form surviving in the forest.

Eashaddir's "children" include beast-men such as minotaurs and fauns, and he is very protective of them.

Tempigone

Tempigone is a rocky isle off the west coast of the Jekkarene peninsula. The whole island is a mountain thrust up above the sea and its coastal waters are treacherous to those unfamiliar with them. For generations the inhabitants have supplemented their subsistence by plundering ship that founder on their shores.

It is a rather dismal little island just over 60 kilometres long and barely 30 wide at its broadest, whose inhabitants are mostly fishermen or herders. The total population is about 5,000, of which almost a quarter is resident in the main town, Guberan. The remainder is spread between five fishing villages and two inland farming settlements. In addition, there is a mining

complex on the north side of Mount Tempiger, where a number of slaves are housed. The majority of the population is of Islander stock, claiming to be Guyuntars by descent and speaking a dialect of Archipelagan. The well-to-do tend to claim Korantine heritage as well or instead, and Korantine is used as the language of officialdom.

Tempigone is a territory of Himela, which inherited control upon the fall of the Korantine Empire. About 60 years ago it was given over to the Duke of Solarne to govern as his place of exile, his principal task being to maintain the fortress at Guberan and ensure the efficient removal of ore from the mines and its transport back to the mainland. The current duke, Arko of Solarne, still fulfils these obligations but otherwise rules with a free hand.

Arko's Rule

Arko rules Tempigone by edict with only a nominal regard to Himelan law. Wrongdoers may be imprisoned, enslaved or executed. Incarceration is really only an option for debtors, who can enjoy a stay in Guberan's gaol until they or a supporter have cleared their debt. Otherwise any punishment short of execution is converted to enslavement to work in the mines at Mt Tempiger. Life expectancy in the mines is rather short, so even those who are given a fixed period of enslavement do not usually expect to come out the other side. Only those who particularly upset the duke are executed – perpetrators of recognised criminal acts are hanged in public and left for a week as an example; those who have crossed him personally tend to be thrown extra-judicially from the walls of castle Guberan where they overlook the sea. Arko's guard form the only police force.

Arko also tolerates the practice of human sacrifice, which still sometimes happens in the villages. It is the custom, when the waves have thrown passing vessels onto Tempigone's rocks and the islanders have carried away any salvageable plunder, to offer any shipwrecked sailors found on the shore to as a sacrifice to Father Ocean. Since Arko connives in and benefits from the plunder via a tithe of all proceeds he has allowed what was formerly a clandestine practice to flourish.

Duke Arko has a standing force of just over 100 men, who are usually allocated watch and patrol duties in Guberan, or providing security at the mines and conduct the annual tax collection visits to the villages, where the locals can sometimes be rather unpleasant towards the collectors. The men are organised into duty squads of four men and a sergeant, and certain squads are designated as crew for the artillery pieces or to act as marines in Arko's tiny navy. There is a hard core of 30 old hands in the guard who have been in service since before Arko took power in Tempigone. These men are almost all Korantines by birth, whereas the remainder have been recruited from whatever manpower was available and with an eye from Arko for diluting the influence of the Korantine-born veterans. He can levy the islanders when needed to crew the two warships in Guberan harbour, or to act as a militia to defend the island against intruders.

Guberan Town and Castle

High on the cliffs overlooking Guberan and the sea is a massive brick-built fortress, which is the duke's seat of power. It is already 300 years old, built originally to protect the mines and act as a bastion from which to combat piracy in the southern reaches of the Korantine Empire. Although poorly maintained and thick with moss, the castle's battlements offer a commanding view over both the town and all approaches by land and sea. Beneath them are sheer cliffs at the foot of which the sea boils around jagged rocks where many who displease the duke have met their doom. Within the castle are the duke's residence, a barracks far too big for the current occupants, the treasury and the dungeon (mostly filled with tax debtors). The castle is oversized for the current occupants, and was in times past manned by a garrison of 1,000 men. It sports a barbican, and three siege engines (ballistae), which are placed to cover the harbour and its approaches

Guberan is Tempigone's only market town; however, there is rarely anything other than local produce and goods on sale unless a passing merchant puts in to port and sets up shop. The harbour has the usual complement of fishing boats plus Arko's two small 50-oared war galleys, which are usually on props out of the water and rarely in the best state of repair. It would take at least a couple of days to get the ships ready to sail and assemble crews by levy from the fishing villages if the need arose. The vessels are only manned in a known emergency, since Arko is short of cash and loathe to spend it on equipment, training and pay.

The Outlying Villages

The remainder of Tempigone's populations lives in or around the seven villages on the island – Enkeleb, Upper Enkeleb, Tempiger, Diotinia, Munda, Tormas and Kolisa. Upper Enkeleb and Tempiger are both situated on the slopes of Mt Tempiger, and mostly subsist on herding (goats and pigs), some arable and orchard crops, hunting and wood-gathering. The five other villages are all situated close to beaches where fishing boats can be drawn up out of the water, but set back from the shore to give some distance and protection from sea-borne raiders.

The fishing villages all have shrines to Diotimar and Dagomar (Mother and Father Ocean). Buildings are single story, timber framed and mostly flat roofed. The stonework is usually rendered and the render often painted an earthy red or white.

There is some game on the island – mostly wild cousins of the pigs and goats kept by the islanders – and the island is quite rich in bird life, so hunting the sea cliffs for eggs is a favourite pastime for young boys. However, much of the island's forestry has been long stripped away for use as building material, props for the mines, firewood and ships' timber, and Tempigone now has barely enough lumber for its own needs.

Fishing Villages

The five fishing villages each have a good beach for dragging boats up on to the shore, where they stand on the grassy dunes above the beach proper when not in use. The dwellings are all situated on higher ground overlooking the sea as a precaution against pirates. Each village has a total population of 2d4x75 of whom half are children and a quarter of whom are adult males.

Fishermen have their own boats, and most of the remaining adult males and some of the older children will work on the boats when the fleet is at sea, and perhaps, work on the farms when it is not. The majority of women and younger children work on cleaning and preparing the catch.

Demographics

Population Breakdown	
Craftsmen	10%
Hunters	5%
Herdsman	50%
Farmers	35%

Farming Villages

The two farming villages produce some arable crops, mostly emmer wheat and vines, with some orchard, mixed in. Herding here involves pigs, goats and sheep, but only the goats on Tempigone are reckoned to be good specimens.

Farmers are those who have their own arable plots and orchards, which are worked on by the other villagers in key seasons.

Tempiger Mines

The mines are publicly owned by the city-state of Himela, but the way they are managed is Duke Arko's problem. As long as he ships iron back to the mother city every year he is left alone. The mining complex is manned by some 200 slaves with a community of 30 or so overseers, engineers and other free labour. There are usually up to a dozen of Arko's guards here to help maintain security and control of the workforce. The settlement is right by the diggings and consists of slave barracks, a collection of shacks and one or two better houses for the staff, as well as the necessary processing and storage facilities for the mining operations. There is also a small shrine to Tempiger, the spirit of the mountain.

Important People

Arko of Solarne

Tempigone's ruler resides in Guberan castle with his wife, his retainers, and his company of guardsmen. His ancestry and titles derive from the town of Solarne in Himela, but the family estates were confiscated and the family exiled to Tempigone 60 years ago. Arko, who was born the wrong side of the blanket and secured his inheritance by the disposal of his half brother, is a greedy self-serving ruler. His principal aim is the acquisition of sufficient wealth to provide him with the standard of living he thinks a duke deserves. Tempigone's meagre resources allow him only to play at the role, and Arko spends his time scheming new ways to supplement his wealth. Arko is terribly unpopular with the Korantine citizen population of Tempigone, who regard him as a tyrant. He has in recent years refrained from calling public assemblies altogether and has converted the civic centre into a boarding house to his own profit. He nevertheless has some support among the other islanders – his mother was one of them, and he tolerates their salvaging practices, which frequently stray into wrecking.

Tiamankore

This Jekkarene woman is Arko's mistress. Thought by everyone to be a witch or sorceress, Tiamankore is in fact a spy, a lady of some stature who carries out her distasteful duties as Arko's mistress as a patriotic act. In league with Baron Solfernoy of Lyortha, this woman has plans to use Arko and his connections to the outside world to spread Solfernoy's trade links, influence and power through the sea lanes. Tiamankore is accompanied everywhere by a big, taciturn servant with a monkey on his shoulder.

Thyrta

Tiamankore arrived in Guberan three years ago and she at once caught Arko's eye and won his favour. Within a month Arko had installed her in a private house in the town, and, from then on, regularly entertained her at his table. She is his lover, and wields enormous influence over him. Indeed her excessive behaviour would have deeply embarrassed a ruler who had a care for public opinion. She affects a hauteur that demands she is addressed as 'mistress', although she holds no claim to any official status. There is an often-repeated story of how she beat one of Arko's slaves to death with a whip, having first asked him to give her the slave who had offended her over some trifle as a gift. Her relationship with the duke is the subject of a great deal of gossip and there is rampant speculation as to her origins.

Tiamankore is well versed in using her sorcery in clever and interesting ways. Besides being the ability to listen in on conversations with her Eavesdrop spell, Abjure Love can be used to manipulate a social situation, especially when converted to a charm using Enchant (and when she cannot bear Arko's more passionate advances, she uses it on him); Transfer Wound to take immediate and painful revenge on anyone who strikes her; and Bypass Armour on her own blade, or more usually, on Tallik's blade and club, to give armoured bullies – or those who think to stand up to Tallik – a very nasty surprise

Tiamankore is rarely seen in town, spending most of her time at home or in the castle. Errands are run for her by her henchman Tallik, who is equally the object of fear and suspicion. Tall and gaunt, swathed in a robe and headwrap of red and gold over a white linen shift, this mute servant Tallik carries his mistress', purse and her pet monkey is often riding on his shoulder. Ripcheep is rather more attached to Tallik than his mistress, and it is Tallik who uses him, via the Pet spell, as a spy or thief.

Alexianis of Sarestra

Arko's wife. Alexianis' wealthy father gave her in marriage to Arko with a healthy dowry and return for preferential trading rights in Guberan. He has long since found out he was sold a pup. Alexianis is in no way enamoured of her husband, so, all in all, it is an unhappy union, with Alexianis seeking annulment with the support of her father, but he wanting to secure the return of the dowry, which is long since spent.

When adventurers first arrive in Guberan a delegation from Duke Alexiandus is in town, negotiating the terms under which Alexianis may be returned to her father. They are destined to spend several months here while Arko delays, frustrates and prevaricates over the deal. Until some progress is made, or another vessel arrives that can return them to Sarestra, they eke out their time in quarters in the castle, and Alexianis spends as much time as she can with them.

For now, Alexianis' only hope is that a deal is done – and if not, that something unpleasant happens to Arko. She is completely outmatched as a plotter by his mistress however, so feels powerless. Her only light relief is Arko's one annual visit to Himela, stopping en route at Thyrta, in order to make his reports and account of himself to the council, on which she gets to accompany him.

Aldus the Bandit

Not really a bandit but rather someone who considers himself a concerned Himelan citizen, he is to Arko a common robber who interferes with his tax collection. His real name is Thurio, a stoical carpenter form Upper Enkeleb, who is well liked, if thought a little intense. To many among the Korantine population, he is a freedom fighter because he makes Arko's position difficult. They reckon that anything that suggests Arko is incompetent could hasten a review of his situation here and perhaps some direct action by the mother city is a good thing. Banditry doesn't pay as a full-time profession on Tempigone, so Aldus and his five men all have normal day jobs as farmers, fishers or craftsmen and live as ordinary citizens in Guberan and Enkeleb. Aldus rarely takes out his anger on fellow Korantines, but he regards the non-Korantine islanders as complicit in Arko's abuse of power, and hence fair game. Despite a reputation that makes him a bit of a hero (or a murderous monster depending on whom you ask), Aldus is neither particularly handsome nor charismatic. He is some 35 years of age, with lank brown hair and pale eyes. He is, however, a thinker and a talker, and it is his willingness to take action and persuade others to join him that has been his making. His cautious planning and careful management has so far kept him and his men safe. His gang numbers only seven, for recently two of his recruits have been killed by Arko's soldiers and their families sent to the mines. Aldus' gang are lightly armed with slings, knives, and the occasional sword or a woodman's axe. They wear leather hoods that cover the upper part of their faces, since Tempigone is a small place and the threat of recognition is significant. In any event, Aldus and his band carry out no more than one or two outrages per year.

Aldus can be a useful Games Master device to provide help to characters who have fallen foul of Arko.

Rosper

This man captains Duke Arko's guard, and is the most experienced and competent warrior on the island. He is also a seafarer who has retired to his position after a career as a pirate to spend his closing years enjoying his ill-gotten gains. Although thoroughly Korantine in his dress and habits, and rigged out in Imperial style when on duty, he nevertheless wears his moustaches long and carries traditional weapons in keeping with the customs of his homeland in Ostricur. This burly man of no great height stays close by Arko as a bodyguard at all his public audiences; otherwise, he goes about his duties in a casual if high-handed manner. When off duty, he can be found with his family in the castle or in one of the taverns where he might hang out with itinerant islanders from friendly clans. Rosper is sufficiently confident of his influence and standing with the Archipelagan population of Tempigone, with his off-island network of friends and collaborators, that he frequently considers murdering his master and taking over. Only the thought that a force from Himela might turn up in response holds him back. So if there's a way to ensure that's not going to happen, Rosper is keen to explore it.

The Sarestran Delegation

Duke Alexiandus' delegation is headed by Ronablus, the duke's steward, a richly dressed man of about 30 with great confidence in his own station and in his master's importance. He is accompanied by a high status slave-retainer by the name of Perigon, old and wise but still quite strong; and a lawyer from Himela named Velon of Nysa, who is thin, unhealthy and prone to coughing fits. Velon is also engaged by the ruling magistrates at Himela to report back on the state of affairs on Tempigone. Arko is not aware of this, neither are the other two delegates.

Arko finds their mere presence terribly irksome, and frets constantly about it. He further resents that the laws of hospitality require they stay in Guberan at his expense, his wife encourages them to consume as much as possible out of spite, and all of his stalling merely runs up his bills.

At the end of protracted negotiations, Ronablus will at the very least be be returning home to Sarestra with a letter sealed by both sides that provides for the very minimum that Arko must agree to under Korantine tradition. This letter, upon being lodged at the temple of Orayna, will annul the marriage and require Arko to return Alexianis and one quarter of the dowry (12,000SP). Alexianis he can do without, the money he cannot. As yet Arko has not come up with a scheme to either avoid paying the money altogether, or find it. Alexiandus is unlikely to be generous in agreeing installments.

Tiamankore regularly intrudes on the privacy of the delegation through her magical arts, and is biding her over how to turn this situation to Solfernoy's advantage.

Non-Player Characters

Aparinaon, Priest of Kos, Torthil Acolyte, Anayo Initiate

Characteristics	Attributes	1D20	Location	AP/HP
STR: 16	Action Points: 3	1–3	Right Leg	0/5
CON: 13	Damage Modifier: +1d2	4–6	Left Leg	0/5
SIZ: 12	Magic Points: 12	7–9	Abdomen	0/6
DEX: 12	Movement: 6 metres	10–12	Chest	0/7
INT: 14	Initiative Bonus: 13	13–15	Right Arm	0/4
POW: 12	Armour: None (if on army duty, full hoplite plate, 5AP, -6 SR)	16–18	Left Arm	0/4
CHA: 12		19–20	Head	0/5

Skills: Athletics 42%, Command 67%, Custom 97%, Devotion (Borissa) 85%, Endurance 55%, Evade 60%, Influence 71%, Insight 69%, Lore (Tactics and Drill) 91%, Perception 45%, Unarmed 68%, Willpower 75%

Passions: Loyalty (Borissa) 65%; Dispassionate 78%

Magic

Folk Magic (Rites 94%) Alarm, Avert, Bladesharp, Demoralise, Magnify, Tire, Vigor

Theism

(Devotion (Kos) 92%, Exhort 80% Devotional Pool = 6; Dismiss Magic, Extensino (3), Obliterate (3), Thread of Life (2)

(Devotion (Torthil) 58% Exhort 35% Devotional Pool = 3) Burn Fields, Consecrate (2), Extension(2) Perseverance, Steadfast

Combat Style: Citizen Infantry (Spear, Hoplite Shield, Shortsword – Phalanx) 78%

Weapon	Size/Force	Reach	Damage	AP/HP
Spear	M	L	1d8+1+1d2	4/10
Shortsword	M	S	1d6+1d2	6/8
Hoplite Shield	H	S	1d4+1d2	6/15

Aromvelos of Tysil, Adventurer

Characteristics	Attributes	1D20	Location	AP/HP
STR: 10	Action Points: 3	1–3	Right Leg	3/5
CON: 12	Damage Modifier: -	4–6	Left Leg	3/5
SIZ: 12	Magic Points: 10+4 stored	7–9	Abdomen	5/6
DEX: 16	Movement: 6 metres	10–12	Chest	5/7
INT: 17	Initiative Bonus: 8	13–15	Right Arm	3/4
POW: 10	Armour: Wyrmscale hauberk(5AP), Brigantine/reinforced leather armour (3AP each limb) and a fancy open helm (4AP)	16–18	Left Arm	3/4
CHA: 10		19–20	Head	4/5

Skills: Athletics 59%, Boating 40%, Brawn 34%, Commerce 40%, Custom 67%, Dance 26%, Deceit 53%, Drive 26%, Endurance 42%, Evade 58%, First Aid 76%, Influence 20%, Insight 27%, Language (Thennalt) 28%, Language (Djesmiri) 27%, Literacy (Korantine) 47%, Literacy (Djesmiri) 30%, Locale (Korantine Shore) 72%, Mechanisms 33%, Perception 79%, Ride 59%, Seamanship 42%, Sleight 76%, Stealth 85%, Swim 67% Unarmed 58%, Willpower 68%

Passions: Loyalty (Self) 99%; Wanderlust 84%

Magic

Folk Magic (Korantine Rites 47%) Detect Magic, Heal, Light, Speedart, Voice

Sorcery (Evoke 36%, Shaping 0%): The Assassin's Edge 41%: Damage Enhancement, Form/Set Iron, Smother

Combat Style: Swordsmanship 98%, Knife Fighting 45%, Archery 74%

Shores of Korantia

Aromvelos is a competent all-rounder, with excellent stealth skills, a lot of brains and a bit of magic alongside his experience as a fighter. If he uses his Damage Enhancement spell, his sword will hit for 8 points every time. He rarely makes use of the Smother spell. In the setting, Smother is a Concentration spell – and Aromvelos is unlikely to take himself out of an active fighting role long enough to make it effective.

Aromvelos's Kit

The Wyrmstones: These gems are found in the skull of a wyrm, and have the ability to store Magic Points. The MP value of a wyrmstone depends on the age of the wyrm it comes from. Wizards have been known to breed these creatures in order to harvest their stones. Aromvelos has one taken from a juvenile, which stores 4MP and he uses himself. He has another taken from an adult that stores 12MP. This is an extremely valuable item, and Aromvelos could reasonably expect a sorcerer with the necessary cash to offer him more than 5,000SP for it. So he is looking for a sorcerer with that sort of money to spend who is not the kind of wizard who will just take it.

Wyrmskin Armour: Not magical, but still very showy, this armour is made by removing the scales from the (presumably) dead wyrm and treating each one to toughen it further then punching the holes necessary to use them for Korantine-style scale armour. The scale cuirass has an AP value of 5 at no extra ENC cost.

Obsidian Chip: A small chip of shiny black obsidian on a thong around his neck. Boosts the Magnitude of any sorcery spell cast by 2, but sucks 2 Magic Points from the user to do so.

Weapon	Size/Force	Reach	Damage	AP/HP
Broadsword	M	M	1d8	6/10
Buckler	M	S	1d3	6/15
Dagger	S	S	1d4+1	6/8
Bow	L	-	1d6	4/4

Arko of Solame, Exiled Aristocrat, Governor-Acolyte of Himelan Anayo

Characteristics	Attributes	1D20	Location	AP/HP
STR: 10	Action Points: 2	1–3	Right Leg	0/6
CON: 13	Damage Modifier: +1d2	4–6	Left Leg	0/6
SIZ: 16	Magic Points: 11	7–9	Abdomen	0/7
DEX: 9	Movement: 6 metres	10–12	Chest	0/8
INT: 14	Initiative Bonus: 12	13–15	Right Arm	0/5
POW: 11	Armour: None	16–18	Left Arm	0/5
CHA: 8	Abilities: Inviolate. Arko is subject to an Ostracism spell	19–20	Head	0/6

Skills: Athletics 30%, Command 35%, Commerce 61%, Customs 70%, Deceit 92%, Endurance 40%, Evade 30% Influence 55%, Insight 38%, Literacy 84%, Perception 50%, Oratory 29%, Ride 40%, Unarmed 45%, Willpower 50%

Passions: Greedy and Ambitious 78%

Magic

Folk Magic (Rites 45%) Calculate, Cleanse, Cool, Disruption

Theism (Devotion 41%, Exhort 45% Devotional Pool = 1) Backlash, Extension (2), Inviolate (2) (Extension and Inviolate active)

Combat Style: *Korantine Citizen Infantry (Spear, Sword, Shield) – Phalanx 45%*

Weapon	Size/Force	Reach	Damage	AP/HP
Broadsword	M	M	1d8	6/10
Buckler	M	S	1d3	6/15
Dagger	S	S	1d4+1	6/8

Thyrta

Typical Member of Arko's Guard

Attributes	1D20	Location	AP/HP
Action Points: 3	1–3	Right Leg	3/6
Damage Modifier: +1D2	4–6	Left Leg	3/6
Magic Points: 10	7–9	Abdomen	4/7
Movement: 6 metres	10–12	Chest	4/8
Initiative Bonus: 8	13–15	Right Arm	3/5
Armour: Scale with laminated greaves and vambraces and an open helm	16–18	Left Arm	3/5
Abilities: None	19–20	Head	4/6

Skills: *Athletics 45%, Brawn 40%, Endurance 45%, Evade 40%,%, Locale (Tempigone) 45%, Lore (Tactics and Drill) 52%, Perception 45%, Survival 30%, Torsion Artillery 30%, Unarmed 50%, Willpower 35%*

Passions: *Loyalty (Arko) 50%*

Magic

Folk Magic (Rites 30%): Bladesharp, Heal, Ignite, Repair

Combat Style: *Korantine Citizen Infantry (Spear, Hoplite Shield, Javelin) 65%*

Weapon	Size/Force	Reach	Damage	AP/HP
Hoplite Shield	H	S	1d4+1d2	6/15
Spear	M	L	1d8+1+1d2	4/5
Javelin	H	-	1d8+1d2	3/8

Belisar Nine-Scar, Adventurer

Characteristics	Attributes	1D20	Location	AP/HP
STR: 12	Action Points: 3	1–3	Right Leg	4/5
CON: 15	Damage Modifier: +1D2	4–6	Left Leg	4/5
SIZ: 16	Magic Points: 8	7–9	Abdomen	5/6
DEX: 16	Movement: 6 metres	10–12	Chest	5/7
INT: 11	Initiative Bonus: 8	13–15	Right Arm	4/4
POW: 11	Armour: Scale hauberk, hoplite plate arms,	16–18	Left Arm	4/4
CHA: 9	legs and head	19–20	Head	4/5

Skills: *Athletics 55%, Brawn 56%, Command 60%, Custom 82%, Dance 30%, Deceit 25%, Devotion (Lanis) 51%, Drive 54%, Endurance 62%, Evade 35%, First Aid 87%, Influence 28%, Insight 58%, Language (Archipelagan) 24%, Language (Thennalt) 45%, Literacy (Korantine) 38%, Locale (Korantine Shore) 62%, Lore (Tactics and Drill) 66%, Perception 68%, Rites (Korantine) 40%, Ride 41%, Sing 20%, Stealth 42% Swim 35%, Track 42%. Unarmed 62%, Willpower 55%*

Passions: *Loyalty (Mersin) 45%*

Magic

Folk Magic (Korantine Rites 40%) Bladesharp, Fireblade, Protection, Speedart

Combat Style: *Archery 80%, Paladin (Javelin, Sword, Spear, Shield) 79%*

Weapon	Size/Force	Reach	Damage	AP/HP
Broadsword	M	M	1d8	6/10
Buckler	M	S	1d3	6/9
Dagger	S	S	1d4+1	6/8
Bow	L	-	1d6	4/4

Belisar's Kit

Miracle Healing Salve (5 doses) Adds 1/10 its POT of 50 to Belisar's CON for determining healing rate. One dose works on one location

Typical Thyrtan Constable

Attributes	1D20	Location	AP/HP
Action Points: 2	1–3	Right Leg	0/6
Damage Modifier: +1d2	4–6	Left Leg	0/6
Magic Points: 9	7–9	Abdomen	0/7
Movement: 6 metres	10–12	Chest	0/8
Initiative Bonus: 11	13–15	Right Arm	0/5
Armour: None	16–18	Left Arm	0/5
Abilities: None	19–20	Head	0/6

Skills: Athletics 38%, Brawn 45%, Endurance 46%, Evade 28%, Insight 35%, Locale (Thyrta) 40%, Perception 45%, Survival 31%, Unarmed 38%, Willpower 30%%, Stealth 39%

Passions: Uphold the Law 65%

Magic

Folk Magic (Rites 30%) Knock

Combat Style: *Constable (Club) 55%*

Weapon	Size/Force	Reach	Damage	AP/HP
Club	M	S	1d6+1d2	4/4

Eashaddir, the Wizard of Sard

Characteristics	Attributes	1D20	Location	AP/HP
STR: 12	Action Points: 3	1–3	Right Leg	0/6
CON: 18	Damage Modifier: +0	4–6	Left Leg	0/6
SIZ: 12	Magic Points: 17	7–9	Abdomen	0/7
DEX: 13	Movement: 6 metres	10–12	Chest	0/8
INT: 18	Initiative Bonus: 16	13–15	Right Arm	0/5
POW: 17	Armour: None	16–18	Left Arm	0/5
CHA: 9	Abilities: none	19–20	Head	0/6

Skills: Athletics 55%, Brawn 37%, Command 48%, Deceit 81%, Endurance 65%, Evade 45%, Influence 35%, Insight 37%, Locale (Sard) 135%, Perception 70%, Survival 75%, Unarmed 38%, Willpower 85%, Stealth 60%

Passions: Bears, Boars and Wyrms 77%

Magic

Folk Magic (Rites 77%) Avert, Bladesharp, Demoralise, Dullblade, Heal, Repair, Slow, Speedart

Sorcery (Invocation 127%, Shaping 125%) Enchant, Enhance SIZ, Regenerate, Shapechange Human To Wyrm, Shapechange Human To Boar, Shapechange Human To Bear, Shapechange Human To Aurochs, Shapechange Human To Wolf, Repulse (Humans), Spirit Resistance, Spell Resistance Switch Body

Notes: Intensity 13 Spirit Resistance (3MP charm, Magnitude 5, monthly)

Combat Style: *Bestial Fury 52%* (Uses natural weapons for the appropriate creature)

Thyrta

Ivanthus of Tysil, Initiate of Torthil, Mercenary Leader

Characteristics	Attributes	1D20	Location	AP/HP
STR: 15	Action Points: 3	1–3	Right Leg	5/6
CON: 14	Damage Modifier: +1d2	4–6	Left Leg	5/6
SIZ: 13	Magic Points: 12	7–9	Abdomen	4/7
DEX: 12	Movement: 6 metres	10–12	Chest	4/8
INT: 14	Initiative Bonus: 8	13–15	Right Arm	3/5
POW: 12	Armour: Hoplite plate greaves and helm,	16–18	Left Arm	3/5
CHA: 12	scale hauberk, Studded bracers	19–20	Head	5/6

Skills: Athletics 65%, Brawn 45%, Command 42%, Endurance 65%, Evade 42%, Locale (Brotomagia) 45%, Perception 60%, Survival 45%, Unarmed 78%%, Willpower 55%, Stealth 50%

Passions: Loyalty (Tysil) 42%, Loyalty (Ivanthus' Gang) 78%

Magic

Folk Magic (Rites 44%) Bladesharp, Demoralise, Heal, Might, Repair

Theism (Devotion 43%, Exhort 38%; Devotional Pool = 3) Burn Fields, Steadfast

Combat Style: *Korantine Infantry (Spear, Hoplite Shield, Javelin) 92%, Sidearm and Shield (Shortsword, Falchion, Hoplite Shield) 81%*

Weapon	Size/Force	Reach	Damage	AP/HP
Falchion	M	M	1d6+2+1d2	6/10
Hoplite Shield	H	S	1d4+1d2	6/15
Spear	M	L	1d8+1+1d2	4/5
Javelin	H	-	1d8+1d2	3/8

Typical Member of Ivanthus' Patriotic Band, Initiate of Torthil

Attributes	1D20	Location	AP/HP
Action Points: 3	1–3	Right Leg	3/6
Damage Modifier: +1d2	4–6	Left Leg	3/6
Magic Points: 11	7–9	Abdomen	4/7
Movement: 6 metres	10–12	Chest	4/8
Initiative Bonus: 8	13–15	Right Arm	3/5
Armour: None when in town. Linen and scale, metal helms	16–18	Left Arm	3/5
Abilities: None	19–20	Head	4/6

Skills: Athletics 45%, Brawn 40%, Endurance 55%, Evade 35%,%, Locale (Thyrta) 45%, Lore (Tactics and Drill) 76%, Perception 45%, Survival 40%, Unarmed 50%, Willpower 45%%, Stealth 35%

Passions: Loyalty (Ivanthus's Gang) 70%, Loyalty (Tysil) 45%

Magic

Folk Magic (Rites 30%): Bladesharp, Heal, Ignite, Polish, Repair

Combat Style: *Korantine Citizen Infantry (Spear, Hoplite Shield, Javelin) 75%, OR Archery 75%. Trait: Formation Fighting; Sidearm and Shield (Falchion, Hoplite Shield) 55%*

Weapon	Size/Force	Reach	Damage	AP/HP
Falchion	M	M	1d6+2+1d2	6/9
Hoplite Shield	H	S	1d4+1d2	6/15
Spear	M	L	1d8+1+1d2	4/5
Javelin	H	-	1d8+1d2	3/8

Kortano the Syndic, Priest of Sabateus, Anayo Initiate

Characteristics	Attributes	1D20	Location	AP/HP
STR: 8	Action Points: 3	1–3	Right Leg	0/6
CON: 12	Damage Modifier: +0	4–6	Left Leg	0/6
SIZ: 15	Magic Points: 16	7–9	Abdomen	0/7
DEX: 10	Movement: 6 metres	10–12	Chest	0/8
INT: 18	Initiative Bonus: 14	13–15	Right Arm	0/5
POW: 16	Armour: None	16–18	Left Arm	0/5
CHA: 14		19–20	Head	0/6

Skills: Athletics 55%, Commerce 110%, Custom 71%, Devotion (Borissa) 65%, Endurance 38%, Evade 26%, Influence 87%, Insight 72%, Literacy 85%, Lore (Accounting) 125%, Locale (Brotomagia) 55%, Locale (Korantine Shore) 40%, Perception 46%, Unarmed 35%, Willpower 70%

Passions: Loyalty (Borissa) 80%

Magic

Folk Magic (Rites 60%) Appraise, Calculate, Lock, Translate, Voice

Theism (Devotion 92%, Exhort 80%, Devotional Pool = 12) Assay, Backlash, Consecrate (2), Excommunicate (3), Extension (3), Mindlink, Pacify

Combat Style

Flat-footed Civilian (Dagger, Knife) 35%

Weapon	Size/Force	Reach	Damage	AP/HP
Dagger	S	S	1d4+1	6/8

Lord Skelfus, Thennalt Noble and Honorary Paladin

Characteristics	Attributes	1D20	Location	AP/HP
STR: 15	Action Points: 3	1–3	Right Leg	5/5
CON: 11	Damage Modifier: +1d2	4–6	Left Leg	5/5
SIZ: 14	Magic Points: 12	7–9	Abdomen	5/6
DEX: 8	Movement: 6 metres	10–12	Chest	5/7
INT: 15	Initiative Bonus: 6	13–15	Right Arm	5/4
POW: 12	Armour: Hoplite Plate Panoply	16–18	Left Arm	5/4
CHA: 14	Abilities: Swift – a Gift from Lanis, bestows an additional Action Point	19–20	Head	5/5

Skills: Athletics 82%, Culture (Korantine) 61%, Custom (Thennalt) 55%, Deceit 60%, Endurance 65%, Influence 70%, Insight 51%, Locale (Brotomagia) 102%, Oratory 43%, Perception 68%, Ride 99%, Survival 60%, Track 72%, Willpower 75%

Passions: Loyalty (Emperor) 90%; Love Hunting 85%; Hate Varoteg 80%

Magic

Folk Magic (Rites 86%) Avert, Bladesharp, Firearrow, Heal, Light, Protection, SpiritShield, Vigour.

Theism (Devotion 93%, Exhort 55%, Devotional Pool = 6) Aegis, Clear Skies (2), Dismiss Magic, Heal Wound, Ripen, Sacred Band, Truespear

Combat Style: Paladin (Javelin, Spear, Sword, Shield) – Mounted 88%, Archery – On the Fly 92%

Weapon	Size/Force	Reach	Damage	AP/HP
Spear	M	L	1d8+1+1d2	4/5
Broadsword	M	M	1d8+1d2	6/10
Hoplite Shield	H	S	1d4+1d2	6/15
Javelin	H	-	1d8+1d2	3/8
Bow	L	-	1d6+1d2	4/4

Thyrta

Rikalsos of Vimaylo, Acolyte of Borissan Anayo

Characteristics	Attributes	1D20	Location	AP/HP
STR: 11	Action Points: 2	1–3	Right Leg	0/5
CON: 12	Damage Modifier: +0	4–6	Left Leg	0/5
SIZ: 13	Magic Points: 13	7–9	Abdomen	0/6
DEX: 10	Movement: 6 metres	10–12	Chest	0/7
INT: 13	Initiative Bonus: 12	13–15	Right Arm	0/4
POW: 13	Armour: None	16–18	Left Arm	0/4
CHA: 10		19–20	Head	0/5

Skills: *Athletics 35%, Command 45%, Commerce 29%, Customs 75%, Deceit 30%, Endurance 45%, Evade 38% Influence 71%, Insight 44%, Literacy 92%, Perception 60%, Oratory, 78%, Unarmed 45%, Willpower 47%*

Passions: *Loyalty (Borissa) 75%; Closet Demagogue 55%; Love Simbale 55%*

Magic

Folk Magic (Rites 66%), Deflect, Protection, Voice

Theism (Devotion 71%, Exhort 55%, Devotional Pool = 5) Backlash, Consecrate (2), Inviolate (2), Ostracism(2)

Combat Style: *Korantine Citizen Cavalry (Spear, Sword, Shield, Dart – Skirmisher) 45%*

Weapon	Size/Force	Reach	Damage	AP/HP
Dagger	S	S	1d4+1	6/8

Rilados the Navigator, Acolyte of Pyrolus

Characteristics	Attributes	1D20	Location	AP/HP
STR: 12	Action Points: 3	1–3	Right Leg	0/6
CON: 17	Damage Modifier: +0	4–6	Left Leg	0/6
SIZ: 13	Magic Points: 9	7–9	Abdomen	0/7
DEX: 13	Movement: 6 metres	10–12	Chest	0/8
INT: 14	Initiative Bonus:14	13–15	Right Arm	0/5
POW: 9	Armour: None	16–18	Left Arm	0/5
CHA: 10	Abilities: None	19–20	Head	0/6

Skills: *Athletics 55%, Boating 93%, Brawn 58%, Commerce 48%, Craft (carpentry) 72%, Endurance 88%, Influence 75%, Literacy 28%, Locale (Western Ocean) 45%, Locale (Korantine Shore) 91%, Language (Archipelagan) 55%, Navigate 90%, Perception 65%, Seamanship 112%, Seduction 45%, Survival 85%, Swim 76%, Unarmed 62%, Willpower 25%*

Passions: *Loyalty (Thyrta) 60%; Dedicated Follower of Fashion 80%*

Magic

Folk Magic (Rites 66%) Beastcall (marine creature), Breath, Deflect, Dry, Glue, Heal, Might, Preserve, Repair, Sea Legs, Shove, Vigor

Theism (Devotion 63%, Exhort 70% Pool 5) Call Winds(2), Consecrat (2), Propitiate (Ocean) (2), Elemental Summoning (Sylph), Lay to Rest (at Sea)

Combat Style: *Marine (Falchion, Dagger, Javelin, Pelte) – Sure Footed 76%*

Weapon	Size/Force	Reach	Damage	AP/HP
Falchion	M	M	1d6+2	6/9
Pelte	L	S	1d4	4/12
Dagger	S	S	1d4+1	6/8
Javelin	H	-	1d8	3/8

Tallik, Mute Henchman to Tiamankore

Characteristics	Attributes	1D20	Location	AP/HP
STR: 17	Action Points: 2	1–3	Right Leg	0/6
CON: 16	Damage Modifier: +1d4	4–6	Left Leg	0/6
SIZ: 17	Magic Points: 11	7–9	Abdomen	0/7
DEX: 11	Movement: 6 metres	10–12	Chest	0/8
INT: 11	Initiative Bonus: +11	13–15	Right Arm	0/5
POW: 11	Armour:	16–18	Left Arm	0/5
CHA: 6	Abilities: None	19–20	Head	0/6

Skills: *Athletics 50%, Endurance 70%, Evade 35% Intimidate 61%, Insight 50%, Literacy 40%, Perception 75%, Unarmed 85%, Willpower 50%*

Passions: *Loyalty (Tiamankore) 99%, Likes Hurting Things 80%*

Magic

Folk Magic (Rites 45%) Bludgeon, Demoralise, Pet

Combat Style: *Murderous Brute (Club, Dagger), Impromptu Weapons – reduce penalty for use of unfamiliar weapons by one grade – 77%*

Weapon	Size/Force	Reach	Damage	AP/HP
Iron Shod Club	M	S	1d6+1d4+1	6/4
Dagger	S	S	1d4+1+1d4	6/8

Tiamankore, Jekkarene 'Devoted Daughter', Spy

Characteristics	Attributes	1D20	Location	AP/HP
STR: 10	Action Points: 3	1–3	Right Leg	0/6
CON: 13	Damage Modifier: +0	4–6	Left Leg	0/6
SIZ: 14	Magic Points: 16	7–9	Abdomen	0/7
DEX: 15	Movement: 6 metres	10–12	Chest	0/8
INT: 16	Initiative Bonus:16	13–15	Right Arm	0/5
POW: 16	Armour: None	16–18	Left Arm	0/5
CHA: 15	Abilities: None	19–20	Head	0/6

Skills: *Customs 85%, Deceit 75%, Endurance 56%, Evade 40%, Dance 84%, Insight 65%, Influence 50%, Language (Korantine) 40%, Literacy 57%, Seduction 79%, Sleight 68%, Willpower 69%*

Passions: *Loyalty (Jekkarenes) 100%, Love Secrets 88%*

Magic

Folk Magic (90%) Avert, Befuddle, Cleanse, Coordination, Heal, Tire

Theism (Devotion 76%, Evoke 58%. Devotional Pool = 6) Miracles: Absorption, Enthrall, Moonbright, Synchronise

Sorcery (Invocation 56%, Shaping 48%) Abjure Love, Bypass Armour, Enchant, Intuition, Mystic Vision, Project Sense (Hearing), Regenerate, Spirit Resistance, Transfer Wound

Combat Style: *Guardian (Rapier, Dagger, Morning Star and Buckler) 65% – Swashbuckling*

Weapon	Size/Force	Reach	Damage	AP/HP
Buckler	M	S	1d3	6/9
Dagger	S	S	1d4+1	6/8

THYRTA

Varoteg, Thennalt Bandit, Freedom Fighter

Characteristics	Attributes	1D20	Location	AP/HP
STR: 15	Action Points: 3	1–3	Right Leg	3/6
CON: 13	Damage Modifier: +1d2	4–6	Left Leg	3/6
SIZ: 13	Magic Points: 17	7–9	Abdomen	3/7
DEX: 16	Movement: 6 metres	10–12	Chest	3/8
INT: 16	Initiative Bonus:13	13–15	Right Arm	3/5
POW: 17	Armour: Bezainted	16–18	Left Arm	3/5
CHA: 17	Abilities: Lucky	19–20	Head	4/6

Skills: *Athletics 75%, Brawn 37%, Command 48%, Deceit 81%, Disguise 62%, Endurance 65%, Evade 75%, Locale (Brotomagia) 110%, Perception 70%, Ride 44%, Survival 75%, Unarmed 78%%, Willpower 55%, Stealth 60%*

Passions: *Loyalty (Thennalts) 70%; Hate (Thyrta) 70%; Pragmatic 85%*

Magic

Folk Magic (Rites 77%) Avert, Bladesharp, Demoralise, Dullblade, Heal, Repair, Slow, Speedart

Combat Style: *Thennalt Bandit (Sling, Battleaxe, Pelte, Dagger) 98%*

Weapon	Size/Force	Reach	Damage	AP/HP
Battleaxe	M	M	1d8+1+1d2	4/8
Pelte	L	S	1d4+1+1d2	4/12
Dagger	S	S	1d4+1+1d2	6/8
Sling	L	-	1d8+1d2	1/2

Volsenna, Priestess of Borissa

Characteristics	Attributes	1D20	Location	AP/HP
STR: 7	Action Points: 2	1–3	Right Leg	0/8
CON: 7	Damage Modifier: -1d2	4–6	Left Leg	0/8
SIZ: 12	Magic Points: 12	7–9	Abdomen	0/9
DEX: 10	Movement: 6 metres	10–12	Chest	0/10
INT: 14	Initiative Bonus: 12	13–15	Right Arm	0/7
POW: 17	Armour: None	16–18	Left Arm	0/7
CHA: 18	Abilities: Robust – Hit Points Based on CON+SIZ+POW; Resilience – immune to the effects of physical pain.	19–20	Head	0/8

Skills: *Craft (spinning) 71%, Custom 65%, Endurance 25%, Evade 29%, First Aid 91%, Influence 77%, Insight 62%, Perception 35%, Unarmed 30%, Willpower 59%*

Passions: *Loyalty (Thyrta) 100%; Loyalty (Borissa) 80%; Love Yezereus 80%; Mother's Love 90%*

Magic

Folk Magic (Rites 94%) Avert, Calm, Cleanse, Heal, Loyal Oath, Voice, Witchsight

Theism (Devotion 95%, Exhort 70%, Devotional Pool = 10) Aegis, Consecrate (2), Excommunicate(3), Extension (3), Heal Body (2), Fortify, Pacify, Spirit Block

Combat Style: *None*

Yezereus, Acolyte of Sabateus

Characteristics	Attributes	1D20	Location	AP/HP
STR: 14	Action Points: 3	1–3	Right Leg	0/5
CON: 12	Damage Modifier: +1d2	4–6	Left Leg	0/5
SIZ: 13	Magic Points: 12	7–9	Abdomen	0/6
DEX: 11	Movement: 6 metres	10–12	Chest	0/7
INT: 14	Initiative Bonus: 13	13–15	Right Arm	0/4
POW: 12	Armour: None	16–18	Left Arm	0/4
CHA: 14	Abilities: None	19–20	Head	0/5

Skills: *Athletics 55%, Commerce 73%, Culture (Thennalt) 50%, Customs 65%, Deceit 40%, Endurance 55%, Evade 50% First Aid 46%, Influence 70%, Insight 54%, Language (Thennalt) 60%, Literacy 52%, Navigate 82%, Oratory 54%, Perception 40%, Ride 55%, Survival 73%, Unarmed 68%, Willpower 47%*

Passions: *Love (Volsenna the Younger) 80%, Loyalty (Borissa) 60%, Open Minded 55%*

Magic

Folk Magic (Rites 66%), Appraise, Calculate, Lock, Polish, Translate

Theism (Devotion 88%, Exhort 54%; Devotional Pool = 6) Assay, Backlash, Consecrate (2), Extension (2), Mindlink, Pacify

Combat Style: *Sabatine (Bow, Buckler, Dagger, Shortsword) 78%*

Weapon	Size/Force	Reach	Damage	AP/HP
Shortsword	M	S	1d6+1d2	6/8
Buckler	M	S	1d3+1d2	6/9
Dagger	S	S	1d4+1+1d2	6/8
Bow	L	-	1d6+1d2	4/4

Varoteg's Rascals

Varoteg and his bandits are a regular problem to those travelling the Thyrtan countryside, and if they seem to have a penchant for robbing Korantine settlers, they also take enormous pleasure in harassing the estates of Lord Skelfus, the local Thennalt bigwig who has done so much to promote settlers' interests over those of his own people.

Running Varoteg to ground is no easy task; after all, Skelfus has spent much time and treasure trying to do just that and so far he has failed. The problem: Varoteg is extremely popular with the downtrodden natives, to whom he is a folk hero; few people know his face, and he is a very clever bandit. A reward of 5,000SP on Varoteg alone, as well as a bounty of 50SP for any of his accomplices, has not achieved any results either.

But outside the protective circle of Varoteg's ardent supporters are a gang of misfits and outlaws whom Varoteg has taken under his wing. They are his Rascals, those whom Varoteg keeps at arm's length from the rest of his network and has set up in a hideout in an abandoned mineworking in the hills. He knows that even his supporters in the general population don't like them because they are outsiders, and so not to be trusted. And one of them is a *monster*. Varoteg also observes caution; he makes sure the Rascals don't know enough about him to be a threat if they turn traitor or simply get caught and interrogated. He uses them for little jobs that might tarnish his own reputation as a champion of the oppressed if he were directly connected and meanwhile they provide a guard to a little cache of treasure he has set aside in case of emergency.

In this scenario, the player characters have acquired some valuable information that gives them the opportunity to set out into the countryside to track down bandits, and win a reward and booty for bringing them to justice. When they set out, they may believe they are actually on the trail of Varoteg himself, and only later realise they have encountered just a part of his organisation. The complication is that there are more bandits in them there hills than you might expect, and they can have conflicted loyalties or reasons for doing what they do. The characters may end up quite confused as to which ones they are chasing.

The scenario is intended to introduce the players to the locale, to get them involved with some of the local personalities, and provide hooks for both the other scenarios in this book and for others devised by the Games Master.

Introducing the Scenario

There are several ways the characters can find themselves on this quest. Information about bandits, their hideouts and so forth is all currency in Thyrta. Rewards and booty are at stake, and while there are some who will dutifully go straight to the authorities with any useful intelligence, the majority will look to how to exploit such information for personal gain. The different situations presented here offer the choice of a straightforward call to action or a more complex and investigative opening to the scenario.

The Turncoat

One of the Rascals gang has abandoned his fellows and snuck into Thyrta to claim the reward for capturing or killing his

comrades. He needs a gang to work with to do the job, and he doesn't want to end up confronting Skelfus who he is convinced will just torture him for his information and kill him afterwards anyway. The Games Master can invent a new gang member to play this role, or pick one of those provided. There may be a reason the individual chosen singles out the characters to be his accomplices, perhaps he comes from the same city, or perhaps they are foreigners with no local loyalties or connections. The promise is not to get Varoteg himself, but to take out part of his gang, hopefully bring back some valuable prisoners (or heads) and at the very least grab and share the loot that Varoteg stashes there.

The Disgruntled Thennalt

Not one of the Rascals but a supporter, or even a follower, of Varoteg who simply objects to the existence of this distasteful gang of outsiders being linked to Varoteg's cause, and considers them a liability and Varoteg's attachment to them a folly. He may also have a personal grudge against one of them – perhaps Orinastron has made advances on his sweetheart, or they have committed some outrage in his home village. This person, a Thennalt who calls himself Dannil, simply offers to sell the location of the Rascals' hideout. He doesn't want to be directly involved.

The Tell-Tale

One of Varoteg's people has been captured and interrogated, and offers up that the abandoned mine as Varoteg's hiding place, thus hoping to give up something to his captors to stop the torture, or trade for his life without hurting the cause too much. The characters are hired to go and find out if the information provided is accurate (or it may be they who captured the fellow in the first place and get this information directly).

The Conspiracy Revealed

Varoteg disposes of some of his loot in Tersippa, but he also makes clandestine trades with the merchant Valsus through the medium of a caravan master called Athlazo. Valsus then fences Varoteg's plunder by selling it on to the Jekkarenes. Athlazo's caravans travel between Thyrta and Tersippa via Bilinthus, and on the way, an exchange takes place in which basic supplies and the occasional special order are traded for bandit loot.

The characters may discover this because they have reason (or orders) to make discreet enquiries into Athlazo's business, or because they have reason to search Valsus' house and find evidence there (see the next scenario: The House of Valsus).

The Counter-Conspiracy

If Valsus or Athlazo suspect someone is snooping around into their affairs, Varoteg is their go-to guy to deal with the problem. Varoteg won't risk his core gang or supporters to help them out, but he will call on the Rascals. Five or six days after the characters come to the attention of the conspirators, one or more of the Rascals gang slips into Thyrta and attempts to ambush the characters in the street or at their lodgings. In this case, the characters may find themselves using information extracted from a captured assailant (who will offer location of his hideout and his stash for his life and/or freedom) to follow the thread to the abandoned mine and back to Valsus and/or Athlazo. In this instance, the informer will tell about the horrible 'THING' (Gorkas) that lurks in the darkness.

THE ROUTE

There is no detailed map that can be used, but it is possible to plot out the route to be taken using notable landmarks as waypoints. Any set of directions will indicate first the boundary of Thyrtan territory (one day's march from the city), then a little under two day's onward march (circa 40km), then a final day picking their way through the hills to reach a spot referred to as "the Thennalt Stone". The instructions state that the traveller should then move north with the woods on their left and the Clumps (a pair of conical hills each topped with a copse) on their right until they reach a broad pasture, containing cattle bearing the "Mark of Theyna". For those investigating where Athlazo trades with bandits, this is the end of the journey unless they subsequently discover the whereabouts of the Rascals' hideout.

For those with instructions to go further to where the Rascals have their hideout, then due east of this pasture, skirting north of the nearby village (Simblay), they will strike a stream bed, which leads to a defile, at the head of which is the abandoned mine where the Rascals hide.

For most of the journey, the route follows little-used tracks through open country, punctuated here and there by a farm or hamlet, orchards, wheat fields or grazing herds. If the characters are guided, they will arrive in good time, and they may avoid the attention of the local toughs (see below). If they navigate by their own wits using written or verbal directions and have no assistance or knowledge of the locale, a successful Navigation or Survival test is required to work out exactly what to do. If this is failed, they will lose 1d3 days blundering around until eventually a local man will be found, who speaks no Korantine;

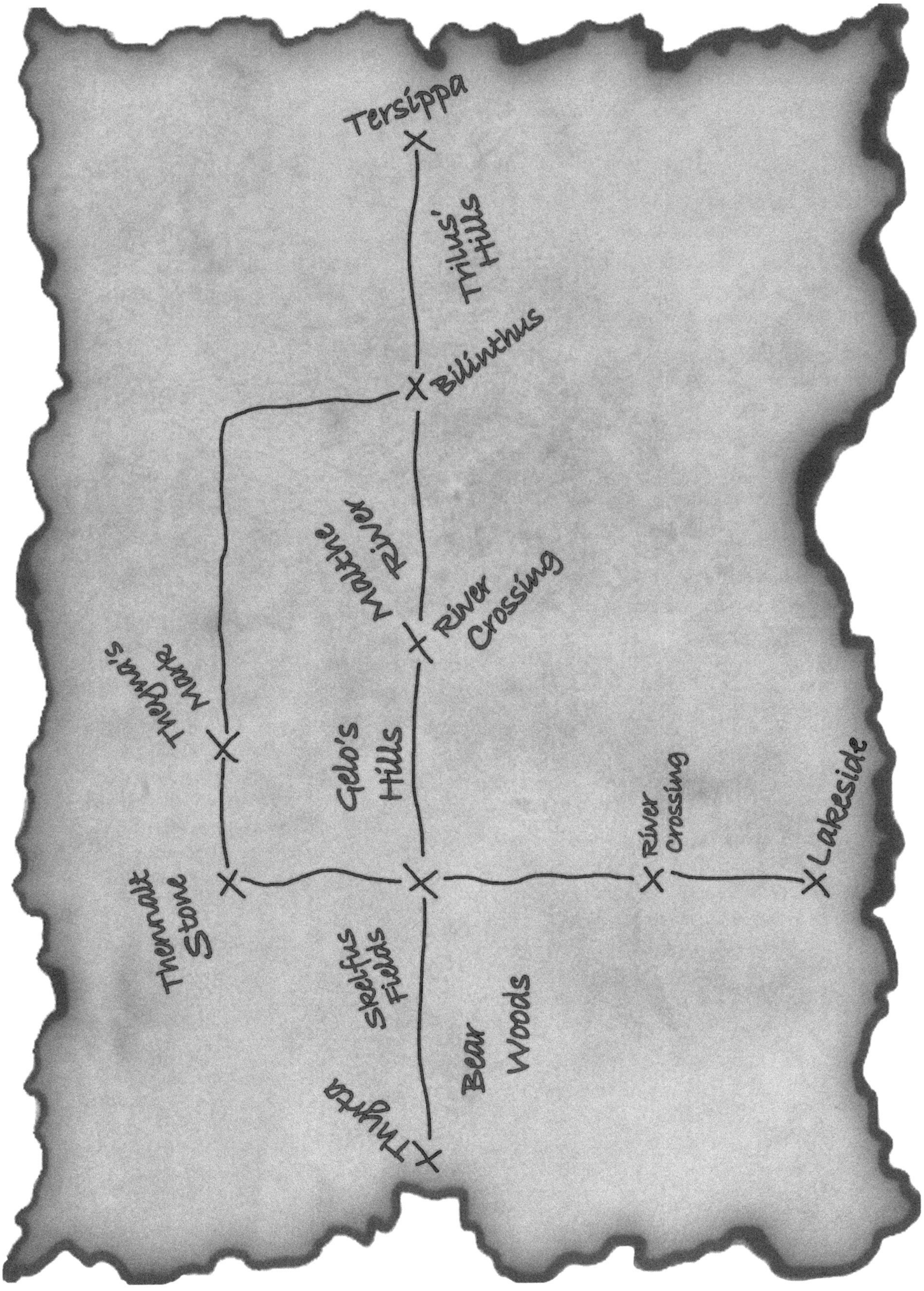
Tersippa
Trilus' Hills
Bilinthus
Malthe River
River Crossing
Thegma's Marke
Gelo's Hills
River Crossing
Lakeside
Thennalt Stone
Skelfus Fields
Bear Woods
Thyrta

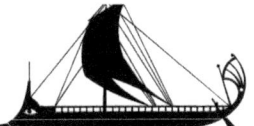

but if communication can be established some other way he can set the characters back on course to the Thennalt Stone. The natives are swiftly alerted to their presence in the area, and some of them will decide to ambush the characters on their arrival.

Random Encounters

While in Thyrta's territory, and thereafter so long as using the main track that runs from Thyrta to Bilinthus and on to Tersippa, use the Korantia encounter table, with the dice results for the Rural Backwater and Minor Routes column.

If the characters stray from the trail, roll 1d6 and on a roll of 4-6 use the Wilderness encounter table instead. There is obviously nothing wrong with checking the dice roll against both tables and picking the most interesting result!

Take note of whether the characters wander into the area known as The Skelfic Fields. This is all the personal domain of Lord Skelfus, and large parts of it are deliberately returned to wilderness. However, if Lord Skelfus hears of people travelling through his territory who have information about Varoteg, he wants it handed over and will be very insistent. This extends to holding people against their will unless they are Borissan citizens or fellow Solarists (Lanis cultists), in which case he is rather more hospitable and careful not to commit an act that amounts to assault or false imprisonment.

The Thennalt Stone

This is a natural rock formation; a boulder covered in weathered carvings. In the sheltered spots are painted designs, some of them animals, some of them people, some of them too stylised or roughly drawn to tell. However, in one place a Perception test reveals a crude graffito depicting a bearded (Thennalt) figure 'penetrating' a beardless (Korantine) and submissive figure wearing nothing but a surprised expression. This particular image does not look like it is very old.

A Thennalt Culture or Customs roll allows the deduction that the Stone is a sacred place that in ancient times was once the gathering spot for a Thennalt warrior society. These cults no longer exist in Brotomagia, at least not openly. Even the spirits are now gone.

This is the place where characters who fail to get a proper guide, or who are otherwise blundering through the countryside and in need of a dangerous encounter, are ambushed by a gang of local lads indulging in some banditry of their own.

Bandit Ambushers: Franskum and his Gang

These men are all Thennalts from the village of Simblay, and all have some connection to Varoteg. The number of bandits should be adjusted to slightly outnumber the characters – they will not attack otherwise. Their objective is not necessarily to kill, but they are willing to do so. Subduing the characters, stripping them of anything valuable or useful and sending them on their way is enough. These bandits have no plans to die for a cause, and only Franskum, the best-equipped but none-too-bright warrior in the mix, is dead set on showing his prowess in a face-to-face duel. As soon as two of them have been badly wounded (taken a serious wound) – or it looks like there is no prospect of overpowering the characters without severe risk to themselves, the bandits will withdraw as quickly as they can. Those who can't will beg for mercy or ransom. Bear in mind they are the largest part of the menfolk of Simblay, and their loss would be a disaster for the community.

Franskum's Tactics

Franskum likes to fool his enemies by offering single combat, drawing them into a trap. He makes a great display, arriving bareback on a big white draft horse (the pride of his home village). He will always dismount before combat – but his party trick is then to strike his heel on the ground, (summoning a gnome, though this may not be apparent), and 'surf' the earth by riding it to where he takes his stand, literally drawing a line in the ground with his axe, inviting a challenger to come forward with taunts and insults.

The gnome takes a position in front of Franskum, acting as a mobile pit trap. Franskum's companions will stay out of sight if possible. Any character who does charge him will find himself falling into the earth just before they come to blows. Franskum will then brain the attacker with his axe while the gnome holds him fast. At this point, his companions should break cover and start pelting the rest of the characters with sling stones.

Theyna's Mark

A broad pasture on the sunny side of a shallow vale that supports a herd of cattle sacred to the Thennalt mother goddess. Each bears a runic symbol in the form of a spoked wheel on its

Varoteg's Rascals

flank, and each has a natural patch of white of a similar pattern on its face. Should any characters decide to take any of these cattle, they will bring an almighty retribution from the locals upon themselves. There is nothing to find here unless Athlazo and his caravan have been by in recent days, in which case wheel marks and tracks from the draft and baggage animals are easily found, a stopping place can be identified at the bottom of the pasture, and the onward track that eventually rejoins the trail towards Bilinthus and Tersippa discovered. There is also a well-used track from the pasture down and along the vale and about 2km south east from the pasture is a hamlet, Simblay. In this village is found Igramsa, the local Theyna priestess who has charge of this sacred herd, and a small community of farmers and herders who take responsibility for its upkeep and protection. The young men of the community are the very same Franskum and his lads that can be encountered as bandits.

SIMBLAY

Simblay contains five houses, all of them large, thatched buildings accommodating an extended family of D6+4 people, built of timber and wattle on a stone foundation. Inside each house are two areas, one for livestock and one for the inhabitants. A fine temple to Theyna is its principle feature, the thatched roof reaching nearly to the ground on either side, its walls plastered and painted in ochre and blue, several impressive sets of bulls horns fixed above the lintel and terracotta figures of serpentine creatures fixed to its ridge. A number of little outhouses, granaries, bee hives and a barn complete the picture, and a stream runs by the village providing a ready source of fresh water.

Nobody who is not at least a lay member of Theyna's cult is allowed inside the temple unless invited in – should anyone trespass there with evil intent then the Games Master should feel free to unleash a Beast Form Miracle that transforms the transgressor into a bull, and, if necessary, persistent offenders will be confronted by an 8 cubic metre gnome.

Strangers in Simblay are hardly welcome. Strangers arriving loaded with weapons and wearing armour are even less so, and depending on their number will provoke the locals to grab arms and attempt to ward them off or everyone to run for the hills. Nobody here speaks Korantine, so again if the characters do not speak Thennalt and have no local guide they may find communication difficult.

If the characters have captured any of Franksum's gang, here is where they can claim ransom or give instructions as to how the transaction should proceed.

Karosus

The headman is a tough looking wiry fellow probably in his 50s, his face weathered and showing a scraggy ill-kept beard. Karosus is Franskum's father, and while his son is a constant cause for fret, Karosus will do whatever he can to protect the young man if he gets into trouble. Otherwise his main concern is to avoid calamity to the village he has lived in all his life, to see its people and the temple there left in peace. Sometimes that involves violent confrontation, but only as a last resort, in which case he will not shrink from it. He is deeply parochial in his outlook, so he cares only for the well-being of people of his village. Karosus harbours a deep distrust of outsiders and will require significant demonstrations of good faith before letting down his guard, but is wise enough not to let this show.

Igramsa

The priestess of Simblay's earth temple is a mature woman who was married once to Karosus' brother Karsil, whom she buried seven years past. One of her sons is a close companion of Varoteg, the other three have made their homes on land beyond the Malthe river. She will see out her days in Simblay, but not before she has found a suitable candidate to inherit her position – who will most likely come from outside the immediate area as she herself did. Igramsa's concerns are all for the temple, and for the villagers in so much as they provide for its basic needs in supply and maintenance. Since worshippers come to the temple from far afield, Igramsa is rather more open to outsiders than is Karosus, but that does not extend to a liking for the Korantine folk at Thyrta, nor for lord Skelfus for whom she has nothing but disdain. Igramsa fears one day her temple may become some backwater shrine visited only by the peasant slaves and tenants of some Korantine landowner.

Getting Information

There is nothing the characters can do that will persuade Franskum or the locals in Simblay to betray Varoteg that does not involve cruel and deeply unheroic action, like threatening the village's children or its sacred cattle, or torturing the priestess. If they commit any outrage, eventually word will get around and they will find the whole countryside up in arms against them. Their journey home will turn into a nightmare pursuit through unfamiliar territory as armed men from the surrounding villages bent on bloody retribution try to run them to ground. Unless the characters make great haste to get out of the area news of their crimes may travel before them enabling an ambush to be set. If they get away with their lives they will have earned the enmity of local people and become a target for Varoteg himself.

Nevertheless, for Igramsa, Karosus and even Franskum, giving up the Rascals is preferable to handing over ransom and they may even propose it to be left alone. They don't know that Varoteg uses the Rascals' hideout to stash some of his loot, so it does not occur to them that they may be harming their hero's interests by doing so. So they will ultimately sell the information to see their village left unharmed or even to have Franskum returned to them for less than the two cows he has promised. They are well aware that the abandoned mine is just one place that Varoteg uses, that he is not there right now and not at risk, and that the current occupants are not their relatives – indeed they are odd and frightening outlanders, just like the characters.

The Abandoned Mine

The mine is a place where the Rascals can hunker down between raids while their comrades can melt away to the villages and hamlets they came from. They are not amongst Varoteg's closest confidants either, and their isolation at the abandoned mine is a deliberate decision on Varoteg's part. Among their number are Orinastron, a Jekkarene exile; Tessenber, a rootless Thennalt; Cardrerus, a Korantine outlaw with a price on his head; Hebdomar, an islander from Tempigone; Shelsum, a woodsman from Sard; and Gorkas, a minotaur.

Games Master Note: This scenario is presented to suit beginner-level characters; except for Gorkas, none of the Rascals are individually very dangerous, and it is possible to take them on in ways that prevent the Rascals making use of clever group tactics. However, if you feel your players need more of a challenge, you might reduce the chance of them finding the Rascals scattered or surprised (perhaps equip them with one or more Alarm spells) or simply beef up the bandits' skill levels. They are not unlike a gang of adventurers, and their main weakness is the lack of spell-caster, which could make all the difference if one were added.

Achieving Surprise

There is every possibility the characters will achieve surprise and have a considerable advantage in taking on the bandits. If they reach the bandit lair with no news of their approach having preceded them, then their quarry may be scattered. 1d4+1 of the Rascals will be outside the mines during the day (Gorkas almost never leaves). Those who are outside will be disposed as follows (check for each individual, but assume those who are doing the same activity are doing it together):

If the characters take up a hidden position and watch events until the sun begins to set, the bandits' activities may change as some return and others go out of the hideout. Once the sun

1D20	Activity
1-3	Out hunting, 1d2 hours away
4-6	Out fetching water at a stream, returning in 2d10 minutes
7-9	Relaxing at the stream, returning in d6x10 minutes
10-14	Relaxing, exercising, relieving themselves or at play immediately around the mine entrance
15-17	Actively keeping watch from the mine entrance
18-20	Asleep in the sun on a patch of open ground by the ruined buildings

goes down activities cease and all traffic is back towards the mine. Canny adventurers could set up surprise attacks on individuals in order to change the odds in their favour.

After dark they are usually all at home, with a fire lit at the entrance – after all, there is usually nobody around to see it. At least three of the bandits will be here at any one time.

A way to approach undetected as far as the foot of the slope up to the mine entrance (1) can be devised by an character using Lore (Tactics and Drill) or Survival. If this fails, an undetected approach requires individual Stealth tests. Anyone who fails is at risk of being seen or heard. A single sorting test for Perception should be made for all bandits in the immediate vicinity (but not deep inside the mine). When intruders are detected, the bandits' first priority is to warn each other, grab as much war gear as they can and take up defensive positions. If they think they are heavily outnumbered, they will confer with one another over whether flight is possible and do so as a team – unless it is clearly a case of every man for himself. Gorkas the minotaur will not flee, even if the others abandon him.

The Gang's All Here

Orinastron

Orinastron is a deserter from one of the Jekkarene units posted to the border region of Sard. Once a strapping fellow, he is now drawn and pale, the result of a wound that never healed properly that is the cause of his low CON. He is tight-mouthed about the reason for his desertion, saying his own commanding officer had contrived for him to get killed because he had 'seen something' he shouldn't have.

Tessenber

Tessenber is from somewhere east of the Malthe river, or at least claims to be, but even his comrades are convinced

Varoteg's Rascals

everything Tessenber says about his past is a lie. He tells it as if he was in some warrior society, has been to Marangia and back, seen the world, done his share of fighting, rape and pillage and 'came home from the wars' to find his village abandoned. Most assume he is an outcast from his own village carrying some terrible burden of shame, and they are probably right. He cannot help but tell a lie; however, he is not very good at it.

Hebdomar

Hebdomar was spat out of the ocean, a reaver from Tapropiscur who found himself on these shores after a shipwreck, naked and alone, the assumed sole survivor of his crew. His luck held out and he fell in with some locals who took him to Varoteg, and Varoteg gave him clothing, food and equipment and put him with his Rascals. Hebdomar is very grateful to his new 'captain', and would never betray his new crew.

Shelsom

Shelsom is little more than a boy, an orphan with no clan or family to call his own. He says he comes from the Forest of Sard, the only child of parents who were killed when a terrible storm washed their house away. The Rascals are his family now, although he is treated by the others almost as a thrall. He was regularly bullied until he formed a strange sort of bond with Gorkas who remains a weird or terrifying monster to the other members but in whom Shelsom recognised another lost soul. The rest of the gang now know that they will have Gorkas to deal with if they treat the boy too roughly

Cardrerus

Cardrerus is Varoteg's pet Korantine, and is well aware that his membership of the gang is not entirely based on free will. Caught thieving in Thyrta, he escaped custody before Aparinaon passed sentence on him and made it to open country where he found refuge with Varoteg's people. Cardrerus hopes one day to slip away from the Rascals and continue his journey to Tersippa, but despite offering to run errands there many times Varoteg has denied him any such opportunity. Cardrerus knows if he is returned to Thyrta the best he can hope for is a swift execution so will do anything to avoid capture. Cardrerus thinks Gorkas a foul abomination and keeps as far away from him as possible.

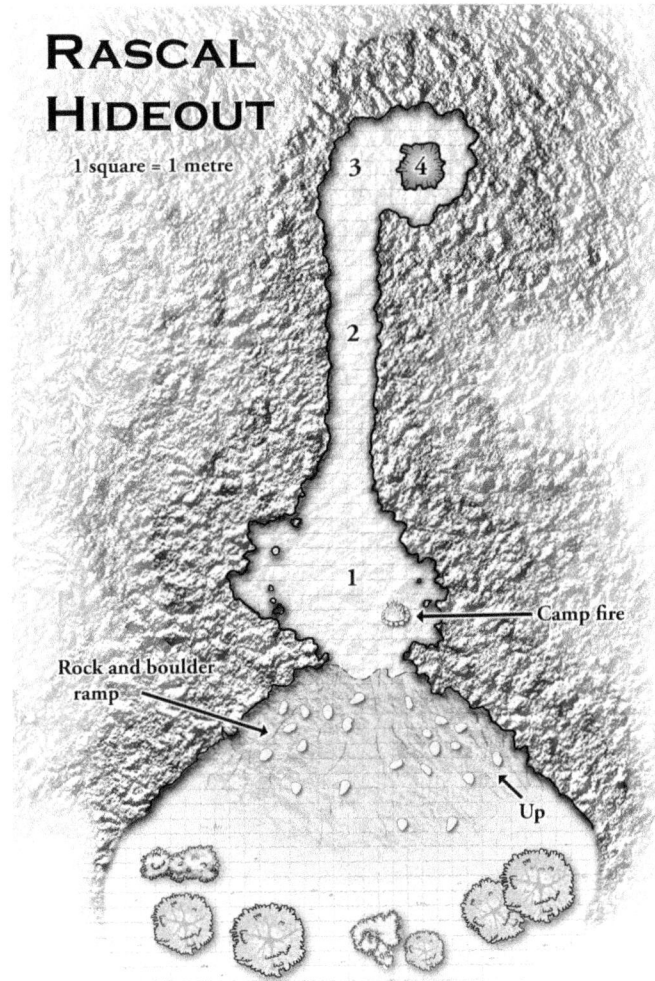

Gorkas

Gorkas is a huge and terrifying creature; he is immense and muscular, his shaggy hide is black as night, his amber eyes are terrible to behold. Igramsa, the priestess at Simblay, rescued Gorkas when he was very young, declaring him a god-child rather than a monstrosity and protecting him from fearful folk who would soonest have him smothered. When he started to grow too big, strong and prone to aggression for her to keep in the village Igramsa handed him over to Varoteg to find some kind of place for him in the world. And so Varoteg spirited Gorkas away to one of his hideouts, gave him a home and made him guardian of his treasure. Gorkas almost never leaves his den; however, when it is raining hard outside he emerges to stand in the downpour as still as a statue, sometimes for hours on end.

Gorkas shares the hideout with the Rascals but is not really one of them. Varoteg has been the only human being that treats him with any true humanity – except now for Shelsom. Gorkas is a very simple soul. He will fight or flee with the rest of the

gang, but if somebody tries to get at Varoteg's treasure, or he sees someone harm young Shelsom, he will throw himself into battle and give no quarter.

Key to the Mine

1. Entrance

An Athletics test is required to climb directly up to the mine entrance; none is needed to make headway by scrambling up the ramp created by a great pile of loose rock unless hurrying or under attack, in which case a roll is required not to stumble, losing a turn (fumble means the character falls prone). Characters fighting while on this material are limited by their Athletics skill unless they have a relevant Combat Style Trait.

If the Rascals get to defend their hideout, then at least two of them will be at the top making life difficult for the characters and will have an ample supply of fist-sized rocks to throw at their opponents using their Athletics skills.

At the top is a broad cavern with a campfire at its mouth. Postholes mark where the old lift system used to be.

Searching: The bandits have their personal gear in this chamber. Their stash is hidden amidst a pile of rocks, and will be discovered if the characters spend more than 15 minutes thoroughly searching the place, or if a hard Perception roll is made in a more cursory inspection. The stash includes a nice-looking shortsword worth 50SP, and 1d10+10SP in various denominations for each bandit residing at the cave when it is attacked. The shortsword may be recognised if sold back in Thyrta, its former owner being a mercenary working for Skelfus who was killed in an ambush some weeks ago.

2. Mine Passage

A 3-4m wide tunnel leads directly off to the north with timber props set at regular intervals. A pair of shallow ruts, 1m apart, runs the length of the passage. Unless some form of light source is on hand, it is pitch black, with the range of the light source being the absolute limit of vision.

As the characters proceed up the tunnel, they hear a rumbling and grating sound up ahead. Gorkas the Minotaur is pushing a mining truck down the passage towards them at some speed in an effort to disconcert or scatter them. Anyone in the tunnel needs to make an Evade roll to get out of the way, or take d6+ Gorkas' 1d10 Damage Bonus to one location – roll 1d10 for location unless they are prone or crawling. If the Evade test is fumbled then 1d2+1 locations are struck. Gorkas, meanwhile, is covered by the truck from missile fire down the passage.

3. Gorkas' Chamber

A small side chamber with a foul atmosphere, and a pile of litter scooped together in one corner with a depression in the top. The stench here is powerful, it is Gorkas' smell; the stink of his waste and the dirty straw and rags from which he made a bed are pretty heady.

4. The Shaft

In the centre of the chamber is a 3m wide rough shaft; the bottom seems strewn with rubbish. There are animal bones, bits of straw, broken pieces of wood. But there is a gleam there, for at the bottom of this shaft, 4m down, is where Varoteg has tossed items of loot. He knows Gorkas has no use for this stuff and will protect it even from the Rascals, so he is the most trustworthy guardian.

The treasure here consists of the following items:

- A scatter of coins: 47SS, a jumble from different cities.
- 3 Gold imperials, worth 20SP each
- A silver ingot (0.5kg), worth 80SP
- A bronze shield boss of Korantine type engraved with a sunburst, and 5 shield ornaments in the shape of stars (Perhaps worth 3 SP overall)
- A dagger with a bone (or ivory?) handle and a fine iron blade with nicely wrought pommel and lozenge hilt (perhaps 20SP)
- A rather dirty but fine helm to fit SIZ 13 comfortably, with cheek plates and reinforced brow ridge (4 AP, value 30SP)
- The broken halves of an amphora (wine jar) of a distinctively Jekkarene style. It retains a faint trace of sweetened wine. Underneath there is another smaller pot which contains a trove of 9SP, 22CP, 9 little chunks of gold (worth 5SP each) and 3 small rough-cut stones.

Varoteg's Rascals

Bullion: the following items are made of precious metal, but all dented, twisted or deliberately broken and/or torn; their value appears to be only in the metal content:

- Y A small silver cup (32SP)
- Y A broken gold brooch shaped like a grasshopper (20SP)
- Y Several pieces of silver, perhaps decorative mounts for a belt or bridle, that have spilled out of a leather bag (7 x 2SP)
- Y Scraps of gold and silver decorative mounts that seem torn from a very fancy sword hilt of Korantine workmanship (60SP)
- Y A bent gorget of copper and gold, small in size, intricately designed with foliage and flowers.

The little grasshopper brooch with the broken pin is a simple enchantment, activated by using a Rites skill (easy roll if using Thennalt Rites) that replicates the Folk Magic spell, Voice. The use of this costs a Magic Point as normal.

The copper and gold gorget is a special thing, a wedding gift from Skelfus to his wife, a nymph. It could be used to bind her.

Returning Victorious

If the characters bring prisoners back to Thyrta, then Aparinaon will pay the 50SP bounty for each one on behalf of the state; any so traded will soon find themselves on the gallows.

The characters will now be noted in Thyrta for their deeds, and how they went about their business and the success they have achieved will colour the way people deal with them in future. Varoteg regards the Rascals as disposable and will not incur risk to revenge or rescue them, except perhaps for Gorkas, whom he considers his ward. He similarly knows there is little advantage in pursuing those who stole his loot unless they should be very careless and make it easy for him. Far more dangerous is Valsus, since he may believe his clandestine dealings with the bandits via the caravan master Athlazo are at risk of being uncovered. He will take steps to cover his tracks and has the money and contacts to do so.

Non-Player Characters

Cardrerus, Fugitive from Justice

Characteristics	Attributes	1D20	Location	AP/HP
STR: 11	Action Points: 3	1–3	Right Leg	0/6
CON: 10	Damage Modifier: +0	4–6	Left Leg	0/6
SIZ: 13	Magic Points: 12	7–9	Abdomen	2/7
DEX: 12	Movement: 6 metres	10–12	Chest	2/8
INT: 15	Initiative Bonus: 11	13–15	Right Arm	2/5
POW: 12	Armour: Padded arming jacket	16–18	Left Arm	2/5
CHA: 14	Abilities: none	19–20	Head	0/6

Skills: *Athletics 60%, Brawn 35%, Deceit 65%, Endurance 40%, Evade 30%, Perception 60%, Sleight 45%, Stealth 62%, Survival 30%, Unarmed 47%, Willpower 30%*

Magic

Folk Magic: *(Korantine Rites 45%) Ignite, Bladesharp*

Combat Style: *Banditry (Sword, Dagger, Pelte) 50%*

Weapon	Size/Force	Reach	Damage	AP/HP
Shortsword	M	S	1d6	6/8
Pelte	L	S	1d4	4/12
Dagger	S	S	1d4+1	6/8

Franskum, Bandit Leader

Characteristics	Attributes	1D20	Location	AP/HP
STR: 16	Action Points: 2	1–3	Right Leg	3/6
CON: 14	Damage Modifier: +1d4	4–6	Left Leg	3/6
SIZ: 15	Magic Points: 12	7–9	Abdomen	3/7
DEX: 12	Movement: 6 metres	10–12	Chest	3/8
INT: 12	Initiative Bonus: 8	13–15	Right Arm	0/5
POW: 12	Armour: Fine tooled horned leather helmet, cuirass and greaves	16–18	Left Arm	0/5
CHA: 12		19–20	Head	3/6

Skills: Athletics 65%, Brawn 50%, Endurance 45%, Evade 30%, Locale (Hills) 60%, Perception 45%, Survival 45%, Unarmed 47%, Willpower 30%, Stealth 52%

Magic

Devotion (Theyna) 35%, Exhort 30% Miracles: Elemental Summoning. Devotional Pool = 1

Folk Magic (Rites 40%): Avert, Bladesharp, Protection

Combat Style: *Earth's Champion (Axe, Shield, Dagger)*

Weapon	Size/Force	Reach	Damage	AP/HP
Battle Axe	M	M	1d8+1+1d4	4/8
Target	L	S	1d3+1+1d4	4/9
Dagger	S	S	1d4+1+1d4	6/8

Pitt, Franskum's Gnome (Intensity 4, 4 Cubic Metres)

Characteristics	Attributes	1D20	Location	AP/HP
STR: 23	Action Points: 2	1–20	Mass	2/27
CON: N/A	Damage Modifier: +1d10			
SIZ: 15	Magic Points: 13			
DEX: 10	Movement: 4 metres			
INS: 9	Initiative Bonus: 10			
POW: 13	Armour: 2 points of gravelly, soilly protection, plus impervious to non-magical damage			
CHA: 12				

Skills: Brawn 66%, Evade 64%, Perception 57%, Unarmed 75%, Willpower 82%

Ablities

Engulfing, Immunity (Earth), Vulnerable (Water)

Combat Style: *Smash, Engulfing*

Weapon	Size/Force	Reach	Damage	AP/HP
Fist Smash	L	M	1d10+1d10	2/27
Engulf		Can Engulf opponents of up to SIZ 13.		

Varoteg's Rascals

Franskum's Thugs (6 in Total – Share the Same Statistics)

	Attributes	1D20	Location	AP/HP
Action Points: 2		1–3	Right Leg	0/5
Damage Modifier: None		4–6	Left Leg	0/5
Magic Points: 9		7–9	Abdomen	1/6
Movement: 6 metres		10–12	Chest	0/7
Initiative Bonus: 11		13–15	Right Arm	0/4
Armour: Leather girdle/clout		16–18	Left Arm	0/4
Abilities: None		19–20	Head	0/5

Skills: Athletics 38%, Brawn 25%, Endurance 36%, Evade 28%, Locale (40%, Perception 41%, Survival 31%, Unarmed 38%, Willpower 22%, Stealth 39%

Magic

Folk Magic (35%) Heal, Speedart, Pathway

Combat Style: *Banditry (sling, club, dagger, buckler) 50%*

Weapon	Size/Force	Reach	Damage	AP/HP
Club	M	S	1d6	4/4
Buckler	M	S	1d3	6/9
Dagger	S	S	1d4+1	6/8
Sling	L	-	1d8	1/2

Gorkas, Minotaur Monstrosity

Characteristics	Attributes	1D20	Location	AP/HP
STR: 23	Action Points: 3	1–3	Right Leg	0/8
CON: 14	Damage Modifier: +1d10	4–6	Left Leg	0/8
SIZ: 24	Magic Points: 12	7–9	Abdomen	0/9
DEX: 12	Movement: 6 metres	10–12	Chest	0/10
INT: 9	Initiative Bonus: 11	13–15	Right Arm	0/7
POW: 12	Armour: Hides and Horns	16–18	Left Arm	0/7
CHA: 7	Abilities: Gorkas' SIZ makes him immune to the impaling effect of Small weapons and missiles (daggers, darts, knives, arrows, crossbow quarrels)	19–20	Head	3/8

Skills: Athletics 65%, Brawn 80%, Endurance 70%, Evade 40%, Insight 45%, Perception 55%, Survival 45%, Unarmed 60%, Willpower 50%

Magic

None

Combat Style: *Brutal 70% Trait Blind Fighting (Gorkas spends most of his time in the dark)*

Weapon	Size/Force	Reach	Damage	AP/HP
Great Axe	H	L	2d6+2+1d10	4/10
Gore	M	S	1d6+1d10	As for Head

Shores of Korantia

Hebdomar, Archipelagan Ex-Pirate

Characteristics	Attributes	1D20	Location	AP/HP
STR: 15	Action Points: 3	1–3	Right Leg	0/6
CON: 14	Damage Modifier: +1d2	4–6	Left Leg	0/6
SIZ: 12	Magic Points: 8	7–9	Abdomen	0/7
DEX: 13	Movement: 6 metres	10–12	Chest	0/8
INT: 12	Initiative Bonus: 11	13–15	Right Arm	0/5
POW: 8	Armour: Padded leather cap	16–18	Left Arm	0/5
CHA: 10	Abilities: none	19–20	Head	2/6

Skills: *Athletics 45%, Boating 55%, Brawn 45%, Endurance 45%, Evade 30%, Perception 60%, Seamanship 40%, Stealth 30%, Survival 45%, Unarmed 46%, Willpower 30%*

Magic

Folk Magic (Archipelagan Rites 40%): Bladesharp, Breath, Protection

Combat Style: *Reaver (Sabre, Dagger, Buckler) 60%*

Weapon	Size/Force	Reach	Damage	AP/HP
Sabre	M	M	1d6+1+1d2	6/8
Buckler	M	S	1d3+1d2	6/9
Dagger	S	S	1d4+1	6/8

Igramsa, Priestess of Theyna

Characteristics	Attributes	1D20	Location	AP/HP
STR: 12	Action Points: 3	1–3	Right Leg	0/5
CON: 14	Damage Modifier: +0	4–6	Left Leg	0/5
SIZ: 12	Magic Points: 13	7–9	Abdomen	0/6
DEX: 10	Movement: 6 metres	10–12	Chest	0/7
INT: 15	Initiative Bonus: +13	13–15	Right Arm	0/4
POW: 13	Armour: none	16–18	Left Arm	0/4
CHA: 14	Abilities: none	19–20	Head	0/5

Skills: *AAthletics 35%, Endurance 45%, Evade 30%, First Aid 70%, Influence 55%, Insight 65%, Locale 75%, Perception 40%, Survival 45%, Unarmed 27%, Willpower 55%*

Magic

Devotion (Theyna) 77%, Evoke 57%. Miracles: Bless Crops, Banish Satyr, Cure Malady, Consecrate, Extension, Lay to Rest, Rejuvenate, Soul Sight

Devotional Pool = 7

Folk Magic (90%) Beastcall (Bovid), Bladesharp, Endurance, Heal, Pathway, Pet, Warmth

Combat Style: *Wily Fighter (Club, Dagger, Javelin) 60%*

Weapon	Size/Force	Reach	Damage	AP/HP
Dagger	S	S	1d4+1	6/8

Varoteg's Rascals

Karosus, Village Headman at Simblay

Characteristics	Attributes	1D20	Location	AP/HP
STR: 13	Action Points: 2	1–3	Right Leg	0/5
CON: 12	Damage Modifier: +0	4–6	Left Leg	0/5
SIZ: 12	Magic Points: 16	7–9	Abdomen	0/6
DEX: 9	Movement: 6 metres	10–12	Chest	0/7
INT: 14	Initiative Bonus: +12	13–15	Right Arm	0/4
POW: 16	Armour: none	16–18	Left Arm	0/4
CHA: 11	Abilities: none	19–20	Head	0/5

Skills: *Athletics 40%, Brawn 65%, Devotion (Theyna) 70%, Endurance 50%, Evade 35%, Locale 75%, Perception 45%, Survival 35%, Unarmed 50%, Willpower 60%*

Magic

Folk Magic: Folk Magic (Rites 65%) Bludgeon, Heal, Ignite, Pathway, Vigor, Warmth

Combat Style: *Wily Fighter (Club, Dagger, Javelin) 60%*

Weapon	Size/Force	Reach	Damage	AP/HP
Shortsword	M	S	1d6	6/8
Pelte	L	S	1d4	4/12
Dagger	S	S	1d4+1	6/8

Orinastron, Jekkarene Refugee, Gang-Member

Characteristics	Attributes	1D20	Location	AP/HP
STR: 12	Action Points: 3	1–3	Right Leg	2/5
CON: 8	Damage Modifier: +0	4–6	Left Leg	2/5
SIZ: 13	Magic Points: 12	7–9	Abdomen	2/6
DEX: 17	Movement: 6 metres	10–12	Chest	2/7
INT: 15	Initiative Bonus:11	13–15	Right Arm	2/4
POW: 12	Armour: Padded armour, bezainted cap	16–18	Left Arm	2/4
CHA: 11	Abilities: none	19–20	Head	3/5

Skills: *Athletics 65%, Brawn 45%, Endurance 35%, Evade 50%, Locale 50%, Perception 60%, Stealth 35%, Survival 45%, Unarmed 47%, Willpower 40%*

Magic

Folk Magic (Jekkarene Rites 40%) Heal, Pierce, Speeddart

Combat Style: *Jekkarene Skirmisher (Bow, Dagger, Buckler) 65%*

Weapon	Size/Force	Reach	Damage	AP/HP
Bow	L	-	1d6	4/4
Buckler	M	S	1d3	6/9
Dagger	S	S	1d4+1	6/8

Shelsom, Rootless Thennalt Youth

Characteristics	Attributes	1D20	Location	AP/HP
STR: 9	Action Points: 3	1–3	Right Leg	0/6
CON: 15	Damage Modifier: +0	4–6	Left Leg	0/6
SIZ: 12	Magic Points: 7	7–9	Abdomen	2/7
DEX: 14	Movement: 6 metres	10–12	Chest	2/8
INT: 13	Initiative Bonus: 13	13–15	Right Arm	2/5
POW: 7	Armour: Padded arming jacket	16–18	Left Arm	2/5
CHA: 12	Abilities: none	19–20	Head	0/6

Skills: Athletics 40%, Brawn 35%, Endurance 30%, Evade 45%, Locale 65%, Perception 50%, Stealth 50%, Survival 35%, Unarmed 35%, Willpower 30%

Magic

Folk Magic (Thennalt Rites 35%) Slow

Combat Style: *Banditry (Club, Dagger, Pelte) 50%*

Weapon	Size/Force	Reach	Damage	AP/HP
Club	M	S	1d6	4/4
Pelte	L	S	1d4	4/12
Dagger	S	S	1d4+1	6/8

Tessenber, Rootless Thennalt

Characteristics	Attributes	1D20	Location	AP/HP
STR: 11	Action Points: 2	1–3	Right Leg	0/5
CON: 12	Damage Modifier: +0	4–6	Left Leg	0/5
SIZ: 13	Magic Points: 12	7–9	Abdomen	2/6
DEX: 10	Movement: 6 metres	10–12	Chest	0/7
INT: 13	Initiative Bonus: 11	13–15	Right Arm	1/4
POW: 12	Armour: Leather Thennalt girdle, bracers	16–18	Left Arm	1/4
CHA: 9	Abilities: none	19–20	Head	0/5

Skills: Athletics 40%, Brawn 45%, Deceit 28%, Endurance 40%, Evade 30%, Locale 40%, Perception 45%, Survival 45%, Unarmed 40%, Willpower 30%, Stealth 32%

Magic

Folk Magic (Thennalt Rites 40%) Bludgeon

Combat Style: *Banditry (Club, Dagger, Pelte) 60%*

Weapon	Size/Force	Reach	Damage	AP/HP
Club	M	S	1d6	4/4
Pelte	L	S	1d4	4/12
Dagger	S	S	1d4+1	6/8

THE HOUSE OF VALSUS

Valsus of Kela has many reasons to find himself a 'person of interest' to inquisitive adventurers. He conducts business with Haliskome, the Jekkarene navy captain; he is involved in trade with the bandits out in the countryside, whom he covertly supplies with basic goods and supplies in return for items of plunder that he ships out via the same Haliskome; and he is busy forging relationships with Duke Arko of Solarne, who, like Valsus himself, is an exile (in Arko's case not such a willing one) from the city-state of Himela, and is an avid conspirator in any scenario where money or influence is to be gained.

Valsus' name may come to the characters' attention because they discover Athlazo the caravan master indulges in questionable trade, and Athlazo himself implicates Valsus (see Varoteg's Rascals). Alternatively if the characters are engaged by Safra AmPrishad (see the next scenario: Prishad's Daughter) to help her seek vengeance for her murdered father, they may reasonably surmise that Valsus had something to gain by Prishad's killing and investigate him further.

WORKING FOR KORTANO

If you want to run the raid on Valsus' house as a stand-alone episode or as a starting point to some of the other adventures provided here, then Kortano the Syndic contacts the characters and suggests he needs an 'unofficial visit' to be paid to Valsus' house to discover if his own suspicions about the merchant's clandestine dealings are justified. This scenario requires the characters to have cunning and some suitable skills for thieving and misdirection if they are to avoid turning a housebreaking into a violent scene.

Kortano has suspicions that Valsus of Kela may be profiting more from his trade with the Jekkarenes than the assessment of goods bought and sold at the docks would suggest. Rather than conduct a formal investigation with no evidence and create a scene, Kortano seeks people of discretion and a malleable moral compass to break in and rummage about for evidence of private accounts, or for goods that are being smuggled past his tax assessors. Consequently, it would be rather helpful if at least one of the party has some skill in Literacy and Commerce, or can follow instructions about what to look for and bring it away with armfuls of other stuff to be pored over by an expert eye.

Breaking in is of course just one strategy. Enterprising characters may try trickery, deceit and even seduction to get access to Valsus' home.

Common Knowledge

Valsus of Kela is an outsider who is entitled to trade in Jekkarene goods, something the guild itself does not do. Trading with the Jekkarenes is likened to trading in slaves – it is regarded as suitable for resident foreigners, but not for respectable locals. Of course the guild applies duties to the trade just like any other import/export business. Valsus has no family, at least none who live here with him in Thyrta (in fact, he is a widower).

Valsus' House

Valsus lives in a plush two-storey residence in the area south of the central plaza with an adjoining storehouse and stable. The house has narrow barred windows on the ground floor, shuttered windows on the first floor; a front door of heavy wood that is locked with a key; a side door into the courtyard, also locked with the same key as the front door; and double gates from the street into the courtyard that are closed with a wooden bar. The courtyard gives access to the double doors of a storehouse, which has its own lock and key.

Three people live here: Valsus, and his two slaves: Modatis, who his steward, and Modatis' wife, Lorena, the cook and housekeeper. The chance that any of them are at home at a random point during the day is 30% for Valsus, 50% for Modatis and 65% for Lorena.

Modatis

This old family slave travelled to Thyrta with Valsus. Tall despite a slight stoop, and with lank white hair surrounding a bald pate, Modatis appears to be in his late 50s. He has been with the merchant for many years, and well remembers happier days in Himela when Valsus' wife still lived. Modatis' is entirely loyal to Valsus, since he cannot imagine any other life than the one in which he and his wife are part of Valsus' household. At any time Modatis' loyalty to Valsus is tested, it is likely that his rather stronger devotion to his wife will also play a part, and the same is true of Lorena.

Lorena

Lorena is short and wiry, with straggled grey hair – and despite appearing to be older than her husband still rather spry and certainly sharp witted.

Warehousemen

At any time, there are also 1d3 hired hands who work in the warehouse or assist Valsus in his business dealings. They generally arrive early, soon after sunrise, work until midday and then return in mid-afternoon to continue their chores until sunset. If they are onsite it is quite likely the courtyard doors to the street stand open, and characters will be able to get a peak at the layout inside – and note the presence of the two dogs.

Keys to the Door

Modatis usually carries keys with him when he is out, and has keys to both the front and side door of the house and to the warehouse. Lorena sometimes carries a key to the house only, and does so if she knows she leaves the house empty and needs to lock up behind her and let herself in, but not otherwise. Lorena also knows the Lock cantrip, which she uses when in sole charge of the house. Valsus never carries keys unless it is Modatis' night off and he expects to be home late when Lorena will be asleep. At all other times he expects his staff to be there to greet him at the door.

Routines

Watching the routines of the house reveals that when Valsus is out he tends to stay out for most of the day on business, whereas Lorena pops out for chores and shopping for perhaps an hour or two at a time at most. When she shops, she makes the rounds of the various market stalls and shops, closely inspecting the goods on offer and taking care to buy at the best price possible. She carries small items home with her in a covered basket but anything large and bulky – sacks of grain or flour, jars of oil and wine and large joints of meat – is delivered to the door in due course.

Modatis rarely leaves the house except to accompany his master on an errand; however, once per week, he is entitled to take a few hours spending his small stipend at a local tavern. A clever character might befriend him there, ply him with drink and ensure that when he returns home it is late and he is drunk. At night all three occupants are usually at home in their beds, although Valsus accepts a dinner invitation about once per month, which brings him home in the early hours of the morning. Valsus is always the last to retire, as he sits up in his study working late.

A carefully planned operation would eventually be able to establish when, for some reason, Modatis and Lorena would both be away from the house – perhaps Modatis helps his wife collect a particularly big food order to restock the larder once per month. There may also be some ruse by which the characters manage to steal a key – such a loss will quickly be noticed, unless they can take a wax impression and then replace the original where it belongs.

Valsus almost never entertains at home – he prefers to meet business contacts at a neutral place such as the Sabatean temple, the market or the Floundering Turtle. He is perfectly able to break this habit if given a good enough reason to do so, which would most likely mean that he is persuaded someone represents an unmissable business opportunity for him and that for some reason discussions are best held in complete privacy. This provides another means for the characters to trick their way into Valsus' house – but to make it work would require a very convincing and well-considered plan.

The House of Valsus

Courtyard Wall and Guard Dogs

The courtyard wall is only a little over two metres high but fairly smooth, so scaling it requires a Hard Athletics test; Standard if the character is tall, Easy if boosted by an accomplice or something is found to stand on. A character with the Acrobatics skill can use that to expertly propel himself to the top of the wall at one grade easier than the Athletics test.

The courtyard to the warehouse is occupied by two dogs, which are not especially vicious but are effective at warning of intruders. During the hotter parts of the day, there is a 50% chance that one, and a 30% chance that both are snoozing, and during the night that increases to 90% and 60%. If one or both are awake there is no chance of someone clambering over the courtyard wall avoiding their notice. If they are both asleep, the intruder needs to succeed in an opposed test of his Stealth skill against their Perception skill (90%) to slip into the courtyard unnoticed, and succeed in another every round thereafter until he succeeds in getting into the warehouse. The dogs are not trained guard dogs, and can be distracted or dealt with by magic if characters come up with a suitable plan to do so.

If the dogs are barking in the courtyard, one of the occupants of the house first looks out of the balcony window in the dining room to try and appraise the situation. The same window is a useful spot from which to call for help.

Should the dogs bark and growl continuously for more than 4 rounds, or if there are sounds of a struggle between dogs and intruders, then one or more of the occupants arrives at the side door in a further 1d6+3 rounds to investigate. During the day, the barking attracts the attention of people in the street, and one of them eventually calls a constable (arriving in 1d4+2 minutes).

The Balcony

Once a character has gained the top of the courtyard wall they may be able to make for the small balcony. This gives direct access to the dining room window, the largest in the house, where the shutters are rarely if ever closed. Leaping for the balcony from the wall and hauling oneself up requires a difficult Acrobatics test; alternatively, it can be reached via an Easy Acrobatics or Hard Athletics test by going into the courtyard and using the stable as a route to the balcony window.

Response to Intruders

If intruders are in the house or attempting to break in Lorena arms herself with a big kitchen knife, Modatis with a big stick (club), and Valsus with a dagger, before confronting any intruders. Valsus pushes Modatis forward, but does not treat Lorena that way: he has some standards. Whoever does respond, one of them brings a lantern (if at night). If real danger threatens, they shout for help from neighbours or the constabulary.

If a break-in or disturbance occurs during the day, when Valsus' employees are onsite, these fellows happily call and run for help, but only put up a fight to defend Valsus or his property if they have some advantage in numbers or surprise (treat them as underlings with 5 HP, 2 Actions, Initiative Bonus 12+, and 35% in any skills or combat styles that may be tested).

Only if intruders have reached as far as the secret door in the cellar does Valsus attempt to deal with the situation alone, in order to preserve his secrets and prevent a public scene.

House Plan

See page 183 for diagram.

1. Entrance Hall

The front door is secured with a bolt, and there is a small shuttered window to peer at whoever might be knocking. The entrance hall within is always lit by an oil lamp, except in the dead of night, hung from the ceiling or placed on a small table set against the wall. There is a small cloak closet under the staircase.

2. Storeroom

Serves as both pantry and tool shed for household repairs. It smells mostly of cheese from the wheels lined up on the shelves, but there are hams, sausages and bundles of herbs hung on the walls, sacks of grain and flour, and some baskets containing vegetables.

3. Kitchen

Managed by Lorena, Modatis' wife, this room is kept clean and is excellently equipped. It has a door giving onto the courtyard and the only floor window that is shuttered rather than barred, looking onto the courtyard. This is the warmest room in the house thanks to the oven, and in winter, the two slaves often move their bed in here.

4. Servants' Hall

This room doubles as a sitting room for the servants and a storeroom where all the gear required for running the household is kept.

5. Servants' Room

Modatis the steward and his wife sleep here on a simple wooden bed topped with a straw mattress. They have no furniture to speak of, just a three legged stool and a small home-made table by the bed.

6. Stairway to Cellar

7. Dining Room

A central table with couches around. A fine wine bowl decorated in the classical Korantine style, with pictures of little ships plying their trade in and out of a harbour, takes pride of place, displayed on a carved and polished stone pedestal.

8. Privy

This little room sits directly above the stairway down to the cellar. A simple wooden seat is set above a chute that flushes into street drains. Next to it is an evil-smelling earthenware pot into which is thrust a short stick of carved bone topped with a piece of sea-sponge.

9. Valsus' Bedroom

A large double bed with fine linen and a richly embroidered bedspread. A patterned rug from distant Rasputana graces the floor, a small table by the bed holds a pitcher of water. Two wooden trunks are set by a wall, each of them with bronze fittings to the corners and one secured with a bronze lock.

Valsus' clothes are folded in the unlocked trunk. The locked trunk (the only key usually on Valsus' own person) contains various personal possessions.

If this trunk is opened with a successful Mechanisms test, or noisily broken open by a blow with a Medium size weapon or bigger that inflicts more than 7 points of damage, inside can be found:

- An almanac written in Jekkarene that describes the phases of the moon through the (Lunar) year, offers some detail on the ritual significance of different months and the meaning of the various patterns and shades that can be discerned on the moon's face. Much of this information is fairly obscure, but a close study of this book would allow someone who already has a Culture (Jekkarene) or Rites (Jekkarene) skill to gain an Improvement Roll in them. More importantly, some of the pages have notes and marks in Valsus' own hand in Korantine. A successful Literacy test gleans that Valsus uses the almanac to work out the scheduled visits to Thyrta of his Jekkarene contacts, translating the lunar terminology in which he is informed of their expected sailing dates into the reckonings used in a regular Korantine calendar.

- A fine polished bronze mirror wrapped in a black cloth, its handle and edge decorated in relief with images of Korantine deities. The mirror can be detected as magical. The mirror accepts an offering of a Magic Point, and if this is done, the viewer sees not his own reflection but that of a fine-looking lady of early middle age. The image persists for 10 minutes, occasionally moving, and then fades, to be replaced with a normal reflection. An Insight test detects the lady is attempting to conceal a terrible sadness with a mask of serenity. This item depicts Valsus' dead wife, and is immensely dear to him, being the

The House of Valsus

most important relic of her that he has. Her sadness is a reflection upon Valsus' own dishonesty, and he knows it, so increasingly he cannot bear to look upon his wife's face that was once such a comfort.

- A small box of tortoiseshell, itself worth some 15SP, containing some modest but good quality jewels. These include a pair of pendant earrings with sapphire stones worth 40SP, and two fine rings in gold, one with an intricately carved stone in the bezel with a traditional Korantine design depicting the Queen of Heaven (28SP), the other decorated with red and blue enamel (35SP). These items belonged to Valsus' late wife and are his mementos of her. Anyone viewing the magical image in the mirror will recognise this jewellery.

- A fine doeskin purse (worth 2SP) containing 18SP and 2 Imperials (gold pieces)

- An old shortsword in its scabbard, the kind carried on militia duty. This looks like it has not been used in many years. Valsus will attempt to retrieve the weapon if he may be fighting for his life with an intruder

- A letter from Arko, styled "Duke of Solarne, Regent of Tempigone, lord of Guberan, Enkeleb, Tormas, Diotinia, Mendo and Solisbund". The letter refers to "mutual interests" and "mutual friends", and suggests that Valsus of Kela should be ready to receive Arko as a guest upon his next visit, probably to be in the late summer. Someone who makes a difficult Locale (Korantia) or Locale (Methalea) will have heard of one or two of the names of the places listed, and can confirm they are actually places on the isle of Tempigone, owned by the state of Himela. Most of the names are however, clearly not Korantine, which reflects the fact that most of the island's inhabitants are not Korantine either. Similarly a Locale (Korantia) reveals that Solarne is a region in the mainland state of Himela, Korantia's most radical democracy.

A successful roll against Perception (automatic for someone who is actively looking) detects a concealed door that gives access to the warehouse loft. This is Valsus' escape route in the event he is attacked by robbers or has some other reason to make a surreptitious exit from the house

10. Library and Office

This area contains shelves of books that Valsus has collected over the years. There is a good selection of poetry, including some racy stuff that is fashionable in Himela, as well as copies of some celebrated Korantine epics that date back to before the Cataclysm when the ancient homeland was lost. Some duller reading includes treatises on management of household and estate, and on the shelves nearer his desk, piles of paper and parchment, much of it used more than once, with old accounting records. These date back some years, and obviously include Valsus' business dealings in the years before he arrived at Thyrta. The literature is quite valuable – each scroll would fetch 1d4x10SP on the market, and there are quite a few of them.

Making use of this library, a character could use his Literacy skill to gain a starting percentage in Commerce; and if he has it already, studying these tomes for a month offers two Improvement Rolls in the skill.

The Map

A thorough search of his desk area reveals a hand-drawn map among his papers, with notes and commentary showing how to get to a location somewhere in the hills. It is clearly an obscure place to have a map to – there is no settlement there, simply a pasture close by a local landmark. The map assumes some local knowledge, so details are scanty and it is more or less useless without the relevant Locale skill.

This map leads to the location where Valsus' agents exchange goods with Varoteg on Valsus' behalf. Apart from being of possible use to the characters, this document, if passed in secret to Lord Skelfus, may bring a rich reward if it helps Skelfus to track down the bandit.

The Books And Records

A detailed examination of some of his accounting sheets reveals:

- Records of goods received, prices paid and value assessed for import duty for his shipments arriving from the Jekkarid aboard the Purple Wanderer. A Literacy test reveals that Valsus is taking delivery of goods reckoned at 30,000SP per year by the tax assessors of the Borissan Syndics, but that the means by which these are paid for is hard to discern, since each entry notes only a cash sum and an unspecified "other goods" that are paid for the imports. A Commerce test reveals that the cash sums add up to no more than 14,000SP, and this is the amount

that he uses to enter into his books to track the cost of his stock.

- Records of goods sold at market in Thyrta. An uninteresting record of his sales at the regular markets held in the town.
- Records of goods purchased for sale "to the caravans", mostly commodities such as food, metal ingots and mundane or essential goods. In here there are also records of costs paid out to a man named Athlazo in respect of transportation – carts, mules for draft, drivers and boys. A Commerce test will highlight that the fees paid are quite excessive. This Athlazo is an outfitter and sometime caravan master based at Thyrta. Athlazo is the man employed by Valsus to carry goods out to the hills, and exchange them with Varoteg's bandits.
- Records of goods sold for export (the majority to named Korantine merchants from other cities). Nothing of any interest here, simply to note that there are clearly people across the Korantine world who rely on Valsus to supply a range of Jekkarene goods for their markets.
- Records of goods sold direct to private clients. These include most of the prominent people of Thyrta, but also Arko of Solarne, ruler of Tempigone (an island to the south). None of these items or transactions are incriminating; however, eyebrows may be raised by just how much money some of his clients have to spend on individual objets d'art.

11. Wine Cellar

The cellar walls are set with racks containing amphorae. Many of these are Jekkarene Sweetwine, something Valsus has a vested interest in offering to his houseguests in order to help build a taste for it. Others contain olive oil of various grades or the Korantine wines that are Valsus' preferred personal choice.

Searching: At the very back of the cellar is a disguised door that requires a successful Perception test to find (a Hard test down here in the dark by lamp or torchlight). A Mechanisms test or use of a luck point reveals how to unlock it, by twisting a particular empty amphora in its rack. This gives access to Valsus' secret store.

Trap: As the wards to the secret store are magical they cannot be detected by normal means. This door is always covered with an Alarm spell. Anyone other than Valsus who attempts to push open the door triggers both the alarm and a spell trap with a Magnitude 3 Palsy affecting locations with 8 Hit Points or less and lasting for 60 minutes. To resist this attack, the victim must beat an opposed roll of 53 with his Resilience. A second attempt to open the door, whether by the first victim or someone new, triggers a second Palsy attack; however, once this trap is triggered the enchantment becomes inert, which it does anyway after 15 minutes. This trap is set up by a sorcerer brought here by Haliskome at some expense to Valsus. He doesn't want anyone snooping in his cellar.

12. Secret Store

Valsus' secret store contains the items that he has good reason not to leave lying around in the warehouse where business callers might see them. The goods here are stolen property, purchased from the bandit Varoteg with food, supplies and sometimes (but rarely) ready cash.

The store contains:

- A sack of clothes – cloaks, tunics, leggings, dresses, gloves, boots and shoes, stripped from various victims of highway robbery. While they are "used", many of these clothes are high class and highly valuable, and some are likely to be recognisable. Perhaps 200-300SP in total value.
- A stack of exotic and fine furs taken from animals hunted on the fringes of Sard: 24 cleaned pelts, amounting to 60SP in value altogether.
- A box containing a jumble of costume jewellery and various items of personal adornment, perhaps amounting to 300SP value in total.
- A box of fine jewellery in bronze, silver and gold, some of it sporting precious or semi-precious stones: 15 finger rings in various styles worth on average 15SP each; a gold diadem worth 160SP as bullion or 200SP as a piece of art; a collection of fine silver fittings from a man's belt worth 18SP.
- A box of military fittings in silver, gold and enamelled bronze and iron, stripped from sword hilts, scabbards, shields and helmets; worth some 250SP as scrap. The adventurers may later discovery that some of these come from items carried by Lord Skelfus's personal retinue.

13. Courtyard

The dirt-floored courtyard contains a cart, and is guarded by a Valsus' two dogs. To the left by the house is a stable, home to a single mule. A big pair of double doors opens into the warehouse. These are generally open in the daytime, but locked by key at night.

The House of Valsus

14. Stable

Valsus keeps a mule in a stable within the courtyard area. The stable provides a viable route for a sneak thief to climb up to the balcony of the main house. The mule will happily kick or bite intruders, but a successful Drive or Ride test will calm the animal and persuade it to provide its services if required.

15. Warehouse

Not a massive building, but enough for Valsus' specialist trade, and besides if he needs more he can rent space elsewhere.

The warehouse is a single room open to the rafters 5 metres above, with a partial floor accessed via a wooden ladder, and a block and tackle used for hauling heavy loads up for storage. This area hides a hatch, big enough for a man stooping to pass through, that connects to Valsus' bedroom in the main house, an escape route for Valsus in an emergency – this is a common enough provision in case of fire; however, Valsus has gone to the trouble of concealing his.

House of Valsus

Ground Floor

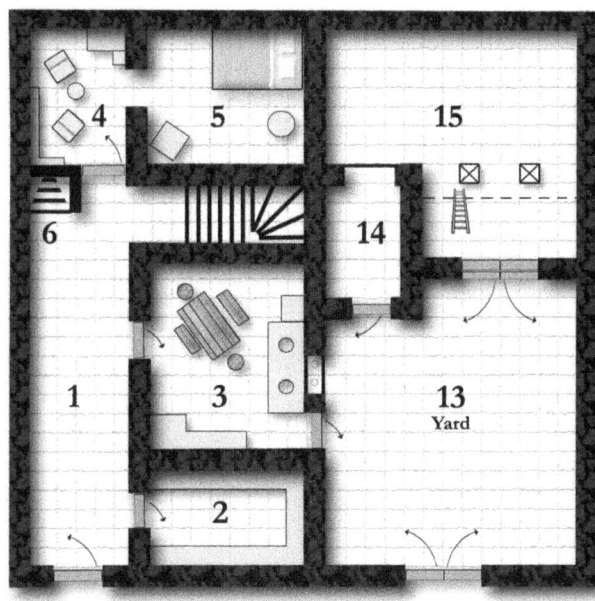

Cellar

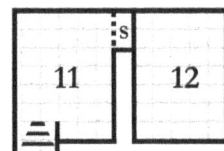

Upper Floor

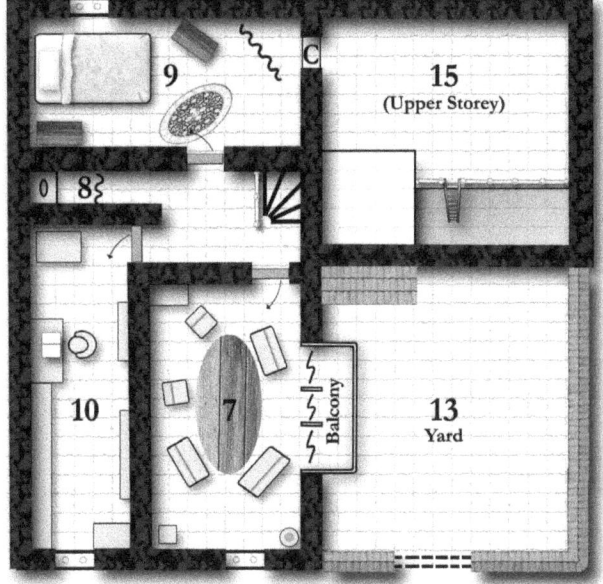

Key

- Wall
- Column
- Door
- Window
- Stairs
- Curtain
- Balustrade
- Ladder
- Scale (0 1 2 3m)

Non-Player Characters

Valsus of Kela, Merchant

Characteristics	Attributes	1D20	Location	AP/HP
STR: 9	Action Points: 3	1–3	Right Leg	0/6
CON: 13	Damage Modifier: 0	4–6	Left Leg	0/6
SIZ: 13	Magic Points: 12-1 (Alarm) = 11	7–9	Abdomen	0/7
DEX: 8	Movement: 6 metres	10–12	Chest	0/8
INT: 17	Initiative Bonus: 13	13–15	Right Arm	0/5
POW: 12	Armour: none	16–18	Left Arm	0/5
CHA: 13	Abilities: none	19–20	Head	0/6

Skills: Commerce 102%, Deceit 68%, Endurance 40% Evade 30%, Influence 67%, Language (Jekkarene) 37%, Literacy (Korantine) 76%, Orate 45%, Unarmed 30%, Willpower 60%

Magic

Alarm

Combat Style: *Himelan Militia (spear, sidearm, shield) 40%*

Weapon	Size/Force	Reach	Damage	AP/HP
Shortsword	M	S	1d6	6/8
Dagger	S	S	1d4+1	6/8

Lorena, Slave Housekeeper to Valsus

Attributes	1D20	Location	AP/HP
Action Points: 2	1–3	Right Leg	0/6
Damage Modifier: -1d2	4–6	Left Leg	0/6
Magic Points: 10	7–9	Abdomen	0/7
Movement: 6 metres	10–12	Chest	0/8
Initiative Bonus: 13	13–15	Right Arm	0/5
Armour: None	16–18	Left Arm	0/5
Abilities: None	19–20	Head	0/6

Skills: Athletics 22%, Brawn 18%, Commerce 55%, Custom 70%, Endurance 36%, Evade 26%, Insight 55%, Perception 38%, Streetwise 65%, Unarmed 22%, Willpower 39%

Magic

Folk Magic (Rites 45%) Appraise, Cleanse, Lock, Tidy

Combat Style: *Desperate Housekeeper 28%*

Weapon	Size/Force	Reach	Damage	AP/HP
Knife	S	S	1d3-1d2	5/4

The House of Valsus

Modatis, Slave-steward to Valsus

Attributes		1D20	Location	AP/HP
Action Points: 2		1–3	Right Leg	0/6
Damage Modifier: 0		4–6	Left Leg	0/6
Magic Points: 9		7–9	Abdomen	0/7
Movement: 6 metres		10–12	Chest	0/8
Initiative Bonus: +12		13–15	Right Arm	0/5
Armour: none		16–18	Left Arm	0/5
Abilities: None		19–20	Head	0/6

Skills: *Athletics 34%, Brawn 39%, Endurance 40%, Evade 28%, Insight 35%, Locale 40%, Perception 41%, Sleight 38%, Streetwise 56% Unarmed 38%, Willpower 27%*

Magic

Folk Magic (Rites 45%) Polish

Combat Style: *Brawler (club, dagger, impromptu weapons) 36%*

Weapon	Size/Force	Reach	Damage	AP/HP
Club	*M*	*S*	*1d6*	*4/4*
Dagger	*S*	*S*	*1d4+1*	*6/8*

PRISHAD'S DAUGHTER

Prishad's Daughter is a classic wilderness adventure involving a voyage to a desert island, weird and dangerous creatures and a forgotten sorcerer's lair. However, there is a complex intersection of plots and circumstance that forms the backdrop to the adventure as presented here, and depending on the way the characters approach things, they could spend much of the scenario blundering into dangers that they barely understand.

The opponents encountered in this scenario can be tough, and, in some cases, have a significant numerical advantage. It is quite possible to use stealth, guile and planning to ensure a good chance of survival, but it is likely that Luck Points will be needed and that one or more characters will not make it through. The rewards, however, are significant. Some powerful magic items, treasure, pay and even a ship to take as a prize are all on offer.

The Merchant's Bane

Twice a year a Jekkarene vessel, the Purple Wanderer, arrives at Thyrta from Lyortha, a sleek war galley captained by Haliskome, a pale and slightly built woman sporting a jewelled eye patch. Haliskome deposits a pile of goods in crates, baskets and pottery vessels on the quayside, and Valsus has it removed to his stores, having offered up goods and cash of his own. The Jekkarene crew almost never venture into town, and Aparinaon's constables hover about looking serious, attempting to prevent a crowd pressing round this strange foreign vessel. Nobody is allowed on board the ship.

This process serves two purposes for Baron Solfernoy, the Jekkarene nobleman in charge of their port at Lyortha, and Haliskome's patron. He profits from the trade, gains some intelligence from Valsus and from Haliskome's observations concerning matters in Thyrta as part of the package, and also Haliskome's smart and magically enhanced vessel serves as a reminder, every time it arrives in a port, that the Jekkarene Theocracy (and Baron Solfernoy, in particular) are a force to be reckoned with. The foundation and rapid growth of the Korantine colony of Thyrta is a genuine and not unjustified concern for the Jekkarenes, who fear its presence will stir up conflict on the theocracy's northern borders – if not now, then surely in future generations – and the Jekkarenes always have an eye to the long term.

Last year Valsus' monopoly was challenged by a merchant from Largil in Morkesh who arrived with a mixed cargo including a fine selection of prestige Jekkarene goods. His name was Prishad, master of the Foamfollower. Prishad paid his dues to set up shop in the market place for a few days, and Valsus was not at all impressed by the arrival of this unexpected competition. When next the Purple Wanderer arrived in Thyrta, Valsus passed a message to its captain that they must do something to stop this Morkeshite merchant from interfering with his profits.

As it happens, Haliskome and Solfernoy took this message very seriously. Not content just to frustrate the man's business in Lyortha, Haliskome had a gang of sailors from her crew waylay the merchant at the docks, put an end to him and dump his body in the water. Unfortunately, the corpse was later discovered, caught in a fish trap near the port, and from even casual inspection, there could be no doubt that Prishad met a violent

Prishad's Daughter

end. When Prishad was murdered, his crew were at a loss what to do, and received many assurances but little or no help from the local authorities in finding out who was responsible for the outrage. So they returned to Largil aboard the Foamfollower with their master's remains in a barrel, and he was buried in his native land.

Whether or not Valsus expected such a definitive solution to his problem, and whether Solfernoy actually ordered the killing or Haliskome exercised her own discretion, the matter was clearly settled in a way that removed the threat to their trade with Valsus and that should have been that.

The Patron

The sole heir to Prishad's estate and a dutiful daughter, Safra AmPrishad has vowed not to set aside mourning, nor to accept any of the flood of marriage proposals with which she was immediately beset, until her father is revenged. Indeed she has devoted considerable funds from her inheritance to seek personal justice, as is the way amongst her people.

Safra set out aboard the Foamfollower as soon as the seas were open in spring of the current year, and first made port in Lyortha. There she approached Baron Solfernoy demanding satisfaction over the death of her father under his jurisdiction. Solfernoy informed her that he had thoroughly investigated the matter and discerned that a woman of the Jekkarene navy called Haliskome was responsible. Solfernoy regretted that he could not present the criminal to her, because she had clearly got wind that the authorities were about to make an arrest; Haliskome and her crew stole a ship (the Purple Wanderer) and deserted – and are now wanted for this rather more serious crime.

Before setting sail from Lyortha, Safra received a messenger, a young woman, who told her that the most likely place to find Haliskome was the island of Solisand. This woman did not provide the source of her information, but so far as Safra is concerned she was clearly someone of status. The identity of the informant may never be revealed, but it is likely to be Aximasadra, a priestess of the Jekkarenes' moon cult with an axe to grind against Haliskome, who suspects that Solfernoy may not exercise sufficient diligence in bringing her to justice.

Safra will arrive in Thyrta direct from Lyortha, probably around the beginning of the month of Arribeus. She takes rooms in the Floundering Turtle where she will attempt to discover more about her father's killing, find out where Solisand actually is, and identify hirelings to take part in her quest to go there in pursuit of Haliskome. Discretion is not the plan – she is planning an open tender for bodies to form a posse.

Safra is 22 years of age, beautiful and determined, unmarried and adventurous. With her head swathed in a mourning veil you cannot see much of her face other than big, dark eyes. She dresses demurely, long pants tight at the ankle, and a long-sleeved tunic, usually in brown with rich embroidered edging and detail in crimson, and a loose robe overall.

Safra is in a foreign place and does not speak the language – and she relies very much on the opinion of those who earn her trust. Her first need is for a translator or advisor, and someone who fulfils this role has the opportunity to wield great influence over her. Unless the Games Master or the characters have other ideas, then the Syndics (cult of Sabateus) will provide her with the services of a secretary who is fluent in Morkeshite or Djesmiri. Cerebos is a stout middle-aged man, short in stature with thick eyebrows and a jutting lower lip. Influencing Cerebos is a good way to influence Safra; however, he is not interested in bribes.

Getting Hired

Safra intends to summon all the would-be sell-swords of Thyrta to the Floundering Turtle to hear what she has to say at an open meeting held in the inn's courtyard. Word gets around this small town quickly and a decent-sized crowd is guaranteed to hear her tale. The open meeting at the Floundering Turtle can be used as a simple way to bring together the adventuring party, even if they come from rather disparate backgrounds.

Ivanthus of Tysil and his gang are likely to be trying to dominate the meeting and make a forceful case for being hired in whole or in part. Nevertheless, their prices are high and Safra may well be circumspect about taking such a large group of grizzled old veterans aboard her ship, in case they decide that she and the Foamfollower make a better prize than the wages on offer. A small team of up to 6 adventurers, backed up by her crew, is more what she has in mind. Ivanthus and his gang are determined, however, and not beneath using violence and intimidation to see off competition on a lucrative contract.

Once they are employed, Safra may ask the characters to dig into the facts of her father's visit here and discover if there is some connection with his murder. In doing so it is possible they uncover the depth of Valsus' connection to the Jekkarenes, and also stumble across the merchant's clandestine dealings with the bandit Varoteg. The other episodes in this book (Varoteg's Rascals and House of Valsus) then become sub-plots of this larger scenario.

Safra expects to pay regular rates – a maximum of 2SP per day, although she will pay up to 5SP for a premium service such as a spell casting or up to 100SP reward if the characters actually find out some critical information by which she understands who killed her father and why. Her price for Haliskome's head is 5,000 Dinars (2,500SP), and that is a lot of money. Safra expects a quarter share of any booty gathered, the rest to be distributed among the hirelings as they decide amongst themselves

The Target

Safra knows only that Haliskome is the name of the woman who captains the Purple Wanderer and who has deserted from the Jekkarene navy complete with a sailing crew and her ship.

The natural assumption of any Korantine who is unfamiliar with Jekkarene culture is that a female sea captain must be a unique phenomenon, although in the Jekkarene navy it is only remarkable that the 'mistress' of a given ship sails it in person.

It should not take long to find someone from the dockside community who can provide a description of the woman, after all her jewelled eye patch is rather eye-catching. Another thing that would not have escaped the notice of the harbour community that the Purple Wanderer is a galley and yet always arrives in port under sail with no rowing crew.

It is common knowledge that Valsus handled all the dealings with this Jekkarene visitor. Valsus, if questioned, denies any involvement in nefarious plots with Haliskome – on the contrary he expresses severe (and sincere) concern verging on mortification that if the woman has absconded with her ship his trade with the Jekkarenes may grind to a halt and all this could be the ruin of him.

Valsus will also profess utter surprise that his last transaction with Haliskome was after she had gone rogue and stolen the Purple Wanderer. So far as he was concerned, all was in order and no different to their earlier trades. Haliskome's current whereabouts are genuinely unknown to him.

The Destination

A long time ago a Korantine wizard called Brasilas made his home on the desert island of Solisand. Brasilas was one of those sorcerers who sensed that the Korantine empire was gearing up for a purge of his kind, and pre-empted any unpleasantness by putting himself beyond the emperor's reach – or so he thought. From his island stronghold, Brasilas made use of his magic to prey upon passing ships, seizing hostages who would be released when Brasilas was brought something he needed or desired – but oftentimes he simply resorted to piracy. It is said he even employed a controlled sea-monster to do so (in fact it was an immense undine). Eventually, his outrages became more serious, and more than one ship was sent to the bottom of the

Prishad's Daughter

sea, its crew drowned, because they had the temerity to attempt to stand up to Brasilas and his monster.

Brasilas had not reckoned with the determination and enthusiasm with which the Emperor Enkilos II would pursue him. A large expedition was sent to deal with the menace and that was the end of Brasilas. For over almost 200 years, Solisand has faded into obscurity – a place visited, if at all, by accident rather than design. But recently something has happened that has changed that – it has become the bolt-hole of the renegade Haliskome who has deserted from the Jekkarene navy with her crew and a ship to boot. Once more Solisand is the source of a danger to those that come within striking distance of her shores.

Solisand can stand alone as an adventuring location, and is a place that adventurers may happen upon by the caprice of wind and currents, or even a failure of navigation. It is not on any regularly travelled route, being in an area of ocean that is used only as a return path towards Korantia from the west, and then only by those who have found themselves, for some reason, forced to use an alternative to the usual and preferred course.

There can be alternative hooks that cause the characters to seek the place out. Some further suggestions are given here:

- Haliskome called at Tempigone on her flight from Lyortha. Arko of Solarne, the local ruler, attempted to hold her there but she and the crew made a daring escape. Arko has his eye on the warship stolen by Haliskome – either to return to Baron Solfernoy to earn his favour or to attach to his own little fledgling navy – and through Tiamankore's eavesdropping he knows where Haliskome was headed. Arko needs some private muscle; his own resources are poor in both men and magic. If the mission fails, Arko will do his very best to ensure he cuts his losses and nobody gets paid.

- Melosson of Thrigos has learned of the Brasilas story. He has managed to squeeze funds from his father and is secretly ploughing them into an expedition to the island to discover if any trace remains of Brasilas and the lost sorceries of the Korantine philosophers. Melosson and his sidekick Bazagar will discreetly weigh up potential hires for their expedition, always preferring mavericks and outsiders over those with traditional Korantine beliefs and prejudices.

Researching Solisand

Information on the island can be hard to come by, but some residents of Thyrta may be able to help. Although it is a reasonably large island, there is a lot of ocean to have to find it in, none of it charted, and some sort of directions are required. Thorough investigation will give the characters advance warning of the reef that protects the island's southern shore, and suggest what their options might be about where to try a landing.

Medanthros the Educator

This fellow loves his books and research, and if the characters can make friends, describe their problem and solicit his help, he may do so free of charge just because he is excited by the challenge.

"Solisand! Well, I declare I have never been there, and have never met anyone who has…although I am sure Rilados the Navigator must have passed that way even if he did not know where he was at the time. And if the Islander folk from across the ocean have been there, which they surely have…well, they don't write books, you see. Now, let me think…it is not a place that anyone writes about you know. At least no-one who matters these days, I'm sure. But in the old days perhaps…"

Medanthros seems pleased with the challenge and starts rooting though scroll tubes and codices…

"Ah, now this isn't literature such as men of quality would pay attention to, so it doesn't often get copied, and you tend to just have a few old rags with faded ink… the kind of thing something interesting might be written on the other side…"

Now the only reason I have this bit is because I like the handwriting, and it's about a part of our world that is not irrelevant to our colony. Exciting stuff too. It's archaic, but lovely. Pre-cataclysmic. Barely two generations before the inundation. A vanished world, you know. Haven't looked at it in a while… here, allow me to recite it for you, as you may struggle with the old letter forms…"

Medanthros can uncover two relevant texts. If the players want a transcript of these passages he will charge for a scribe to copy for them, but this will cost no more than 3SP in labour and materials.

Shores of Korantia

Report of Astangoras, Paladin of Emperor Enkilos II, dated 1014

(Fragment quoted in a secondary work, which attempts to describe the geography of the archipelago):

'By the time our fleet reached the apostate's island we had already lost two ships to the ocean's violent temper. So with land in sight, we put in at the first available beach, on the north side of the island. We set a camp and sent two parties inland to explore. One returned within a few hours, reporting that they had found the ruins of a village to the west. The other party returned the following day with reports of a forest that stretched as far as they could reckon, forming a barrier between our position and the location of the apostate's stronghold – indeed three of their party had already become lost, including the Paladin Nastarios. As a result of this intelligence, I decided to send a ship under Captain Ortantos to circumnavigate the island, rather than risk more of my men on a march into the forest. The captain reported back that the west coast offered anchorage but no beach; the east coast had but few landing places, and those exposed to the elements; yet at the south, closest to our objective, were many miles of fine beaches, however, made treacherous to approach by the presence of a broad reef.

Ortantos had tested the reef in a small boat and was convinced we could make a landing with some good seamanship and our ships' boats leading the way to find viable passage through. With two thirds of my force we attempted a landing – however, as soon as the first boats made it into the lagoon a great sea creature attacked them*, and many men were slain. Some struggled to the shore and in its eagerness to pursue, the monster beached itself, and thus we were able to set about it with sword, spear and arrow until it was dead. Even in its last moments, its tremendous thrashing accounted for more of my men, including the good captain Ortantos."

Games Master Note: The sea creature referred to is not an undine summoned from Brasilas' magic ring, but a sea serpent that Brasilas had acquired and kept in his lagoon. Nothing is left of it now.

Report of Mylomas of Kipsipsindra, dated 1147

'When it became known around port that I sought passage to Solisand, the earlier press of sea captains offering to place themselves and their crews at my disposal quickly evaporated. Eventually I took ship to Tapropiscur, and there found a local who claimed to have landed at Solisand once to collect fresh water, and had encountered nothing to substantiate the island's evil reputation. This same captain found me a crew who would take me to the island, and for a significant rental and deposit, we hired a vessel from a local magnate. The voyage to Solisand took us the better part of 3 weeks, and the only landfalls available in the latter part of that journey were desolate places said to be full of dangers to those who land there.

The Syndics

Visiting the headquarters of the local Sabatean cult is another way to find some information if the characters know where to look and what questions to ask. The Syndics do not keep charts nor maintain their own shipping resources, and can provide no information about Solisand. Enquiries here will not bear fruit other than suggestions of which sailors the characters might talk to for the information they need.

The Valsus Connection

Should the relationship between Valsus and Haliskome be raised with someone at the temple-guild, the characters will be reminded that Valsus is an associate member of their cult, being a resident non-citizen approved to conduct trade in accordance with the rules of the Borissan Syndics. If the characters take that to mean that he is under the Syndics' wing but they can distance themselves from him if he proves to have committed some wrongdoing, that is precisely what is intended. The Syndics have records only of the duties paid for goods shipped in and out of Thyrta, and, from this, it is possible to get a sense of how frequently Valsus and Haliskome did business, and to calculate the value. This information may be made available to a Borissan citizen who succeeds in an Influence roll.

It is absolutely clear from the Syndics' records that Haliskome appeared in Thyrta after the date at which she was reported to have absconded from Lyortha. As such, it is obvious that the last person known to have dealings with her is Valsus.

Elkanos

Valsus has a paid informer at the Sabatean temple, a slave-secretary called Elkanos. Born of a Taskan father taken captive in the Camtric War, he has been brought up with Korantine as his native tongue but is also fluent in Djesmiri and Taskan. Taking money from Valsus accelerates the rate at which he can save up to buy his freedom, which all slaves of the Syndics are entitled to do as a sort of performance-related bonus. Elkanos can act as a secretary block, promising to arrange meetings with important officials that never happen, offering to look into the records but reporting he has found nothing, and all the while letting Valsus know if the characters are snooping around and what sort of questions are being asked. He won't risk getting

Prishad's Daughter

into serious trouble on Valsus' account, so is more of an obstacle than an enemy.

Rilados the Navigator

When seafaring advice is called for, most people in Thyrta would recommend talking to Rilados the Navigator, who is most readily found carousing at the Blue Fin tavern.

"Solisand...Solisand you say?...Hmmm, can't say it's on my list of regular places to visit. After all, any land where there are native women to throw themselves at a Korantine sailor you can be assured I have been to, but the only place I know of by that name is by all accounts deserted."

Rilados will certainly know about Safra's call for adventurers:

"So some foreign woman arrives in port, a pretty little fish so I hear, puts out word she is going to Solisand and needs some muscle (but not that one, eh?), and what do you know, but in no time at all a couple of clumsy sailors go casually dropping the name of this otherwise obscure place into conversation with Thyrta's leading seaborne adventurer. For the record, I am now retired, thank you. Done plenty well for myself. And if I wanted to be putting myself up for this job with this lady at this time I could have done so, right? But no, this sounds like just the job for a bunch of wet-behind-the-ears young bucks to cut their teeth on. Or wind up dead, maybe. Or just...lost, right....?"

Once he is done with grandstanding, Rilados will actually take an interest in the characters' search for information if it might profit him. 'Thyrta's leading seaborne adventurer', can provide navigation instructions to reach Solisand. There are others who claim to do so, but Rilados has a name to maintain and is the most reliable source. He can also provide transport; Rilados has a dilapidated ship that hasn't been to sea in over a year, which he offers for hire crewed by whoever he can rope together (since he laid off his own crew ages ago), for a handsome sum of money...and has no intention of personally setting foot on a ship if it can be avoided, far less on Solisand. Hiring vessel, crew and getting bearings from him will come to several hundred Silver Pieces, but he can be persuaded to simply part with the necessary information for 150SP.

Rilados' coordinates require taking a bearing off the shore of Tempigone, although it is not necessary to make a stop there.

Morses

Without Rilados' information a Streetwise roll will eventually turn up a drunken sailor who, according to regulars in At Salty Mari's, has been to Solisand. This fellow, by the name of Morses, will sail with the adventurers as a navigator. His Navigation skill is no more than 35%. If it were once rather higher, as he claims, his drunkenness ensures he is not possessed of his full faculties and Morses is likely to get everyone lost or at least take much longer to find Solisand than he should, leaving ample time for inconvenient encounters or changes in the weather.

Failing these measures, the expedition can proceed to Tempigone, where, as everyone agrees, there will be people who can point the way.

THE JOURNEY

The characters may have their own ideas about how to get to Solisand and where they might get a ship. Otherwise, it is assumed that Safra provides transport aboard the Foamfollower.

The Foamfollower is a handsome vessel built in the Assabian style with curved lines and a lateen sail. She has a raised rear deck where the helmsman Zenduf usually sits at the steering oars under an awning, and it is decked out with all manner of little religious images, symbols and charms placed there by the crew.

The main deck has a hatch down to the hold and to the crew quarters. There is a cabin for the ship's owner (currently Safra), another area reserved to the officers (Zenduf, Joresh and Senduk). The other crew and any passengers are expected to doss down in the hold or on deck, such as suits them.

Any character who has any Seamanship skill at all will be aware that there is a serious drawback to the Foamfollower – as a cargo ship she is deep-draughted and not suitable for beaching. The only way to land on an island, if it has no natural harbour, is to take the ship's boat to shore.

The Crew of the Foamfollower

Safra's crew are mostly old hands in her father's service, trusted and loyal, and some of them as keen to see her father avenged as she is.

- Zenduf – The ship's captain and helmsman (Seamanship 88%, Navigate 75%), a grizzled seaman, perhaps 40 years or more of age
- Joresh – First mate, and trusted to look out for Safra (Seamanship 95%, Boating 85%). Small and wiry with

The Foamfollower, A Trade Ship From Morkesh	
Power	Sail (2 masts – one main, one forward; square rigged)
Crew	11 officers, sailors, and hands
Dimensions	Length 24m, Beam 7m, Freeboard 2m
Capacity	160 Tons
Hull Type	T
Size	M
Armour Points	6
Hit Points	60
Seaworthiness	75%
Armaments	None. Ramming Damage 3d6.

Notes: The Foamfollower has a broad bottom, but is deeper draft than a galley. She trails a little ships' boat, a skiff, in her wake.

nut-brown weathered skin and a lined face. Looks tough though.

Y Senduk – A man from Perlak. He's the ship's doctor (First Aid 78%, Healing 55%) but quite willing and able to pitch in to the sailing work.

Y Kallish, Midrim, Valosh, Vashtar and Horsum, the sailors, the core of the crew (Seamanship 30%-65%). Varying in age between early 20s and mid 30s.

Y Zebos is the ship's cook and storekeeper. He's painfully thin – just the way he is, so he says – because he's smart enough not to touch his own cooking, so say the rest of the crew.

Y Bessum and Zoshi, two deck hands. Bessum is a big dumb brute with little more than his muscle power to offer, Zoshi hardly more than a boy – he is 14.

Travel Time

Solisand is approximately 3-4 day's sailing from Thyrta, or 2-3 days west-south-west of Tempigone.

Safra will not set sail in dangerous conditions but rather wait in port until a fair wind is given, and the Games Master should check for weather conditions and encounters as normal.

Stopping at Tempigone

If the party call at Guberan, whether by choice or to shelter from adverse weather, they will surely be brought before Arko of Solarne (by force if necessary), who will take a keen interest in their plans. Appropriate Deceit or Influence rolls are required if they wish to keep their mission a secret – if he gets the impression they are holding out on him he will attempt other means to learn what their purpose is (see stats for Tiamankore, Arko's mistress).

Asking around the little port will soon uncover that Haliskome and the Purple Wanderer made port here in the late summer, but made their escape when Arko attempted to impound the vessel. Arko's two little naval ships are habitually in dry dock and would take days to get ready for sailing, so no chase was attempted.

Eventually someone can be found who is willing to be hired to direct the ship to Solisand for 30 pieces of silver. If the Games Master wishes it, this may be a spy planted by Arko, or his Jekkarene mistress Tiamankore.

Overview of Solisand

The island of Solisand is unusually busy. Circumstances have brought the crews of three vessels to its shores even before the characters arrive, and these groups are becoming aware of the others' presence and working out what they are doing here and who is the greatest threat.

Haliskome and her Gang

In one corner, Haliskome and her crew are hiding out, planning how they will live, how they will use their skills and the ship at their disposal to make their fortune as pirates, and what they will do with a fortune once it is made. They have now been on Solisand for several months, and have had ample opportunity to explore their immediate environment and scout beyond it, to maintain their ship and even take it out to sea.

The pirates do not yet know of the Jekkarene force landed on the north side of the island, but will do so soon enough as the Jekkarenes extend their patrols towards the south. They have found wreckage from the orcs' ship and found more than one body in the lagoon or washed up on the beach. As yet they have seen evidence that they are not alone, but have not yet encountered any orcs, as their preference is to maintain security by restricting themselves to the immediate surroundings of their camp where they are close by their ship.

Only Haliskome's lover, Melantos, wanders alone on the island – and then only at full moon when he may not be able to control his lycanthropy and is a danger to his shipmates.

The Orcs

On another corner of the island is a band of shipwrecked orcs led by Bandestrap, a lapith (orcish sorcerer) and his lieutenant, Sandula, who is an experienced and scarred warrior. Bandestrap and his gang are an off-shoot of a small orcish colony on Fierla who occupy Herosida, one of the now abandoned Korantine colonies that has lain in ruins since the Cataclysm. Their ship was driven off course and onto the reefs off Solisand by an ill wind. Those who survived, some two-thirds of the original crew, are those who managed to swim to shore from the wreck.

They are far from home and making do with what they can forage or scavenge from the island's natural resources. Despite being short on equipment, the orcs are quite at home in the environment, well able to fashion what they need from the raw materials they can find, but have lost several of their men to an unknown attacker (the Woses) and are thus rather edgy.

What they really want is to get their hands on a vessel to get off the island and return home. They have been on Solisand for several weeks, lost a few more men to its dangers, and have scouted out the western end of the island. They regard the Orc Hills (Zone G) as their home turf and the ruins at the Crag (Zone A) as a place they might make a stronghold if necessary to settle in for a long stay, but at present are deterred by the lack of fresh water on the crag and the harpies who make a nuisance of themselves whenever the orcs try to camp there. They are aware of the pirates and have avoided them so far.

The orcs are keen on taking prisoners if they can. Bandestrap likes a sacrifice just to keep his hand in. Even if he can't make good use of one because of the Evocation requirement, he will keep trying with gradually increased range on his Evoke spell to determine if there is a Hungry God anywhere in the vicinity (this worked for the orcs of Fierla). There isn't.

If the characters somehow manage to parlay with these orcs, they could be negotiated with. The orcs want transport back to Herosida, and if there is a way to offer this in a way that makes Bandestrap believe the characters can deliver on the promise, the Orcs might become unlikely allies.

The Jekkarenes

The last group of visitors to the island are a Jekkarene expedition that has arrived aboard the *Moonglory*, a light galley with a full crew of 50 rowers plus sailors and marines. This expedition is in pursuit of Haliskome, to bring her to justice for the crime of apostasy, desertion and the theft of state property – but even more importantly to bring the *Purple Wanderer* back to Lyortha. The commander is Valontermus, who is highly methodical and cautious in his approach, very concerned not to make any dumb mistakes by rushing into action before establishing his base and fully scouting the terrain. He is accompanied by the moon-priestess Pelusinne, who is there to supervise his activities but has her own interest in exploring Brasilas' old lair.

They have encountered the orcs, and think them 'monstrous, murderous natives'. Assuming therefore there could be many of them, they are wary of running into more, and this has made their progress even more slow and cautious. Valontermus believes there is a native village on the crag, having seen from afar signs of activity and mistaking distant ruins for primitive dwellings.

When the characters first encounter the Jekkarenes, they may mistake them for Haliskome's pirates and vice versa. They will have to convince Valontermus they are 'innocent' of piracy. Nevertheless Valontermus can make good use of prisoners, both to interrogate for information (he is very thorough) and to ensure he can crew both the *Moonglory* and the *Purple Wanderer* back to port. For these reasons, he will have them either kept prisoner at his stockade or immediately pressed into service, perhaps even used to help take on the pirates or make the ruins of Brasilas' lair safe for Pelusinne's exploration.

Solfernoy's Intrigue

Although Baron Solfernoy is responsible for equipping and sending the expedition and is accountable to his local trio of moon-priestesses for the same, he may not wish it every success. Valontermus is officially briefed to kill or, if possible, capture the deserters, including Haliskome, but Solfernoy has privately informed him that should the pirates be captured alive this may be inconvenient for him. All this is kept secret from Pelusinne, and Valontermus has to negotiate the tricky business of fulfilling his mission instructions to the letter while trying to accommodate Solfernoy's requirements too, all under the watchful eye of a moon priestess.

Pelusinne's Plan

Pelusinne is a surprise addition to the expedition – a surprise to Solfernoy at least. While Valontermus may believe she is there to spy on him, she is actually happy for him to get on with his job and confident in his abilities. Pelusinne's real interest is in the island's history. There are significant references to Brasilas and Solisand in Jekkarene records, and apparently he was being courted by the priestesses to assist in calling on Father Ocean to lay low the Korantine Empire. The Korantine emperor got to Brasilas before he could participate in The Glorious Day, as the Jekkarenes refer to the Cataclysm that sank Korantis,

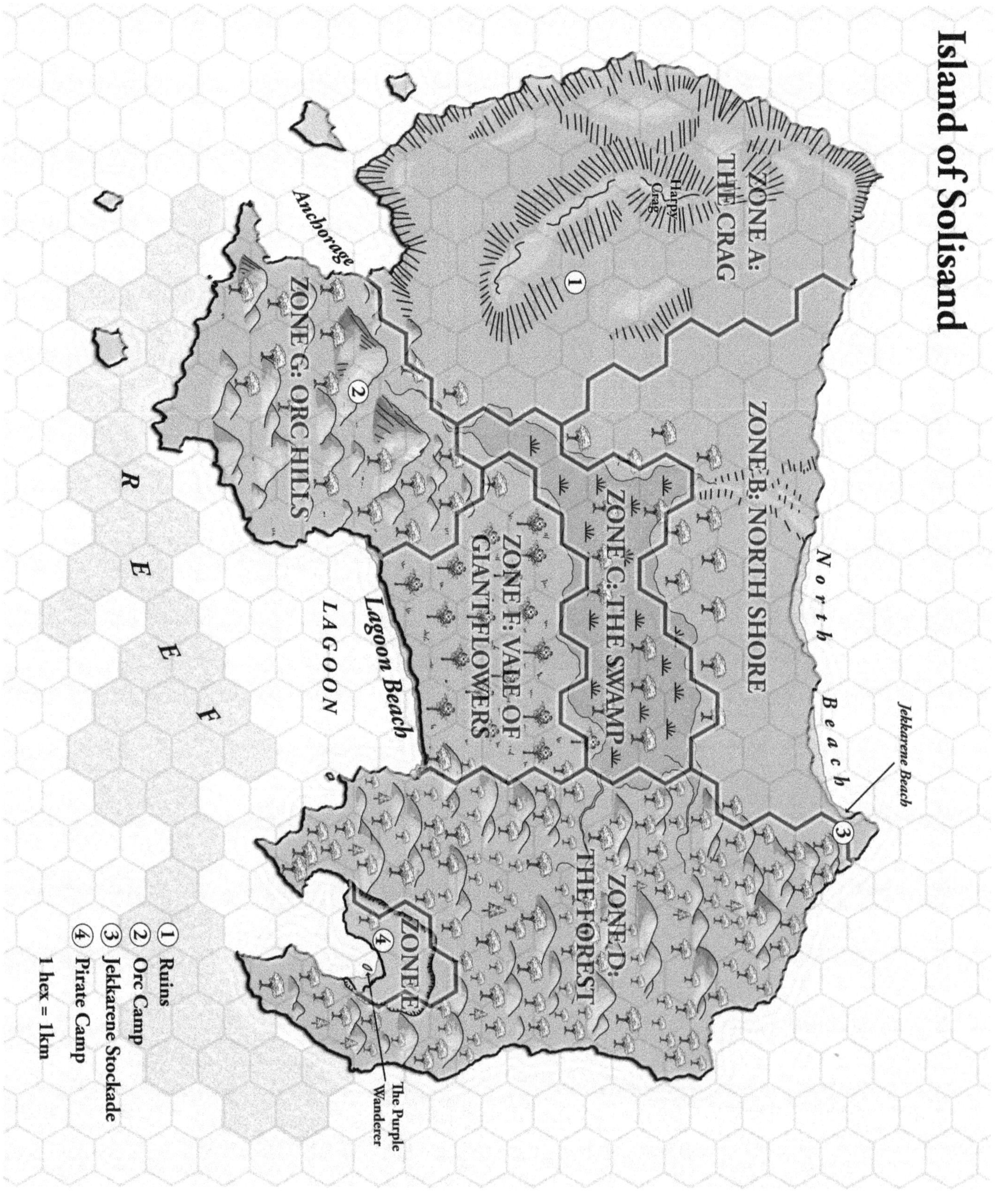

Shores of Korantia

Island of Solisand

- ① Ruins
- ② Orc Camp
- ③ Jekkarene Stockade
- ④ Pirate Camp

1 hex = 1km

Zone A: The Crag
Zone B: North Shore
Zone C: The Swamp
Zone D: The Forest
Zone E: (Pirate Camp area)
Zone F: Vale of Giantflowers
Zone G: Orc Hills

Harpy Crag
Anchorage
Lagoon Beach
LAGOON
REEF
North Beach
Jekkarene Beach
The Purple Wanderer

but he, nonetheless, is still remembered as a 'good Korantine'. Pelusinne wants to investigate Brasilas' former home to find out what trace of him and his magic remains.

Alternative Foes

Depending on the set-up, you can substitute all Jekkarene encounters for a similar encounter with members of an expedition sent by Arko of Solarne under the command of his guard captain, Rospur. In this case, the Jekkarene woman with the crew is Tiamankore, Arko's mistress.

Denizens of Solisand

The island has its own denizens, both magical and physical. Of these the only organised community are the Woses, diminutive vestiges of the island's earlier human population, who were mostly wiped out by Brasilas. They have been preserved through the power of the Bakru, a supernatural denizen of the island who even the local nymph, Solisma, looks up to. These Woses have little or no experience of foreigners. The pirates have been no trouble, but the Jekkarenes have been butchering the trees of their forest to make their stockade and the orcs have previously captured one of their number and eaten him so are clearly very bad people. On the whole, they will attempt to protect their forest and themselves from intrusion and will use ruse and magic to do so before resorting to anything truly dangerous.

In appearance they are quite peculiar, their facial features and extremities still being the same size as for a normal human but applied to a body half the size. For Wose characteristics, use MYTHRAS Halfling, but with SIZ 1d6+3. They are dressed in nothing but loincloths made of twisted grasses, and the pelts from small woodland animals.

The bakru is a physical manifestation of a vegetation-daemon, who dates back to Brasilas' day and was perhaps summoned from the Many Hells or transported here by the wizard. It is rarely met, but if either Solisma's grove or the survival of the Woses is at stake, it will act, using its magic to the best effect possible.

Solisma is the nymph of the island, one who suffers a feeling of guilt for having once been persuaded by Brasilas to assist in the destruction of the human community on Solisand. The bakru made her see the right of it, and she subsequently helped protect the few survivors and nurtured the Woses that the Bakru created from them. Solisma is shy but can be stirred to action in defence of the Woses and, of course, protect her grove.

The Crag supports a small community of eight harpies, who can be a great nuisance to those who travel in open country. When the characters arrive, the Jekkarenes have managed to kill a harpy attempting to harass one of their patrols, and crucified the body outside their stockade as a warning to others.

Flora and Fauna

There are some poisonous snakes on Solisand, constrictor snakes in the swamp, a great many biting insects and some super-sized carnivorous plants. More mundane wildlife incudes a native breed of wild boar which is the largest surviving mammal; colourful bird life; small, furry critters of the forest, and some very large spiders, beetles, butterflies and moths that are harmless enough but can be disconcerting. The megaflora has allowed some of these to reach enormous proportions – a butterfly as big as a dinner plate, a spider as big as your head. A few examples are much, much bigger, and are dangerous.

The waters immediately around Solisand offer only mediocre fishing, and while there are sharks, there is nothing for the biggest sort to feed on in the area, so there is little to fear in the water unless it is summoned or awakened by magical action.

Hauntings

Solisand has its share of hauntings, in almost all cases the spirits of the former human population who were wiped out by Brasilas once he had no further use of them as slave labour. Their language and customs were an idiosyncratic off-shoot of Archipelagan culture. The Woses refer to these Haunts as The Sad Ancestors, and do not fear them.

Landfall

It is likely the characters arrive from the east, in which case there are some narrow beaches suitable enough for making a landing with a rowboat without any trouble. Beaching a larger vessel such as a galley is possible in places but at risk of damage (requires a Seamanship roll). The east coast offers the best chance of landing without detection, since nobody is watching this shore unless they have been given reason to do so by unfolding events.

Solisand's only natural harbour is on the west coast, where there is a bay that offers an anchorage with some shelter from the elements, but the rocky shore is no good for beaching anything larger than a rowboat. This bay is also overlooked by the orcs, and any ship anchoring here will be spotted within hours of arriving. The orcs will be delighted at this god-send, and proceed to work out how they can capture the ship and take it for their own so they can head home.

Sailing round to the north presents the prospect of long beaches, broad enough to draw up a galley, but there are Jekkarenes camped on the bluff at the east end of this shore, their galley on the beach below, and they may well spot the characters approaching the island. The Jekkarenes are not expecting visitors and their attention is turned inland. If the characters approach the coast by ship within 4km of the Jekkarene camp, there is a 40% chance they will be spotted. The Perception roll becomes Easy (60%) if the approach is within 2km and automatic if under 1km; adjust the difficulty if the approach is at night and the characters have the wit to do so with lights doused.

Sailing to the south introduces the problem of the reef, which is situated roughly 2 km from shore. The reef is some 300-500m wide at its narrowest points. It is possible to find a way through it using a galley or other shallow draft vessel – indeed to cross it in a rowing boat – but a transport ship has no chance without magical help to lift it over the reef, perhaps by summoning undines to carry it across. Once across, the lagoon within offers a long fine beach that is within the zone patrolled by the orcs, and to the west a secluded bay where Haliskome's camp can be found.

The pirates do not keep watch out to sea until alerted to the presence of the Moonglory and its crew on the north side of the island. Once this is the case, there is no chance of making it to shore unseen within 2km of Zone B, unless a special plan is devised to do so.

Movement

Ask the players for a plan for each day. If they are on the move, they must choose 'Search', 'Marching' or 'Pursuit' speed.

Search: Speed 2km per hour, 3km in open country. The characters are moving cautiously, taking care to examine the surroundings, keeping an eye out for trails and ready to go to ground or use stealth if they suspect an encounter is near. Characters always get a chance for Track and Perception rolls before running into an encounter, and may have a chance to avoid traps by detecting their presence before they are triggered.

Marching: Speed 3km per hour, 5km in open country. Moving at normal pace, forging a path though the surroundings to reach a destination. Track rolls are only awarded if the party states they are stopping for the task. Traps avoided or evaded on an opposed roll basis. Counts as Light activity for the purposes of fatigue.

Flight/Pursuit: 5km per hour, 10km in open country. When haste is the main concern, perhaps in flight or pursuit or in a hurry to reach an objective. No opportunity for perception, tracking or spotting/avoiding traps. Counts as Medium activity for the purposes of fatigue.

Encounters

Rolled encounters are one of the key elements of this scenario, and many of them tell a story, act as a catalyst to events, or provide clues as to who is on the island and what is going on. Encounter checks should be made quite regularly, in accordance with the following table:

Encounter Frequency

Terrain	Encounter Probability	Frequency Day/ Night
Forest	25%	3 hours/2 hours
Marsh	10%	4 hours/ 3 hours
Shore	30%	2 hours/ 4 hours
Open Ground	20%	2 hours/ 6 hours

The island has been divided into seven 'zones' each of which represents a different type of terrain and/or the territory where particular enemies and creatures are likely to be encountered.

General Encounters Table

1D100	Encounter Type
01-05	Corpse
06-20	Jekkarenes
21-25	Pirates
26-34	Orcs
35-37	Woses
38	The Bakru
39-42	Giant Plant
43-50	Insect Swarm
51-60	Harpies
61-70	Tracks
71-75	Campsite, Abandoned
76-80	Campsite, Occupied
81-83	Snake
84-94	Small Game
95-98	Wild Pig
99-00	Spirit

Prishad's Daughter

Whenever an encounter occurs, roll 1d6 – if the result is 1-3, the local encounters provided for each zone are used. On a 4-6, roll d100 and refer to the General Encounters table, below. Some of these encounters should only be used once and if they reoccur the Games Master can use discretion and change the description or roll again.

Encounter Descriptions

Corpse

The party comes across a recent corpse, already flyblown or being devoured by ants. Roll 1d6 or choose what is most appropriate to the area:

1D6	Corpse Type
1-2	An orc; to most people a bizarre looking individual – pale grey or purplish skin and hairless, near naked. Examination detects a small dart in the fellow's neck, as from a blowgun, and a blow to the back of the skull (he has been darted and killed by the woses).
3-4	A sailor – one of Haliskome's men. His body has been stripped. A broken arrow shaft protrudes from his chest, which if retrieved looks like it was made from local resources, with a flint point (he has been killed by orcs).
5-6	A deadfall pit contains the remains of a Jekkarene sailor, whose neck has been broken. The body is unlooted and with it is a waterskin, a sidearm of some kind; a silver pendant round his neck. In his belt pouch and still grasped in his fist is a bunch of edible roots. If the characters wait long enough an orc patrol will come and check this trap.

The Games Master should adjust the numbers of whichever group has lost a man accordingly.

Jekkarenes

Valontermus sends out two 10-man parties at a time, one to explore and search the island, the other on patrol or on water-fetching duty. Each party consists of two marines and eight lightly-armed rowers, one or two of whom have been given a spear. When encountered far from their stockade the Jekkarenes are well beyond their comfort zone, and very jumpy. They will always attempt to withdraw from an encounter if someone has the drop on them; they are only up for taking casualties when there is a specific objective to be achieved. If these patrols are encountered, roll 1d6:

1D6	Jekkarenes
1	Lost and looking for a way back to their camp
2	Lost and fleeing a skirmish with the orcs. 1d3 members of their group have been left behind
3	Searching for 1d3 lost companions (perhaps having recovered their composure after fleeing a skirmish)
4	In good order and picking out a suitable trail towards the pirates' zone
5	In good order, collecting food and/or water
6	In good order, tracking a suspected foe, which may be the characters, orcs, pirates, or some sort of monster

Statistics for the Jekkarenes can be found from page 219.

Pirates

An encounter with pirates outside their home zone means they are on a mission. It is possible they have realised that other people are now on the island and have sent out a team to investigate. This team will normally be headed by Kisethentyes and Ankaskron, two very tough individuals, and backed by four of the sailors. If they encounter anyone unexpected, the pirates will be keen to snatch a prisoner or two for questioning, and will subsequently take them back to Haliskome.

The pirates have been on the island longer than the orcs and Jekkarenes, and understand its dangers. They are far less jumpy, and far more able to act with intelligence and cunning than the other groups characters may encounter.

Orcs

Most orc encounters are with a 5-strong gang of warriors out hunting, patrolling, checking traps. There is a 50% chance that such a group is led by Sandula, Bandestrap's second in command. The 5-man patrol is only likely to attack if they can set up an ambush or otherwise have a clear advantage. Otherwise they are likely to go and fetch support.

The more dangerous possibility is a run-in with Bandestrap himself; a strong force of 10 warriors led by Bandestrap in person. Finally, Bandestrap has brought a familiar with him, a small therapod dinosaur known as Grrruff. This creature roams quite freely, enjoys hunting the local wild pigs, and often basks somewhere on the Crag.

Select or roll 1d6:

1D6	Orcs
1-3	5 man patrol.
4-5	10 man expedition.
6	Grrruff, Bandestrap's familiar.

Woses

The Woses' typical Stealth skill is 67%, as long as they remain in the forest their skill roll is Easy and therefore treated as 100%. They may observe intruders in their forest for a while, and perhaps use their Folk Magic to scare them away by producing mysterious lights, sounds and events. A favourite is to cast Pet on a small creature, send it towards the characters and make it speak by using Ventriloquism – although their language is unintelligable to almost anyone, requiring a Formidable roll in Archipelagan to get the gist of. At night, a Light spell is applied as well to add to the overall effect.

If Woses are rolled as an encounter, their default starting position is hidden in cover observing the adventurers, 1d6+2 in number. Their weapon of choice is a blowgun, and their choice of Special Effect is always Deliver Poison, combined with Choose Location or Bypass Armour if required to assure a dart strikes flesh. The poison used is a natural toxin that paralyses the victim. If they have time to prepare, they have cast Pierce spells on their blowgun darts, up to two each. Woses carry clubs to stun or dispatch victims, and some carry sharpened sticks as little spears, but they will always try to avoid going toe to toe with a human. If caught in the open, their first concern is to run and hide.

The Bakru

This creature will only reveal himself to the characters if previously convinced of their good will by their behaviour towards the Woses, or perhaps towards Solisma. The bakru can communicate by a Translate spell, and so may come forward to speak

Typical Woses

Attributes		1D20	Location	AP/HP
Action Points: 3		1–3	Right Leg	0/6
Damage Modifier: -1d4		4–6	Left Leg	0/6
Magic Points: 11		7–9	Abdomen	0/7
Movement: 4 metres		10–12	Chest	0/8
Initiative Bonus: +14		13–15	Right Arm	0/5
Armour: none		16–18	Left Arm	0/5
Abilities: None		19–20	Head	0/6

Skills: Athletics 41%, Brawn 35%, Endurance 62%, Evade 68%, Insight 54%, Locale 90%, Perception 65%, Sleight 55%, Stealth 67% Unarmed 41%, Willpower 42%

Magic

Folk Magic (Solisand Rites 39%) Pathway, Pet, Pierce, Ventriloquism

Combat Style: *Forest Hunter (spear, club, blowgun) 55%*

Blowgun Poison (Honeytrap Juice)

Application: contact

Potency: 66

Resistance: Endurance

Onset time: 1d3 Rounds

Duration: 1d3+1 hours

Condition: Paralysis. If the victim successfully resists then the location is stunned (as the Special Effect) for the Duration. If the poison wins, their whole body is paralysed

Weapon	Size/Force	Reach	Damage	AP/HP
Club	M	S	1d6-1d4	4/4
Spear	M	M	1d6-1d4	6/8
Blowgun	-	-	Poison	

with the characters on behalf of other denizens. His voice creaks like branches in the breeze. The bakru has no agenda of his own except to protect his followers. He may beg or demand that the characters stop doing something destructive, or he can promise help from the Woses, from Solisma, or just from himself. His help most likely comes by the use of Folk Magic in support of the characters' actions if they are doing something good. He has no antipathy towards the pirates, would see the Jekkarenes kept out of the forest to prevent further logging or hunting, and would happily see the orcs exterminated.

The bakru will make clever use of Folk Magic to hinder or frighten away the characters if they are perceived as a threat.

Bakru statistics can be found in MYTHRAS page 228. The Games Master can allow the Bakru to have any Folk Magic spells that he thinks will be useful to the game.

Giant Plants

If not in the Vale of Giant Flowers, the most common encounter is with a Honey Trap, a carnivorous horror that has hidden itself among the native plants. Roll 1d6

1D6	Plant Type
1-2	Lone Honey-Trap lying in ambush
3-5	Megaflora colony, d6 x 10m diameter (in the Vale of Flowers, treat as Insect, Giant)
6	A Honey Trap plant, its flower closed but swollen with the remains of a creature still stuck in it, half digested – the chitinous husk of a giant insect or the partially dissolved remains of a man.

The Honey Trap is so called because it releases chemicals into the air that cause a creature picking up the scent to smell whatever it finds most delicious, attracting them towards the source. Match a Potency of 60 against Willpower; those who fail to resist feel compelled to head towards the source of the scent. Once familiar with the danger the Resistance roll is one grade easier.

As soon as the target is within range (VL) the Honey Trap attempts to entangle it with its sinuous tendrils and pull it towards its centre, where it is paralysed and slowly digested.

The main part of the flower is very large, its mass being just below ground level, and big enough to attempt to fully envelop anything up to a SIZ of 12. Above ground is a discreet flower shaped like an artichoke until its tendrils have caught something, at which point its dull green exterior unfurls to reveal a fringe of yellow petals around its pink, dewy centre.

A Honey Trap has 1d3+1 tendrils, and each has an Action Point. The tendril always attempts the Entangle Special Effect, and if it succeeds its next action is an opposed Brawn test (40%, made one grade easier for each additional tendril) to drag the victim into the plant's maw, which is ringed with a sticky contact poison that can paralyse the victim on the following action.

The Honey Trap is an inanimate object, its tendrils having 2 AP and 4HP each, its main body 2 AP and 10HP. Characters hacking at a Honey Trap can choose where to strike without using the Choose Location effect.

Honey Trap

Attributes	1D20	Location	AP/HP
Action Points: 1d3+1	N/A	Body	2/10
Damage Modifier: 0	N/A	Tendril	2/4
Magic Points: NA			
Movement: 0			
Initiative Bonus: 8			
Armour: 2 points for thick vines and coating			
Abilities: Entangle			

Skills: *Brawn 40%*

Combat Style: *Flower Power 40%*

Honeytrap Juice

Application: contact

Potency: 66

Resistance: Endurance

Onset time: 1d3 Rounds

Duration: 1d3+1 hours

Condition: Paralysis. If the victim successfully resists then the location is stunned (as the Special Effect) for the Duration. If the poison wins, their whole body is paralysed

Weapon	Size/Force	Reach	Damage	AP/HP
Tendril	M	VL	Entangle	2/4
Maw	H	T	Paralysing Touch	2/10
Digestion	-	T	1 HP per location per hour	

Insect Swarm

See the MYTHRAS *rules, page 251.*

The Games Master should feel free to put in something more frightening such as a giant insect or spider instead, but the island is not big enough to support a colony of giant ants and the most likely encounters would be with flying insects or with beetles that grub around among the damp litter of the Vale of Giant Flowers.

Harpies

Harpies are essentially harmless if you are moving under cover of the forest, as the canopy prevents them attacking from the air and they have no desire to pick a fight on the ground. If you are routinely climbing trees to look around, or traversing the Swamp, North Shore or Crag, then you are in danger of being attacked. The harpies might also attack those on boats within 2km of the shore.

The number of harpies encountered depends on the area. Near their home atop the Crag then 1d4+3 will appear, anywhere else, 1d3 harpies.

Harpy statistics are found in MYTHRAS, *page 250.*

Tracks

The characters come across a trail in the forest. Roll 1d6:

1D6	TRACKS
1	A successful Tracking roll determines small bipeds made the trail (Woses). However, this trail will abruptly and inexplicably end after a few dozen metres at most.
2-4	An animal trail, an excellent spot to set snares or lay traps for game
5-6	Human trail, either orcs, Jekkarenes or pirates, depending on the zone, leading to their camp..

Campsite, Abandoned

A cold campfire in a small clearing. There are a few bones scattered around. Searching the site may give some clues as to who was here:

1D6	NATURE OF CAMP
1-3	Jekkarenes – remains of ships's biscuit, a piece of torn clothing, a worn out shoe
4-5	Orcs – remains of a kill from the hunt, or of making arrows and armour from found materials.
6	Pirates – as for Jekkarenes, but a much smaller camp, maybe half a dozen people at most were here.

Campsite, Occupied

The characters come across one of the other parties on the island in camp. Roll 1d6:

1D6	NATURE OF CAMP
1-3	Jekkarenes
4-5	Orcs
6	Pirates

Snakes

The adventurers may frequently be within spitting distance of a snake – this encounter means they have disturbed one, and come so close as to give it the chance to attack.

In the swamp, there are giant constrictor snakes. These are not the monsters provided in MYTHRAS, page 266, being half the size, but still of terrifying proportions. Their first attack is likely to be submerged and camouflaged beneath the swampy waters, taking the legs of the victim and so dragging them under water to drown while they are crushed. The snake's second attack will target the chest or abdomen and so begin squeezing.

For Snake statistics, see opposite and page 202.

Small Game

Harmless small game that provides an opportunity for hunting

Wild Pig

1d6 wild pigs; up to two of them are aggressive, tusked adults.

See MYTHRAS, *page 230, for statistics.*

Prishad's Daughter

Constrictor Snake

Characteristics	Attributes	1D20	Location	AP/HP
STR: 22	Action Points: 3	01-02	Tail Tip	2/8
CON: 17	Damage Modifier: +1d8	03-04	Mid End-Length	2/8
SIZ: 19	Magic Points: 10	05-07	Fore End-Length	2/8
DEX: 19	Movement: 4 metres	08-10	Rear Mid Length	2/9
INS: 12	Initiative Bonus: 13	11-13	Mid Mid-Length	2/9
POW: 10	Armour: 2 point skin	14-16	Fore Mid-length	2/9
	Abilities: Camouflaged, Cold Blooded, Grappler, Swimmer	17	Rear Fore-Length	2/8
		18	Mid fore-Length	2/8
		19-20	Head	2/8

Skills: Athletics 79%, Brawn 66%, Endurance 66%, Evade 68%, Perception 59%, Stealth 71%, Willpower 54%

Combat Style: Squeeze and Bite 60%

The snake can use each action to coil itself round an additional location, to crush a location already constricted or to bite. A SIZ 20 example can up to four locations at once on a man-size target. Add or reduce one location for every 5 SIZ the target is smaller or larger than the snake. If the head, chest or abdomen are affected, the target must oppose the attack with his Brawn or make checks for Asphyxiation as well. Armour only reduces damage from crushing until its value is exceeded by the cumulative damage.

Weapon	Size/Force	Reach	Damage	AP/HP
Bite	S	T	1d6+1d8	As for Head
Constrict	H	T	1d4+1d8	4/12
Dagger	S	S	1d4+1	6/8

Spirit

The haunts of Solisand fall into 2 types:

- Apparitions, very weak (intensity 0) spirit entities that produce only a specific 'glamour' that may be experienced by characters who encounter them, and

- Haunts, which have some element of will left to them that can interact with mortals in a variety of ways (see haunts in Mythras, page 150).

A mortal who wishes to deny an apparition, or prevent a haunt from attacking him, can resist its Manifestation ability with his Willpower. The haunt's Manifestation skill is set at 5x POW. If the mortal succeeds, he can avert all effects upon himself of the haunt's presence.

These haunts are well known to the pirates, who tend to avoid the places where they are encountered, having learned that an apparition may be harmless but is often a warning that a haunt is present, which can be very dangerous indeed. Apparitions and haunts have a Manifestation skill that represents their ability to impress themselves upon a mortal. Roll 1d6:

1D6	Apparition
1-2	Sight Apparition (Manifestation 25%, MP 5). A fleeting glimpse of an islander from ancient times, in some macabre situation that tells of the unspeakable brutality with which Brasilas crushed Solisand's inhabitants. A bleeding corpse hung upside down from a bough; a figure buried up to the neck and left for wild animals; a stumbling figure with flesh blasted from bones by a spell...each momentarily turns its eyes to the characters and tries to speak. A successful Insight test on the part of the character plagued by these apparitions is enough to understand that they are in some disjointed way narrating the story of a massacre.
3-4	Sound Apparition (Manifestation 20%, MP 4). Simply a scream, a cry, or a long demented babbling. The ghost may just be making a cry of frustration and wants to be heard by the living, or drawing the characters towards a haunt's locus as a trap.
5-6	Haunt (Manifestation 50%, MP 10). The islanders who met dreadful deaths at the hands of Brasilas haunt the island as tormented souls. In general, each ghost is restricted to a zone where it can manifest as an apparition, and within that zone there is a locus within POW metres of which it can manifest fully as a haunt.

The only means of removing the island's hauntings, short of banishing the ghosts one by one, is to devise some right of appeasement, guided by the bakru or Solismar.

Venomous Snake

Characteristics	Attributes	1D20	Location	AP/HP
STR: 6	Action Points: 3	01-02	Tail Tip	1/3
CON:11	Damage Modifier:	03-04	Mid End-Length	1/4
SIZ:5	Magic Points: 8	05-07	Fore End-Length	1/4
DEX: 20	Movement: 6 metres	08-10	Rear Mid Length	1/4
INS: 12	Initiative Bonus: 16+	11-13	Mid Mid-Length	1/4
POW: 8	Armour: 1 point skin – no penalty	14-16	Fore Mid-length	1/4
	Abilities: Cold Blooded, Venomous	17	Rear Fore-Length	1/4
		18	Mid fore-Length	1/4
		19-20	Head	1/4

Skills: *Endurance 33%, Evade 80%, Stealth 80%, Willpower 24%*

Combat Style: *Squeeze and Bite 60%*

If injected via bite, the venom will inflict a burning pain shortly followed by respiratory difficulty which can lead to death. Even surviving a cobra bite comes at a horrible cost, the bitten area suffering permanent necrotic damage.

Application: Injected
Potency: 75
Resistance: Endurance
Onset time: 1d6+4 minutes
Duration: 1d3+3 days

Conditions: Bitten victims begin with Agony but can struggle along until 1d6+6 hours after the bite when Asphyxiation strikes, usually resulting in death, unless First Aid is successfully applied to keep the victim breathing. Survivors will then suffer Necrosis, losing 1 Hit Point per day from the location bitten, until the venom is somehow purged or it naturally ends.

Antidote/Cure: Can be ameliorated with the Healing skill. Each day of Necrosis suffered before successful treatment inflicts permanent damage.

Weapon	Size/Force	Reach	Damage	AP/HP
Bite	S	T	1d4-1d4	As for Head

Solisand Descriptions by Zone:
Zone A – The Crag

The Crag is the highest point on the island. To the west, steep slopes and cliffs drop 200m to the sea. The north is a broad swathe of open rocky ground. To the east the ground descends to a swamp that occupies a large tract of land across the middle of the island, fed by streams at either end.

Many areas in this zone are difficult to travel through and require Athletics rolls to make progress, up or along steep rocky slopes. In these places reduce movement to one hex per hour.

Encounters – Roll 1d6

1d6	Encounter
1	Orcs
2-3	Harpies
4-6	Roll on General Encounter Table

The Ruins on the Crag

Up on the steep rocky hillside, there is evidence of ancient human activity. A Perception roll from anywhere within the zone that has a clear view may spot some unnatural formations. Halfway up the Crag is a pair of megaliths. On the surrounding slopes is evidence of dry stone walling, tumbled houses and enclosures. This is the 'village to the west' mentioned in the report of Astangoras and spotted by the Jekkarenes.

Prishad's Daughter

Approaching the ruins is almost sure to bring attack from the harpies whose eyrie is above. Only a stealthy night approach can avoid this. Nevertheless, there is a 30% chance that there is a five-man orc party camped here. They use the subterranean passages as shelter from the harpies, and move in and out of the zone by night. Bandestrap's familiar often hunts or basks here during the day, and is likely to spot approaching characters and alert his master.

Among the ruins, aligned to the megaliths, is the entrance to a man-made underground complex once used by the vanished inhabitants. Within are several bare chambers, the largest of which is a circular space 15m across with the remains of a deep clay-lined pool or tank (now dry and with no visible means of it being filled) in the centre. This served as the islanders' main holy site, but its consecration has long since expired.

This village and mountain hideout is ideal orc territory – but despite having found it the orcs have not settled here due to lack of water, knowing it is therefore indefensible, and have stuck to their range in Zone A. If it suits the game, then some sort of monster could make a lair there, emerging only at night to hunt and to go to a source of fresh water.

Zone B: North Shore

This part of the island consists of light forest and open, rocky ground. Its shore is one long, sandy beach, mostly backed by low dunes tufted with coarse grasses. In one place, there is a broad wash where the swamp behind sometimes disgorges its overflow after heavy rains. Most of the time, this is just a stony expanse with a few trickles and pools of water. There is a long beach, and the Jekkarenes have dragged their ship up at the eastern end and are busy constructing a stockade on a nearby spur, and surrounding trees have been cut to leave an open field of vision (and fire) around it.

Encounters – Roll 1d6

1D6	Encounter
1-3	Jekkarenes
4-6	Roll on General Encounter Table

The Jekkarene Stockade

The stockade is more or less circular, surrounded by a shallow ditch, the earth heaped up behind and topped with a palisade that is little more than a fence of rough-hewn stakes. The whole thing is maybe 30-40m across. The gate – which is just that, a swing gate – is on the left (west) side facing the beaches. The ground around the stockade has been cleared of brush and small trees in a radius of 60-70m

Outside the stockade and standing well above the height of the palisade is a T-shaped timber construction, on which something large and feathery has been fixed, as if crucified, facing west. If it is a bird, it is clearly massive. A closer inspection reveals that this crucified creature is in fact a harpy – one that had been shot by the marines while harassing the woodcutters and has been nailed up to act as a warning to the others.

Inside the stockade the Moonglory's crew is camped under canvas, 8 men to a tent, with private pavilions for Valontermus and Pelusinne, and Pelusinne's manservant, Orgogoron (treat as an underling with 6 Hit Points, 2 Action Points and all skills at 30% except for Custom and Craft (Cookery) which are both at 90%).

At least half of the Jekkarene force is occupied at the stockade at any one time. Of the ten marines, two will be with each of the patrols somewhere on the island, three on guard duty at the ship and the remainder at rest or escorting the commanders.

The ten sailors are employed in restoring the ship (Moonglory) to full seaworthiness after the voyage, guarded by marines, and 1d3+4 of them are at the beach during the day.

The 50 rowers are divided between local duties near the stockade such as wood cutting, digging latrines or clearing the ditch, and patrol duties. Spare hands will be at rest in the stockade or put to work assisting the sailors.

The Warrior and the Priestess

Valontermus and Pelusinne are here with a job to do. As explained on earlier, their mission is to locate Haliskome and her ship, returning with both to Lyortha so that Haliskome can be subjected to proper Jekkarene justice. Both Valontermus and Pelusinne are dutiful servants of the matriarchy and not about to jeopardise their mission through foolish or rash action. It is possible that the character may be mistaken for Haliskome and her allies (and perhaps the Jekkaranes are similarly mistaken by the characters), but neither Valontermus or Pelusinne will let themselves be distracted once it becomes clear that the characters represent another faction on the island. Indeed, the

characters can be highly useful – as sources of information; as potential scouts in hostile territory; as spies once Haliskome is located; and as potential crew members for Haliskome's ship and the journey back to Lyortha.

Valontermus is a typical, no-nonsense Jekkarene commander. Stern, stentorian, efficient and not given to displays of unnecessary emotion. He views the characters as practical adjuncts to his mission, but essentially dispensible once their objective is complete. He is all for forcing the characters to co-operate through the most expedient means. He punishes swiftly and harshly – especially if he feels someone is trying to make a fool of him.

Pelusinne, by contrast, is easier to deal with: although just as dutiful as Valontermus, she is pragmatic, willing to listen to all sides of a story, and more keen to manipulate the characters into helping than forcing them through threats or actual violence. Nevertheless, Pelusinne is no push-over. She is an experienced priestess with all the political acumen that goes with the role: she is also not averse to making tough or harsh decisions (the crucifixion of the harpy as a deterrent was her idea). The characters would do well to be wary of her.

The main objective of the Jekkarenes then, is to take prisoners and evaluate their usefulness to the mission. Both Valontermus and Pelusinne want to minimise the risk to their own forces, and so using the characters as a form of intelligence, whether-willingly or reluctantly, is their primary aim.

Zone C: The Swamp

This reeking, insect-infested wetland is a mixture of wooded swamp and open marshes. Crossing the swamp is arduous and dangerous; reduce movement by one half and increasing activity level for fatigue checks by one grade. It is easy to lose footing to submerged roots, or to lose shoes and boots to sucking mud. In places, it is necessary to wade into chest-deep water; there are poisonous snakes lurking there in great numbers as well as some big constrictor snakes capable of pulling a victim under, and biting insects swarm about the head. Each of the streams that offers a fresh water supply to people on the island runs into the swamp, and the swamp spills its contents out onto the north shore and creates seasonal streams that empty into the sea.

Encounters – Roll 1d6

1d6	Encounter
1-2	Insect Swarm
3	Snake
4-6	Roll on General Encounter Table

Zone D: Solisma's Forest

This area is an extensive forest, for the most part trackless and with a heavy canopy that can make it dark even at the height of the day. The forest contains Solisma's Grove. Within 210m radius of her grove, Solisma can use her magical abilities freely. Beyond that range – and up to 2.1km radius from her grove, she can use her abilities if physically manifest. Outside that range, she can also use her powers if manifest, but loses 1MP per hour when doing so to maintain her manifestation.

Unrequited Feelings?

A possible plot intrigue or complication is to introduce a little emotional or sexual tension into the Valontermus/Pelusinne relationship. Perhaps one has feelings for the other, and those feelings are unrequited – or known, but deliberately rejected. For instance, the gruff Valontermus may desire Pelusinne, but their professional standing makes it impossible for him to make his show his feelings. Pelusinne knows this, of course, and is occasionally flirtatious with Valontermus, allowing her to get her own way when she feels it is necessary. Conversely, Pelusinne has fallen for the commander but cannot let her feelings show: this results in a tension that manifests as a short temper towards, or dismissive attitude that Valontermus finds bewildering. A successful Insight roll by one of the characters could determine the nature of their true feelings and be used to some advantage, especially if the characters are made prisoner by the Jekkarenes.

Prishad's Daughter

Encounters – Roll 1d6

1d6	Encounter
1-2	Woses
3	Supernatural Denizen
4-6	Roll on General Encounter table

This whole area is thickly forested, and the forest floor is in places very dark. All Stealth rolls are one grade easier, and Perception rolls are one grade harder.

Solisma's Grove

Solisma is a dryad, and her locus is a grove deep within the forest. Other than a family of wild pigs, there are few animals that dwell in the area large enough to do any more than operate as minions or spies if she takes control of them; so she has a snake pit, in which the Woses throw venomous serpents they have captured. Solisma picks the ones she likes and keeps them as pets. She usually has 1d4+1 snakes at her command. Her power over nature is such that her Pet spell is capable of having creatures attack intruders on her behalf. Most dangerously, Solisma is able to take the form of an Elemental, at 1 cubic metre per Magic Point. Although a 6 cubic metre version may suffice in most situations, in defence of her grove and with sufficient Magic Points in hand she can become a real monster and will go for the 12 cubic metre option, which is the version provided here.

On the whole, she will not tolerate the use of fire in her grove, or anyone hacking at the trees or being mean to the Woses. And if anyone harms the bakru she will be driven into a cruel and murderous fury. Other than that, Solisma has no need to be hostile to those who stumble into her domain, and in any case the Woses will probably warn intruders off way before that happens.

The Bones of Nastarios

In Solisma's grove is something special – the bones of a paladin who was lost in the expedition of Astangoras 200 years ago. Solisma fell in love with this man, they remained together until he died some years later, and she has cherished his remains ever since. However, should anyone of initiate rank or higher in a solar cult enter the grove, Nastarios will manifest to them and ask his remains be returned to the mainland. Solisma will not tolerate this to happen, and she will have to be dealt with before the remains can be excavated and removed.

Once Nastarios' remains are recovered he becomes an allied spirit to his rescuer. They must provide him with 1MP as a Pact to establish the link (for a maximum of one year and a day, but potentially renewable). He cannot recover any Magic Points unless his bones rest in a place consecrated to the sun god, and the process can be accelerated through veneration. Nastarios has an agenda, which is to be laid properly to rest at Hilanistra – however, he would settle for being the focal point in the establishment of a shrine somewhere else. Lord Skelfus would kill – or pay handsomely – to have control of Nastarios' bones to help establish an important centre of solar worship in his domain.

Zone E: Pirate Lair

This area is thickly wooded, grading down to light forest at the shore. The area is watered by a stream that springs from a cave in the limestone cliffs. Haliskome and her pirate gang camp close by the beach and in sight of the Purple Wanderer, which rides at anchor in plain view in the shallow (maximum 1.5m deep) water 50m from the shore. One kilometre from their camp is the entrance to Brasilas' ruined lair, and the pirates keep their loot there, unafraid that anyone else will get in and steal it.

Encounters – Roll 1D6:

1d6	Encounter
1-2	Pirates Hunting or Fishing
3	Melantos and Haliskome
4-6	Roll on General Encounter table

In all there are 15 pirates: Haliskome, Melantos, Jereboas the Sailing Master, Kisethentyes the weapons master, Kalish (a man of Morkesh) and Ankaskron, Haliskome's trusted enforcers; and nine other sailors of whom six are native Jekkarenes and the remainder are hired from Assabian crews. The pirates rarely leave their zone; however, they do take their ship out to sea once in a while – when they do it is likely Melantos is the only one left behind to keep an eye on things.

The Pirate Camp

Halsikome and her gang have had ample opportunity to build good shelters using some canvas and timber from their ships' supplies, matting woven from local leaves and vines, and even provided with a few home comforts and personal touches.

Melantos and Haliskome have their own hut; the sailing crew are divided between two larger shelters with screens set up to divide areas or for privacy.

The crew are aware of others on the island and so keep careful watch. Haliskome also maintains Alarm spells that cover any obvious tracks and routes into their zone (this has Haliskome's Magic Points at -5).

The Purple Wanderer

Typically only two pirates guard the vessel at a time, and are situated on the deck, camping out there at night. One of them is supposed to keep an eye out to sea, but there is only a 30% chance this watch is maintained even in daytime unless the pirates are aware of an imminent threat.

The pirates have no problem with keeping their vessel within the reef as the lagoon is well sheltered except in the worst storm. They only beach the galley if the weather is very bad, as they are nervous to slow their getaway in the event of an emergency. The undine bound to the hull can be commanded (via the captain's baton, an enchantment stolen by Halsikome along with the ship itself) to raise the hull above the reef. This, however, can only be done once per day.

The Purple Wanderer, A Jekkarene Galley	
Power	Sail (1 mast, square rigged), oars x 60
Crew	12 officers and sailors, plus 60 rowers if at full complement or 16-man skeleton or 30-man half-crew). A further dozen men as marines when fully fitted for war.
Length	Length 27m, Beam 4m, Freeboard 1.5m
Capacity	50 Tons
Hull Type	T
Armour Points	8
Hit Points	45
Seaworthiness	55%
Range	6
Armaments	Spur. Ramming Damage 3d6

Notes: The Purple Wanderer is heavily enchanted. On the deck near the stern is the 'Mark' or homing circle for a Teleport spell enchanted to the captain's baton. In the keel is an enchantment into which is bound an 8 cubic metre undine (STR 46, DEX 18, INS 18, POW 29, HP 54), large enough for the ship to make (slow) progress without even oars or sail, and only capable of being released by using the Captain's Baton. All Seamanship roll and Seaworthiness tests are one grade easier while this undine is bound.

Haliskome

An almost unheard-of example of a former Temple Guardian turned renegade, Haliskome was disaffected above all else because her lover Melantos fell under suspicion (thanks to Solfernoy) of treasonous behaviour, in particular consorting with foreigners in unapproved ways. Solfernoy used the man, who was until that point a favoured henchman, as a scapegoat for his own indiscretions. He was arrested by the authorities, taken before the high priestess and cursed with Lycanthropy. Before he could be transported to the Badlands, Haliskome broke Melantos out of prison and escaped with him aboard the Jekkarene naval ship she commanded. She first fled to Tempigone but after a run-in with Arko of Solarne, who unkown to Haliskome was in league with Solfernoy, Haliskome and her crew eventually set out west again and made their base at Solisand.

Haliskome is now saddled with a lover suffering from Lycanthropy; she has been told that the further she can take him from the moon's shadow over the Jekkarid itself, the more power he can assert over his affliction. The pirates put to sea during the full moon, leaving Melantos ashore on his own. It is safer that way.

Haliskome is charismatic and has managed to carry her crew with her. She has promised them a new life outside the restrictive world of the Theocracy – but first to use the tools at their disposal to set themselves up for life and put themselves beyond the reach of their enemies for good. However, her choice of refuge is limited – she has been brought up to distrust Korantines (something Arko of Solarne has done nothing to change) and her choices are to head south or west. If Haliskome and her crew survive the scenario, she will most likely surface again in Zarland (Fierla), Othrikor or one of the Sultanates of Djesmirket.

Haliskome relies on speed and spell in a toe to toe fight. She'll cast Protection first, then attempt to Befuddle one of her opponents if outnumbered. If things go badly wrong, she will, if within range, use the portal enchantment on the captain's baton she carries to escape back to the ship.

The Crew

All of Haliskome's gang are fiercely loyal and will stay with her through thick and thin.

Melantos

Burly and rather hairy with black eyebrows that meet above his nose, Melantos is devoted to Haliskome, who he knows has risked everything to spring him from prison, and is now coping

Prishad's Daughter

as best she can with his lycanthropy. He will unquestionably give his life for her if the situation calls for it.

Kisathentyes

The master-at-arms is an expert archer, and even better in a hand to hand duel on a slippery deck. He wears no armour, relying on his skills and dexterity to avoid blows and missiles. If the crew get into a fight, he prefers to stand off and pick out targets with his arrows, shouting commands and encouragement to his 'boys'. He relies on Kalish to provide the aggression and fight at the front; Kisathentyes is no coward but his job is to see an action managed to a successful outcome. Once in a while, he might call out a handy-looking fighter or leader from an enemy crew to single combat, a display intended to remind everyone of his skills.

Jereboas

An experienced old hand allocated to the Purple Wanderer because of his impeccable record in the navy, Jereboas is something of a mascot for the crew who will do their best to keep him out of harm's way of a fight begins knowing how critical he is to all their fortunes.

Ankaskron

Charged with being Jereboas' lieutenant, and with keeping him safe from harm, Ankaskron is an enthusiastic plunderer and has turned to the pirate lifestyle with gusto. In an emergency Ankaskron and Jereboas are detailed with making for the ship as quickly as possible with some extra hands to make her ready to get under way at a moment's notice.

Kalish

The non-Jekkarene amongst the senior crew, Kalish has been found to be a vicious and effective fighter so has been elevated from among the other sailors. His skill comes from the kind of demon pact common among his countrymen, but as is usual comes at a price – not only a dedication of three Magic Points to his demon ally, but a passion that compels him to kill any foe he bests in combat.

If the pirates are under serious threat, they will make for the ship. However, the pirates will not easily abandon their loot, and will either counter-attack or come back later, perhaps via a different part of the coastline to attempt to retrieve it.

Brasilas' Lair

See map on page 208

The sorcerer's old hideout is still a depressing place that bears the supernatural scars of its former occupant's aberrant behaviour. Few creatures and even fewer people choose to wander its long dark passages. It is barely accessible, and, for all these reasons, Haliskome has chosen to hide her gang's loot there.

Carved from the rock, almost certainly with magical or supernatural help, Brasilas' lair was sacked amid violence and has been abandoned for some 200 years since. It is in a poor state although the actual walls, ceilings and floors are solid enough.

The lair is barely populated, but what does lurk here is dangerous. Haliskome and her gang, if not previously dealt with, will quickly make their way to the lair if Haliskome's Alarm spells is tripped by intruders (there is one on the ledge by the main entrance). They are aware of the lair's denizens, so restrict themselves to certain rooms and will not pursue characters deeper into the complex.

1. Main Entrance

A rope ladder leads 30m from the forest floor to a wide ledge. It is clearly a recent installation. Not so the enormous portal accessed from the ledge, an open doorway into a pitch dark complex of rooms and tunnels. Also on the ledge is a wooden frame, made to support rope and tackle that are not present (found in room 7).

Perception roll reveals much recent traffic.

2. Hall

A high-ceilinged hallway, the floor strewn with debris and large amounts of old splintered bone. The plaster render that remains bears traces of geometric designs painted in blue and red. A pair of unfinished caryatids flanks the exit ahead. These seem bizarre sculptures – and on closer inspection the stone has been torn away in places, revealing real human remains within around which the statues have been formed.

Games Master Note: These caryatids have been created by sculpting rock around a living body, although the process was fatal to the model.

3. Vestibule

A chamber where guests and visitors were held prior to entering the great hall beyond. Carved stone seats line the walls. There is a stack of torches soaked in pitch placed here. These

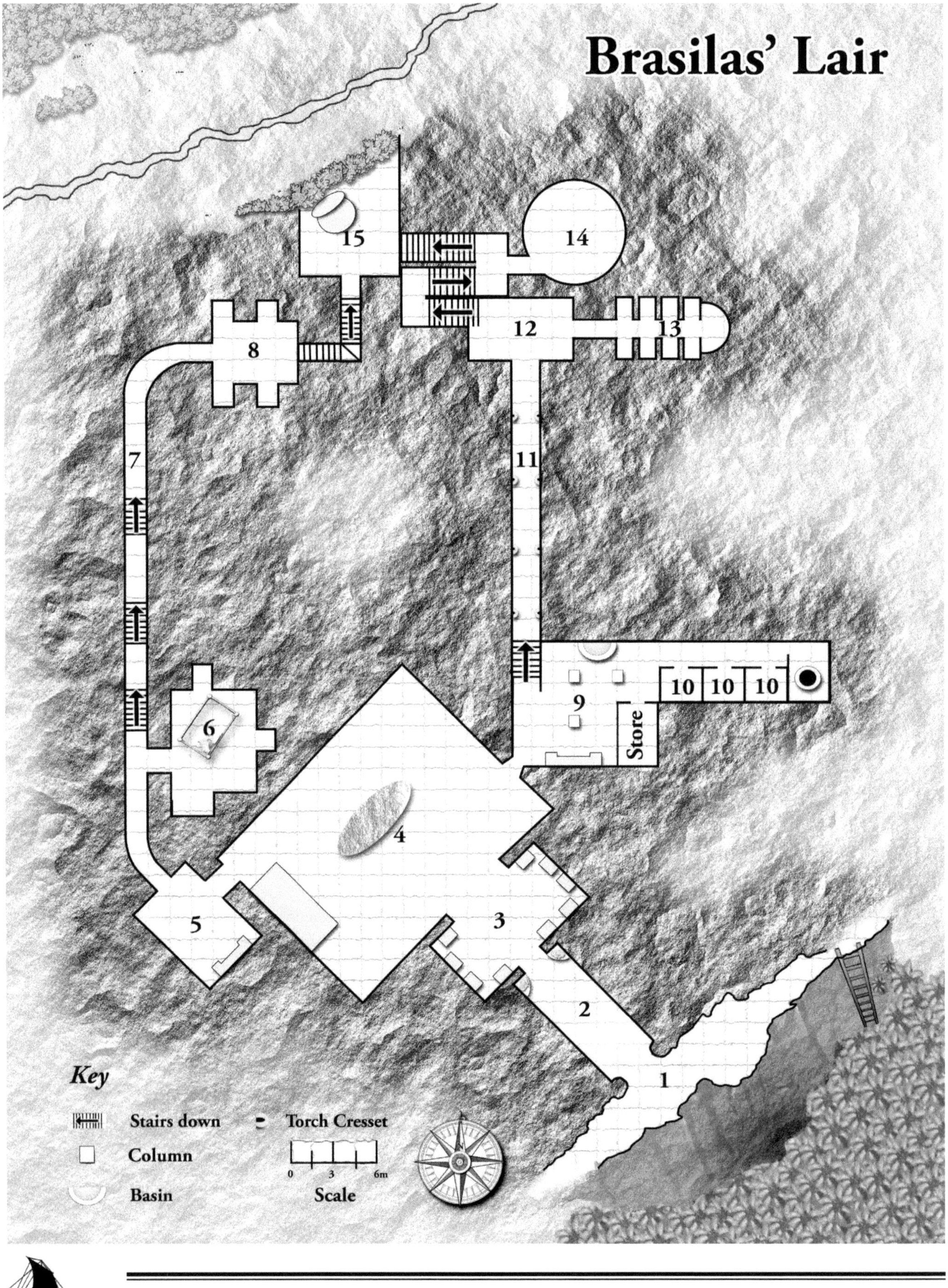
Brasilas' Lair
1
2
3
4
5
6
7
8
9
10
10
10
Store
11
12
13
14
15
Key
Stairs down
Torch Cresset
Column
Basin
0
3
6m
Scale

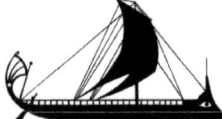

Prishad's Daughter

are a precaution for the pirates against the spider that inhabits the parlour (room 5).

4. Banqueting Hall

A great rectangular room with a raised dais at one end. Around a huge stone table carved in situ are the remains of 12 seated statues, in various poses of shock and fear. A Culture (Korantine) test reveals they are dressed in an archaic Korantine style. A critical test recognises details that identify the statues as diplomats – representatives of the Emperor. Behind the dais are remains of an elaborate mural, and what is left suggests that a great gorgon's face once graced the wall.

Games Master Note: These are the victims of a delegation sent to Brasilas with an ultimatum from the Emperor himself to allow shipping to pass by Solisand or put in for fresh water unmolested. The negotiation went badly.

The doors to the west are intact and lie half open. The exit to the east is an open passageway.

5. Parlour

A chamber where Brasilas would relax or hold more intimate audiences with his guests. There is little to see except pieces of broken furniture scattered around the floor and sherds of high class pottery. There is a hearth on the south wall, but no chimney.

A Perception roll, or any closer examination of the floor, reveals that amongst the other debris there are also dessicated parts of various creatures; nothing bigger than SIZ 8, but including parts of one or two Woses that could be mistaken for the remains of children. Clinging to the ceiling above the doorway is a giant spider (see MYTHRAS, page 267), which will attack if someone enters the room. The spider will defend itself against two opponents but if confronted by more attackers, or as soon as it suffers a serious wound, it will try to make a rapid retreat. This spider hates fire, and brandishing a torch in its face may force it to back off or at least make its attacks one grade of difficulty harder – information that might be gained from one of Haliskome's crew.

Games Master Note: If your party is particularly strong, this spider can be part of a small colony nesting in room 8. The spiders are ambush predators, and mostly hunt the forest or Vale of Giant Flowers at night, moving in and out of the complex through room 15.

6. Bed Chamber

This room contains a huge bed frame of cracked and dry black wood. It would seem to be the bed of a giant, fully 4 metres long. Recesses are cut into the walls – the remains of storage spaces and cupboards – but otherwise it appears bare. There is a curious atmosphere about the place caused by an apparition that instils a sense of doom and despondency. This produces an effect identical to the Folk Magic spell Demoralise. Anyone who spends more than a minute or two in the room must resist a Manifestation of 30%, and if they fail, the effect persists as long as they are in the complex.

7. The Narrow Passage

A long (more than 30m) passageway, only 2m wide, which was Brasilas' private route to and from his work spaces.

8. Library

Brasilas' valuable library and collection of arcana was systematically plundered and burned by the Korantines who stormed this place. There is nothing of value to find here, only a story to tell from witnessing the number of fragments of pottery storage jars of the type often used to hold scrolls, and the splintered ruins of racks and shelves, most of which are turning to dust. Characters in this room who are have limited light available may notice a greenish glow coming from down the stairway that exits on the east side.

9. Pirate's Treasure

A large open chamber that from the fittings appears to have once been a kitchen. There is a well at one end, a stairwell at the other, and very large open hearth. Over this hearth is a chimney, a simple irregular shaft less than 1m wide rising up to the ground 10m above, but this is now blocked by 200 years of detritus. Piled up at one end of the room are all manner of crates, boxes and sacks. Here is where Haliskome's crew are accumulating the loot.

A search through this material turns up the following list:

14 Amphoras of wine (each holds 20 litres), worth 1SP per litre

2 x 5 litre Jars of Jekkarene Sweetwine, worth 2SP per litre

4 jars of olive oil (5 litres each) worth 1 SP per litre

2 x 2 litre jars of perfumed oil worth 7SP per litre

16 bolts of cloth (each 40m of cloth), being 10 bolts of wool (1SP per metre) and 6 of cotton (1.5SP per metre)

A length of silk (4 square metres, worth 1,000SP)

A quantity of SS coins from various places, as well as some bronze and copper pieces. In all 265SS, 120CP and 37BP

A large piece of canvas, 20 square metres, suitable material for reparing or patching sails (3SP per square metre).

A barrel of salted fish (14kg)

A barrel containing 38 half-finished bronze spearheads and 45 bronze arrowheads (value 40SP)

A sack containing a large quantity of fine down feathers (value 5SP)

A breast-plate and back-plate, each fashioned from a single piece of turtleshell, with hanging plates also of the same material to protect the abdomen (3AP, ENC 2 per Location, fits SIZ12-13 lithe or medium frame), bronze fittings and some gilded decoration. Possibly worth up to 100SP either as a fine set of fancy armour or in salvageable turtleshell. This is a prestige item among Archipelagans.

20kg of iron in five 4kg ingots,

24kg of copper in six 3kg ingots

A pair of copper candlesticks, 0.5KG total and of little worth – except that they are enchanted with an Ignite spell that can be used by anyone willing to gift a Magic Point to them.

10 grain sacks, each containing a bushel (28kg) of barley.

10. Staff Quarters

This is where a handful of Brasilas' most trusted henchmen were housed. These chambers were long ago stripped and looted, and only one even has a door still remaining.

11. Broad Passage

The stairwell leads down into the darkness. Those descending begin to come across human bones, and small metal items such as buckles, clasps and fittings for weapons that have survived the ages they have rested here. This is the scene of a furious battle as the Korantines attempted to force their way into the heart of Brasilas' lair.

The passageway at the foot of the stair is almost 3m across. Every few metres there is an (empty) torch cresset. The floor shows more bone scatter, and slopes gradually downwards while the ceiling stays level, thus gradually increasing the ceiling height.

12. Antechamber

This room is stripped of any furnishings, but is notable for the luminous glow that comes from down the grand staircase to the west, a green, sickly hue. The walls show signs of burning. Standing here, looking towards the stairs, are three statues of Korantine warriors in full battle gear and action poses. To the east is an exit to the dungeons.

13. Dungeons

The place where Brasilas kept captured enemies, prisoners being held ready for magical experiment or sacrifice, is simply a corridor flanked with tiny cells, and with an apse at the far end where somebody could be chained to the wall for convenient interrogation.

14. Summoning Chamber

Here is where the wizard would summon entities, not to control them and bind them to his service, but to enter into Pacts with them as a means to increase his own knowledge and power. There is no trace of any signs or sigils here now, only a plastered domed ceiling rising to an apex that shows evidence of colour, deep blues and geometric patterns traced across it. This once was a diagram showing the Vault of Heaven, and it can be determined that the representation is precisely aligned with the real sky beyond it.

Searching this chamber for 10 minutes or more will reveal a sequence of letters inscribed in the floor, and these letters spell a name: D-E-M-US-K-E-R-A. This is the true name of a daemoness, a gorgon, with whom Brasilas had a Pact. She fought for him in defence of his lair but was eventually banished (a temporary block on her ability to manifest, now long expired). If the means of summoning a gorgon are researched or acquired, possession of this name is a key component in successfully completing the rite.

She can perceive what happens in the summoning chamber and can materialise here of her own will at a cost of only 1 Magic Point. Once she does so, she can move freely around areas 12-15. The giant spider in room 5 is immune to Demuskera's gaze attack.

Demuskera does not have a serpentine body, but she does have scaly skin and little tusks protruding from either cheek, and cruel bronze talons and a curious otherworld bow made entirely of bronze. She carries 10 shafts in her quiver.

The pirates know of her and carefully avoid an encounter, never passing beyond the kitchens. Damuskera is prevented from moving outside the dungeon by the efforts of Solisma and the Bakru. She just might allow an intruder to live if she thinks they could be up to the task of killing the nymph for her.

Prishad's Daughter

15. Brasilas' Study

As the stairwell descends the glow becomes a little brighter. The floor of chamber below is entirely covered in some sort of lichen or moss, which gives off the greenish glow and a sickly smell. The stuff gives gently under foot. Here and there great clumps of fungus sprout from this glowing carpet. In the southwest corner lies an enormous (3m high) cauldron of bronze, thrown on its side. The far wall seems to be tangled with a mass of twisted vines and branches, both living and dead.

The north-west corner of the room is in fact gone, carried away by a landslide and now open to the elements but blocked by vegetation that (in daytime) shows chinks of light from the outside world. The giant spider from room 5 is able to squeeze through. A human will find it easy enough using a Pathway spell, otherwise it would be necessary to strip off any bulky or awkward equipment and rely on some Brawn to force through or Athletics to squeeze through in 1d3 rounds per attempt. Thirty minutes or more of hacking and ripping away at the obstruction with suitable implements will cut an exit wide enough to use without a struggle.

Beyond is a rocky watercourse, now no more than a trickle yet thickly clothed in giant ferns, which descends to the Vale of Giant Flowers. The contents of Brasilas's cauldron were spilled here, and carried by a stream running down the hillside – ultimately creating the mutations found in the plants growing below.

For the same reason, the fungal growths in the chamber are mutated and unnatural, and contain traces of Brasilas' magic. While the stuff that covers the floor may be disconcerting, it is harmless, except that someone who spends time here will find their Magic Points slowly leeched away at the rate of 1 point per hour. The fungi themselves can have a variety of effects at the Games Master's discretion, and different varieties crop up at different times – assume there are 1d4+1 varieties present in a given season. Anyone brave enough to eat them may get one of the effects on the Fungi Table (see page 212).

These fungi could potentially be harvested and taken back to civilisation; but without the benefit of a Preserve spell, it must be assumed they remain potent for only a limited period. In any event, they may make excellent alchemical ingredients.

Brasilas' Cauldron

The cauldron is green with age, covered in engraved arcane symbols. These are recognisable as the set of esoteric runes used with the Djesmiri script, but Korantine characters are recognisable amongst them.

This cauldron is Brasilas's Spellbook, and it contains an extensive set of spells of which the following are still legible and could be copied:

Enchant, Abjure Self*, Dominate Ghost, Diminish SIZ, Enhance SIZ, Tap SIZ

This spell removes a passion or trait from the target for the duration of the spell.

These spells will for most sorcerers require a new Invocation skill, as they belong to an idiosyncratic tradition of Korantine sorcery based on an amalgam of Djesmiri Lore.

The walls of the cauldron are quite thin, and in places corroded through. The whole object weights some 100kg, and appears too large to remove from the chamber in one piece. Breaking it up without damaging the precious inscriptions is not easy, and requires a Craft (Metalwork) or similar to achieve it.

Studying the inscriptions in situ is an alternative. A sorcerer could either use an Extended Task to copy down the inscriptions for later study (each Task Round being 1 full day, and each 25% less than the target, meaning that the transcription is sufficiently shaky that two of the spells are unlearnable). Critical results delivering progress in excess of 100% will allow the sorcerer to piece together an additional spell by filling in gaps.

Zone F: Vale of Giant Flowers

This is a well-watered forest of giant plants. The western side is a forest of giant ferns that form a canopy at about 6 metres, allowing easy passage between the massive stems; the rest is spread with giant wild flowers, some truly immense specimens growing to a height of 20m. In parts, shafts of sunlight filter through to the forest floor, which in many places is a stinking mass of rotting vegetation. While beautiful in its way, the area feels eerie and there is a sense of being watched.

Fungi Table

1D20	Description	Effects
01-03	A greyish, lumpen cluster looking like discarded pie crusts	Foul tasting, but harmless
04-05	A broad, yellow dish-shaped cap almost 30cm across	Harmless, edible and delicious
06-09	Long fingers of white spotted with purple	Mildly Poisonous; Resist a Potency of 50% or suffer a level of Fatigue Loss (onset 1d6+4 minutes, duration 1d3 days).
10-11	A magnificent large conical toadstool, its cap a bluish hue	Quite Poisonous; Resist a Potency of 60% or suffer 1d3 damage to the abdomen (onset 1d4 minutes, duration instant).
12-13	A riot of small, button-shaped mushrooms with glossy black caps.	Deadly Poisonous; Resist a Potency of 70% or suffer complete incapacitation followed by death (onset 1d6+4 rounds, character becomes comatose (see fatigue table) until death 1d6+4 hours later).
13-14	Small, round puff balls, the colour of flesh, containing spores that seem to fizz on the tongue	Magical; Restore 1d3 Magic Points (onset 1d3 minutes), no effect if the character has no spent Magic Points to restore.
15-16	A large and ragged fan-shaped mushroom	Magical; Gain knowledge of one use of a sorcery spell cast at INTx5% (onset 1d10+10 minutes, duration POW days)
17-18	A coral-like structure of deep blue	Magical; Temporary Mystic Vision bestowed upon the character at POWx5% Intensity (onset 1d6+4 rounds, duration POW minutes)
19	Tiny arrow-shaped toadstools, growing in clumps of three	Multiple Effects; Roll twice and ignore results of 01-05
20	A spongiform fungus that gives off an unpleasant smell like a rotting corpse	Multiple Effects; Roll three times and ignore results of 01-05

Encounters – Roll 1D6

1D6	Encounter
1-2	Giant Insects
3	Carnivorous Plant
4-6	Roll on General Encounter table

Encounters Roll 1d6

1D6	Encounter
1	Orc Patrol
2	Orc Trap
3	Orc Ambush
4-6	Roll on General Encounter table

Zone G: Orc Hills

Two dome-shaped, wooded hills are the main feature of this zone. From between the two, a stream runs to the swamp, which provides a source of water to the orcs camped here. This whole area is thickly forested and all Stealth rolls for hiding from sight are one grade easier.

Orc Traps

The orcs have made the area secure for themselves as best they can. The whole area is laced with traps, both to hinder intruders and to catch game. When a trap is encountered, roll 1d6 to determine the type. All orc traps have a difficulty of 55%.

Prishad's Daughter

Solisand - Orc Camp

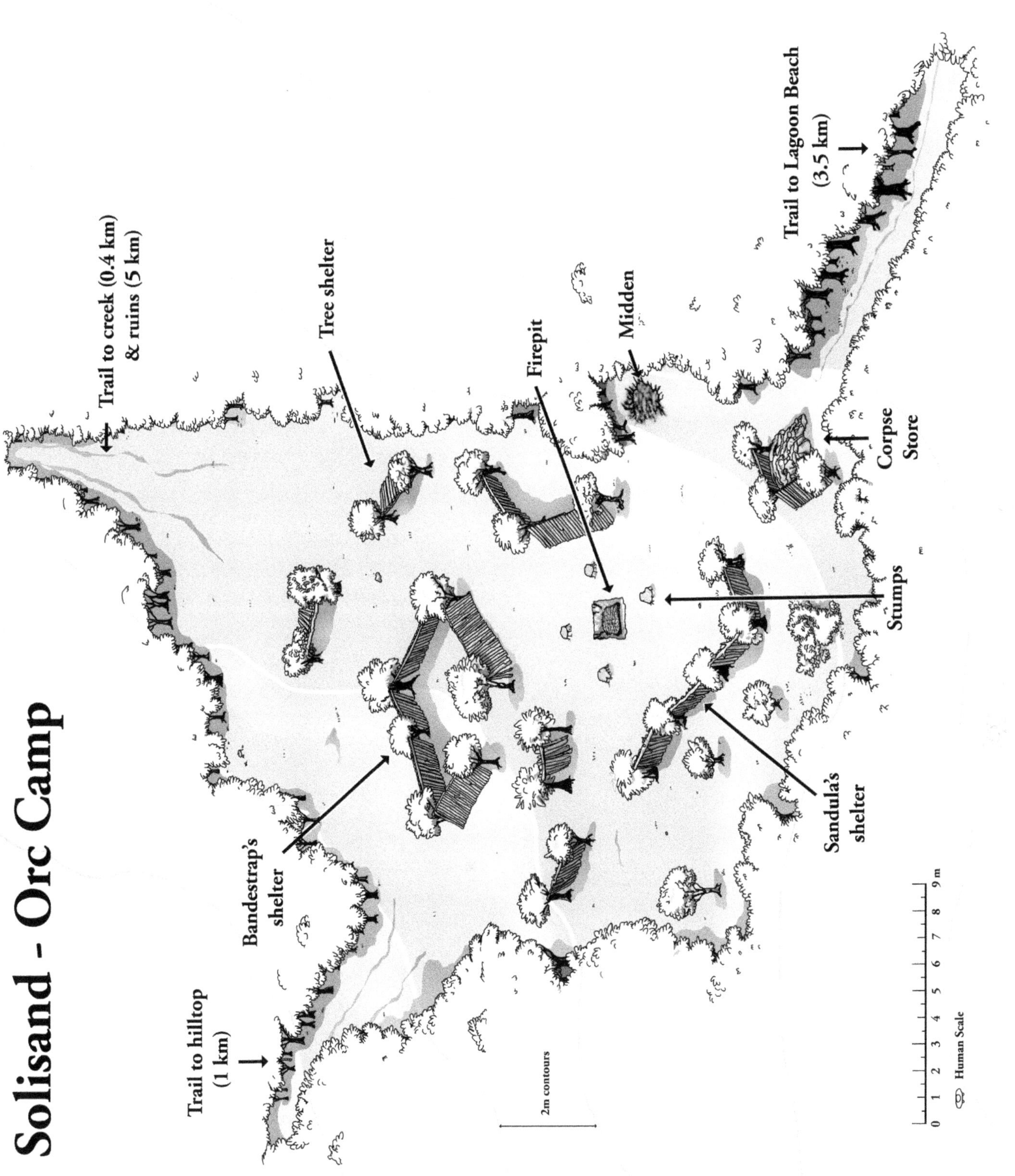

- Trail to creek (0.4 km) & ruins (5 km)
- Trail to Lagoon Beach (3.5 km)
- Tree shelter
- Firepit
- Midden
- Corpse Store
- Stumps
- Sandula's shelter
- Bandestrap's shelter
- Trail to hilltop (1 km)

2m contours

0 1 2 3 4 5 6 7 8 9 m
Human Scale

1-2: Punji Stakes

A trap in which the victim's leg is caught in a hole that is lined with sharp stakes pointing downwards, so making extracting the trapped limb dangerous and painful.

Purpose: Maiming

Trigger: Stepping into the camouflaged hole

Resistance: A Hard Evade Roll. The character can choose not to attempt to resist; if he does and the resist fails, the trap automatically does its damage.

Effects: A random leg is trapped. No damage initially unless the character tries and fails to avoid the trap, however, check Endurance or character suffers a twist or sprain that reduces movement by 2 until his next wound recovery (whether natural, magical or from First Aid or Healing). If character attempts to extricate his leg, it will take 1d8 damage. Armour protects; however, there is a 25% chance he is impaled, and a 10% chance that the damage bypasses armour. The safe way to get out is to be dug free.

3-4: Pitfall.

1d6 Damage to a random location; the character is now trapped in a pit 3m deep.

5-6: Boar Trap

Purpose: Death

Trigger: Tripwire (concealed)

Resistance: Evade, or a Hard shield parry (weapon size Huge)

Effect: Tripwire of twisted vine releases a sharpened stake at leg height, which hits with a 55% chance and can impale. 2d6 damage to location 1d8. Characters who are less than SIZ 11 or who are crawling may use differing Hit Location dice (1d10, 1d12, 1d20).

Orc Ambush

The orcs had a campsite, now disused, which they can make look occupied – by lighting a fire for example – to draw the characters towards it.

The orcs spring their trap when the characters are in the campsite, and, ideally, have split-up to poke around. Two orcs will cut the trail, the remaining 8 will make the assault.

If the characters have made their landing in this area and discovered the spring, the orcs will assume they will return there at some point and lay a trap on the trail.

The Lagoon Beach

The lagoon is excellent fishing. If equipped with a hook and line and something for bait it would be possible for one man to feed himself in just 1d2 hours work.

The Orc Camp

See map on page 213.

A simple campsite with shelters created by use of boughs set against or between trees supporting layers of foliage used to screen the elements. The shelters are scattered about haphazardly, as there are usually no more than two orcs to each one, and many are often unoccupied as members of the crew are off hunting or exploring.

A single firepit is made in the middle, and a large midden has accumulated already which is full of discarded animal and fish bones, sea shells and putrefying scraps. The nearest source of fresh water is 400m away to the north.

Bandestrap, Orc Sorcerer

Short, broad and squat in stature, standing only shoulder high to most of his followers, Bandestrap cuts a slightly whimsical figure. However, he has saved his people from disaster when they got shipwrecked here, and the other orcs follow him loyally. He is usually to be found in command of the larger expedition party of 10 warriors.

Bandestrap is fascinated by the sapience awoken in Grrruff, his familiar. Their Mindlink allows the orc to experience a life-view through a wholly reptilian intellect – something that is governed by heat, primal urges, and an amoral curiosity about the world. As a result, Bandestrap often spends hours in Mindlink communication with Grruff, questioning it on its opinions, motives, desires, needs and overall world-view. It would be true to say that Bandestrap is falling in love with his familiar: the two certainly share a highly developed relationship that goes disturbingly beyond the usual master-servant paradigm of sorcer and familiar.

Grrruff, Familiar, Small Therapod Dinosaur

Grruff is a sapient creature, its intelligence awakened through Bandestrap's Mindlink spell. It is a therapod dinosaur and is often basking somewhere in open territory, particularly in the Crag area, or by one of the beaches. He is in Mindlink with Bandestrap, so if he spots anything interesting he can instantly alert his master.

Grrruff appreciates the attention lavished by Bandestrap and is happy to converse with his master whenever Bandestrap feels the need arise. While sapient, Grrruff is not naive and it knows the growing feelings Bandestrap seems to be developing. It is no use: Grrruff is, at heart, a dinosaur and views the world opportunistically. If the need should ever arise – or the opportunity – Bandestrap is just another meal.

Orc Warriors

The weaker members of Bandestraps's crew have not made it this far. Man for man, the remaining orcs are a tough and resourceful bunch. Their weapons are mostly made on the island, using stone tips and wood. Their spears consequently do d8 Damage instead of 1d8+1 unless Bandestrap has had the chance to cast Bladesharp on them.

They have scraps of armour made in the field including pieces of hide, woven grasses and even tree bark. Where they have armour, it can be bypassed as a standard Special Effect, without need of a Critical roll. Their improvised but effective kit can lead those who encounter them to believe they are some sort of primitive native band.

Revivified Orc Warriors

Bandestrap will use his Revivify spell to turn dead followers or enemies into useful zombies, so ideally his men secure the used bodies of any of the fallen. These corpses are kept in a shelter in the orc camp in case of need, and there are three bodies in various states of decay to choose from at present. A revivified follower +5 STR and CON compared to their living brethren, -2 in each other Characteristic.

The zombie orcs must be in sight and in range of his spell for him to control them, and if there is more than one he must direct them to the same purpose, or all their skill rolls become one grade harder per zombie after the first as Bandestrap tries to cope with coordinating their actions.

End Game: Stealing Haliskome

The characters can succeed in their mission by killing Haliskome and bringing adequate proof to Safra of the deed. Precisely how this is achieved is dependent entirely on how the characters approach the island, what preparations they make, and how they deal with the three different factions present and with the island's denizens. The *Adventuring on Solisand* section offers some additional advice and guidance. There are, however, certain practicalities the characters need to consider.

How will they get off the island?

If the characters have their own ship or are using the Foamfollower, then this is the logical choice. However, there is also the opportunity to steal The Purple Wanderer or even the Jekkarenes' galley. Indeed both might be the only alternatives if the characters' own vessel is compromised somehow. Bear in mind Bandestrap and the orcs are determined to secure themselves a ship to get away from Solisand – if they are not allied to the characters then they may well remove one of the possible ways off the island from the game by stealing it.

Haliskome will not go quietly

Whether her final destination is to be properly tried for piracy, returned to the Jekkarid or handed over to Safra AmPrishad, it will end badly for Haliskome and she knows she has nothing to lose. The same goes for her crew. They will use every means available to prevent capture, and the characters should take this into consideration as they formulate their plans. If Haliskome is captured, any of her crew who remain at large will look for an opportunity to rescue her.

Haliskome's Guilt

Haliskome is indeed responsible for Prishad's death, although the knife was wielded by her crewman Kalish of Morkesh, enabling Haliskome to claim it was a situation that got out of hand.

Should Haliskome be taken alive, she will not demean herself by begging for mercy, but she will use all her wiles and any convenient lies she can come up with to convince her captors she deserves to live. Haliskome's ship, her treasure and her magic ring, are all of no use to her if she is dead; so, if they are still in her possession, she might as well offer them up in return for being set free. She might otherwise attempt to implicate Solfernoy and Valsus, establishing she is a pawn in a bigger game. Haliskome is smart enough to drip bits of information – true or false, but always plausible, rather than blurt out her story in one go, playing for time to come up with a plan or to win the sympathy of her captors.

Taking a captive Haliskome back to Safra is tantamount to killing her – Safra has only one purpose and that is to see her father's killer dead. All the better if she gets to watch. The characters may feel uncomfortable about this – especially if Haliskome has managed to earn their respect while under their power or just convince them it is not quite such a cut and dried case that they should indulge Safra AmPrishad's desire for extra-judicial killing.

The Jekkarenes

If the characters do the Jekkarenes' job for them by taking out Haliskome, that is all very well.

However, should they enable Haliskome's escape, or even take Haliskome off the island as a prisoner, this will cause considerable embarrassment to the Jekkarene expedition leaders. Valontermus will take the blame back in Lyortha and will be keen to restore his reputation or gain revenge. Baron Solfernoy will need to set new plots into motion in order to make sure Haliskome never gets to reveal his involvement in her earlier crimes. If this is achieved through a rapprochement between them that is all very well – but her silence is much better assured by seeing her dead. This goes for anyone to whom she may have blabbed.

The Purple Wanderer

It is an essential part of Valontermus' mission that he recovers the Purple Wanderer, if at all possible. Should the characters secure Haliskome's ship they become the Jekkarenes' primary target. Pursuit is assured unless something has been done to limit Valontermus' ability to give chase.

Thwarting Valontermus' attempt to recapture the Purple Wanderer guarantees the enmity of the Jekkarene state. If the characters have taken the ship, it could be held for ransom or reward – its replacement value is some 18,000SP, so it has a bargaining value of some 10-15,000SP. At any port where the Jekkarenes can rely on Taskan influence, the characters will simply find the ship seized and themselves thrown into a dungeon until someone decides what to do with them. Sailing the Purple Wanderer into a Korantine port where they are safe from Jekkarene retribution will likely cause a diplomatic incident, sparking a furious negotiation for its return between the Jekkarenes and the local authorities exacerbated by the old emnity between Jekkarene and Korantine. There is one exception – if they take the Purple Wanderer to Tempigone, Arko of Solarne will sell them out to the highest bidder in a heartbeat. And that is likely to be Solfernoy.

Alternatively the characters may decide that possession of such a fine vessel is too good an opportunity and set sail for foreign shores.

The Island

There are reasons that characters may return to Solisand. They may try to redress the terrible effects of Brasilas' magic, to come back for his spell cauldron, search for more magic fungi, or even make their own base on the island once Haliskome has been dealt with and the other visitors have gone. The abandoned settlement on the Crag could be brought back to life if only a means could be found to restore access to fresh water. Brasilas' lair, once cleared of its horrors, might be turned into an adventurers' den or a hideaway when the characters get into trouble with someone powerful. In most cases, it will be necessary to stay on friendly terms with Solisma, the bakru and the woses to make a success of a long-term stay on the island. Like Brasilas before them, Haliskome's gang chose Solisand for good reason – it is an excellent jumping-off point to launch into a seafaring campaign. Of course Pelusinne's exploration may pave the way for the Jekkarenes to create their first – and secret – offshore base, so there is every opportunity to weave a campaign thread that continues the conflict and rivalry with these people.

Adventuring on Solisand

This scenario can be run in several ways:

- First, as the mission to find and bring-back Haliskome to Safra: this is the core of the scenario as presented and perhaps the easiest way to integrate the characters into the interplays on Solisand.

- Second, as a setting the characters stumble upon through general adventuring through the Korantine Empire (being ship wrecked, perhaps, or simply deciding to explore Solisand when they spy its coasts).

- Third, the characters might be in the employ of the Jekkarenes and so form part of Valontermus and Pelusinne's crew. Their mission, in this case, is to capture both Haliskome and the Purple Wanderer.

- Fourth, the characters may even be part of Haliskome's crew, in which case they are looking to avoid capture by the Jekkarenes or by those Safra hires back in Thyrta.

Whatever the framing for the scenario, there are a number of elements Games Masters should encourage once the action moves to Solisand.

Exploration

Whether Haliskome is the prize or not, exploring Solisand is key. The characters, if they are to be successful, need to establish the lay-of-the-land, hideouts, territories, threats and hazards. This is where sandbox play (see below) comes into its own. The characters need to strategise their travel plans, clearly note where they will observe and/or act; and they should, if smart,

plan exit and contingency strategies. Spending time watching and observing will give them a significant advantage, especially when it comes to exploiting relationships.

Relationships

The interplay between the different factions on Solisand are key to the scenario. The pirates, Jekkarenes, orcs and character have conflicting agendas. Haliskome wants to avoid capture; the Jekkarenes and characters want to capture her; and the orcs want to displace invaders, securing Solisand as their own territory. The opportunity for creating alliances, temporary or sustained, and betrayals/double-crosses is huge – but this hinges upon the characters forging relationships first. If that is to happen, the characters need to bear a few things in mind:

- They may well be outnumbered. Going on the offensive may well prove futile. The orcs will almost certainly want the characters as slaves, the Jekkarenes prisoners to act in another capacity, and Haliskome will work to preserve her own skin. Taking a more cautious approach is likely to be the most sensible thing to do.

- The other factions know more about the island than the characters. They know something of its secrets, its perils and so on. A little knowledge goes a long way: exploiting someone's knowledge aids survival and may aid success, too.

Solisand as a Sandbox Campaign

A sandbox setting lays out the geography, ecology, cultures and settlements of a region, then scatters it liberally with encounters and scenario ideas with which to tempt the players. It does not present a structured series of adventures, nor offer any order in which to perform them; the idea being that players decide what they would like to do and create a quest arc by their character's own actions. Here are some basic guidelines about how this should work...

Not Everything is Meant to be Killed

Solisand consists of three intelligent factions, each of which has a degree of friction with the others. However, there are no objective Good Guys or Bad Guys; such concepts depend on the traditions and customs of each culture and are very malleable. Just because the orcs have a certain reputation, it does not mean they are depraved... merely *different*. The Jekkarenes have a similar goal to the characters, but, of course, serve a different patron and have their own agenda – which, to them, is the correct one. So, whilst players are, of course, free to undertake a crusade of genocide, the Solisand factions are there to provide characters with moral choices and more interesting roleplaying experiences. Games Masters should take some time to sketch-out the motivations and likely reactions of the key Non-Player Characters, bearing in mind their own reasons for being on the island. This will help make the NPCs become three-dimensional and help manage the tendencies of some players to view all NPCs as sword-fodder.

All the factions on Solisand can be interacted with, forming relationships or providing plot hooks for further adventures. Social bonds forged through relationships can be powerful driving forces within a campaign without the need to directly harm or threaten player characters at all. Indeed, the interesting political balance means that characters are far better forging strong ties with potential allies if they are to succeed in capturing Haliskome and, indeed, survive.

Another aspect to bear in mind is that MYTHRAS is not forgiving of repetitive combat. The island are already dangerous enough with roaming beasts, without players making a rod for their own backs by unilaterally declaring war on the orcs, Jekkarenes and pirates too. Since magical healing may be limited, every potential fight should be approached with caution, and avoided if at all possible, by clever use of other skills; Deceit, Influence, or Stealth for example. Prudence is by far a character's best protection!

There is No Game Balance

A common misconception when starting a sandbox campaign, or with those playing MYTHRAS for the first time, is the concept of Game Balance. Games Masters should emphasise that not everything the characters encounter can be beaten, since the island and its inhabitants do not scale in step with the characters' own skills. Thus players should be willing to retreat or give up in some situations, since they can always come back another day and try again.

Solisand contains some very dangerous spirits and monsters which should be avoided until ways are found to conquer that particular encounter; perhaps by setting a trap, asking for advice from the natives, or organising a hunting party to take it down en masse. Rather than seeking to frustrate players, this style of play is there to encourage imagination.

On the other hand, Games Masters should feel free to lower the challenge presented by some creatures or NPCs if it is felt they are overly demanding. This is easily done by reducing the skills, difficulty levels or damage inflicted by such challenges if the desire is to make such adventures more survivable.

Every Action has a Consequence

Whilst such things might not be directly observable by the players, every action taken by their characters should have a consequence. Solisand and its factions are dynamic – not inert targets waiting for something to come along and kill them.

A critical part of developing this dynamic process is to remember that people learn from their mistakes and that time continues to pass. Nothing remains static. So if characters continue to assault the Jekkarene compound, they are likely to encounter nasty traps and a heightened level of alert – which may escalate into violence the characters simply cannot control, talk their way out of, or easily flee.

Some Places are Deliberately Left Blank

Whilst Solisand presents a large number of interesting locations to explore, it does not comprehensively cover the entire island. There is simply no practical way to detail everything which might be found there.

However, this give Games Masters the scope to add their own locations as and when they need to. What this adventure does is simply offer a starting point, and give tantalising hints of what sorts of thing already exist. For example, if you have access to MONSTER ISLAND, many of the places described in that book, and the scenarios presented, can be dropped straight into Solisand. Indeed, this section on Sandbox campaigns is taken directly from MONSTER ISLAND.

Provide Options and Objectives

A good sandbox offers many different places to explore and people to interact with. Overarching campaign plots are not absolutely necessary, although can be fun. For example, the focus of the game where the characters are shipwrecked might be to find a way off the island, forging alliances with the factions to help with that simple goal.

Player characters will not take every lead or hook, nor should they be overwhelmed by every possibility provided in these pages – just enough so that they have choice. Once they begin to form relationships and antipathies with the island's inhabitants, or discover the lure of ancient magics and long lost treasure, the characters will create their own plot lines.

Non-Player Characters

Safra Am Prishad, A Wealthy Merchant's Daughter from Morkesh

Safra is 22 years of age, beautiful and determined, unmarried and adventurous. With her head swathed in a mourning veil you cannot see much of her face other than big, dark eyes. She dresses demurely, long pants tight at the ankle, and a long-sleeved tunic, usually in brown with rich embroidered edging and detail in crimson, and a loose robe overall.

Characteristics	Attributes	1D20	Location	AP/HP
STR: 9	Action Points: 3	1–3	Right Leg	0/6
CON: 13	Damage Modifier: 0	4–6	Left Leg	0/6
SIZ: 12	Magic Points: 12	7–9	Abdomen	0/7
DEX: 13	Movement: 6 metres	10–12	Chest	0/8
INT: 15	Initiative Bonus: +14	13–15	Right Arm	0/5
POW: 12	Armour: None	16–18	Left Arm	0/5
CHA: 16		19–20	Head	0/6

Skills: *Athletics 35%, Brawn 25%, Commerce 55%, Endurance 45%, Evade 30%, Insight 52%, Language (Djesmiri) 57%, Locale (Largil) 60%, Perception 40%, Unarmed 35%, Willpower 65%, Stealth 34%*

Passions: *Hate 'those that let me down' 68%, Thirst for Vengeance 112%*

Magic: None

Combat Style: *Hell Hath No Fury (any impromptu weapon, dagger or knife) 45%*

Weapon	Size/Force	Reach	Damage	AP/HP
Dagger	*S*	*S*	*1d4+1*	*6/8*

Prishad's Daughter

Valontermus, Jekkarene Navy Officer, Zygas Taga Initiate

Of moderate height, moderate appearance and even of a seemingly unassuming personality, Valontermus is, nevertheless, a decorated, respected, dedicated officer of the Jekkarene navy. He is dutiful and follows his orders diligently. The navy is his life and his true love. When in control and issuing orders, he is in his element. As a fighter, he acts defensively: in combat Valontermus will throw up his Aegis Miracle (buckler becomes Size L and gains the characteristics of Hoplite Shield) before going into action, and cast Protection as well if there is time. Valontermus's rapier is a 'presentation sword' inscribed with a message from the Iron Simulacrum stating how it is bestowed as a gift in recognition of the Emperor's high opinion of his family. His priest has cast Truesword and Extension on it. It is a prize worth a considerable sum in blood, honour and cash if lost; however, its magical potency will expire as soon as news reaches Valontermus' temple that he is no longer in need or possession of it.

Characteristics	Attributes	1D20	Location	AP/HP
STR: 12	Action Points: 2	1–3	Right Leg	0/5
CON: 11	Damage Modifier: +0	4–6	Left Leg	0/5
SIZ: 13	Magic Points: 13	7–9	Abdomen	1/6
DEX: 13	Movement: 6 metres	10–12	Chest	1/7
INT: 14	Initiative Bonus: +14	13–15	Right Arm	1/4
POW: 13	Armour: Fine Padded Jerkin, 1 AP (Chest, Abdomen, Arms).	16–18	Left Arm	1/4
CHA: 15		19–20	Head	0/5

Skills: *Command 68%, Deceit 35%, Endurance 55% Evade 40%, Influence 67%, Insight 44%, Orate 45%, Seamanship 76% Willpower 60%*

Passions: *Loyalty to Jekkarenes 100%, Love Order 90%*

Magic:

Folk Magic (Jekkarene Rites 55%) Protection, Translate, Voice

Devotion (Zygas Taga) 46%, Exhort 50% Devotional Pool 3. Miracles: Aegis, Dismiss Elemental, Fortify, Heal Wound.

Combat Style: *Swordsman 78%*

Weapon	Size/Force	Reach	Damage	AP/HP
Rapier	L	M	2d8	5/8
Buckler	M	S	1d3	6/9

Pelusinne, Jekkarene Moon-Priestess

Pelusinne is a stern and proud woman. Her features are angular and striking, and she is not unattractive (indeed, in the moonlight, is appears quite beautiful). She is utterly devoted to her goddess and is a dutiful servant of the theocracy. When travelling she dresses practically in a leather kilt, good, linen shirt, high sandals, the ensemble set-off by an azure cloak hemmed with the runes of her temple.

She is a formidable magician. Pelusinne's most useful party trick is her Behold spell. Haliskome knew full well that the priestesses could follow her if she did not renounce her cult, and she made her crew do likewise. But here on the island Pelusinne can at key moments – so long as there is a moon in the heavens to work the magic – make use of her Behold Miracle to scry what is going on with one of the patrols. The marines at least are all lay members of the cult, and can provide the focus she needs. She will only do this if a patrol is long overdue or known to be set for an important confrontation.

Pelusinne carries two special items. A Moon Bowl – a large, shallow ritual vessel that Pelusinne uses for her Behold Miracle. To perfom the Miracle she fills it with water and

places it so that she can see the moon reflected in the bowl. The Behold Miracle only works on targets visible by the moon (bear in mind the moon is stationary and present in the sky night and day). Value 75SP

A Moonblade: a crescent-bladed knife used by the priestesses of Jekkara. Nothing magical about it, but worth 20SP

Characteristics	Attributes	1D20	Location	AP/HP
STR: 10	Action Points: 3	1–3	Right Leg	0/5
CON: 9	Damage Modifier: +0	4–6	Left Leg	0/5
SIZ: 11	Magic Points: 16	7–9	Abdomen	0/6
DEX: 13	Movement: 6 metres	10–12	Chest	0/7
INT: 15	Initiative Bonus: +14	13–15	Right Arm	0/4
POW: 16	Armour: none	16–18	Left Arm	0/4
CHA: 14		19–20	Head	0/5

Skills: *Custom 85%, Deceit 55%, Endurance 40%, Evade 42%, Insight 75%, Influence 80%, Perception 49%, Willpower 65%*

Passions: *Loyalty to Jekkarene Theocracy 60%, Love Moon Goddess 110%, Hate Traitors 95%, Arcane Curiosity 65%*

Magic:

Folk Magic (Rites 90%) Avert, Befuddle, Cleanse, Coordination, Light, Heal, Tire

Devotion (Jekkara) 86%, Evoke 76%; Devotional Pool 8. Miracles: Absorption, Behold, Consecrate (2), Enthrall, Moonbright, Rejuvenate (3), Synchronise

Combat Style: *Guardian (Rapier, Dagger, Morning Star and buckler) 46% – Swashbuckling*

Weapon	Size/Force	Reach	Damage	AP/HP
Rapier	L	M	2d8	5/8
Buckler	M	S	1d3	6/9
Moonblade	S	S	1d3+1	5/4

Jekkarene Rowers and Sailors

A standard crew for a Jekkarene naval vessel: strong, dense, dutiful, obedient and in-awe of Pelusinne.

Attributes	1D20	Location	AP/HP
Action Points: 2	1–3	Right Leg	0/5
Damage Modifier:+0	4–6	Left Leg	0/5
Magic Points: 10	7–9	Abdomen	0/6
Movement: 6 metres	10–12	Chest	0/7
Initiative Bonus: +12	13–15	Right Arm	0/4
Armour: none	16–18	Left Arm	0/4
Abilities: None	19–20	Head	0/5

Skills: *Athletics 45%, Boating 55%, Brawn 65%, Endurance 40%, Evade 25%, Seamanship 45%, Sing (Lewd Sea Shanty) 100%, Unarmed 35%, Willpower 45%*

Magic: None

Combat Style: *Jekkarene Crew (Dagger, hatchet, club or spike) 40%*

Weapon	Size/Force	Reach	Damage	AP/HP
Dagger	S	S	1d4+1	6/8
Hatchet	M	S	1d6	3/6
Club	M	S	1d6	4/4
Boat Hook/Shortspear	M	L	1d6+1	4/5

Prishad's Daughter

Jekkarene Marines

Decent warriors loyal to Valontermus.

Attributes	1D20	Location	AP/HP
Action Points: 3	1–3	Right Leg	3/5
Damage Modifier: +1d2	4–6	Left Leg	3/5
Magic Points: 10	7–9	Abdomen	4/6
Movement: 4 metres	10–12	Chest	4/7
Initiative Bonus: +13-4 = 9	13–15	Right Arm	3/4
Armour: Lamellar haunberk, cuirboilli greaves and bracers, crested helm	16–18	Left Arm	3/4
Abilities: None	19–20	Head	5/5

Skills: Athletics 40%, Boating 55%, Brawn 40%, Endurance 45%, Evade 35%, Swim 40%, Unarmed 35%, Willpower 35%

Magic: Folk Magic (Rites 40%) Speedart, Heal

Combat Style: Jekkarene Marine (sidearm, shield) 70% Trait – Sure-Footed; Marksman (Crossbow) 60% Trait – Hawkeye

Weapon	Size/Force	Reach	Damage	AP/HP
Falchion	M	M	1d6+1+1d2	6/10
Shield	L	S	1d4+1d2	6/12
Heavy Crossbow	H	-	1d10	4/8

Solisma the Dryad

Solisma's grove is dominated by Kermes Oaks – a thorny tree that can reach 12 metres in height and has leaves with a pale green upper surface and greyish underside and thorns along their edges. Solisma manifests cloaked in these leaves, giving her a strange, rippling, greeny-grey sheen as she moves, the thorns making it appear that she is spine-covered. She is ambivalent towards intruders unless her trees, the Woses or the Bakru have been threatened or hurt. If any have, then she is murderously vengeful.

Characteristics	Attributes	1D20	Location	AP/HP
STR: 10	Action Points: 3	1–3	Right Leg	0/5
CON: 16	Damage Modifier: +0	4–6	Left Leg	0/5
SIZ: 9	Magic Points: 21	7–9	Abdomen	0/6
DEX: 9	Movement: 6 metres	10–12	Chest	0/7
INT: 19	Initiative Bonus: +14	13–15	Right Arm	0/4
POW: 21	Armour: None	16–18	Left Arm	0/4
CHA: 18	Abilities: Dryad to Elemental; Solisma can become a Gnome with a volume of 1 cubic metre per Magic Point spent.	19–20	Head	0/5

Gnome Characteristics: (12m gnome): Actions 4, SR24, HP75, Brawn 130%, Evade 94%, Perception 76%, Willpower 105%, Combat 117%, Envelop (Colossal, 2d10 Damage).

Skills: Athletics 65%, Endurance 64%, Evade 27%, Locale 152%, Perception 76%, Seduction 85%, Stealth 55%, Unarmed 50%, Willpower 105%

Passions: Love Grove and its Inhabitants 115%, Hate Fire 115%, Guilt and Shame (for her part in Brasilas' takeover of the island) 55%, Lost Love (Nastarios) 84%

Magic:

Folk Magic (84%): Beastcall (any native animal), Avert, Befuddle, Bypass, Demoralise, Heal, Mindspeech, Pathway, Phantasm, Pet, Witchsight

Nastarios Lanis, Paladin and Haunt

When he was alive and stranded on the island, Nastarios dreamed of returning home. Solisma's love provided a certain amount of comfort, but, in the end, he tired of it. A jealous creature, Solisma resented Nastarios' previous life and the paladin felt suffocated and isolated from what he had had before. In his spirit form, Nastarios therefore hates Solisma: intruders – especially Solar Cult intruders – offer a way for his remains to be returned to his homeland, which is all he ever craved. Naturally Solisma will not tolerate the remains of her beloved to be removed from the grove and so love turns to anger and vengeance.

Once Nastarios' remains are recovered, he becomes an allied spirit to his rescuer. They must provide him with 1 Magic Point as a Pact to establish the link (for a maximum of one year and a day, but potentially renewable). He cannot recover any Magic Points unless his bones rest in a place consecrated to the sun god, and the process can be accelerated through veneration. Nastarios has an agenda, which is to be laid properly to rest at Hilanistra – however, he would settle for being the focal point in the establishment of a shrine somewhere else. Lord Skelfus would kill – or pay handsomely – to have control of Nastarios' bones to help establish an important centre of Solar worship in his domain.

Characteristics	Attributes
INT: 14	Action Points: 3
POW: 15	Damage Modifier: 0
CHA: 16	Magic Points: 4
Intensity: 2	Movement: 8m, or instantaneous at cost of 1MP (within POW metres of his bones only)
	Initiative Bonus: 15

Traits and Abilities: *Locus. Nastarios is bound to his own bones and cannot move more than POW (16m) from them; Allied Spirit; Wither; Spellcasting.*

Nastarios can manifest if within POW metres of a sun worshipper (initiate or higher) at no cost to himself by taking the 1MP cost from the mortal, who may resist using Willpower; or within any area consecrated to the sun god at 0MP; in all other cases Manifestation costs him 1MP as for Haunt. Nastarios can only use his Theist magic when manifested in this way. As an ordinary Haunt, he is limited to the use of his Folk Magic.

Skills: *Manifest 62% Influence 55%, Insight 36%, Stealth 30%, Willpower 82%,*

Passions: *Hate Solisma 84%, Homesick 100%*

Magic:

Folk Magic (83%) Avert, Bladesharp, Firearrow, Heal, Light, Polish, Warmth, Vigour

Theism: (capped by Manifest skill of 62% unless in a Consecrated space)

Devotion 92%, Evoke 69%, Devotional Pool 4. Miracles: Aegis, Consecrate (2), Dismiss Magic, Summon Salamander, Heal Wound, Ripen, Sunspear (2)

Combat Style: *Spiritual Paladin 41%, 1d6 Damage*

Haliskome, Pirate Captain, Lapsed Initiate of Jekkara

In her early 30s, with fair hair, a small, round mouth and missing her , Haliskome is charismatic, headstrong, determined and devious. As a child, she was uncontrollable and it was thought that the cult of Jekkara would instil some discipline. It worked – until the priestesses cursed her lover, Melantos, with lycanthropy, forcing her to break him free and go on the run with their captured ship. In truth, Haliskome prefers this free-spirited life, despite its dangers, but her first priority is to get Melantos to somewhere where the moon's influence is reduce, giving him greater control over his curse.

Haliskome's lively personality usually encourages people to like her. Her crew is loyal, and she uses her personable charm as a way to win-over others. If that fails, she is not beyond resorting to violence, but her first tactic is to talk her way out of trouble. If combat is inevitable, she relies on speed and spell, casting Protection first, then attempting to Befuddle one of her opponents if outnumbered. If things go badly wrong she will, if within range, use the portal enchantment on the captain's baton she carries to escape back to the ship.

Haliskome carries the following:

Captain's Baton (POW6, INT2) Spells cast at Intensity 9, Range 5, Magnitude 4.

This item has two enchantments; one is a Portal spell linked to a mark set on the deck of the Purple Wanderer (and cannot be made to go anywhere else). With a range of 300 metres, she takes care to try to remain within easy escape distance to her ship; hence her camp is close by the shore. The portal closes as soon as the baton-holder passes through it, but allows Haliskome to usher through her crew before entering herself.

The baton also holds an enchantment for Dominate Undine at Intensity 8, Range 5, Magnitude 4, which is effective on Undines with a INS of 18 or less (risky therefore where Undines of 6 cubic metres or greater in size are concerned). This item has been extremely useful in light of the artefact the pirates have found here that enables them to summon an undine of immense proportions.

A Jekkarene Rites roll is required to use the baton, although Assabian rites might work at Hard difficulty. A sorcerer who studied it could begin a new Invocation skill to use its power. It powers itself, however, each use costs 3 Magic Points, and so the baton can only be used twice before it runs out of Magic Points, which it recovers at a rate of 1 per day. For purpose of resistance rolls, the baton's spells are deemed cast at 90%

The Ocean's Call

This artefact dates back to the days of Brasilas, and enables the summoning of Undines. A simple ring of a lightweight grey metal, inscribed on its outer surface with various runes. The summoner must stand in the sea (fresh water will not do), and expend 1 Magic Point per cubic metre of undine they wish to summon – with no limitation. The problem is that the Undine only obeys someone who also has a devotion to Father Ocean. In all other circumstances, it must be dominated and commanded using an appropriate Sorcery spell or Miracle, which is not included. Otherwise, the undine will attack the summoner, with the intent to take the ring and deposit it back in the ocean. The undine will remain for the summoner's CHA in minutes – there is no means to manipulate the summoning; however, once summoned the undine could be bound to further service. The ring will not allow the user to regain the Magic Points expended until the undine is released.

Shores of Korantia

Characteristics	Attributes	1D20	Location	AP/HP
STR: 10	Action Points: 3	1–3	Right Leg	1/5
CON: 14	Damage Modifier: +0	4–6	Left Leg	1/5
SIZ: 11	Magic Points: 16-5=11	7–9	Abdomen	1/6
DEX: 13	Movement: 6 metres	10–12	Chest	1/7
INT: 15	Initiative Bonus: +14 -2 = 12	13–15	Right Arm	1/4
POW: 16	Armour: Black leather jerkin, bracers and leggings	16–18	Left Arm	1/4
CHA: 14	Abilities: none	19–20	Head	0/5

Skills: *Athletics 40%, Brawn 25%, Endurance 51%, Evade 68%, Influence 58%, Navigation 32%, Perception 58%, Seamanship 71%, Swim 64%, Unarmed 60%, Willpower 72%*

Passions: *Love Melantos 85%, Hate Jekkarenes 44%, Love Freedom 71%*

Magic:

Folk Magic (65%): Alarm, Avert, Befuddle, Heal, Tire

Combat Style: *Guardian (Rapier, Dagger, Morning Star and buckler) 75% – Swashbuckling*

Weapon	Size/Force	Reach	Damage	AP/HP
Rapier	M	M	1d8	6/8
Buckler	M	S	1d3	6/9
Morningstar	M	M	1d8	5/8

Melantos, Haliskome's Lover, Werewolf

Melantos' were-form statistics are in parentheses.

Burly and rather hairy with black eyebrows that meet above his nose, Melantos is devoted to Haliskome, who he knows has risked everything to spring him from prison, and is now coping as best she can with his lycanthropy. He will unquestionably give his life for her if the situation calls for it. He is fearsome in battle and his combat style is always augmented by his Love Haliskome Passion. He casts Protection on himself before any battle and, if time permits (and fire is available), he casts Ironhand so that he can grasp and then throw red-hot stones or burning brands from a nearby campfire.

In wolf-form he is a massive, black-furred wolf with a darker crest running between his eyes and down the length of his spine. He uses both his Intimidate and Leaping Attack abilities to scare the life out of enemies, and to render them prone before savaging them, aiming attacks at the head and limbs, attempting to open arteries (Bleed effect) so that death comes slowly and painfully. Melantos is immune to non-magical weapons when in were-form. At the full moon, Melantos's STR when in were-form is doubled, giving him a Damage Modifier +1d8.

Prishad's Daughter

Characteristics	Attributes	1D20	Location	AP/HP
STR: 14 (28)	Action Points: 3	1–3 (1-2)	Right Leg	0(1)/5
CON: 16	Damage Modifier: +1d2	4–6 (3-4)	Left Leg	0 (1)/5
SIZ: 14	Magic Points: 8	7–9 (5-7)	Abdomen	0(1)/6
DEX: 12	Movement: 6 metres (8)	10–12 (8-10)	Chest	0(1)/7
INT: 12 (INS12)	Initiative Bonus: +12	13–15 (11-13)	Right Arm	0(1)/4
POW: 8	Armour: 1 Pont Skin	16–18 (14-16)	Left Arm	0(1)/4
CHA: 13	Abilities: See description on page 224	19–20 (17-20)	Head	0(1)/5

Skills: *Athletics 66%, Boating 58%, Brawn 55%, Endurance 50%, Evade 48%, Seamanship 65%, Swim 60%, Tracking 44% (88%), Unarmed 60%, Willpower 45%*

Passions: *Love Haliskome 95%, Love Freedom 80%*

Magic:

Folk Magic (Rites 51%) Deflect, Ironhand, Protection

Combat Style: *Swashbuckler 77%, (Dagger, Buckler, Club) – Swashbuckling; Weremonster 66% – Intimidate, Leaping Attack*

Weapon	Size/Force	Reach	Damage	AP/HP
Dagger	S	S	1d4+1+1d2	6/9
Buckler	M	S	1d3	6/9
Club	M	S	1d6+1d2	4/4
Bites	S	T	1d3+1d8	As for Head

Kisethentyes, Master at Arms of the Purple Wanderer

Bald, burly, tanned and tattooed, the master-at-arms is an expert archer, and even better in a hand to hand duel on a slippery deck. He wears no armour, relying on his skills and dexterity to avoid blows and missiles. If the crew get into a fight, he prefers to stand off and pick out targets with his arrows, shouting commands and encouragement to his 'boys'. He relies on Kalish to provide the aggression and fight at the front; Kisathentyes' job is to see an action managed to a successful outcome. Once in a while he might call out a handy-looking fighter or leader from an enemy crew to single combat, a display intended to remind everyone of his skills.

Characteristics	Attributes	1D20	Location	AP/HP
STR: 11	Action Points: 3	1–3	Right Leg	0/5
CON:12	Damage Modifier: +0	4–6	Left Leg	0 /5
SIZ: 13	Magic Points: 8	7–9	Abdomen	0/6
DEX: 16	Movement: 6 metres	10–12	Chest	0/7
INT: 13	Initiative Bonus: +15	13–15	Right Arm	0/4
POW: 9	Armour: none	16–18	Left Arm	0/4
CHA: 12	Abilities:	19–20	Head	0/5

Skills: *Athletics 66%, Boating 58%, Brawn 55%, Endurance 50%, Evade 78%, First Aid 70%, Perception 54%, Seamanship 45%, Swim 65%, Unarmed 60%, Willpower 45%*

Passions: *Loyalty to Haliskome 80%, Love Freedom 80%*

Magic:

Folk Magic (Jekkarene Rites 60%) Bladesharp, Fanaticism, Firearrow, Heal, Pierce

Combat Style: *Archery 92% Trait – Rapid Fire; Jekkarene Marine 96% (Buckler, Sidearm) Trait – Sure Footed*

Weapon	Size/Force	Reach	Damage	AP/HP
Dagger	S	S	1d4+1+1d2	6/9
Buckler	M	S	1d3	6/9
Mace	M	S	1d8+1d2	6/6
Moon Bow	H	-	1d8+1d2	4/6

Shores of Korantia

Jerboas, Sailing Master of the Purple Wanderer

An experienced old hand allocated to the Purple Wanderer because of his impeccable record in the navy, Jereboas is something of a mascot for the crew who will do their best to keep him out of harm's way of a fight begins, knowing how critical he is to all their fortunes.

Characteristics	Attributes	1D20	Location	AP/HP
STR: 13	Action Points: 3	1–3	Right Leg	0/5
CON: 10	Damage Modifier: +1d2	4–6	Left Leg	0/5
SIZ: 13	Magic Points: 12	7–9	Abdomen	0/6
DEX: 13	Movement: 6 metres	10–12	Chest	0/7
INT: 14	Initiative Bonus: +14	13–15	Right Arm	0/4
POW: 12	Armour: none	16–18	Left Arm	0/4
CHA: 10	Abilities: none	19–20	Head	0/5

Skills: *Athletics 41%, Boating 78%, Brawn 55%, Endurance 50%, Evade 48%, Insight 38%, Locale (Inner Ocean) 51%, Navigation 69%, Perception 82%, Seamanship 95%, Swim 60%, Unarmed 40%, Willpower 45%*

Passions: *Loyalty to Haliskome 80%, Love Freedom 80%*

Magic:

Folk Magic (Jekkarene Rites 56%) Calculate, Cool, Deflect, Preserve, Sea Legs, Shove, Vigor

Combat Style: *Reaver (Sabre, Dagger, Buckler) 51%*

Weapon	Size/Force	Reach	Damage	AP/HP
Dagger	S	S	1d4+1+1d2	6/9
Buckler	M	S	1d3	6/9
Sabre	M	M	1d6+1d2	6/8

Ankaskron, Jekkarene Deserter, First Mate of the Purple Wanderer

Charged with being Jereboas' lieutenant, and with keeping him safe from harm, Ankaskron is an enthusiastic plunderer and has turned to the pirate lifestyle with gusto. In an emergency, Ankaskron and Jereboas are detailed with making for the ship as quickly as possible with some extra hands to make her ready to get under way at a moment's notice.

Characteristics	Attributes	1D20	Location	AP/HP
STR: 15	Action Points: 3	1–3	Right Leg	0/5
CON: 8	Damage Modifier: +1d2	4–6	Left Leg	0/5
SIZ: 14	Magic Points: 9	7–9	Abdomen	2/6
DEX: 12	Movement: 6 metres	10–12	Chest	2/7
INT: 12	Initiative Bonus: +12 (–2 for armour)= +10	13–15	Right Arm	1/4
POW: 9	Armour: Bracers, Leather Cuirass and helm	16–18	Left Arm	1/4
CHA: 7	Abilities: none	19–20	Head	2/5

Skills: *Athletics 65%, Boating 80%, Brawn 75%, Deceit 41%, Endurance 45%, Evade 38%, Perception 50%, Seamanship 77%, Stealth 42%, Survival 38%, Swim 62%, Unarmed 47%, Willpower 42%*

Passions: *Loyalty to Haliskome 80%, Love Freedom 80%*

Magic:

Folk Magic (Jekkarene Rites 40%) Bludgeon, Speedart

Combat Style: *Jekkarene Marine (sidearm, shield) 70% Trait: Sure-Footed; Thug (Club, Dagger, Knife) 67% Trait: Intimidation*

Weapon	Size/Force	Reach	Damage	AP/HP
Dagger	S	S	1d4+1+1d2	6/9
Buckler	M	S	1d3	6/9
Club	M	S	1d6+1d2	6/8

Prishad's Daughter

Haliskome's Crew

Mixture of Jekkarene renegades and riff-raff pirates recruited along the way. Loyal to Haliskome.

Attributes	1D20	Location	AP/HP
Action Points: 3	1–3	Right Leg	0/5
Damage Modifier:+0	4–6	Left Leg	0/5
Magic Points: 10	7–9	Abdomen	0/6
Movement: 6 metres	10–12	Chest	0/7
Initiative Bonus: +12	13–15	Right Arm	0/4
Armour: none	16–18	Left Arm	0/4
Abilities: None	19–20	Head	0/5

Skills: Athletics 45%, Boating 60%, Brawn 40%, Endurance 40%, Evade 25%, Seamanship 45%, Sing (Lewd Sea Shanty) 100%, Unarmed 35%, Willpower 45%

Magic: None

Combat Style: *Jekkarene Crew (Dagger, hatchet, club or spike) 40%*

Weapon	Size/Force	Reach	Damage	AP/HP
Dagger	S	S	1d4+1	6/8
Hatchet	M	S	1d6	3/6
Club	M	S	1d6	4/4
Boat Hook/Shortspear	M	L	1d6+1	4/5

Shores of Korantia

Kalish, a Sailor of Morkesh, Demonist

The non-Jekkarene among the senior crew, Kalish has been found to be a vicious and effective fighter so has been elevated from amongst the other sailors. His skill comes from the kind of demon Pact common amongst his countrymen, but as is usual comes at a price – not only a dedication of 3 Magic Points to his Demon ally, but a passion that compels him to kill any foe he bests in combat.

Characteristics	Attributes	1D20	Location	AP/HP
STR: 12	Action Points: 4	1–3	Right Leg	0/6
CON: 13	Damage Modifier: +0	4–6	Left Leg	0/6
SIZ: 13	Magic Points: 7	7–9	Abdomen	3/7
DEX: 15	Movement: 6 metres	10–12	Chest	3/8
INT: 12	Initiative Bonus: +14 (–2 for armour)= +12	13–15	Right Arm	0/5
POW: 10	Armour: Bezainted cuirass and helm.	16–18	Left Arm	0/5
CHA: 11	Abilities: Pact: Puissance. Kalish is pacted with a combat demon, raising his skill as a swordsman to 100%. This costs 1 MP, and if the pact lapses his skill reverts to 65%; Unnatural Speed; Kalish has an additional Action Point (2MP)	19–20	Head	3/6

Skills: *Athletics 55%, Boating 65%, Brawn 55%, Endurance 55%, Evade 59%, Perception 60%, Seamanship 40%, Stealth 40%, Survival 45%, Tracking 40%, Unarmed 66%, Willpower 40%*

Passions: *(From Pact): Killing Without Compunction 65%. Every time Kalish incapacitates a foe he rolls against this Passion. If the roll succeeds Kalish will quickly deliver a coup de grace to his enemy.*

Magic:

Folk Magic Folk Magic (Assabian Rites 50%): Dullblade, Protection

Combat Style: *Swordsman (Falchion, Scimitar, Tulwar, Dagger, Buckler) 100% Trait: Excellent Footwork; Marksman (Crossbows) 79% Trait: Hawkeye*

Weapon	Size/Force	Reach	Damage	AP/HP
Dagger	S	S	1d4+	6/9
Buckler	M	S	1d3	6/9
Scimitar	M	M	1d8	6/8
Heavy Crossbow	H	-	1d10	4/8

Demuskera, the Gorgon of Solisand

Demuskera is the true name of a daemoness, a gorgon, with whom Brasilas had a Pact. She fought for him in defence of his lair but was eventually banished. If the means of summoning a gorgon are researched or acquired, possession of her true name is a key component in successfully completing the rite.

Demuskera can instinctively perceive what happens in the summoning chamber and materialise there of her own will at a cost of 1 Magic Point. Once she does materialise, she can move freely around areas 12-15 of the lair. The giant spider in room 5 is immune to Demuskera's gaze attack. Demuskera has a humanoid body (unlike the depiction in the Mythras rules, page 247), but she does have scaly skin and little tusks protruding from either cheek, cruel bronze talons and a curious Otherworld bow made entirely of bronze. She carries 10 shafts in her quiver.

Damuskera is prevented from moving outside Brasilas' lair by the efforts of Solisma and the Bakru. She just might allow an intruder to live if she thinks they could be up to the task of killing the nymph for her: indeed, the manipulative Demuskera would even be tempted to enter into negotiations if she thought revenge against Solisma was possible.

Prishad's Daughter

Characteristics	Attributes	1D20	Location	AP/HP
STR: 18	Action Points: 3	1–3	Right Leg	2/7
CON: 19	Damage Modifier: +1d4	4–6	Left Leg	2/7
SIZ: 17	Magic Points: 16	7–9	Abdomen	2/8
DEX: 16	Movement: 6 metres	10–12	Chest	2/9
INT: 15	Initiative Bonus: +14	13–15	Right Arm	2/6
POW: 17	Armour: Scales on lower body	16–18	Left Arm	2/6
CHA: 10	Abilities: Gaze Attack, Immunity (poisons) Terrifying, Venomous	19–20	Head	2/7

Skills: Athletics 65%, Brawn 66%, Deceit 55%, Endurance 74%, Evade 70%, Insight 62%, Perception 76%, Seduction 55%, Track 62%, Willpower 70%

Passions: Hate Solisma 112%

Magic:

None

Combat Style: Gorgon Horror 74% (Talons, Snakes, Bow, Gaze Attack)

Demuskera's Gaze Aatack costs 1 Magic Point to initiate. Anyone meeting her gaze directly must succeed in an opposed roll of their Willpower versus Demuskera's. If Demuskera wins, immediate petrification – instant death – is the result. If she is in a benevolent mood, she warns potential victims of her power and averts her own face so that she can converse safely.

Her Snakes inflict a poison with 74 Potency, taking effect on the next Combat Round after entering the system and causing paralysis to 1d4+3 Hit Locations unless resisted.

Weapon	Size/Force	Reach	Damage	AP/HP
Talons	M	S	1d6+1d4	As for Arms
Snake Hair	S	S	Poison	As for Head
Bronze Bow	H	-	1d10+1d4	8/8
Gaze			Special	

Bandestrap, Orc Sorcerer

Short, broad and squat in stature, standing only shoulder high to most of his followers, Bandestrap cuts a slightly whimsical figure. However, he has saved his people from disaster when they got shipwrecked here, and the other Orcs follow him loyally. He is usually to be found in command of the larger expedition party of 10 warriors, directing their actions from the rear rank. If threatened, warriors close around him swiftly.

Bandestrap is cunning in his use of magic. Enslave Humans is a very effective spell and the sorcerer ensures that he has enough protection around him to allow time for its casting at multiple foes when possible. Enslaved humans are forced to drop their arms and prostrate themselves before Bandestrap, allowing him and his orcs to humiliate these victims in some inventively foul and vile ways. Failing his Enslave spell, Hinder is used to slow assailants to a crawl, giving his warriors time to close to wreak havoc, while Palsy is focused on weapon-holding limbs to ensure that resistance is, indeed, futile. Imprison is used when it is clear he and his orcs are winning a conforntation, casting a barrier around the immediate scene of the battle to prevent survivors from dragging themselves free and allowing his orcs some confined sport. Bandestrap cannot use his Evoke (Hungry Gods) spell because he is out of range of any volcanic features thorugh which they can force their way into the mundane world. Consequently, he cannot make sacrifices to them, and his access to manna is limited to what he can generate himself or tap from others. Bandestrap has used Store Manna to create a storage device, and then tapped fatigue from his followers when he had the chance. Some of these points have been spent revivifying three of his gang who failed to survive the shipwreck but washed up on the beach all the same.

So, despite his small size, Bandestrap is not some one to mess with lightly. He is powerful, devious and wholly sadistic. His warband loves him.

SHORES OF KORANTIA

Characteristics	Attributes	1D20	Location	AP/HP
STR: 14	Action Points: 3	1–3	Right Leg	0/5
CON: 16	Damage Modifier: +0	4–6	Left Leg	0/5
SIZ: 8	Magic Points: 14-3=11 (personal) plus 10 stored	7–9	Abdomen	2/6
DEX: 17	Movement: 6 metres	10–12	Chest	2/7
INT: 15	Initiative Bonus: +16-1 armour = 15	13–15	Right Arm	0/4
POW: 14	Armour: Bone-stiffened leather jerkin, salvaged from the wreck, 2AP chest and abdomen.	16–18	Left Arm	0/4
CHA: 8	Abilities: Blood Magic	19–20	Head	0/5

Skills: *Athletics 63%, Brawn 72%, Endurance 57%, Evade 40%, First Aid 67%, Healing 45%, Influence 50%, Rites 79%, Stealth 39%, Survival 52%, Unarmed 64%, Willpower 68%*

Passions: *Enslaving Others 80%*

Magic:

Folk Magic (Rites 72%) Bladesharp, Bloody Knife*, Calm, Tire, Spirit Shield, Witchsight

Sorcery (Spellcraft 73% Invocation Song of the Crysanthemum Blade 78%): Enchant, Enslave (Humans), Evoke (Hungry Gods), Hinder, Imprison, Palsy, Sculpt (Obsidian), Tap (Fatigue), Revivify

Combat Style: *Club and Dagger 54%*

Weapon	Size/Force	Reach	Damage	AP/HP
Flint Knife	S	S	1d3	4/4
Club	M	S	1d6	5/4

Grrruff, Bandestrap's Familiar, Small Therapod Dinosaur

This creature is often basking somewhere in open territory, particularly in the Crag area, or by one of the beaches. He is in Mindlink with Bandestrap, so if he spots anything interesting he can instantly alert his master.

Characteristics	Attributes	1D20	Location	AP/HP
STR: 14	Action Points: 2	01-02	Tail	3/6
CON: 15	Damage Modifier: +1d2	03-05	RH Leg	3/6
SIZ: 14	Magic Points: 8	06-08	LH Leg	3/6
DEX: 11	Movement: 8 metres	09-11	Hind Quarters	3/7
INT/INS: 5/14	Initiative Bonus: +13	12-15	Fore Quarters	3/8
POW: 8	Armour: 3 point hide – no penalty	16	R Claw	3/6
CHA: 4	Abilities:	17	L Claw	3/6
		18-20	Head	3/6

Skills: *Endurance 50%, Evade 45% Perception 50%, Stealth 40%, Tracking 75%, Willpower 25%*

Passions: *Love Bandestrap 90%*

Combat Style: *Claws and Teeth 45%, Leaping Attack*

Weapon	Size/Force	Reach	Damage	AP/HP
Claws	M	S	1d6+1d2	As for Claw
Bite	M	S	1d8+1d2	As for Head

Prishad's Daughter

Sandula, Orc Lieutenant

Commanding the rest of the orc warbands, Sandula is gruff and uncompromising. Sandula owns a polished piece of black obsidian streaked with red. An item of orcish blood magic, this amulet provides Sandula with a bonus to Willpower tests when resisting any kind of supernatural attack, making the roll one grade easier. This item can be attuned by a new owner by immersing it in their own blood and leaving it to soak overnight (1 STR of the stuff would do it, recovered at normal rates).

Characteristics	Attributes	1D20	Location	AP/HP
STR: 15	Action Points: 3	1–3	Right Leg	3/5
CON: 11	Damage Modifier: +1d2	4–6	Left Leg	3/5
SIZ: 14	Magic Points: 16	7–9	Abdomen	1/6
DEX: 13	Movement: 6 metres	10–12	Chest	0/7
INT: 13	Initiative Bonus: +13-3=10	13–15	Right Arm	0/4
POW: 9	Armour: Splinted wooden armour on legs, thick hide girdle and cap.	16–18	Left Arm	0/4
CHA: 12		19–20	Head	1/5

Skills: *Athletics 45% Boating 40%, Brawn 50%, Endurance 60% Evade 45%, Stealth 40%, Survival 45%, Swim 50%, Unarmed 45% Willpower 50% (+20%)*

Magic:

None

Combat Style: *Orc Warrior 76%, (Spear, Club and Shield) Trait – thrown weapon*

Weapon	Size/Force	Reach	Damage	AP/HP
Club	M	S	1d6+1d2	4/4
Spear	M	L	1d8+1d2	4/5
Hide Shield	L	S	1s3+1d2	4/9

Orc Warriors

These orcs are a tough and resourceful bunch. Their weapons are mostly made on the island, using stone tips and wood. Their spears consequently do 1d8 Damage instead of 1d8+1 unless Bandestrap has had the chance to cast Bladesharp on them.

They have scraps of armour made in the field including pieces of hide, woven grasses and even tree bark. Where they have armour it can be bypassed as a standard Special Effect, without need of a Critical roll. Their improvised but effective kit can lead those who encounter them to believe they are some sort of primitive native band.

Attributes	1D20	Location	AP/HP
Action Points: 3	1–3	Right Leg	0/5
Damage Modifier: +1d2	4–6	Left Leg	0/5
Magic Points: 11	7–9	Abdomen	1/6
Movement: 6 metres	10–12	Chest	1/7
Initiative Bonus: +11	13–15	Right Arm	0/4
Armour: Tree bark, ,plaited grass, hide and bone	16–18	Left Arm	0/4
Abilities: None	19–20	Head	1/5

Skills: *Athletics 40%, Brawn 40%, Evade 40%, Endurance 50%, Stealth 35%, Survival 40%, Swim 35%, Willpower 45%*

Combat Style: *Bandestrap's Boys 55%*

Weapon	Size/Force	Reach	Damage	AP/HP
Club	M	S	1d6+1d2	4/4
Spear	M	L	1d8+1d2	4/5
Bow	L	-	1d6+1d2	4/4

Revivified Orc Warriors

Bandestrap will use his Revivify spell to turn dead followers or enemies into useful zombies, so ideally his men secure the used bodies of any of the fallen. These corpses are kept in a shelter in the orc camp in case of need, and there are three bodies in various states of decay to choose from at present. A revivified follower +5 STR and CON compared to their living brethren, -2 in each other Characteristic.

The zombie orcs must be in sight and in range of his spell for him to control them, and if there is more than one he must direct them to the same purpose, or all their skill rolls become one grade harder per zombie after the first as Bandestrap tries to cope with coordinating their actions.

Attributes	1D20	Location	AP/HP
Action Points: 2	1–3	Right Leg	0/5
Damage Modifier: +1d4	4–6	Left Leg	0/5
Magic Points: 9	7–9	Abdomen	1/6
Movement: 6 metres	10–12	Chest	1/7
Initiative Bonus: 11—2=9	13–15	Right Arm	0/4
Armour: Tree bark, plaited grass, hide and bone	16–18	Left Arm	0/4
Abilities: Immune to Fatigue; requires Major Wound to head or chest to incapacitate	19–20	Head	1/5

Skills: *Athletics 63%, Brawn 72%, Endurance 57%, Evade 40%, Stealth 39%, Survival 52%, Unarmed 64%, Willpower 68%*

Combat Style: *Bandestrap's Boys 55%*

Weapon	Size/Force	Reach	Damage	AP/HP
Club	M	S	1d6+1d4	4/4

INDEX

A

Abandoned Property 117
Age Of Heroes 10
Agissei 9
Agissene 12, 14, 15, 16, 19, 21, 22, 24, 25, 28, 37, 58, 77, 81, 122, 143, 144
Albirs 35, 49, 50
Albulo 35
Aldus the Bandit 151
Alexiandus 151, 152
Alexianis of Sarestra 151
Allies, Contacts, Rivals and Enemies 44
Anayo 25, 55, 83, 84, 93, 94, 96, 99, 136, 137, 153, 154, 158, 159
Anayo Of Vestrikina, Cult of 93
Animist Traditions 69
Ankaskron 197, 205, 207, 226
Ankwar 33, 49
Antekos II 11
Aparinaon 136, 137, 140, 153, 169, 171, 186
Archipelagans 47
Aristocracy and the Super-Rich 41
Arko 149, 150, 151, 152, 154, 155, 177, 181, 182, 189, 192, 195, 206, 216
Arko of Solarne 149, 150, 154, 177, 182, 189, 192, 195, 206, 216
Armour 78
Armour And Weapons 25
Arms and Armour 75
Army On The Move 123
Aromvelos of Tysil 145, 146, 153
Arribeus 84, 85, 95, 142, 187
Arribeus Of Vestrikina, Cult of 95
Ashkor 33
Aspala 30
Assabia 4, 33, 34, 49, 53, 58, 59, 62, 65, 68, 76, 79, 135
Assabians 48
Assabian Sorcerer 53
Astangoras, Paladin 190
Athlazo 164, 167, 171, 177, 182

B

Background Events 39
Badlands Of Methalea 32
Bakru 195, 196, 198, 199, 201, 205, 210, 216, 221, 228
Balbufera 34, 35
Bandestrap 193, 197, 198, 203, 214, 215, 229, 230, 231, 232
Banish Satyr (New Miracle) 102
Barbarians, Someshi 35
Baristates of Velathela 21
Baron Lankermost 32
Baron Solfernoy 32, 150, 186, 187, 189, 193, 216
Bear Woods 146
Beast-Man 120, 121, 122, 123
Beast-Men 125
Beggars 117, 118
Belisar of Mersin 146
Bilinthus 146, 164, 166, 167
Billet 140
Bind Vessel (Miracle) 105
Blue Finn 140
Boar-Kin 125
Boating And Seamanship 110
Bones Of Nastarios 205
Boons 68
Borissa 4, 10, 12, 14, 15, 19, 30, 98, 135, 136, 137, 139, 140, 142, 143, 144, 145, 146, 148, 153, 158, 159, 161, 162
Boundary, Miracle 97
Bows and Accoutrements 79
Brasilas 188, 189, 190, 193, 195, 201, 205, 207, 209, 210, 211, 216, 221, 223, 228
Brasilas' Lair 207
Briga River 34
Brotomagia 5, 14, 30, 31, 33, 135, 142, 148, 157, 158, 161, 166
Burn Fields, Miracle 97
Byotyes 9

C

Calendar, Korantine 26

Camtri 5, 12, 14, 18, 31, 33, 44, 46

Cannibal Coast 35

Cardrerus 168, 169, 171

Careers 52

Cataclysm 11, 12, 21, 28, 37, 48, 80, 88, 90, 100, 133, 181, 193

Celestial Court 25, 83

Celestial Queen 144

Centaurs 125

Changing Weather 110

Characteristics 38

Characters 38

Characters from Foreign Cultures 44

Charms 65

Choosing a City 39

chora, the 16, 18, 97

Citizen Levy, the 24

Citizenship 23

Citizens (Lay Membership) 86

city goddess 17, 44, 84, 87, 144

City Goddess Cults 86

City Matrons (Initiates) 87

City-State Populations 19

City-State Religion 25

City-State, the 16

Civic Trinity 25

Clothing 74, 77

Colonies And Outposts 30

Combat Styles 56

Conditioning, New Skill 52

Constables 140

Constitutions, City-State 23

Continents 6

Copper Pieces 72

Cost Of Living 73

Court 22

Crag, the 202

Creating the Goddess 86

Creatures 125

Cult Hierarchies 25

Cults 83

Cult Structures 84

Culture and Community 38

Culture, Korantine 18

Currency 71

Currency Exchange Rates 73

Current, Dangerous 130

D

Dagomar 35, 36, 48, 84, 104, 105, 150

Dagomils 35, 48, 133

Damaric 35

Dariscur 35

Debt Bondage 22

Deities 67

Dekos 35, 36

Demons 64

Demons, Plague 126

Demuskera 210, 228, 229

Devotion Requirements 68

Dinosaurs 37

Diotima 36, 84

Divine Portent 123

Djesmir 33, 49

Djesmirket 33, 34, 49, 53, 71, 82, 145, 206

Docks (Thyrta) 139

Doldrums Of Hiolanta 35

Domestic 54

Dorasdi 9, 91

E

Earning a Living 73

Eashaddir 145, 148, 156

East, Civilised 31

Eilak 33, 34

Elementals 63

Elephants 36

Elkanos 190

Emperor 4, 10, 11, 12, 13, 14, 15, 16, 21, 23, 28, 31, 33, 42, 43, 44, 45, 58, 67, 72, 82, 88, 89, 90, 106, 137, 146, 158, 190, 209, 219

Emperor Enkilos 10, 14, 21, 190

Enchanting 66

Encounter Chance 117

Encounters 117

Encounters at Sea 130

Index

Enkefalan 35
Entertainment 21
Errabna 37
Estrigel 83, 84, 97
Ethereals 63
Exiles 43

F
Factor of Mikosso 36
Fair Wind Sailing Table 109
Families 43
Father and Mother Ocean 36
Fauns (Goat-Kin) 125
Felsang 33
Fengo 33
Fierla 6, 14, 30, 36, 37, 82, 134, 142, 193, 206
First Matron (Acolyte) 87
Fishing Fleet 130
Fleet 132
Floundering Turtle 139
Foamfollower, the 191
Fog 131, 133
Folk Magic 64
Follies Of Emperor Enkilos 10
Foods 74
Foreign Raiders 123
Forensics, New Skill 52
Forest of Sard 15, 32, 125, 135, 144, 145, 169
Four Kingdoms Of The North 34
Franskum 166, 167, 168, 172, 173

G
Galley 111
Geography 21
Gold Coins 72
Gorgon 209, 210, 228
Gorkas 164, 168, 169, 170, 171, 173
Government, City-State 23
Graveyard, Desecrated 123
Grounded 131
Grrruff 197, 198, 214, 215, 230
Guberan 149
Gulf of Eilak 33
Gumathena 32

gunpowder 33
Guyuntars 12, 47, 149

H
Hags, Evil Nymphs 126
Haliskome 177, 182, 186, 187, 188, 189, 190, 192, 193, 196, 197, 203, 204, 205, 206, 207, 209, 215, 216, 217, 219, 223, 224, 225, 226, 227
Haprosindra 36
Harpies 200
Haunting 124
Hazard 117, 118, 120, 121
Heaven, Vault of 5, 6, 210
Hebdomar 168, 169, 174
Hilantri 9
Himela 4, 11, 12, 14, 15, 19, 21, 22, 23, 30, 77, 85, 109, 142, 144, 146, 149, 150, 151, 152, 177, 178, 181
Hiram Hiram 135
Hispola 20, 30, 36, 109
Historical Timeline for Korantia 7, 14
History 21
History Of The Korantine People 9
Holenyo the Fool 21
Homora 34, 109, 133
Honey Trap 199
horse racing 21
How Magic Works 61
Hunters 121, 122, 150

I
Igramsa 167, 168, 169, 174
Inner Ocean 4, 5, 14, 33, 34, 35, 36, 50, 226
Inns 106
Inquisitive Locals 118
Inviolate (New Miracle) 95
Iron Simulacrum 4, 5, 14, 33, 33, 33, 219
Ivanthus 140, 143, 157, 187
Ivory Sea 36

J
Jal 34
Jandekot 6, 11, 13, 14, 31, 34, 36, 37, 38, 49, 51, 55, 88, 131, 145
Janisdaron 36
Jekkara 14, 32, 46, 47, 102, 104, 220, 223
Jekkara, Cult of 102
Jekkarenes

Jekkarene Theocracy 5, 6, 9, 11, 12, 14, 31, 32, 46, 47, 102, 123, 124, 135, 142, 145, 146, 160, 164, 177, 186, 187, 188, 192, 193, 195, 196, 197, 199, 200, 202, 203, 204, 205, 215, 216, 217, 219, 224

Jelhai 33, 49, 65, 82

Jereboas 205, 207, 226

Jorelso of Sarestra (Sea Captain) 144

K

Kalish 205, 207, 215, 225, 228

Kapoli 36

Karosus 167, 168, 175

Kasperan 6, 10, 35, 37, 50, 51, 65, 125

Keba 14, 15, 16, 19, 23, 30, 76, 109

Kessum 34

Khorala 33, 49

King Arribates 9

Kingdom of Menkh 34

King Koibos 10

King Uskil 30

Kipsipsindra 4, 10, 13, 14, 15, 18, 19, 23, 30, 31, 36, 48, 76, 88, 90, 109, 145, 190

Kisathentyes 207, 225

Koibos 10, 11, 12, 13, 14, 31, 90, 137

Korantia, Land of 4

Korantine League, the 12, 13, 14, 15, 16, 28, 106

Korantine Prices 77

Korantine Social Class 39

Korantine Wealth 71

Korantis 5, 9, 10, 11, 13, 14, 28, 48, 69, 83, 88, 90, 104, 193

Korazoon 33

Koremchai, Demonic Pact 104

Kortano 136, 139, 158, 177

Kos 23, 83, 84, 96, 99, 136, 137, 153

Kos, Cult of 99

Kosimus of Pelostra 137, 144

L

Lakeside 146

Land and Property 75, 80, 81

Landless 39

Land Travel 106

Language And Literacy 19

Lanis 4, 10, 13, 14, 30, 55, 56, 83, 88, 89, 90, 91, 102, 155, 158, 166, 222

Lanis, Cult of 88

Lanthrus 84, 118

Lanthrus-Stones 118

Lapith 55

Lasca Veltis 84, 101

Lasca Veltis, Cult of 101

Law and Order (Thyrtan) 140

Law, Korantine 22

Livestock 75, 78

Lorena 178, 179, 180, 184

Lorsil 36

Lycanthropy (Miracle) 103

Lyortha 32, 150, 186, 187, 189, 190, 193, 203, 204, 216

M

Magic 21, 61

Magical Systems, Alternative 70

Magic, Learning 64

Magic Point Recovery 61

Malstrom 32

Malthe River 148

Many Hells 5, 53, 55, 62, 63, 64, 70, 104, 195

Marangia 5, 14, 18, 28, 31, 169

Marble Simulacrum 33

Material World, the 62

Mathematics 21

Medanthros 137, 139, 142, 189

Medanthros the Educator 142, 189

Melantos 192, 205, 206, 223, 224

Melosson of Thrigos 144, 189

Menkh 34

Men of Property 40

Merat 33

Mercenaries 25

Mercenary, Sabatine 56

Merchants (Encounter) 119

Mersin 14, 15, 19, 30, 32, 76, 109, 146, 155

Messengers 119

Metals 75, 80

Methelea 5, 9, 14, 15, 21, 47, 135

Metics 18, 43

Middling Sort, the 40

Mikosso 36, 37, 109

Military 23

Minotaurs 125

INDEX

Modatis 178, 179, 180, 185
Monstrous Predator 124
Moonbright (Miracle) 103
Moonglory, the 193, 196, 203
Moon, the 1, 14, 32, 47, 65, 67, 70, 102, 104, 219, 220, 223, 225
Morkar 34
Morkesh 33, 34, 37, 44, 49, 71, 135, 145, 186, 192, 205, 215, 218, 228
Morses 191
Mothers of the City (Priestess) 88
Mount Nester 28
Mount Tempiger 30, 149
Mylornas of Kipsipsindra 190
Mysticism 64
Mythology, Korantine 83

N
Nature of Magic 61
Navigation 109
Nereid, the Lonely 134
Nesterin 15, 22, 22
Nishimbakoi 30, 35, 50, 55
Non-Citizen Characters 41
Nymph 121, 127
Nymphs 125
Nysil 12, 14, 15, 19, 31

O
Odi's Fort 146
Official and Retinue 119
Old Korantis 28, 28
Oleg's Hills 148
Orator, Korantie 54
Orayna 15, 16, 83, 84, 86, 137, 152
Orchang 36, 48
Orc Hills 212
Orc Piracy 50
Orcs 35, 50, 217, 229
Orcs, of Solisand 193
Orinastron 164, 168, 175
Ornfeld Spike 148
Oster 12
Othrikor 36
Outer Ocean 5, 34
Outlaws 41, 121

Outlaws and Outcasts 41
Ozyrian mountains 4, 18, 31, 81, 91

P
Pacts 68
Pagans 5, 18, 42
Paladin 55
Palaskil 6, 24, 30, 46, 48, 84, 100, 115
Pandospalam 34, 35
Pantheons 67
Panthotaurs 125
Parlasos 32, 46, 104
Patriotic Bands 24, 25, 58, 96
Peddlers 119
Pelusinne 193, 195, 203, 204, 216, 219, 220
People of Status (Encounter) 119
Peoples' Plaza, The 137
Perlak 33, 49, 62, 192
Phereleukus 9
Philosophy 21
Pilgrims 119
Pirate Lair 205
Pirates 131
Plants, Giant 199
Poetry 21
Poor, the 40
Population 18
Predator 121, 122, 123, 124, 130
Predator, Flying 130
Priests 86
Prishad's Daughter 186
Pryjarna 33
Puissance, New Skill 52
Purple Wanderer 181, 186, 187, 188, 192, 193, 205, 206, 207, 215, 216, 223, 225, 226
Pyrolus 24, 30, 37, 84, 100, 113, 137, 142, 144, 145, 159
Pyrolus, Cult of 100
Pyrolus Stream 37

Q
Queen Semankore 32, 46
Queen Tursiba the Lioness 34

R

Raiders 121
Ramassa 12, 14, 32
Rams 114
Rasputana 6, 33, 34, 35, 64, 65, 131, 180
Rastush 34
Reavers 37
Reef 131
Rekshimetor 37
Religious Practices 25
Retorios of Kelso 21
Rich, the 41
Rikalsos of Vimaylo 136, 159
Rilados 140, 142, 143, 159, 189, 191
Rilados the Navigator 191
River Travel 107
Roads 106
Roads Encounter Table 118
Robbers 120
Roc 127
Rosper 151, 152
Ruin 121
Rukkos the Slight 36
Runes 70
Rustic Shrine 120

S

Sabateus 24, 84, 96, 97, 98, 136, 137, 145, 158, 162, 187
Sabateus, Cults of 97
Sabatines 24, 56, 97, 98
Sacred Bands 24
Sacred Year 26
Safra am Prishad 177, 187, 188, 191, 192, 215, 216, 218
Sailing Conditions 109
Sailing Conditions Table 110
Sailing In Local Time 109
Sailing In Strategic Time 108
Salty Mari's 139, 191
Sarestra 4, 13, 15, 18, 19, 23, 30, 41, 81, 98, 109, 135, 139, 144, 145, 151, 152
Satyr 102, 121, 125, 127, 128, 129, 174
Sea Monster 131
Sea Monster, Colossal 132
Sea Satyrs (Tritons) 128
Seaslaver, the 145
Sea Travel 108
Seaworthiness 111
Semordis 84
Settler Land Grabs 143
Settlers (Thyrtan) 142
Shamans 70
Sharranket 4, 33, 34, 35, 36, 49, 82
Shelsom 169, 170, 176
Sheylo 84, 97, 120
Shields 79
Ship Class 111
Ship Condition Table 112
Ship Quality 113
Ship To Ship Combat 112
Shipwreck 131
Shrine, Abandoned 122
Shrine, Wild 122
Shrinking Hills 146
Shuja 34
Siege Weapons 114
Simbale 136, 137, 159
Simblay 146, 164, 166, 167, 169, 175
Sisanayontes 9
Skelfus 137, 139, 142, 143, 146, 148, 158, 163, 164, 166, 167, 170, 171, 181, 182, 205, 222
Skelfus Fields 146
Skill Progression Limits 38
Sky, The 6
Slargr 37
Slaver, Orc 55
Slavery 22
Slaves, Agricultural and Industrial 42
Slaves, Household 42
Small Cities, the 16
Small City Populations 20
Social Class for Taskan Characters 45
Soldiers (Encounter) 120
Solisand 187, 188, 189, 190, 191, 192, 193, 195, 198, 201, 202, 206, 209, 215, 216, 217, 218, 228
Solisma 195, 198, 199, 204, 205, 210, 216, 221, 222, 228, 229
Solisma's Forest 204
Somadsil 6

Index

Someja 34, 35

Someshi 35

Sorantia 33, 90

Sorcerer-Priest, Orcish 55

Sorcery 65

Sorcery Lores 53

Sostrum of Sustra 21

Southern Draw 34

Spirits 63

Spirit World, the 62

Sports 21

Starting Money 43

Storm 131

Storm, Cataclysmic 132

Supernatural Beings 63

Swamp, the 204

Swarm, Deadly 132

Synchronise (Miracle) 103

T

Tapropiscan Confederacy 35

Tapropiscur 37

Tarankis 84

Tarsang 33

Tarsenia 6, 11, 19, 31, 33, 42, 44, 68

Taskan Empire 5, 10, 11, 14, 31, 33, 34, 45, 57, 68, 71, 76, 90, 106

Taskan Empire, the 33

Taskay 33

Taygus 4, 6, 14, 28, 33, 34, 37, 45, 125, 135

Tempiger Mines 150

Tempigone 15, 30, 109, 148, 149, 150, 151, 152, 155, 168, 181, 182, 189, 191, 192, 206, 216

Temple Dancer, Jekkarene 54

Tersippa 12, 20, 31, 135, 146, 164, 166, 167, 169

Tessenber 168, 169, 176

Tetrapolis, the 14, 16, 30

Thalvi's Place 139

The House of Valsus 177

Theism 66

Thennalt 5, 12, 13, 14, 15, 18, 30, 31, 33, 42, 44, 46, 58, 60, 84, 90, 91, 101, 102, 122, 125, 135, 137, 142, 143, 144, 146, 148, 153, 155, 158, 161, 162, 163, 164, 166, 167, 168, 171, 176

Thennalts 45

Thennalt Stone 164, 166

The Realm 159

Theyna 5, 45, 46, 101, 102, 164, 166, 167, 172, 174, 175

Theyna, Cult of 101

Theyna's Mark 166

Thieves (Encounter) 120

Thread of Life (New Miracle) 99

Three Kingdoms Of The South 34

Three Realities, the 62

Thurina 6, 16, 37, 125

Thyrta 3, 14, 15, 30, 33, 109, 135, 136, 137, 139, 140, 142, 143, 144, 145, 146, 148, 151, 156, 157, 159, 161, 163, 164, 166, 167, 169, 170, 171, 177, 178, 180, 181, 182, 186, 187, 189, 190, 191, 192, 216

Thyrta Town 136

Tiamankore 150

Timolay 14, 31, 145

Tomb, Old 124

Tools 75, 75, 78

Torestal 31

Torrik the Greedy 37

Torthil 24, 25, 26, 30, 84, 94, 96, 97, 100, 120, 136, 137, 153, 157

Torthil Of Vestrikina, Cult of 96

Trade Goods 76, 82

Trade Ship 132

Transients 43, 144

Transport and Shipping 75, 80

Transport (Ship) 111

Travel Conditions 107

Travel Distances, Exceeding 108

Travellers (Encounter) 120

Travelling Korantia 106

Travel Times 107

Tribes of Jandekot 51

Trilus' Hills 148

Triton Hellraisers 134

Tygorus 10

Tysil 5, 15, , 16, 19, 28, 31, 140, 143, 145, 146, 153, 157, 187

U

Unconquerable Heroes of Taskay 33

Usarwi Plain 34

Using Social Class in Play 40

Utility (Ship) 111

Uxmal 6, 34, 35, 36, 131

V

Vale Of Giant Flowers 211

Valontermus 193, 197, 203, 204, 216, 219, 221

Valorik Blueface 36

Valos 12, 13, 14, 15, 22, 24, 28, 37, 106, 143

Valsus' House 178

Valsus' House Plan 180

Valsus of Kela 142, 177, 181, 184

Varoteg 3, 137, 146, 148, 158, 161, 163, 164, 166, 167, 168, 169, 170, 171, 177, 181, 182, 187

Varoteg's Rascals 163

Velontes 9

Veltis 24, 84, 101

Vessel Types and Statistics 114

Vestrikina - City Goddess 91

Volsenna 137, 140, 161, 162

W

War Ship 132

Weaponry, Ship's 114

Weapons 79

Weather 108, 130

What Magic Is For 62

Wilderness Encounters 120

Wooden Walls (Miracle) 105

Woses 195, 198

Wreckers 132

Y

Yaristra 14, 16, 19, 21, 23, 81

Year, The 6

Yegusai 33

Yezereus 137, 140, 142, 161, 162

Z

Zarendra 11, 13, 14, 20, 30, 31, 88, 90, 109

Zarina 33

Zartos of Horaia 11

Zathrum 12, 12, 30, 31, 45, 146

Zibud 34

Zolesta 84

Zombie Ship 134

Zygas Taga 5, 11, 14, 33, 45, 47, 219

www.ingramcontent.com/pod-product-compliance
Ingram Content Group UK Ltd.
Pitfield, Milton Keynes, MK11 3LW, UK
UKHW050714131224
452254UK00013B/64